THE CANADIAN
WRITER'S MARKET

Thirteenth Revised Edition

Jem Bates

with an Introduction
by Adrian Waller

M&S

CANADIAN CATALOGUING IN PUBLICATION DATA
The Canadian writer's market

ISBN 0-7710-8770-5 (13th rev. ed.)
ISSN 1193-3305

1. Authorship – Handbooks, manuals, etc. 2. Publishers and publishing – Canada – Directories. 3. Canadian periodicals – Directories. 4. Advertising agencies – Canada – Directories. 5. Journalism – Study and teaching – Canada – Directories.

PN4908.C3   070.5'2'02571   C92-032255-7

We acknowledge the financial support of the Government of Canada through the Book Publishing Industry Development Program for our publishing activities. We further acknowledge the support of the Canada Council for the Arts and the Ontario Arts Council for our publishing program.

Typeset in Plantin by M&S, Toronto
Printed and bound in Canada

McClelland & Stewart Inc.
The Canadian Publishers
481 University Avenue
Toronto, Ontario
M5G 2E9

1 2 3 4 5   02 01 00 99 98

Contents

INTRODUCTION

Back in the 1970s, when *The Canadian Writer's Market* was first published, the country sported a mere 100 consumer magazines, about 150 trade journals, two dozen or so farm publications that appeared somewhat sporadically, and 147 book publishers. As time went on, however, the industry was caught in an upswing and, five or six years later, there were 225 consumer magazines in Canada, most sold by subscription or delivered to selected households free of charge, and almost as many trade publications distributed in various corners of the workplace and business world. As well, there were 50-odd farm publications and 160 book publishers.

According to *Canadian Advertising Rates & Data (CARD)*, published monthly by Maclean Hunter Ltd., as the 1990s dawned there were over 400 consumer magazines, and trade journals were keeping pace. By Statistics Canada figures, in 1990-91 (the most recent year for which reliable data are available) there were some 1,500 periodicals in Canada. The number of national book publishers had almost doubled.

Publishing, however, has always been an extremely transient business. In today's Canada, magazines come and go faster than they ever did. Thus, keeping *The Canadian Writer's Market* up-to-date over the years has required much research and revision.

Many publications are distributed free as corporate public relations vehicles. However, a large number of magazines are still sold by subscription, while many are kept in business almost entirely by either government grants or funds from specific organizations. Whatever their method of funding or distribution, most Canadian magazines that buy freelancers' work have been included in the thirteenth edition of *The Canadian Writer's Market*, making it a useful tool for all who seek to sell their words.

This edition again focuses on English-language publishers and publications. In earlier editions we carried many francophone magazines and trade publications. By 1991, however, we had become uncomfortably aware that to do full justice to Quebec's dynamic publishing industry was beyond our resources, yet any halfway point seemed to us an unacceptable compromise. So, as with the last three editions, this is a guide to the English-language publishing world, though we have retained many bilingual publishers. We would refer readers looking to work in Québécois to the *CARD* directory for French-language magazines, and to *Quill & Quire*'s biannual guide, the *Canadian Publishers Directory*, for a full listing of French-language book publishers.

Again we have chosen in general not to list the specialist educational and professional publishing houses, which offer few opportunities for the unspecialized writer, while retaining those publishers that also have a trade operation, and not to carry many of the very small publishers who produce, on an ad hoc, occasional basis, perhaps no more than one or two volumes a year.

Few could have imagined, when *The Canadian Writer's Market* first appeared, the impact on the writer's trade of technological advances – from fax machines and personal computers to e-mail, the Internet, and searchable databases. Now it is possible to transmit story ideas across the country electronically almost instantaneously with a single keystroke. Where, four years ago, many editors would solicit faxed story proposals and manuscripts to save time, today they are increasingly requesting electronic submissions.

Except where editors have asked us not to, we have included e-mail, phone, and fax numbers with each listing. Writers are generally advised to try to sell their work by letter or fax. While it is often perfectly acceptable to phone a publication to ask for its contributor's guidelines (which usually say how much it pays for those articles needed for its various editorial departments), business with editors is nearly always more effectively accomplished with a carefully compiled story proposal. However, editors have differing needs, and many of the entries that follow carry their specific requirements in this regard. We have also added publishers' web sites wherever possible: these are becoming increasingly useful as a first-stop source of practical information.

We have again opted to arrange the magazines into logically appropriate groups. The three main classes remain Consumer Magazines; Literary & Scholarly; and Trade, Business, Farm, & Professional Publications. And to facilitate a quick and easy reference for writers seeking a suitable market for a good idea, or for those wanting to recycle an article to other buyers, we have narrowed down these groups further, according to subject. Inevitably, however, these classifications are somewhat arbitrary and have a tendency to overlap. Even the distinction between consumer and trade publications is sometimes difficult to delineate. Some "trade" periodicals – the book industry's *Quill & Quire*, for instance – have such a general popularity that they are equated to consumer magazines. We include a section of prominent business journals in Chapter 1 in order to describe the market they offer in greater detail. Many comparable business publications retain a simplified listing in Chapter 3. Women's magazines are retained as a sub-group in Chapter 1. These popular, high-circulation magazines are among the most successful areas in Canadian publishing and can offer freelancers some of the best markets.

Consumer magazines appear in fourteen sub-groups: arts & cultural; business; city & entertainment; the environment; feminist; general interest; home & hobby; lifestyle; news, opinions, & issues; special interest; sports & outdoors; travel & tourism; women's; and youth & children's. Trade publications are divided into twenty subsections according to the professions or trades they serve. These groups range from advertising, business, and data processing to electronics, transportation, and travel.

To sharpen this reference book as a marketing tool, we provide thumbnail sketches for each consumer magazine to explain in the limited space available what kinds of articles it carries. This is useful because so many magazines have names that give little indication of what they really are, who reads them, and, consequently, the kinds of articles or stories they buy. No one would ever guess, for instance, that a monthly Vancouver magazine called *Kinesis* is a forum for feminists. Nor that, far from being a farm publication, as one might first suspect, *Grain* is a spunky little literary publication that has been produced quarterly in Regina since 1973.

We use the term publication often throughout this book because, strictly speaking, many of its listings are not really magazines as we have come to know them. Some may be tabloid newspapers, some simple, one-colour, staple-bound periodicals that feed the needs, sometimes sporadically, of a smallish group of loyal readers. Others, however, are magazines in the truest sense: glossy, highly professional consumer or trade journals that boast respectable circulations. The word publication, then, seems to safely cover all listings, both large and small.

Much more important to the writer is that all these publications provide opportunities both for established freelancers wanting to break fresh ground and for neophyte writers seeking to have their work published. Each magazine listed accepts outside contributions with varying frequency and for equally varying fees.

Some publications, particularly among the scholarly journals and the literary and arts magazines, do not pay their writers at all. Others pay fees that are among the highest in North America, and expect high standards of writing and reporting in return.

Marketing

Too few novice writers understand that marketing is as vital an element of their craft as style and subject matter. Without a successful marketing strategy, their words and ideas may never see print.

The professional way to sell your writing is with a coherently written proposal. This eliminates the risks inherent in producing work on speculation. When an idea is accepted, the writer and the editor discuss fee, deadline – an *obsession* in the business, by the way – and the preferred writing style for the finished article.

Writers should always study the magazines for which they would like to write so they can immediately address the question, What does this particular editor want? Ultimately, though, they are aiming to satisfy not the editor but the magazine's readers, and the only way to find out what *they* like is by reading the kind of material they have been purchasing in the past.

Another sure-fire way of becoming acquainted with a specific group of readers, and getting a feel for what they want, is to take careful note of the type and quality of the advertising within the magazine. In other words, you can only really know what to suggest to an editor after diligently studying his or her issues – and lots of them – as regularly as you can, in libraries, on the newsstands, or in doctors' offices.

Unquestionably, the hardest writing to sell is the novel. No matter how timely or ingenious a story may be, the effect a piece of fiction ultimately has on readers will depend almost entirely on how well it is constructed and written. Some of this, of course, also applies to non-fiction writing, particularly first-person experience pieces so much a part of the writer, and essays that must intelligently set out opinions and arguments. But, whereas the worthiness of most suggestions for magazine articles can be demonstrated aptly in a proposal, the power of a novel really cannot.

Some publishers are able to judge the merits of a piece of fiction from two or three sample chapters accompanied by a synopsis of the entire work. Ideally, this should explain the plot and show the very thing that holds fiction together – the theme. On the basis of this initial work, some publishers will give an experienced writer a contract and an advance against royalties to complete the book. Usually, though, they only commit themselves to novels submitted by an unknown author after seeing the completed text.

To help sell their work, fiction writers often seek out literary agents like those we have listed in Chapter 6. But don't expect agents to possess magic wands that they can wave to find a market for everything that crosses their desks. On the contrary, they must work extremely hard to sell whatever they can, and their best acquisitions, usually from experienced writers, are nearly always the first to find a buyer. So, to make their lives easier, reputable agents only ever handle a work they think will sell so well that it will be financially beneficial for both themselves and their clients.

In the United States, it is common practice for agents also to place magazine articles and essays, especially by frequently published and well-known authors. In Canada, however, this is seldom the case. Virtually all articles are sold directly to magazines and publishing houses by authors themselves – with well-crafted proposals.

Not surprisingly, then, the query letter to an editor and the full, detailed proposal or outline that follows it may well be the most significant piece of work the beginning writer ever undertakes. It not only sells a suggestion, after all, but the writer with it. It should serve to demonstrate to an editor that, beyond any shadow of doubt, the person who conceived the idea and refined it really *is* the one best able to turn it into a strong, informative piece of writing for a lot of readers to enjoy.

Copyright

Whatever you sell, and by whatever means you choose to do it, one of the most crucial legal elements of the writing craft is copyright. This is usually discussed the moment an editor responds favourably to a writer's suggestion.

Copyright is an *extremely* complex area of law, and writers are advised to read up on it all they can before negotiating the sales terms of their work, thus putting themselves in a stronger bargaining position. Put simply, copyright means the sole right to reproduce – or allow others to reproduce – a literary or artistic work. It begins upon creation rather than on publication, and exists until fifty years after the creator's death.

The *assignment* or *licensing* of copyright is what is negotiated in any deal between a publisher and a writer. Depending on the nature of the contract, the author can sell rights in many different ways.

Some publishers, often book publishers, will ask an author to *assign* copyright. This means that the publisher has control of all aspects of the copyright, including subsidiary rights such as translation rights, reprint rights, or even film rights, for the period of the agreement. The work is then published with copyright in the publisher's name. Such a contract will generally stipulate that once the publisher has allowed the book to go out of print, the rights revert to the author. The writer will likely find that it is preferable to *grant a licence* to a publisher, specifying the rights of the publisher with respect to territory and time. In this way, the publisher is given the right to use the work in different markets or at a later date, and will be able to negotiate separately for subsidiary rights.

Terms of a copyright agreement may vary greatly in nature or content – a contract, after all, can include whatever conditions one party feels pertinent – but not in principle. Canadian magazines with large circulations most often buy North American rights – the right to publish an article to be read by an audience scattered across the entire continent. Some large Canadian magazines are content simply to buy Canadian rights – the right to publish a work that will be read only within the country. Some acquire serial rights – the right to publish a work in a sister publication without having to pay extra for it.

Many smaller publications, however, simply buy one-time rights. Under this type of agreement, copyright ownership automatically reverts to the writer, either immediately upon publication or shortly afterwards, depending on the agreement. This leaves the writer legally free to sell the same article in the same words to what is called a secondary market. If that new market also buys only one-time rights, the same article may then be re-sold to a third magazine without the need for any alteration, then a fourth, and so on down the line.

Another variation of one-time rights, which is preferred by many of the larger magazines, is for *first-time* rights, giving the publisher the right to be the first to publish an article. In other words, they may indeed want one-time rights, but these must be first-time.

This usually leaves writers with two main options. They can either sell a story several times over to those magazines willing to buy one-time rights, not caring if these are first, second, or even third, or they can take what most experienced freelancers have come to regard as the more lucrative road. That is, they can write a piece for a top fee from a large magazine first, then try selling the same idea to smaller magazines later.

Be careful here, though. While ideas can't be copyrighted, the words used to express or explain them can, and are. This is why our copyright laws came into being: to prevent people from taking and using something – in this case, words, phrases, expressions, literary structures – that does not belong to them. So if you have sold North American, Canadian, or even world rights to a magazine, remember that before being offered elsewhere, your piece must be totally rewritten and restructured. As it passes from the original buyer to others wanting first-time rights, each text must avoid any of the original word combinations, structures, or echoes. If, on the other hand, you have sold one-time rights and the copyright has reverted to you, you may send off your article in its original, unaltered form as many times as you wish.

Some magazines – *Reader's Digest*, for example – buy what are known as reprint rights, yet another corner of the maze of copyright. Under this agreement, editors may pick up and re-publish articles that have appeared elsewhere so long as they pay the original publishers, and/or the writers, fees for their one-time use. This practice is always restricted to publishers and must never be confused with recycling. It is merely an arrangement made between two magazines, with the copyright laws in mind, which gives the writer a little extra money as a bonus for his or her initial efforts.

Here are some of the most frequently posed questions about copyright, with general answers:

Is every piece of written work copyrighted?

No. In Canada, copyright on a work lasts for the life of the author plus fifty years. After that, the work falls into the public domain and may be legally copied at will.

How can I tell who the rightful owner of a copyright is?

In the first few pages of a book or magazine there is a copyright notice. Typically, it will read: Copyright Josephine Blow, 1998; or Joseph P. Blow & Sons, Publishers, 1998. Beneath this will usually appear the publisher's address. Even if the copyright is held in the author's name, it is generally the publisher who has the right by contract to authorize reprints of excerpts. If, however, the author has retained these rights exclusively, which may sometimes be the case, he or she can be contacted through the publisher.

How does copyright infringement occur?

Usually through carelessness or ignorance. Few writers, after all, deliberately set out to steal something that doesn't belong to them. They either quote too much of someone else's work without first seeking permission to do so, or use previously written words without making a sufficiently concerted effort to rework them. (For some comments on the other side of copyright infringement, see page 26.)

What is too much of someone else's work?

The answer to this isn't easy. It depends on several factors, principally the quantity and quality of the portion taken and whether its use will detract from the impact and/or the marketability of the original. No one loses sleep if a writer uses a line or two from a book and attributes its source; to reproduce three or four key paragraphs without permission, however – even *with* attribution – could lead to problems. The writer is always advised to contact the copyright holder, quoting the extract(s) he or she wants to use in full, giving a true indication of context, details of format (magazine article, script, or book), and size of audience, and ask for permission to reproduce it. A neophyte writer wanting to use 100 words for publication in a small magazine probably will not be charged what a name writer would be expected to pay for a similar-sized extract in an article for one of the big players. Many copyright holders, however, do not charge for so few words.

How can I copyright my work?

The moment you have written something it is automatically copyrighted. If, however, you feel there is a chance someone may one day say your manuscript is theirs, you may register it for a fee with the Federal Department of Communications' Copyright and Industrial Design Branch. If your work is registered in this way, should a dispute over copyright arise, you would be in a much stronger position if the case ever went to court. It would be up to the other party to prove that you are not the creator of your work. You can also mail a copy of your manuscript to yourself in a registered package. This would provide you with a dated receipt, which you would be able to produce when opening the package before a judge, should the manuscript's rightful ownership ever become a legal issue.

If I work for a newspaper, who owns the copyright on my work?

Usually, if you are employed by a company, it automatically owns the copyright of everything that is published by it in the course of your work. This cannot be reproduced or re-sold in any form without permission first being obtained. Often, newspapers generously allow articles, or portions of them, to be reprinted without charge.

Can a magazine editor steal the idea contained in my story proposal and assign it to someone else to write?

Yes, but the good ones won't. For this reason, it is not necessary to write copyright on your proposal. You would be wasting words anyway. Ideas like titles are in the public domain and cannot be protected by copyright laws unless they are part of an invention. And that is yet another branch of copyright law. If you intend to sell movie scripts in Hollywood (in which case you will definitely need an agent to negotiate rights on your behalf), have faith in the people you deal with. Good magazines and publishing houses stay in business because their editors are ethical. (See page 26 for a discussion about electronic rights and the Internet and how they are affecting relations between freelance writers and magazine and newspaper publishers.)

Should I copyright the book I have been contracted to write before sending it to the publisher?

No. All publishers will copyright your work for you, under either their name or yours, depending on the terms of the contract you should already have signed. They will also register it for you, at the National Library in Ottawa, as an original Canadian work.

Libel

Jonathan Swift, in *A Tale of a Tub*, complained loudly and logically that writers were no longer able to lash out at particular people for particular vices and had to content themselves with general satire on mankind. More than two hundred years later, we still must take heed. We must do our best not to make any direct, unfair, or inaccurate allusion to the living that might shed bad light upon their reputations.

Libel suits are notoriously complex – and the traps are wide. Many writers hold the mistaken belief that the use of fictitious names, or a statement saying that any resemblance between the characters in the book and living persons is purely coincidental, will automatically protect them from the possibility of a libel suit. This assumption is wrong. If the average reader associates a character described in a manuscript with an actual person, and the description reflects unfavourably on that person's reputation or integrity, there is always the danger of libel.

Fiction writers must always strive to ensure that the resemblance really is coincidence, and must certainly avoid the intention. Apparent intention to libel an actual person, even in fiction, could be interpreted by legal minds as a personal attack, and could possibly lead to an action.

All writers need to understand enough about Canadian libel law to protect both themselves and their publishers against court action. This is absolutely necessary since nearly all publishers' contracts provide for indemnification by the author in cases where a person maligned in a manuscript resorts to a suit.

Libel in Canada is mostly covered by civil law and comes under provincial jurisdiction. Its principles are based on English common law for all provinces except Quebec, where the law stems directly from the French Civil Code. But the principles remain: libel is a printed statement or picture that exposes a person to hatred, ridicule, or contempt, and imputes to that person immorality, crime, or disorderly conduct, or tends to injure that person in the pursuit of a profession, office, or trade. In short, anything that might discredit a person may be construed as libellous. And under some circumstances, this can also apply to corporations or their individual members.

If such a statement or picture is printed, the publisher must be prepared to defend his publication on three fronts: truth of the statement; privilege; and fair comment on a matter of public interest. If the author's statements are accurate and true, there may be no basis for a civil action for libel, but any false or defamatory statement that tends to harm a person's reputation may constitute libel.

Privileged reports fall into two classifications: absolute privilege and qualified privilege. If published at the same time as they took place, a fair and accurate report without editorial comment on proceedings heard before a court of justice is absolutely privileged. Qualified or conditional privilege is enjoyed by reporters while covering proceedings in any government body, whether legislative or administrative, any commission of inquiry or organization whose members represent any public authority in Canada, or municipal council, school board, or board of health meetings.

The defence of qualified privilege extends to the findings or decisions of those Canadian organizations formed to promote the interests of any art, science, religion, or learning; any trade, business, industry, or profession; any game, sport, or pastime to which members of the public are invited as spectators or participants.

Fair and honest comment on matters of public interest, as long as it is true, is privileged. An author who comments on current affairs or writes a biography is permitted to express honest opinions or fair criticism of someone's works or accomplishments because this is usually in the public interest and serves to promote a useful purpose. Fair comment extends to criticism of books, magazines, articles, plays, and films.

Another defence often resorted to by newspapers and magazines is mitigation of damages based on a retraction of a statement that was made in error. While this action does not absolve the publication from libel, it nevertheless tends to show that any injury was purely accidental, and this may lessen the amount of the damages levied by the court.

Simultaneous Submissions

There is absolutely nothing wrong with writers sending the same article, proposal, or book manuscript to more than one potential market at the same time. It is their work, after all, so they can do whatever they please with it. But unless they are sending off material simultaneously to those magazines that are happy to buy second, third, or fourth rights, they could run into problems.

The practice can sometimes be unethical. Busy magazines need about a month to assess an idea or a manuscript properly, sometimes more. During this time, several people may be assigned to the job of writing an informed critique explaining to both the writer and the senior editor how the manuscript or article is effective, how it isn't, and what revisions may be necessary.

In publishing houses, this work takes considerably longer and is correspondingly more expensive. Judging a promising book proposal or an intriguing manuscript of several thousand words usually means that an editor must set aside present work. If the editor is rushing to complete a book for the upcoming spring list, an outside reader might have to be hired to do this job instead. Readers are also hired for their specialized expertise, to judge whether a writer has covered a topic, fact or fiction, properly and accurately. If an idea or manuscript appears tempting, the publisher may recruit market researchers to assess its sales potential. By sending the same material to several houses, the writer may automatically involve them all in the expense of assessing something only one of them would eventually be able to acquire.

Indeed, to established writers, the idea of simultaneous submissions is distasteful. Knowing how busy editors can be, they give them reasonable time to respond – about six weeks on a magazine and as long as three months in a publishing house. If after that they have heard nothing, they fire off a reminder, then turn immediately to other productive work. The publishing business is notorious for its slowness and, unfortunately, this is something all writers have to learn to accept.

Personal Computers

Thanks to modern technology, most writers now craft their poems, articles, and books on personal computers. Publishers prefer (indeed, many insist) that authors use computers, not because it saves them money, but because typesetting from disk speeds up the production process and helps prevent errors from creeping into the manuscript at a later stage.

The personal computer enables the writer to compose words and keep them in files – one file per story or article, perhaps, or one per chapter – then recall them. As long as a file has been properly stored, it can be retrieved at any time. The PC enables writers to edit, cut, and paste limitlessly, without resorting to such traditional and perfectly respectable writers' tools as scissors, stapler, or glue. Thus they are spared the drudgery of seemingly endless retyping while striving to make their prose sparkle or their narrative flow in a smoother, clearer line. At the end of the day, with the final text saved on a disk, a clean copy can be printed out in a matter of minutes.

Most word processing programs contain a spell-check and a thesaurus. The spell-check, of course, helps eliminate poor spelling and typographical errors, and the thesaurus gives the writer instant access to a wide choice of synonyms and antonyms. With just another keystroke, any word can be selected from the thesaurus to replace one that is no longer wanted in the text.

In recent years, as personal computers have flooded the market, the consumer has become increasingly confused about what product to buy. Strange as it may seem, the least important part is the computer itself. This – the hardware – is really nothing more than an electronic box with switches, coils, and microchips. It is only as good as whatever program – the software – is inserted into a drive to make it perform in a specific way. Thus, software capabilities must always be foremost in the writer's mind, and he or she is far better off seeking out the most suitable word processing program first, then buying the right computer to accommodate it. Your choice of program will ultimately determine the type of hardware you buy to run it. Powerful software packages need equally powerful computers to absorb them, make them run, and still have enough working memory, or RAM.

For books, by the way, a powerful computer and decent software is essential. Some writers do manage to write books on small home computers, but all too often their software restricts them, and the computer's capacity is such that they can only get one or two chapters on a single disk. If you find yourself with half a chapter on one disk, and the other half on another, you can bank on awkward technical problems when the time comes for you to print out your work.

Power, memory, and software capability are one thing. Another aspect of word processing worthy of almost equal consideration is your working speed, which lies largely in using a good keyboard, one with which you feel comfortable.

It is also important to remember that just how quickly a manuscript can be produced does not necessarily depend on how good or expensive your printer is, but how suitable. Your printer should provide a clear, draft-quality text in an easy-to-read typeface. Script typefaces resembling italics or Old English should be avoided because they are harder to read. This rule applies to both a computer and a typewriter, electric or otherwise.

Another component of the home computer, and one more integral to comfort than any other, is the piece of equipment you must stare at for hours on end – the screen. Best is what is called a high-resolution screen. This not only costs significantly less than a colour screen, but helps to reduce eyestrain. Suffice it to say that endlessly watching your work spring to life on a screen you are not comfortable with will make word processing a chore, and certainly not a pleasure.

Before buying a PC, shop around, and talk to other writers to ascertain what computers and software packages they bought, and why. Judge your needs by theirs. And make certain you obtain the type of software best suited to a writer's needs.

Manuscripts

Manuscripts should be clean, well-prepared, and printed out double-spaced on white bond letter-size paper, with a covering page bearing a title. If your article is accepted, it is doubtful that the title you gave it will survive. It is likely to undergo several changes as editors put their heads together to dream up something that suits it better, according to the style of their magazine. When first submitting a piece, then, its title is of little consequence. Your job is merely to call your work *something* so it can be recorded as such when the editorial department receives it. Much more of a priority is the other information you must put on the title page – your name, complete address, and telephone number.

Of course, editors are most interested in such ingredients as uniqueness or importance of subject, and whether it has been properly covered and deftly illustrated with anecdotes. They look, too, for good writing – this does not translate to clever or fancy as much as it does to clear and coherent. Editors do find, however, that a neat manuscript is infinitely more inviting to read than an untidy one.

When submitting a book manuscript, each new chapter should be denoted as such by starting partway down the page. All pages must be numbered, double-spaced, and have margins about an inch wide. The text will require a title page, too, and others devoted to a full, accurate listing of any permissions the author needed to acquire to be legally entitled to quote from copyrighted works. Do not bind or staple your manuscript.

While editors used to like to see an entire manuscript, this is usually no longer the case. Many publishing houses will not accept unsolicited manuscripts, and if you do manage to convince a busy editor to take a look at your work, two sample chapters plus a synopsis will be sufficient. You can always courier the balance of the manuscript if required.

Always be sure to discuss with your editor the form in which your disk will be delivered, to ensure the typesetter will have no problem accessing and converting your files. Your editor will likely have some specific instructions for you to follow here, but some are general: 1) each article or chapter should have its own file; 2) never fill your disks – always leave at least 40k "working space" on each for the typesetter's format instructions; 3) always make backup disks; 4) never centre or justify the text, which makes it difficult for the publisher to obtain an accurate word count and creates problems for the typesetter during formatting; 5) set your margins so that there are no more than sixty characters per line; 6) never hyphenate a word at the end of a line unless that word has a hyphen already; 7) make very clear your codes for accents, currency symbols, fractions, and footnote or endnote numbers, and don't overuse bold and italic typefaces.

Style

By style, most book and magazine editors mean the conventions of spelling, punctuation, and capitalization. There is, of course, no universally accepted manual for style because it varies from periodical to periodical, publishing house to publishing house, not to mention from fiction to non-fiction, from genre to genre, and from discipline to discipline. Writers should remember, however, that style is an integral part of their craft and, by showing a blatant disregard for it, they can quite inadvertently prejudice an editor against their work.

Writers are expected to observe at least some of the basic house rules, and these should be obvious in what has already been published by those magazines and book publishing houses for which they aspire to write. If they are not, the writer is always wise to find out as much as possible about what these rules are, and what stylistic traits – as idiosyncratic as many may appear to be – are preferred.

Canadian newspapers generally follow *The Canadian Press*

Stylebook (which also contains some good tips on reporting, by the way), and magazines tend to develop their own standards and preferences from one authoritative source, or a compilation of several. Book publishers, however, usually adhere to well-known manuals. A selection of the best style and resource books is provided at the end of this book.

Very often, a publishing house has compiled its *own* guide to house style, and the aspiring writer should never be afraid to ask for a copy of this.

The Word Count

The number of words a manuscript contains is another consideration for editors. A large part of their job is to ensure that stories will fit into an allotted space. When they order 2,000 words, the manuscript should not be appreciably longer, and preferably 100 words or so less.

For books, the word count is more crucial, because cutting, even merely trimming to a publishable size, is a lot more work than many writers realize. Doing it properly almost always means having to judiciously remove material – a sentence here or a couple of paragraphs there – throughout an entire text and not just from one part of it. The time involved explains why authors lament that they have had potentially good works either rejected out of hand or returned swiftly to them for drastic shortening.

Always remember that the real skill in writing is being able to tell a story, fact or fiction, in the shortest number of necessary words. To achieve this, good writers develop keen powers of self-criticism. They are constantly scrutinizing their work for wordiness, clutter, unnecessarily long quotes, or characters that do nothing to enhance the subject of their story or move the action along. The moment they come upon any of them, they ruthlessly pare away the superfluous material so as to make their text tighter.

They also check regularly to see how many words they are writing. Use the word-count function on your computer, if you have one, or, if you are working on a typewriter, set your left-hand margin at twenty and the right at seventy-five so that each line of type will contain an average of ten words. Twenty-five double-spaced lines on a standard-size page, therefore, will equal roughly 250 words.

Postage

These days all publishers are under pressure to reduce costs wherever possible. Postage rates have soared in recent years and so, for any business that relies heavily on our mail system, they represent a bigger expense than ever. It should now be taken for granted that if you want your manuscript returned you must include a self-addressed, stamped envelope, so that it can be returned without cost. Increasingly, publishers will assume that you do not want your material back if an SASE is not included, and will simply throw it away. Magazine and book editors stress this point again and again, and writers ignore it at their peril. If submitting to U.S. publishers, enclose international postage coupons or keep a supply of American stamps. You can stock up on a visit, arrange for a friend visiting the States to bring some back for you, or buy them through a Canadian dealer (*Canadian Author* magazine often carries advertisements for these).

Income Tax

In Canada, the Income Tax Act is good to writers, allowing them to deduct legitimate work expenses from their taxable incomes. In return, writers are trusted to show all their earnings, particularly fees that are unsupported by T4, T4A, or T5 slips from magazines and publishing houses that have printed their work.

Basically, writers come under three classifications:

- Salaried employees who supplement their incomes by earning a little extra money as occasional freelance writers.
- Part-time writers whose major income comes from another job that will almost certainly be cast aside the moment writing becomes more profitable.
- Totally self-employed, full-time writers not on any payroll, who are expected to file honest returns mindful that no income taxes have been deducted at source.

Writers with other jobs need only attach to their income tax returns a statement summarizing writing income and expenses, and to show whether this extra work resulted in a profit or a loss. Any profit must be added to that taxable income earned from the other job. Losses, however, may be used to reduce it.

Writers living entirely from their craft must keep many more details – a list of all income and its sources, and receipts and vouchers to support expenses. Maintaining proper financial records not only serves as a reminder of cash that has flowed both in and out, but also helps to reduce problems that might be encountered should a tax return be audited.

All writers may reasonably deduct the cost of all stationery, including letterhead, envelopes, typewriter ribbons, computer and fax paper and ink cartridges, pencils, pens, and paper clips. Telephone costs, particularly long-distance calls, are also deductible, as are postage, membership dues in writers' organizations, union dues, accountants' fees, secretarial help, research assistance, subscriptions to newspapers and magazines, reference books, copyright costs, and photocopying charges.

Many writers find that their biggest annual deduction is for their work space. Those who work in an outside office may claim its rent as an expense. If, however, they work at home, they may write off a reasonable portion of their living space. A writer using one room as an office in a six-room apartment, for example, may claim one-sixth of the rent plus one-sixth of such other expenses as municipal taxes, heating, lighting, minor repairs, and ordinary maintenance. However, work space related costs can only be deducted from your *net income from writing* after you have deducted all your other costs.

An area of tax deduction often overlooked is the depreciation of office furniture and equipment. Both may be written off according to a fixed percentage determined by the income tax regulations. A computer or typewriter can be depreciated by 20 per cent of the total cost each year for five years. The same tax saving may be applied to printers, modems, fax machines, cameras, tape recorders, filing cabinets, desks, chairs, and telephone answering machines.

Travel is also an allowable expense, whether it is to visit a publisher or to gather research for an article. Here the non-fiction writer is at a distinct advantage, because in many cases, interviewing people in a different town personally is absolutely necessary. This could conceivably mean a bus trip from downtown Vancouver to nearby Burnaby, on the one hand, or a flight from Halifax to Istanbul, on the other.

The simple rule is that to be tax deductible, travel must relate to work. For the novelist who cannot secure an advance commitment from a publisher, a legitimate business trip may be extremely hard to prove. All is not lost, however. If a visit to Turkey is necessary to gather material that cannot be found elsewhere, it can either be claimed as an expense when the work is published, or written off against royalties.

Car travel, hotels, meals, and entertainment – the drinks you may want to buy a useful contact, the dinner you host for a person who is figuring prominently in your story, or the editor on your latest book – are also legitimate writers' expenses. Remember, though, that you cannot claim on your income tax form any expenses that a magazine or publishing house may already have refunded to you. Apart from being illegal, it is dishonest.

American Markets

The English-speaking Canadian who has begun to sell with some consistency enjoys a unique geographical advantage over colleague writers overseas. Canada has a southerly neighbour with a population of some 260 million people, most of whom speak English and are thus potential readers of English writing.

The American-published *Writer's Market* (see Chapter 11, Book Resources) lists more than 4,000 paying markets in the United States for novels, short stories, fillers, plays, gags, verses, even photographs the freelancer may take during travels. This book also gives the names and addresses of editors, and sets out their requirements – what they expect from a manuscript in content and length, and how long it takes them to report back to a writer with a decision on whether or not to publish.

Two U.S. monthly magazines are also indispensable to Canadian writers seeking new markets south of the border – *Writer's Digest* itself, the publisher of the annual *Writer's Market*, produced in Cincinnati for practical-minded freelancers, and *The Writer*, published in Boston for those with more literary tastes. These journals not only keep readers informed about markets and trends, but provide both a stimulus and a constant flow of fresh ideas. Writer's Digest Books, by the way, publishes an astonishing range of practical books for writers – from guides to writing genre fiction to manuals on magazine article writing.

The much-repeated rule about studying markets, as you must when writing for Canadian magazines, applies more than ever in the United States, because the array of American publications is awesome, and those that may at first appear similar most certainly are not on closer examination. Nearly all magazines have their own special character and narrow, specific needs to go with it.

The enormous selection of American magazines, however, in no way diminishes the difficulty in breaking into the huge market they have come to constitute, particularly with a Canadian story. The first point to ask yourself here is, "Why would an American magazine be interested in Canada?" A quick answer to the question is that most really aren't unless they can be *made* to be interested, or unless the story has a broad appeal to both nations.

Some Canadian stories, of course, will have an obvious and natural tie-in with American events. A perceptive article on NAFTA from a Canadian perspective might attract the interest of a U.S. business magazine. As a Canadian writer you will have to work hard to penetrate the American market, especially with ideas for the consumer magazines.

Most Canadians who have consistently sold their writing in the United States can thank those opportunities provided by the vast collection of American trade publications. If Canada is related to the United States at all, it is through sharing common trade channels, and having similar concerns about world politics and business. The moment American equipment and/or expertise is brought to bear on a Canadian building site, for example, there could legitimately be the makings of a story for an American trade or professional magazine. Sometimes, there may also be a story in how Canada sees, or deals with, problems specific to both countries.

But there is yet another hurdle to cross. Many American trade magazines are staff-written. This means that a staff writer will travel to Canada to cover an American story rooted here, so a manuscript from a Canadian freelancer must be exceptionally strong to win a place.

The odds can be beaten, though. After accepting a few manuscripts from a Canadian contributor, the editor of an American trade magazine might be willing to publish a monthly feature written by a Canadian on the Canadian viewpoint: what his or her country thinks about mutual problems and issues, and what solutions it can offer.

It is well worth trying to secure a foothold in the American market, for purely economic reasons. It is still extremely difficult, after all, for Canadians to make a satisfactory living by writing exclusively for magazines and publishing houses in their own country, which helps explain why most combine crafting poetry, novels, magazine articles, and non-fiction with other work. The situation may change though. Writing opportunities for Canada's writers have certainly increased since this book first appeared; with more settled economic times they are almost certain to continue to do so. And when they do, *The Canadian Writer's Market* will be there with a richer list than ever.

Adrian Waller

1

CONSUMER MAGAZINES

"Magazines constitute the only national press we possess in Canada. . . . Magazines, in a different way from any other medium, can help foster in Canadians a sense of themselves."
– *Report of the Special Senate Committee on Mass Media*, 1970

At the time of this report, 70 per cent of all magazines sold in Canada originated in the United States. Since then, protective federal legislation has helped to foster the growth of a vigorous local industry: twenty years on, Canadian magazines had captured 40 per cent of the local market, and had done so despite the fact that a mere 6 per cent of Canadian magazines ever reached our American-dominated newsstands. Today, almost half Canadian magazines reach readers through the mail as paid subscriptions, with a further 35 per cent delivered as free, controlled-circulation copies, yet in recent years this remarkable success story has faced threats from all sides. The first was to the postal subsidy.

Canada's enlightened federal postal subsidy program was established more than a century ago to help compensate for the isolation of many Canadian communities. The guiding principle was that all Canadians, wherever they lived, should have equal access to their nation's magazines, with the full range of individual and communal points of view they represented. The preferential postal rates for subscriber magazines have played a vital role in fostering the growth of the local industry by subsidizing distribution costs for magazines heavily reliant on subscription sales. The Canadian Magazine Publishers Association and other industry advocates had long warned that removing or reducing the subsidy would threaten many fragile publishing operations. Nevertheless, in December 1989, a cash-strapped federal government announced the incremental phasing out of the program. By 1995 it had been cut by two-thirds (it was removed from controlled-circulation magazines in 1992), and soon it may be removed altogether.

Magazines struggling with extra postal costs also faced strong consumer resistance to price hikes in the wake of the 7 per cent increase imposed by GST. Coinciding with the recession, the introduction of the GST in January 1990 was a body blow to the industry. According to a report by the CMPA, the first year of GST brought a devastating 62.5 per cent decrease in magazine profits. On top of the direct impact on subscription and advertising sales, Canadian magazines stood at an extra 7 per cent competitive disadvantage in relation to their U.S. competitors, as more than 50 million copies of U.S. magazines enter Canada each year without being taxed.

The stealthy introduction of split runs from across the border presented another threat. Split runs are special editions of magazines imported into Canada with rerun U.S. editorial content but deeply discounted Canadian advertising. They siphon off advertising that would otherwise go to Canadian magazines, eroding their market share. Consumer magazines simply cannot survive without a reliable level of advertising, their main source of revenue. (In the fall of 1997, the World Trade Organization, supporting the U.S. position, came down in favour of split runs in a ruling that, in the words of *Masthead*'s Doug Bennet, "effectively dismantles 30 years of legislation aimed at keeping out cheap Canadian advertising editions of powerful U.S. magazines." At the same time, the WTO decision ruled against *all* measures used to artificially prop up Canada's magazine industry, which included postal subsidies. The next year or so should see a clarification of the Canadian government's response to this ruling.)

As a result of these combined assaults, Canadian magazines have suffered heavy losses in revenue during the 1990s. The number of full- and part-time magazine employees decreased by more than 30 per cent between 1990 and 1993, while the number of unpaid voluntary staff increased by some 60 per cent. To underscore just how fragile the magazine publishing industry is, 47 per cent of the periodicals surveyed by Statistics Canada in 1984 ran at a loss, while only 41 per cent reported after-tax profits. In 1990-91, according to StatsCan, average pre-tax profit was 2 per cent, but a breakdown of this figure reveals how unequally this "profit" was spread: while the market leaders averaged a 4 per cent profit, a larger number of magazines – those with modest annual revenues below $100,000 – were averaging pre-tax losses of 22 per cent. The big players will often use the profits from their successful, high-circulation publications to support a smaller one not making a profit – an option not available to solo magazines. As the recession eased, however, magazines continued to show an extraordinary resilience. In 1993, according to figures from the industry magazine *Masthead*, 120 new magazines were launched while 89 ceased operations; the following year saw a similar number of launches (117), while only 54 were forced to close down. In 1996, the last year for which we have reliable data, the figures show further signs of stabilizing, with 90 launches and 34 certain closures.

Years of corporate consolidation have led to an environment in which the majority of Canadian newspapers and magazines are now controlled by a handful of media conglomerates, yet large numbers of independents persist too. It is perhaps a cause for wonder that the industry survives at all, let alone as the dynamic profusion of voices that it is. It is also a tribute to those who make it happen – to loyal Canadian readers, who continue to support their national press through their subscriptions; to the freelance writers who are its creative backbone; and to the publishers, editors, designers, and production staff who dream up and sustain the magazines. So when you're feeling especially frustrated about how poorly paid you were for that last article, perhaps you should spare a thought for your "tight-fisted" employer. When researching this book, it is often striking how many publishing ventures (smaller arts magazines stand out especially) are kept alive – indeed, in creative terms, are flourishing – through the enthusiasm, hard work, and sheer willpower of a few stubborn, committed, underpaid (often unpaid) individuals.

There are good reasons, however, why freelance writers' sympathy for many of their employers has become increasingly strained in recent years. These reasons pivot around the new electronic media and the impact they have had on questions of copyright.

Probably no development has affected the writer's environment more profoundly in recent years than the technological revolution of the Internet. Publishing on-line is very cost effective compared to conventional printing, and over the next few years we can expect more and more newspapers, magazines, and journals to operate a web site or a database service. Many of the larger magazines have already licensed their editorial content to commercial databases, who sell on the full text to subscribers. For some smaller magazines unable to meet ever-rising printing and distribution costs, the Web offers the only medium through which they can continue publishing and sharing their ideas.

The explosion of the new electronic media should, in theory, have significantly increased market opportunities for writers; in fact, their incomes, which have scarcely shifted in twenty years, are falling. Why? Simply, copyright infringement.

Copyright is a complex issue (for more discussion on this subject, see Adrian Waller's introduction). In general, however, it is in the writer's interest always to limit the transfer of rights. By giving up more than one-time rights, she may be giving up several opportunities for milking further payment from her efforts. Until quite recently, most magazines have sought only first Canadian serial rights – that is, first-time publication in a Canadian periodical. Once the piece has appeared in print, the writer is free to recycle it elsewhere if she can. (Before signing a contract, check out the Periodical Writers Association of Canada's Standard Agreement, contained in their *Copyright Information Kit* – see below.)

Traditionally, successful freelancers' earnings depended on their ability to license their work several times to non-competing markets. The rise of the Internet and commercial databases, and a new publishers' offensive over contracts, however, have greatly restricted writers' opportunities to gain more than one payment for their work. Large publishers especially have taken to placing freelancers' material on their web site or on commercial databases without securing permission from the writers, thus flagrantly contravening the Canadian Copyright Act. They have also developed new contracts seeking rights in perpetuity and requiring that freelancers surrender electronic rights for little or no extra payment. To add insult to injury, writers who refuse to sign have been denied further work from that source.

PWAC's response, already endorsed by a variety of writers' advocacy groups, is an initiative called TERLA – The Electronic Rights Licensing Agency, through which publishers would negotiate a fee for electronic usage. The agency would also collect and distribute these fees. As yet many publishers appear resistant to the plan, but something of the kind would seem essential if freelance writers are to retain any control over their creative work in the future, let alone be adequately paid for it.

Of course, the great boon the Internet offers writers is as a research tool, allowing the writer to tap into a practically infinite and ever-growing repository of information and opinion. While magazine writers can uncover all kinds of specialized data to help them write well-informed and authoritative articles, they can also visit numerous web sites that offer searchable databases of magazines and other periodicals to help them find new markets for their work (www.mediafinder.com, for example, carries information on over 20,000 publications). The challenge for the writer is to learn to use the Internet efficiently and avoid being endlessly sidetracked down intriguing but time-consuming false trails.

Despite the rather gloomy backgrounder above, most consumer magazines continue to rely heavily on freelancers, and the range of opportunity for the skilled and imaginative writer remains broad. Large-circulation consumer magazines that are heavily supported by advertising can usually afford to pay most for a writer's work – fifty cents to a dollar a word at the top of the scale. Standouts remain high-calibre general interest magazines like *Equinox*, *Canadian Geographic*, and *Saturday Night*, inflight magazines like *Canadian* and *enRoute*, top women's magazines like *Chatelaine* and *Homemaker's*, and leading business journals like *Profit* and the *Globe*'s *Report on Business Magazine*.

Many other magazines pay fees that can amount to between $1,000 and $1,500 for a professionally written feature article. Magazines with smaller circulations, which include the majority of those listed in the following pages, for obvious reasons tend to pay less – anything from $100 to $800 for an article of up to 3,000 words – though there is often some room for negotiation over the fee, depending on the writer's experience and the amount of research needed.

A last class comprises those magazines and journals that either generate much of their own editorial copy, or rely almost entirely on the voluntary contributions of professional colleagues or qualified readers. They may pay only occasionally for freelance contributions, or offer a modest honorarium or free copies. The committed freelance writer should consider contributing to these too, recognizing the long-term benefits in terms of experience and professional development. It is a sign of the times that more entries than ever before fall into this class in the present edition of *CWM*. More positively, however, it also reflects the large number of exciting and stimulating small magazines that are determinedly holding their own despite hostile market conditions, and deserve our support.

Today, more than ever, writing for publication is an intensely competitive business, and to succeed requires the right approach, good research, and plenty of hard work. The first, golden rule is to familiarize yourself thoroughly with the magazine's agenda and style before you approach the editor with a proposal. Find out whether they have an editorial calendar or run special or theme issues (the *CARD* directory and its annual supplement, *Publication Profiles*, sometimes list these – see Chapter 11, Book Resources). Always check out their web site if they have one, where you'll often find information about upcoming themes as well as writer's guidelines, fee schedules, and other information useful for contributors. You will often have time to prepare your submission ahead of schedule. Seasonal stories may need to be submitted up to six months in advance.

The successful freelancer keeps abreast of changes and developments in the industry. One excellent conduit for this information is the Periodical Writers Association of Canada. PWAC membership entitles you to a subscription to their informative bimonthly newsletter, *PWAContact*; a comprehensive listing in their annual directory, sent to editors and publishers nationwide; a free subscription to *Sources*, a biannual directory of contacts for journalists and other writers; and, not least, the opportunity to exchange market information and make important contacts with other writers. PWAC also offers for sale the very useful *Copyright Information Kit* ($18.00) and *Freelance Writers in Canada*, a 1997 report on the threats and opportunities facing the freelancer today ($12.50). Among other sources, the monthly *Canadian Author* magazine carries a useful section on new magazine markets for writers, and you'll also learn about new magazine launches in the pages of *Masthead*.

The most financially secure freelancers are those who are most versatile. They may feed feature articles steadily to a handful of consumer magazines, develop a working relationship with the editors of a couple of specialist trade publications, and write a regular column for a weekly newspaper. Or perhaps they have approached the director of communications of a government department or corporation and now have irregular (but comparatively lucrative) commissions to write reports, newsletters, or information packages. As professionals, they are ready to practise their craft in unexpected – even initially unappealing – contexts as well as in their chosen areas of interest.

Target your articles, but remember that other, independent publications might also be interested in the fruits of your research. Always look for research follow-on ideas. Research for a feature on city gardens for a general interest consumer magazine might also turn up useful background material for an article on the gardening centre phenomenon for a business journal or a more technical piece for a trade publication. Again, you'll need to be very wary about rights in such cases.

Note the magazines that interest you in the following pages and send for sample copies, or search them out in a good bookstore or your public library. Generally, it is not a good idea to send unsolicited work without an initial written inquiry. Always request contributor's guidelines where these are available in hard copy only (enclosing an SASE with your request). They may be a few short, practical remarks or several pages of background and detailed instructions, but close attention to these guidelines will often make the difference in the way your submission is received. Be sure to check what form your submission should take. Many magazine editors prefer to receive them on disk. Ensure that you provide it in the appropriate program, or in a readily convertible, text-only form. Provide hard copy back-up, too, in case the disk presents problems or the editor chooses to do an initial edit on paper. Increasingly, e-mail is used as a means of transmitting manuscripts.

Nothing will endear you less to a hard-pressed editor than to present him or her with an unintelligible disk or a poorly presented article. A submission full of spelling and punctuation errors, manifesting an ignorance of basic grammar, will not impress. On the other hand, clean copy, delivered on time, may win you an important ally. Your first submission to a periodical should always include a story outline along with a brief summary of your professional experience and clippings of previously published stories (tearsheets). Mention any experience that qualifies you to write on the topic. For most editors, evidence of previous experience is initially the single most attractive feature in a submission. Always be businesslike in your dealings with editors – respond immediately to letters, phone calls, or e-mail messages, and be friendly and cooperative. And *always* include an SASE with *every* inquiry or submission that requires a response.

Arts & Cultural

Aboriginal Voices
116 Spadina Avenue, Suite 201, Toronto, ON M5V 2K6
Phone: (416) 703-4577 Fax: (416) 703-4581
E-mail: abvoices@inforamp.net
Web site: www.cacmall.com
Contact: Millie Knapp, editor
Circulation: 20,000
Published bimonthly

A non-profit charitable organization whose purpose is to reclaim Aboriginal writings, images, sounds, dance, and arts, and to inspire the reclamation of First Nations culture. Received the Native American Journalists Association's 1995 award for excellence. Articles 1,500 to 2,000 words. Rates vary, depending on project.

Applied Arts
885 Don Mills Road, Suite 324, Don Mills, ON M3C 1V9
Phone: (416) 510-0909 Fax: (416) 510-0913
E-mail: app-arts@interlog.com
Web site: www.interlog.com/~app-arts
Contact: Sara Curtis, editor
Circulation: 12,000
Published bimonthly

Canada's leading graphic arts magazine, targeting visual communicators who work in both traditional and new media. Spotlights the work of graphic design, advertising, photography, and illustration professionals, featuring outstanding examples of their work. Pays 40¢ to 50¢/word on acceptance for articles of 1,200 to 2,500 words. Guidelines available.

Artfocus Magazine
P.O. Box 1063, Station F, Toronto, ON M4Y 2T7
Phone: (416) 925-5564 Fax: (416) 925-2972
E-mail: info@artfocus.com
Web site: www.artfocus.com
Contact: Pat Fleisher, publisher/editor
Circulation: 8,000
Published quarterly
   Features art gallery and museum reviews and previews, profiles of contemporary artists, dealers, and collectors, and articles on media and technique by prominent artists. Also comments on controversial issues in the arts. Carries short articles of 500 to 600 words, features of 1,500 to 2,000 words. Fees range from $50 to $200, paid after publication. Query first with samples of written work.

Artichoke: Writings about the Visual Arts
901 Jervis Street, Unit 208, Vancouver, BC V6E 2B6
Phone: (604) 683-1941 Fax: (604) 683-1941
Contact: Paula Gustafson, editor
Circulation: 1,000
Published 3 times a year
   The only nationally distributed magazine consistently presenting and discussing the visual arts in western Canada. Also features articles and reviews about national and international artists and exhibitions, analysis of current and critical issues, and stories connected with the visual arts. Preferred length for features 1,500 to 2,000 words, reviews 1,000 to 1,500 words, book reviews and ArtSeen column 500 to 750 words. Pays on publication: $75 for features and reviews, less for shorter pieces. "Artichoke does not publish academic jargon or artspeak. Articles written with clarity, precision, and a knowledge of art are welcomed." Guidelines available.

ArtsAtlantic

145 Richmond Street, Charlottetown, PE CIA IJI
Phone: (902) 628-6138 Fax: (902) 566-4648
E-mail: artsatlantic@isn.net
Contact: Joseph Sherman, editor
Circulation: 2,700
Published 3 times a year

Award-winning arts review carrying features, reviews, and reports on Atlantic Canada's fine arts, cinema, video, artisanship, performance, literature, and topics with national resonance. Reviews are 600 to 800 words, feature articles 1,200 to 3,000 words. Pays a flat rate of $75 per review, 15¢/word for features – up to a maximum of $400 – on publication. Welcomes approaches by mail, phone, or fax.

Atlantic Books Today

1657 Barrington Street, Suite 502, Halifax, NS B3J 2AI
Phone: (902) 429-4454 Fax: (902) 429-4454
E-mail: bookatl@istar.ca
Contact: Elizabeth Eve, managing editor
Circulation: 32,000
Published quarterly

Formerly the *Atlantic Provinces Book Review*. Features books, writing, and issues relating to the Atlantic region. Pays 20¢/word on publication for short pieces of 250 to 350 words. Welcomes inquiries by e-mail, mail, fax, or phone.

Azure

2 Silver Avenue, Toronto, ON M6R 3A2
Phone: (416) 588-2588 Fax: (416) 588-2357
Contact: Nelda Rodger, editor
Circulation: 17,000
Published bimonthly

A design review, covering developments in graphic, interior, and industrial design, art, and architecture in Canada and abroad; directed toward designers, architects, and the visually aware. Pays on publication. Guidelines available.

B.C. BookWorld

3516 West 13th Avenue, Vancouver, BC V6R 2S3
Phone: (604) 736-4011 Fax: (604) 736-4011
E-mail: bcbook@portal.ca
Contact: Alan Twigg, publisher
Circulation: 100,000
Published quarterly

Promotes B.C. books and authors. Circulated by more than 600 distributors. Preferred length 500 to 750 words. All fees negotiated on assignment, but most writing is in-house, so phone or write first. This is not a trade publication or a review periodical – it's a populist, tabloid-format newspaper.

Blackflash

12 – 23rd Street E., Saskatoon, SK S7K 0H5
Phone: (306) 244-8018 Fax: (306) 665-6568
E-mail: af248@sfn.saskatoon.sk.ca
Contact: Linda Stark, assistant editor
Circulation: 1,300
Published quarterly

The only magazine in Canada that focuses on critical writing about photography. Pays $100 to $250 for 1,500 to 2,500 words. Accepts proposals/outlines only; no unrequested submissions. Guidelines available.

Books in Canada

50 St. Clair Avenue E., 4th Floor, Toronto, ON M4T 1M9
Phone: (416) 924-2777
E-mail: binc@istar.ca
Contact: Gerald Owen, managing editor
Circulation: 8,000
Published 9 times a year

An award-winning magazine providing reviews of Canadian books, interviews and profiles of Canadian authors, and general articles to entertain the literate reader. Carries reviews by some of the country's best-known writers and critics. Pays 10¢/word on publication. Cannot take responsibility for responding to or returning unsolicited submissions. "All reviews and articles are assigned to our pool of freelancers, most of whom have extensive publication credits. So query first, always. Don't contact us if you've never read *BiC*."

Border Crossings
500 – 70 Arthur Street, Winnipeg, MB R3B 1G7
Phone: (204) 942-5778 Fax: (204) 949-0793
E-mail: bordercr@escape.ca
Contact: Meeka Walsh, editor
Circulation: 4,000
Published quarterly

An interdisciplinary arts review with an educated national and international audience, featuring articles, book reviews, artist profiles, and interviews covering the full range of the contemporary arts in Canada and beyond. Subjects include architecture, dance, fiction, film, painting, photography, poetry, politics, and theatre. Pays a negotiated fee on publication. Use the magazine as your guide when formulating submissions, but first query by letter or phone.

Broken Pencil
P.O. Box 203, Station P, Toronto, ON M5S 2S7
Phone: (416) 538-2813
E-mail: halpen@interlog.com
Web site: www.interlog.com/~halpen
Contact: Hal Niedzviecki, editor
Circulation: 2,000
Published twice a year

A guide to 'zines and alternative culture in Canada. Accepts musings on underground culture and original fiction. Pays $25 to $200 on publication for 500 to 4,000 words. No poetry. "Read the magazine first! Only the knowledgeable and unconventional need apply."

C Magazine
P.O. Box 5, Station B, Toronto, ON M5T 2T2
Phone: (416) 539-9495 Fax: (416) 539-9903
E-mail: cmag@istar.ca
Contact: Joyce Mason, editor/publisher
Circulation: 7,000

Published quarterly

Canada's leading international magazine of contemporary art, criticism, and reviews. Features are 1,000 to 3,500 words, reviews 500 words maximum. Feature rates vary; $100 paid per 500-word review. Pays on publication. Guidelines available.

Canadian Art

70 The Esplanade, 2nd Floor, Toronto, ON M5E 1R2
Contact: Richard Rhodes, editor
Circulation: 20,000
Published quarterly

Covers visual arts in Canada in a lively and opinionated way. Includes articles on painting, sculpture, film, photography, architecture, design, video, and television, with critical profiles of new artists and assessments of established art-world figures. Reviews and features 500 to 3,000 words. Pays $200 for 500 words, up to $1,500 for 3,000 words, on publication. Query first. No unsolicited submissions. Guidelines available.

Canadian Author

776 Colborne Street, London, ON N6A 3Z9
Phone: (519) 438-2011
E-mail: DougBale@netcom.ca
Web site: www.canauthors.org/cauthor.html
Contact: Doug Bale, editor
Circulation: 3,000
Published quarterly

Canada's oldest national writers' magazine. "Includes news, views, reviews, interviews, and how-to's, poetry, fiction, drama, columns on legalities, practicalities, technology, markets, and more." A valuable resource for writers. Pays a basic rate of $20 for short pieces and book reviews, $30 per published page for longer items, on publication. Some content bought with provision for second use on Web pages at extra rate. Written queries only. Guidelines available.

Canadian Musician

23 Hannover Drive, Unit 7, St. Catharines, ON L2W 1A3
Phone: (905) 641-3471   Fax: (905) 641-1648

E-mail: jmckay@nor.com
Web site: www.nor.com.nwc
Contact: Jeff McKay, assistant editor
Published bimonthly

A magazine for professional and amateur musicians, as well as serious music enthusiasts and industry personnel. Most articles (2,000 to 3,000 words) are assigned and fees are negotiable. Pays on acceptance. All writers must be technically and musically literate. Guidelines available.

Canadian Notes & Queries

c/o The Porcupine's Quill, 68 Main Street, Erin, ON NOB ITO
Phone: (519) 833-9158 Fax: (519) 833-9158
E-mail: pql@sentex.net
Web site: www.sentex.net/~pql
Contact: John Metcalf, editor
Circulation: 660
Published twice a year

Represents the antiquarian book trade in Canada. Of particular interest to book collectors, dealers, writers, and librarians. Articles 1,000 to 10,000 words. Cannot pay but welcomes submission inquiries.

Canadian Theatre Review

Department of Drama, University of Guelph, Guelph, ON NIG 2WI
Phone: (519) 824-4120, ext. 3147 Fax: (519) 824-0560
Contact: the editors
Circulation: 850
Published quarterly

Publishes playscripts, essays of interest to theatre professionals, and interviews with playwrights, actors, directors, and designers. Issues are thematic. Preferred article length 1,500 to 3,000 words. Pay scale and guidelines available on request. Hard copy must be included with IBM WordPerfect disk.

Canadian Writer's Journal

P.O. Box 5180, New Liskeard, ON POJ IPO
Phone: (705) 647-5424 or 1-800-258-5451 Fax: (705) 647-8366

E-mail: cwj@ntl.sympatico.ca
Web site: www.nt.net/~cwj/index.htm
Contact: Deborah Ranchuk, editor
Circulation: 400
Published quarterly

A digest-size quarterly that is a useful source of ideas on professional, motivational, and marketing aspects of the profession. Emphasis on short how-to articles for both apprentice and professional writers. Also opinion pieces, book reviews, and short poems. Length 400 to 2,000 words. "Queries or complete mss. welcome. Writers should present specifics rather than generalities, and avoid overworked subjects such as overcoming writer's block, handling rejection, etc." Runs annual contests for poetry and short fiction. Guidelines available.

Chart Magazine
41 Britain Street, Suite 200, Toronto, ON M5A 1R7
Phone: (416) 363-3101 Fax: (416) 363-3109
E-mail: chart@chartnet.com
Web site: www.chartnet.com
Contact: Nada Laskovski, editor/publisher
Circulation: 20,000
Published monthly

Established 1990. Covers new music for a high school/university audience. Canadian bands, independent/alternative music, campus radio, pop culture reviews and articles. Pays only a token amount for most articles. Guidelines available.

The Church-Wellesley Review
491 Church Street, Suite 200, Toronto, ON M4Y 2C6
Web site: www.xtra.ca/cwr
Contacts: Jeffrey Round, Hilary Clark, and Rod Heimpel, co-editors
Published quarterly (on-line), annually (print)

A literary publication by, for, and about gays and lesbians. Invites submissions of high-quality, innovative writing (up to 5,000 words in any genre). Content for annual print review (distributed as a supplement to *Xtra Magazine*) is chosen from the quarterly on-line issues. Pays a modest honorarium on publication. "Look carefully at opening sentences and paragraphs. Because of the large volume of submissions we receive, you must catch our interest quickly or we will not read past the first pages."

CineACTION!
40 Alexander Street, Apartment 705, Toronto, ON M4Y 1B5
Phone: (416) 964-3534
Contact: editorial collective
Circulation: 3,000
Published 3 times a year
   A film magazine that explores neglected and unconventional cinema, both mainstream and independent productions, from a feminist and socialist perspective. Submission inquiries welcome. It is the magazine's policy to pay for contributions, but limited funds mean payment is sometimes delayed.

Classical Music Magazine
P.O. Box 45045, Mississauga, ON L5G 4S7
Phone: (905) 271-0339 Fax: (905) 271-9748
E-mail: classical_music@inforamp.net
Web site: www.cmpa.ca/pa3.html
Contact: Anthony Copperthwaite, publisher
Circulation: 7,000
Published quarterly
   Featuring classical music in all its aspects, including news stories, photo features, historical articles, personality profiles, and interviews. Pays on publication for articles of 2,500 to 3,000 words. Appropriate short news items (100 to 200 words) earn $50; longer articles up to $300. Send $5 for writer's guidelines.

Coda Magazine
P.O. Box 1002, Station O, Toronto, ON M4A 2N4
Phone: (416) 593-7230 Fax: (416) 593-7230
E-mail: codawest@mars.ark.com
Contact: Bill Smith, editor
Circulation: 3,000
Published bimonthly
   The Canadian jazz and improvised music magazine with an international reputation, published since 1958, with articles, essays,

personality profiles, and reviews – 900 to 3,000 words. Fees are negotiated. "*Coda* is a specialized periodical and only publishes work by experts in this field, so all is negotiable."

Dance International

Roedde House, 1415 Barclay Street, Vancouver, BC V6G 1J6
Phone: (604) 681-1525 Fax: (604) 681-7732
Contact: Maureen Riches, editor
Circulation: 3,500
Published quarterly

Provides a forum for lively and critical commentary on the best in national and international dance, including features, reviews, reports, and commentaries. Preferred length 1,000 to 2,000 words. Pays on publication $100 to $150 for features, $65 to $80 for commentaries, $40 to $60 for reviews, $60 to $75 for notebook. Full guidelines available.

FUSE Magazine

401 Richmond Street W., Suite 454, Toronto, ON M5V 3A8
Phone: (416) 340-8026 Fax: (416) 340-0494
E-mail: fuse@interlog.com
Web site: www.interlog.com/~fuse
Contact: Petra Chevrier, production co-ordinator
Circulation: 2,000
Published quarterly

Addresses all aspects of contemporary art. Special emphasis on issues relating to different cultural communities, including feminist issues, gay and lesbian culture and politics, minority struggles, and economic and policy analysis. Reviews visual arts, from independent production to mass media, including video, film, television, music, performance art, theatre, and books. Articles 1,400 to 5,000 words. No fiction. Pays 10¢/word on publication, $100 for reviews. "Please send SASE for guidelines before submitting unsolicited copy."

In 2 Print Magazine

P.O. Box 102, Port Colborne, ON L3K 5V7
Phone: (905) 834-1539 Fax: (905) 834-1540
Contact: Jean Baird, editor

Circulation: 25,000
Published quarterly

A national forum for young emerging artists (12 to 21 years), featuring poetry, short stories, and plays (up to 1,500 words), paintings, photography, computer art, and cartoons. Publishes an eclectic array of interviews and reviews of books, music, and theatre. "A terrific magazine" – Peter Gzowski. Fees range from $25 to $200, paid on publication. Guidelines available.

Inuit Art Quarterly

2081 Merivale Road, Nepean, ON K2G 1G9
Phone: (613) 224-8189 Fax: (613) 224-2907
E-mail: iaf@inuitart.org
Web site: www.inuitart.org
Contact: Marybelle Mitchell, editor
Circulation: 4,000

Devoted exclusively to Inuit art, and directed toward art specialists, artists, historians, teachers, and all interested readers with the purpose of giving Inuit artists a voice. Carries feature articles, profiles, interviews, news and reviews, and reader commentary. Most features (2,000 to 3,000 words) pay $500 to $700. Pays on acceptance. A knowledge of Inuit art and culture essential. Query editor first. Guidelines available.

The Lazy Writer

P.O. Box 977, Station F, 50 Charles Street E., Toronto,
    ON M4Y 2N9
Phone: (416) 538-0559
E-mail: lzwriter@interlog.com
Contact: Cheryl Carter, editor
Circulation: 2,500
Published quarterly

Offers information and inspiration for writers in all genres. Publishes articles about the profession and craft of writing, a cross-country calendar of events and deadlines, reviews, news, and poetry and prose. Look at back issues to get a sense of the type of work published. Will begin paying contributors in spring 1998. Guidelines available.

Matriart
401 Richmond Street W., Suite 389, Toronto, ON M5V 3A8
Phone: (416) 977-0097 Fax: (416) 977-7425
E-mail: warc@interlog.com
Contact: Linda Abrahams, editor
Circulation: 2,000
Published quarterly
   Established 1990. A journal of contemporary women's art for a general audience as well as academic and feminist communities. Committed to cultural diversity. Issues are thematic. Reviews 750 to 1,000 words; feature articles 2,000 words. Pays 7¢/word, $48/image page. Guidelines available.

Mix: The Magazine of Artist-Run Culture
401 Richmond Street W., Suite 446, Toronto, ON M5V 3A8
Phone: (416) 506-1012 Fax: (416) 340-8458
Web site: www.mix.web.net/mix
Contact: Jennifer Rudder, editor
Circulation: 3,000
Published quarterly
   A national magazine that traces developments in contemporary art, including painting, sculpture, installations, video, new music, dance, and performance. Articles 2,000 to 2,500 words. Contact editor for guidelines and pay rates.

Musicworks: The Journal of Sound Exploration
179 Richmond Street W., Toronto, ON M5V 1V3
Phone: (416) 977-3546 Fax: (416) 208-1084
E-mail: sound@musicworks.web.net
Web site: www.musicworks.web.net/sound
Contact: Gayle Young, editor
Circulation: 2,500
Published 3 times a year
   Distributed with audio component – cassettes or CDs – to illustrate articles and interviews covering a broad range of contemporary classical and experimental music. Also ethnic music and sound related to dance and visual art. Features are 1,000 to 3,500 words. Fees depend on length, complexity, and other factors. Pays on publication. Welcomes inquiries. Guidelines available.

The Mystery Review
P.O. Box 233, Colborne, ON K0K 1S0
Phone: (613) 475-4440 Fax: (613) 475-3400
E-mail: 71554.551@compuserve.com
Web site: www.inline-online.com/mystery
Contact: Barbara Davey, editor
Circulation: 5,000
Published quarterly

For readers of mystery and suspense. Carries information on new mystery titles, book reviews, interviews with authors, real-life unsolved mysteries, puzzles, and word games relating to the genre. Pays honorarium on publication. Contact editor for guidelines. Query before submitting an article or review.

The New Reader
1701 West 3rd Avenue, Vancouver, BC V6J 1K7
Phone: (604) 732-7631 Fax: (604) 732-3765
Contact: Celia Duthie, publisher
Circulation: 11,000
Published quarterly

A free-circulation book review of new titles of interest to the general reader. One issue each year is devoted to reviews of children's books. Length 200 to 800 words. Pays on publication with a $100 gift certificate for major reviews, a $50 gift certificate for brief reviews. Welcomes unsolicited reviews, but acceptance not guaranteed. "Submissions should be succinct, interesting, and positive." Guidelines available.

ON SPEC: More Than Just Science Fiction!
P.O. Box 4727, Edmonton, AB T6E 5G6
Phone: (403) 413-0215 Fax: (403) 413-0215
E-mail: onspec@earthling.net
Web site: www.icomm.ca/onspec
Contact: Katerina Carastathis, publisher's assistant
Circulation: 2,000
Published quarterly

Specializes in science fiction, fantasy, horror, and magic realism by Canadian authors. Publishes short stories and poetry. Stories up to 6,000 words are paid 3¢/word, stories under 1,000 words earn $30;

poems up to 100 lines earn $20 each. Pays on acceptance. "Read the magazine (samples $6 including tax and postage), and send SASE for guidelines before submitting – we have unusual format require- ments. We welcome new as well as established writers."

Opera Canada

366 Adelaide Street E., Suite 434, Toronto, ON M5A 3X9
Phone: (416) 363-0395 Fax: (416) 363-0396
Contact: Jocelyn Laurence, managing editor
Circulation: 5,000
Published quarterly

Devoted for more than 30 years to Canadian opera. Reviews international performances, interviews Canada's best singers, and addresses opera-related cultural issues. Reviews up to 300 words; features 1,200 to 1,500 words. Accepts submissions and submission inquiries. Pays $300 on publication for 1,500 words.

Parachute

4060 St. Laurent Boulevard, Suite 501, Montreal, PQ H2W 1Y9
Phone: (514) 842-9805 Fax: (514) 287-7146
Contact: Chantal Pontbriand, editor
Circulation: 3,000
Published quarterly

A bilingual magazine offering readers in-depth articles on the theory and practice of art today – interviews with artists, and arti- cles on music, cinema, photography, theatre, dance, and video. Pays about $100 for reviews and issues column (to a maximum of 1,000 words), up to $500 for articles and interviews (3,000 to 5,000 words), on publication. Guidelines available.

PARSEC

1942 Regent Street, Unit G, Suite 108, Sudbury, ON P3E 3Z9
Phone: (705) 523-1831 Fax: (705) 523-5276
E-mail: parsec@vianet.on.ca
Web site: icewall.vianet.on.ca/comm/parsec
Contact: Chris Krejlgaard, publisher
Circulation: 2,500
Published quarterly

Addresses Canadian contributions to science fiction, fantasy, and horror, and also publishes fiction and artwork in these genres. Length 500 to 5,000 words. Pays a negotiable fee between $70 and $125 on publication. Query first. Guidelines available.

Performing Arts & Entertainment in Canada

104 Glenrose Avenue, Toronto, ON M4T 1K8
Phone: (416) 484-4534 Fax: (416) 484-6214
E-mail: kbell@interlog.ca
Contact: Karen Bell, editor
Circulation: 44,000
Published quarterly

Explores the issues and trends affecting performing arts in Canada – primarily theatre, dance, opera, ballet, and film. Also carries profiles on individual performers, companies, and troupes. Prefers articles of 600 to 1,500 words, which earn $95 to $170, paid on publication. Query first.

Periwinkle

P.O. Box 8052, Victoria, BC V8W 3R7
Phone: (250) 382-5868
E-mail: Hannah@Islandnet.com
Contact: Tanya Yaremchuk, editor
Published quarterly

A new magazine carrying mainstream as well as gay, lesbian, feminist, and alternative poetry and short fiction. Pays $10 to $20 for short fiction, $5 to $10 for poetry on publication. Guidelines available.

Quill & Quire

70 The Esplanade, Suite 210, Toronto, ON M5E 1R2
Phone: (416) 360-0044 Fax: (416) 955-0794
E-mail: quill@hookup.net
Contact: Scott Anderson, editor
Circulation: 7,000
Published monthly

The news journal of the Canadian book trade – for booksellers, librarians, educators, publishers, and writers. Prints news, reviews, lists of recently published and upcoming books, and profiles of authors and publishing houses. Includes the biannual supplement

Canadian Publishers Directory. (Also now publishes the compendious sourcebook of the publishing industry, *The Book Trade in Canada*.) Pays 30¢/word for news articles, $50 for reviews of 400 to 600 words, on acceptance. "We do not accept unsolicited articles. Query by phone or fax."

The Readers Showcase
10608 – 172nd Street, Edmonton, AB T5S 1H8
Phone: (403) 486-5802 Fax: (403) 481-9276
E-mail: suggitt@planet.eon.net
Contact: Tanis Nessler, editor
Circulation: 400,000
Published bimonthly
    Features book reviews, author interviews, and general interest articles. Preferred length 500 to 1,500 words. Fees (paid on publication) vary according to project and writer's experience, and may be negotiated.

Scrivener Creative Review
McGill University, 853 Sherbrooke Street W., Montreal, PQ H3A 2T6
Phone: (514) 398-6588 Fax: (514) 398-8146
Contact: Michelle Lelievre, editor
Circulation: 500
Published annually
    A journal of prose (fiction, non-fiction, drama), poetry, reviews, interviews, art, and photography, focusing on new Canadian and American works. Prose should not exceed 30 pages; 5 to 15 poems. Pays in copies. Submission inquiries welcome. For sample copies, send $3 plus $1 for postage. Submission deadline January 15. Guidelines available.

Shift Magazine
119 Spadina Avenue, Suite 202, Toronto, ON M5V 2L1
Phone: (416) 977-7982 Fax: (416) 977-7983
E-mail: info@shift.com
Web site: www.shift.com
Contact: Joanna Pachner, managing editor
Circulation: 80,000
Published bimonthly

A general interest cultural magazine with a vigorous and youthful editorial agenda and a digital twist. It's about life in a culture of change, where pop culture, technology, music, film, and entertainment collide. Pays 50¢ to 80¢/word on acceptance for stories of 2,000 to 4,000 words. Welcomes submissions, which should include author bio. Guidelines available.

Shiver Magazine
P.O. Box 178, Surrey, BC V3T 4W8
Phone: (604) 581-9111
E-mail: shiver@clubtek.com
Web site: www.clubtek.com/shiver
Contact: T.L Craigen, editor
Circulation: 1,000
Published biannually
Publishes horror, fantasy, science fiction, and related non-fiction, along with interviews relevant to the genres. Length 3,000 to 7,000 words. Pays 1¢/word for first 5,000 words, ½¢/word after that, on acceptance. "We are a concept magazine in which characters from different stories interact." Guidelines available.

Spaceways Weekly
P.O. Box 3023, London, ON N6A 4H9
Phone: (519) 690-0773
E-mail: spaceways@mirror.org
Web site: www.mirror.org/spaceways
Contact: Rigel D. Chiokis, editor/publisher
Circulation: 100
Publishes science fiction and fantasy short stories by e-mail. Specializes in new writers but also publishes established authors. Stories from 100 to 5,000 plus words. Pays a maximum of $50 on acceptance. Electronic submissions preferred. Guidelines available.

Storyteller: Canada's Short Story Magazine
43 Lightfoot Place, Kanata, ON K2L 3M3
Phone: (613) 592-2776 Fax: (613) 236-4246
E-mail: stories@direct-internet.net
Web site: www.direct-internet.net/storyteller_magazine

Contact: Terry Tyo, publisher/managing editor
Circulation: 1,500
Published quarterly

Features popular fiction of all types, "but keep genre 'soft.' Our readers are not necessarily familiar with all genres." Stories 2,000 to 6,000 words. Contributors receive 3 copies. "We're interested in stories about living, not dying, stories about people who show us who they are by what they do." Guidelines available.

Theatre News

619 Yonge Street, Unit 203, Toronto, ON M4Y 1E5
Phone: (416) 961-0900 Fax: (416) 966-8788
E-mail: theatre@interlog.com
Web site: www.durhammall.com/theatrenews
Contact: Alan Raeburn, features editor
Circulation: 28,000
Published monthly

Provides theatre news for theatre patrons. Preferred length 500 to 750 words. Fees are negotiated, paid on publication, but not all articles are paid. Compensation usually reserved for exceptionally well written work by established writers. Guidelines available.

Time for Rhyme

P.O. Box 1055, Battleford, SK S0M 0E0
Phone: (306) 445-5172
Contact: Richard W. Unger, editor
Circulation: 100
Published quarterly

For those who enjoy traditional rhyming poetry. Contains a poem markets column and rhyming verse only. Pays with a copy for well-written (not first-draft) poems up to 32 lines. Read guidelines first. Sample copies $3.25.

Writer's Block Magazine

P.O. Box 32, 9944 – 33rd Avenue, Edmonton, AB T6N 1E8
Contact: Shaun Donnelly, publisher/editor
Circulation: 5,000
Published twice a year

Focuses on genre fiction: fantasy, horror, mystery, romance, science fiction, and western. Also open to poetry and humour. Pays 5¢/word on publication for 500 to 5,000 words. Guidelines available.

The Writers Publishing

P.O. Box 55, Tofino, BC VOR 2ZO
Phone: (604) 725-2588 Fax: (604) 725-2588
Contact: R. Tuck, editor
Circulation: 400
Published quarterly

Presents poetry, short stories, and memoirs up to 1,000 to 1,500 words. Pays a flat rate of $25 on publication. Open submission format – even legible handwriting accepted.

Business

AfriCan Access Magazine

1290 Broad Street, Suite 201, Victoria, BC V8W 2A5
Phone: (250) 598-4940 Fax: (250) 598-4977
E-mail: editor@africanaccess.com
Web site: www.africanaccess.com
Contact: Chris Roberts, publisher/editor-in-chief
Circulation: 5,000
Published quarterly

A new quarterly aimed at the internationally oriented business, travel, NGO, and government markets. Pays 25¢/word plus on publication for 600 to 1,400 words. "We are willing to work with new and experienced writers, so rates vary. Query with unique, practical idea related to growing Canadian–Sub-Sahara African relationship, especially business and travel related or how-to. Photos an asset." Guidelines available.

AgriFamily Business Magazine

93 Lombard Avenue, Suite 108, Winnipeg, MB R3B 3B1
Phone: (204) 985-8160 Fax: (204) 943-8991
E-mail: wnat@fox.nstn.ca
Contact: Stuart Slayen, editor

Circulation: 30,000
Published 5 times a year
   Aims to empower Canadian agricultural producers with the information they need to make effective business decisions. Provides news, features, and columns. Most feature stories run from 1,200 to 2,200 words. Rates vary according to story length and complexity. Pays on acceptance. Guidelines available.

Atlantic Business Magazine
197 Water Street, P.O. Box 2356, Station C, St. John's, NF A1C 6E7
Phone: (709) 726-9300 Fax: (709) 726-3013
E-mail: ehutton@nfld.com
Contact: Edwina Hutton, editor
Circulation: 25,000
Published bimonthly
   An Atlantic magazine carrying business and investment articles with a regional focus. Pays around 15¢/word for 1,500 to 2,500 words. "Please send an outline of any story ideas you have for business in Atlantic Canada. We will respond promptly." Guidelines available.

Atlantic Chamber Journal
275 Amirault Street, Dieppe, NB E1A 1G1
Phone: (506) 858-8710 Fax: (506) 858-1707
E-mail: eastpub@nbnet.nb.ca
Contact: Elie J. Richard, publisher
Circulation: 8,000
Published bimonthly
   A regional business magazine serving Atlantic Canada since 1987, making it, unofficially, the longest continuously running Atlantic business magazine. Uses articles of 300 to 1,200 words. Seldom pays, though sometimes contributes $50 to $100 for a chosen piece.

Atlantic Lifestyle Business Magazine
197 Water Street, P.O. Box 2356, Station C, St. John's, NF A1C 6E7
Phone: (709) 726-9300 Fax: (709) 726-3013
E-mail: ehutton@nfld.com

Contact: Edwina Hutton, editor
Circulation: 25,000
Published bimonthly
Examines culture, lifestyle, and business in Atlantic Canada. Pays 15¢/word on publication for articles of 2,000 to 2,500 words, a fixed rate for cover stories. Story ideas always welcome. Guidelines available.

B.C. Business
4180 Lougheed Highway, 4th Floor, Burnaby, BC V5C 6A7
Phone: (604) 299-7311 Fax: (604) 299-9188
Contact: Bonnie Irving, editor
Circulation: 26,000
Published monthly
A regional business publication covering real estate, telecommunications, personal finance, management trends and technology, and lifestyle. Directed toward business owners, managers, entrepreneurs, and professionals. Pays 50¢/word two weeks before publication for features of 1,500 to 3,000 words, 40¢/word for advertising features. "Read at least six back issues before querying." Guidelines available.

Business Examiner
1824 Store Street, Victoria, BC V8T 4R4
Phone: (250) 381-3926 Fax: (250) 381-5606
E-mail: be@busex.bc.ca
Web site: www.busex.bc.ca
Contact: Bjorn Stavrum, editor
Circulation: 14,000
Published twice a month
Provides news, features, and columns with a strong business angle. Pays $50 to $150 on publication for 300 to 600 words. Fees are negotiated. Submit story ideas first. Vancouver Island and Victoria region subjects, profiles, and trends get preference. Guidelines available.

Canadian Business
777 Bay Street, 5th Floor, Toronto, ON M5W 1A7
Phone: (416) 596-5475 Fax: (416) 599-0901

Contact: Arthur Johnson, editor
Circulation: 90,000
Published biweekly

Canada's premier national business journal, carrying incisive and thoughtful commentary and advice on business issues and profiles of successful business people. Articles 800 to 4,000 words. Pays $500 to $3,000 on acceptance, depending on assignment and experience. However, this magazine draws on a pool of professional writers and rarely uses new contributors. Initial inquiries by mail.

Canadian Money Saver
P.O. Box 370, Bath, ON KOH IGO
Phone: (613) 352-7448 Fax: (613) 352-7700
E-mail: moneyinfo@canadianmoneysaver.ca
Contact: Dale Ennis, publisher/editor
Circulation: 32,400
Published 11 times a year

A national consumer finance magazine offering articles (800 to 1,600 words) on such current topics as personal finance, tax, investment techniques, retirement planning, consumer purchases, small business practice, and discount service. Fees are negotiated. "Contributors have the opportunity to participate in national and offshore conferences, and propose other writing projects." Guidelines available.

The Financial Post Magazine
333 King Street E., 3rd Floor, Toronto, ON M5A 4N2
Phone: (416) 350-6172 Fax: (416) 350-6171
E-mail: fpmag@total.net
Web site: www.canoe.ca/FP
Contact: Jocelyn Laurence, senior editor
Circulation: 200,000
Published 11 times a year plus *FP 500* annual

An executive lifestyle magazine featuring political, business, and general interest articles and personal finance columns, mostly written by experts or seasoned journalists. Articles 1,500 to 3,000 words. Pays top rates (approx. $1/word) on acceptance.

The Home Business Report
2949 Ash Street, Abbotsford, BC V2S 4G5
Phone: (604) 857-1788 Fax: (604) 854-3087
Contact: Barbara Mowat, publisher
Circulation: 50,000
Published quarterly

A magazine to link home-based businesses across the country, providing a network for sharing experiences, including advice for launching new businesses and support for those that are struggling. Articles 600 to 1,200 words. Pay rates depend on assignment – from 10¢/word to $250 to $400 for a 1,200-word feature – paid on publication. Very interested in successful rural and small-town home-based businesses offering an unusual product or service. Guidelines available.

Ivey Business Quarterly
Richard Ivey School of Business, University of Western Ontario,
   1151 Richmond Street, London, ON N6A 3K7
Phone: (519) 661-3309 Fax: (519) 661-3838
E-mail: lverde@ivey.uwo.ca
Web site: www.ivey.uwo.ca/publications/bq
Contact: Linda Verde, acting publisher/editor
Circulation: 15,000

A long-established business journal directed toward senior executives with the purpose of improving the practice of management. Most articles are between 2,000 and 3,000 words. Contributors are unpaid, but submission inquiries welcome. Guidelines available.

London Business Magazine
P.O. Box 7400, London, ON N5Y 4X3
Phone: (519) 472-7601
Contact: Jenine Foster, editor
Circulation: 12,000
Published 11 times a year

Profiles business success stories, trends, and issues with a London connection. Pays $200 to $600 on publication for articles of 1,000 to 2,500 words. Rates depend on kind of story, number of sources, and writer's experience. "Whether it's a trend piece or service journalism, there must be a London link."

Nova Scotia Business Journal
900 Windmill Road, Unit 107, Dartmouth, NS B3B 1P7
Phone: (902) 468-8027 Fax: (902) 468-2425
E-mail: ncc@istar.ca
Contact: Ken Partridge, contributing editor
Circulation: 10,000
Published monthly
Informs and educates Nova Scotia's business community on issues, people, and activities of interest to them. Articles of 500 to 700 words preferred. Pays a flat rate of $40 on publication. Send query letter. Deadline is 15th of month preceding publication.

PROFIT: The Magazine for Canadian Entrepreneurs
777 Bay Street, 5th Floor, Toronto, ON M5W 1A7
Phone: (416) 596-5999 Fax: (416) 596-5111
E-mail: profit@cbmedia.ca
Web site: www.profit100.com
Contact: Rick Spence, editor
Circulation: 100,000
Published bimonthly
Canada's only national magazine that delivers hands-on management advice to business owner-managers. Features regular columns and departments along with articles on management topics and issues of interest to owner/managers of small to medium-sized businesses. Offers insights and practical advice in the areas of marketing, technology, finance, innovators and trends, and personnel management. Pays 60¢ to 75¢/word on acceptance for stories of 250 to 2,500 words. "You must know something about business and be prepared to rewrite." Guidelines available.

Report on Business Magazine
444 Front Street W., Toronto, ON M5V 2S9
Phone: (416) 585-5499 Fax: (416) 585-5705
Contact: Patricia Best, editor
Circulation: 290,000

Published monthly

A news magazine covering the national business scene and international developments affecting Canadian companies. Carries profiles of prominent business and political personalities, book reviews, and regular columns on personal finance and national opinion. Pays about $1/word. Full-length feature fee varies from $1,500 to $4,000, depending on length, complexity of topic, and writer's style and experience. Pays on acceptance.

Saskatchewan Business Magazine
2213C Hanselman Court, Saskatoon, SK S7L 6A8
Phone: (306) 244-5668 Fax: (306) 244-5679
Twila Reddekopp, publisher
Circulation: 12,000
Published bimonthly

Has a provincial focus on the business economy of Saskatchewan. Rates vary according to the project, the negotiable fee paid on publication. First submit a brief outline of story idea.

Small Business Week Magazine
c/o The Bowering Group, P.O. Box 116, Winnipeg, MB R3C 2G1
Phone: (204) 958-7540 Fax: (204) 958-7547
Contact: Lorna Wenger, editor
Circulation: 30,000
Published annually

Provides a range of helpful material for Manitoba-based small business owners, managers, and staff. Articles 700 to 2,000 words. Pays $175 for 1,500 words, on publication. Rates are negotiable, depending on the story. Writers are encouraged to phone the editor to discuss story ideas before submitting. Local writers preferred. Guidelines available.

Trade & Commerce
P.O. Box 6900, 1700 Church Avenue, Winnipeg, MB R3C 3B1
Phone: (204) 632-2606 Fax: (204) 694-3040
Contact: Laura Jean Stewart, editor
Circulation: 10,000
Published 5 times a year

Profiles companies and communities with an emphasis on their contribution to the economy or economic development activity. Pays 25¢ to 35¢/word on publication for 1,500 to 2,500 words. Works with freelance writers all over Canada and the United States. Guidelines available.

City & Entertainment

Calgary CityScope
2032 – 33rd Avenue S.W., Suite 202, Calgary, AB T2T 1Z4
Phone: (403) 240-9055 Fax: (403) 240-9059
Web site: www.cityscopemag.com
Contact: Gary Davies, editor
Circulation: 52,000
Published bimonthly

A general interest city magazine catering to the city's educated and affluent readers, focusing on arts, entertainment, sports, and recreation in and around Calgary. Articles 1,200 to 4,000 words. Pays about 25¢/word two weeks after acceptance, $700 to $900 for a 3,000-word feature. Rate depends on importance as well as length. Guidelines available.

The Coast: Halifax's Weekly
5171 George Street, 2nd Floor, Halifax, NS B3J 1M6
Phone: (902) 422-6278 Fax: (902) 425-0013
E-mail: coast@navnet.net
Contact: Kyle Shaw, editor
Circulation: 20,000

An alternative newspaper serving Metro Halifax. No fiction, but ambitious non-fiction and investigative journalism welcome. Pays 5¢ to 10¢/word on publication for 500 to 2,500 words (pays higher scale for well-researched investigative pieces). "Alternative newspapers are an ideal market for freelancers at all levels of experience. We publish excellent, magazine-style journalism but come out more often and tend to be much more accessible for unknown writers. The pay may be lower, but the clipping and experience are invaluable, and with more frequent publishing there's more opportunity to earn money." Guidelines available.

eye Weekly

57 Spadina Avenue, Suite 207, Toronto, ON M5V 2J2
Phone: (416) 971-8421 Fax: (416) 971-7786
E-mail: eye@eye.net
Web site: www.eye.net
Contact: Bill Reynolds, managing editor
Circulation: 96,000

"Toronto's Entertainment and Opinion Weekly." Carries news, commentary, humour, information, and opinion, with some political/social writing. Preferred length 500 to 1,000 words. Pay rates vary, paid on publication. Query first.

Focus

10608 – 172nd Street, Edmonton, AB T5S 1H8
Phone: (403) 486-5802 Fax: (403) 481-9276
E-mail: suggitt@planet.eon.net
Web site: www.suggitt.com
Contact: Tanis Nessler, editor
Circulation: 40,000
Published bimonthly

A music magazine featuring artist interviews, album reviews, industry news, and more. Pays 10¢/word for 500 to 850 words. Contact editor for more details.

Georgia Straight

1770 Burrard Street, 2nd Floor, Vancouver, BC V6J 3G7
Phone: (604) 730-7000 Fax: (604) 730-7010
E-mail: editor@straight.com
Contact: Beverley Sinclair, managing editor
Circulation: 105,000
Published weekly

Event-oriented yet thoughtful articles on the arts, music, movies, style, food, sports, and outdoor recreation, anchored by a general interest feature story. Articles 200 to 4,000 words. Rates vary according to project; fees for cover features are negotiated. First send an inquiry with writing samples. Don't call on Monday, Tuesday, or Wednesday. Guidelines available.

Hamilton Magazine
875 Main Street W., Hamilton, ON L8S 4R1
Phone: (905) 522-6117 Fax: (905) 529-2242
Contact: Wayne Narciso, publisher
Circulation: 40,000
Published 7 times a year
   A news and general interest magazine for Hamilton and its
suburbs, focusing on public issues, events, and concerns – and the
personalities behind them. Also covers food, fashion, the arts, music,
and interior decorating. Feature length 2,000 to 4,000 words. Phone
with ideas. Fees negotiable.

id Magazine
123 Woolwich Street, 2nd Floor, Guelph, ON N1H 3V1
Phone: (519) 766-9336 Fax: (519) 766-9891
Web site: www.idmagazine.com
Contacts: Sherri Telenko, arts editor; Michael Barclay, music editor
Circulation: 40,000
Published twice a month
   An urban street magazine focusing on music, the arts, enter-
tainment, and non-mainstream political issues. Pays $50 to $150 on
publication for researched features of 1,000 to 2,000 words; 3¢/word
for shorter pieces. "*id*'s features and news section has some room
for national and international issues, but we mainly focus on matters
of concern in our regional distribution area: Guelph, Kitchener,
Hamilton, London, and the Niagara region." Guidelines available.

London Magazine
244 Adelaide Street S., London, ON N5Z 3L1
Phone: (519) 685-1624 Fax: (519) 649-0908
Contact: Jackie Skender, editor
Circulation: 32,000
Published 8 times a year
   Covers lifestyles, fashion, city issues, art, food, history, business,
sports, and entertainment for Londoners and residents of south-
western Ontario. Features regular columns by local writers. Articles
from 200 to 2,000 words. Fees are negotiable, paid on acceptance.
Guidelines available.

Marquee Entertainment Magazine

77 Mowat Avenue, Suite 621, Toronto, ON M6K 3E3
Phone: (416) 538-1000 Fax: (416) 538-0201
Contact: Jack Gardner, editor
Circulation: 664,000
Published 9 times a year

Distributed in newspapers across Canada, *Marquee* continues to carry feature stories, previews, and profiles of upcoming movies and personalities while expanding its coverage of music. Given the magazine's advance deadline, writers need access to on-set and on-location interview opportunities. Articles 300 to 1,000 words. Pays on publication. Fees vary.

Montreal Mirror

400 McGill Street, 2nd Floor, Montreal, PQ H2Y 2G1
Phone: (514) 393-1010 Fax: (514) 393-3173
E-mail: mirror@babylon.montreal.qc.ca
Contact: Annarosa Sabaddini, editor
Circulation: 80,000
Published weekly

An alternative tabloid featuring articles on major issues written from a local perspective. Also reviews and previews music releases and concerts, films, art shows, books, and theatre. Features are 2,000 to 3,000 words. Fees are negotiated, paid on publication. Guidelines available.

Network

287 MacPherson Avenue, Toronto, ON M4V 1A4
Phone: (416) 928-2909 Fax: (416) 928-1357
Contact: Stephen Hubbard, managing editor
Circulation: 90,000
Published quarterly

A national entertainment magazine featuring predominantly pop/rock music interviews and reviews, with some movie and video coverage. Pays on publication $40 to $300 for short pieces between 150 and 700 words. Three-month lead time. Query letter advisable.

The Newfoundland Herald
P.O. Box 2015, Logy Bay Road, St. John's, NF AIC 5R7
Phone: (709) 726-7060 Fax: (709) 726-8227
E-mail: herald@nf.sympatico.ca
Contact: Greg Stirling, editor-in-chief
Circulation: 40,000
Published weekly
   A family entertainment and local interest magazine focusing on people. Articles 1,000 to 5,000 words. Pays 10¢/word on publication. "Read at least three recent issues before deciding on story angles, then contact the editor by phone or mail with ideas."

NOW
150 Danforth Avenue, Toronto, ON M4K INI
Phone: (416) 461-0871 Fax: (416) 461-2886
E-mail: publishers@now.com
Web site: www.now.com
Contact: Glenn Wheeler, associate editor
Circulation: 103,000
Published weekly
   A news, entertainment, and listings magazine covering Toronto region news, music, film, theatre, fashion, and the arts. Story length from 400 to 2,000 words. Most work is assigned. Uses very few out-of-town writers. No freelance entertainment submissions unless they're entertainment news stories. Toronto region news submissions with alternative perspective have best chance. Rates vary. Pays on publication. All fees negotiable. Inquiries welcome.

prairie dog
2201 Hamilton Street, Regina, SK S4P 2E7
Phone: (306) 757-8522 Fax: (306) 352-9686
Contact: Mitch Diamantopoulos, editor
Circulation: 15,000
Published monthly
   An alternative urban news and entertainment monthly. Articles 750 to 2,500 words. Cannot pay but welcomes submission inquiries.

SEE Magazine

The Boardwalk Market, Suite 411, 10310 – 102nd Avenue,
   Edmonton, AB T5J 2X6
Phone: (403) 428-9354 Fax: (403) 428-9349
E-mail: see@greatwest.ca
Web site: www.greatwest.ca/see
Contact: Stew Slater, managing editor

A city magazine covering arts, entertainment, and news within
Edmonton, favouring stories not tackled by the two major dailies.
Preferred length 300 to 1,200 words. Pays $80 for 1,200-word fea-
tures, $40 for regular articles, on publication, but rates vary accord-
ing to project. "Most of our freelance work is assigned by one of our
two co-editors, though we do accept pieces on spec occasionally,
especially opinion pieces."

Starweek Magazine

1 Yonge Street, Toronto, ON M5E 1E6
Phone: (416) 869-4870 Fax: (416) 869-4834
Contact: Jim Atkins, editor
Circulation: 740,000
Published weekly

Carries profiles of top entertainers plus articles on sports, music,
videos, and cooking, to complement Toronto-area weekly television
listings. Pays on publication for articles of 800 to 1,100 words. Mail
or fax queries. Fees negotiated for new freelancers.

Toronto Life

59 Front Street E., 3rd Floor, Toronto, ON M5E 1B3
Phone: (416) 364-3333 Fax: (416) 861-1169
E-mail: lifeline@tor-lifeline.com
Web site: www.tor-lifeline.com/new/tl
Contact: John Macfarlane, editor
Circulation: 100,000
Published monthly

Established 1962. A classy city magazine that tells readers how
Toronto works, lives, and plays. Examines city politics, society,
business, entertainment, sports, food and restaurants, and shopping in a unique mix of hard-nosed reporting and rigorous service journalism. Also publishes supplements. Draws on a stable of

experienced writers and rarely accepts outside submissions. Pays on acceptance between $1,000 and $4,500 for 400 to 4,000 words, depending on assignment. Guidelines available.

TV Guide
25 Sheppard Avenue W., North York, ON M2N 6S7
Phone: (416) 733-7600 Fax: (416) 733-3568
E-mail: tvgletters@telemedia.ca
Contact: Bill Anderson, features editor
Circulation: 760,900
Published weekly
   Carries television listings and articles on the entertainment industry, children's programming, sports, food, and showbiz personalities. Pays competitive, always negotiable rates on acceptance for articles of 500 to 1,600 words. "Read the magazine. Be prepared to submit a single-page proposal with suggested contacts. This magazine is not for neophyte writers."

TV Week
4180 Lougheed Highway, 4th Floor, Burnaby, BC V5C 6A7
Phone: (604) 299-7311 Fax: (604) 299-9188
Contact: Robin Roberts, editor
Circulation: 88,000
Published weekly
   A television and entertainment guide. Pays 40¢/word on publication for stories of 800 to 1,000 words.

Vancouver Magazine
555 West 12th Avenue, Suite 300, S.E. Tower, Vancouver, BC V5Z 4L4
Phone: (604) 877-7732 Fax: (604) 877-4849
E-mail: vanmag@vanmag.com
Web site: www.vanmag.com
Contact: Jim Sutherland, editor
Circulation: 65,000
Published 10 times a year
   The city magazine of the new Vancouver – its people, stories, and ideas – focusing on current affairs and entertainment. Articles must be Vancouver specific. Pays 40¢ to 60¢/word on acceptance for 100 to 10,000 words. Read the magazine before submitting.

View Magazine

149 Main Street E., Hamilton, ON L8N 1G4
Phone: (905) 527-3343 Fax: (905) 527-3721
E-mail: editor@iaw.on.ca
Web site: www.viewmag.com
Contact: Walter Sendzik, editor
Circulation: 20,000
Published weekly

An alternative urban weekly featuring art, music, theatre, and social issues of interest to Hamilton-area residents. Most stories 600 to 1,200 words. Pays $40 for a feature, $70 for a cover story, after publication.

Vue Weekly

10080 Jasper Avenue, Suite 307, Edmonton, AB T5J 1V9
Phone: (403) 426-1996 Fax: (403) 426-2889
E-mail: office@vue.ab.ca
Contact: Amy Hough, managing editor
Circulation: 30,000

An urban alternative weekly featuring Edmonton news and entertainment, with an emphasis on music and the arts. Rates vary. Pays on publication. Guidelines available.

The Environment

Alternatives Journal: Environmental Thought, Policy & Action

Faculty of Environmental Studies, University of Waterloo,
     Waterloo, ON N2L 3G1
Phone: (519) 888-4545 Fax: (519) 746-0292
E-mail: alternat@fes.uwaterloo.ca
Web site: www.fes.uwaterloo.ca/research/alternatives
Contact: Suzanne Galloway, managing editor
Circulation: 4,200
Published quarterly

The most widely read environmental journal in Canada, with 25 years of journalistic experience. Articles provide a blend of practical information and theoretical perspectives from across Canada and abroad. Feature-length articles (3,000 to 4,000 words) are peer-reviewed. Also publishes reports (500 to 1,000 words), notes (up to 500 words), book reviews (750 to 1,000 words), and humour pieces. Readers include environmental professionals, academics, activists, and students. *"Alternatives* is . . . reflective, topical and Canadian; it plays a uniquely important role in the field of environmental journalism" – Susan Holtz, vice-chair, National Round Table on Environment and Economy. Contributors are unpaid. Guidelines available.

Common Ground
P.O. Box 34090, Station D, Vancouver, BC V6J 4MI
Phone: (604) 733-2215 or 1-800-365-8897 Fax: (604) 733-4415
E-mail: cgbc@web.net
Contact: Joseph Roberts, editor/publisher
Circulation: 80,000
Published 10 times a year
   Aims to inform and inspire readers in the areas of personal growth, ecology, and healthy living. Pays 10¢/word on publication for articles from 500 to 1,800 words. "Make your first sentence and first paragraph great, or the article won't even get read." Query first.

Green Teacher
95 Robert Street, Toronto, ON M5S 2K5
Phone: (416) 960-1244 Fax: (416) 925-3474
Contact: Tim Grant, co-editor
Circulation: 5,500
Published quarterly
   A magazine by and for educators that aims to provide ideas, inspiration, and classroom-ready materials to help all educators (including parents) promote environmental and global awareness amongst young people, pre-school to college, in school and in the community. Articles 500 to 3,000 words. All writers are volunteers. Submissions welcome.

Harrowsmith Country Life
11450 Albert-Hudon Boulevard, Montreal-North, PQ HIG 3J9
Phone: (514) 327-4464 Fax: (514) 327-0514
Contact: Tom Cruickshank, editor

Circulation: 160,000

Published bimonthly

A magazine for a thoughtful, critical audience interested in self-reliance and country living. Subject areas most frequently covered include rural issues, home improvement, gardening, energy and ecology, and innovative architecture. Pays a negotiated rate (depending on writer's experience) on acceptance for 1,000 to 1,500 words; rate varies according to complexity and writer's experience. Guidelines available.

Natural Life

R.R.1, St. George, ON NOE 1NO

Phone: (519) 448-4001 Fax: (519) 448-4001

Web site: www.life.ca

Contact: Wendy Priesnitz, editor

Circulation: 20,000

Published bimonthly

An environmental magazine focusing on ways to live a self-reliant, environmentally friendly, and sustainable lifestyle. Pays 10¢/word ($100 maximum) on publication for articles of 800-plus words. Query first with outline, after you have read the magazine. Guidelines available.

Nature Canada

1 Nicholas Street, Suite 606, Ottawa, ON K1N 7B7

Phone: (613) 562-3447 Fax: (613) 562-3371

E-mail: cnf@cnf.ca

Web site: www.magma.ca/~cnfgen

Contact: Barbara Stevenson, editor

Circulation: 20,000

Published quarterly

Mailed to members of the Canadian Nature Federation, a non-profit conservation organization. Began in 1939 as *Canadian Nature*. Focuses on Canadian natural history and environmental issues. Designed to educate, entertain, and increase readers' awareness and understanding of nature. Features 2,500 to 3,500 words. Pays 25¢/word on publication. Guidelines available.

Seasons
355 Lesmill Road, Don Mills, ON M3B 2W8
Phone: (416) 444-8419 Fax: (416) 444-9866
Contact: Nancy Clark, editor
Circulation: 16,000
Published quarterly

A nature and outdoors magazine published by the Federation of Ontario Naturalists and designed to enhance knowledge about natural history and the environment in Ontario. Features Ontario wildlife, wilderness, parks, and conservation issues. Preferred length 1,500 to 3,000 words. Pays up to $700 on publication. "Be familiar with the magazine before querying. We accept phone inquiries." Guidelines available.

The Sustainable Times
1657 Barrington Street, Unit 508, Halifax, NS B3J 2A1
Phone: (902) 423-6709 Fax: (902) 423-9736
E-mail: ip-cuso@chebucto.ns.ca
Contact: Sean Kelly, editor
Circulation: 20,000
Published quarterly

A national newsmagazine addressing solutions to our employment, environmental, and global development challenges. "We believe economics should be guided by environmental protection and fairness, not just profit." Pays $200 on publication for articles of 1,500 to 2,000 words. Send initial query rather than complete article. Guidelines available.

Wildflower
90 Wolfrey Avenue, Toronto, ON M4K 1K8
Phone: (416) 466-6428
E-mail: ann.melvin@sympatico.ca
Web site: www.acorn-online.com/hedge/cws.html
Contact: James Hodgins, editor
Circulation: 5,000
Published quarterly

Devoted to the conservation, cultivation, and study of North American wildflowers and other flora. Contains essays, book reviews, notices of coming events, and plant sources. Articles 1,500 to 5,000 words. Published by the Canadian Wildflower Society, for gardeners, naturalists, field botanists, and teachers. Cannot pay but welcomes submissions. Guidelines available.

Feminist

Fireweed: A Feminist Quarterly

P.O. Box 279, Station B, Toronto, ON M5T 2W2
Phone: (416) 504-1339
Contact: Mary Myers, office manager
Circulation: 1,500

Established 1978. A journal of politics and the creative arts, featuring a wide range of cultural expression, including fiction, poetry, critical texts, interviews, reviews, visual art. Aims to provide a forum for a lively mix of voices, engaging issues of race, class, and sexuality. "A vital, nervy feminist statement" – Judy MacDonald (author). Length up to 5,000 words. Pays $30 for first page and $10 thereafter, on publication. Guidelines available.

Herizons

P.O. Box 128, Winnipeg, MB R3C 2G1
Phone: (204) 774-6225   Fax: (204) 786-8038
Contact: Penni Mitchell, editorial co-ordinator
Circulation: 5,000
Published quarterly

A feminist periodical focusing on women's issues and the women's movement. Articles 500 to 3,000 words. Pays 10¢/word. Send query and sample of previous published work written from a feminist perspective. Guidelines available.

Kinesis

309 – 877 East Hastings Street, Vancouver, BC V6A 3Y1
Phone: (604) 255-5499   Fax: (604) 255-5511
Contact: Agnes Huang, editor
Circulation: 2,500
Published 10 times a year

A nationwide feminist newspaper for all women. Articles of 800 to 1,600 words cover the struggles of women activists in Canada and abroad. Issues of interest include health, politics, poverty, violence against women, and Aboriginal women's news. Also discusses music, dance, literature, film, and the visual arts from a feminist perspective. Contributors are unpaid. Guidelines available.

WE International
736 Bathurst Street, Toronto, ON M5S 2R4
Phone: (416) 516-2600 Fax: (416) 531-6214
E-mail: weed@web.net
Contact: Lisa Dale, magazine manager
Circulation: 2,000
Published quarterly

Formerly *Women & Environments*. A co-operative forum for discussion, review, and research on women's built, natural, social, and political environments for feminists, academics, and a broad base of grassroots groups. Articles 400 to 1,500 words. Contributors are not paid, but submission inquiries welcome. "Clear language is essential – no academic jargon, please. We are cross-cultural and international – avoid parochialism. All issues are theme related." Guidelines available.

General Interest

The Beaver: Canada's History Magazine
167 Lombard Avenue, Suite 478, Winnipeg, MB R3B 0T6
Phone: (204) 988-9300 Fax: (204) 988-9309
E-mail: beaver@cyberspc.mb.ca
Web site: www.cyberspc.mb.ca/~otmv/cnhs/cnhs.html
Contact: Annalee Greenberg, editor
Circulation: 45,000
Published bimonthly

A market since 1920 for lively, well-researched, informative, expository articles on Canadian social history. Articles based on unpublished journals or letters are of particular interest. Interested in submissions from all parts of the country. Pays a varying rate (depending on research necessary and writer's experience) for articles of 3,000 to 4,000 words. Guidelines available.

Canadian Geographic

39 McArthur Avenue, Ottawa, ON KIL 8L7
Phone: (613) 745-4629 Fax: (613) 744-0974
E-mail: editorial@cangeo.ca
Web site: www.cangeo.ca
Contact: Rick Boychuk, managing editor
Circulation: 245,000
Published bimonthly

Published by the Royal Canadian Geographical Society. Describes and illuminates, with fine colour photography, all aspects of Canada: its people, places, natural resources, and wildlife. Concerned with geography in its broadest sense, looking at the way our landscape was formed and the human impact on it, and also reporting on discoveries in the sciences, from archaeology to zoology. The magazine is widely used as a high school and undergraduate teaching resource. Rates vary, depending on project. Fees paid on acceptance for articles of 2,000 to 3,500 words. A large paid circulation helps make it one of the more lucrative freelance opportunities. Written queries essential.

Equinox

11450 Albert-Hudon Boulevard, Montreal-North, PQ HIG 3J9
Phone: (514) 327-4464 Fax: (514) 327-0514
E-mail: equinox@kos.net
Web site: www.equinox.ca
Contact: Sylvia Barrett, managing editor
Circulation: 130,000
Published bimonthly

Canada's award-winning magazine of discovery is dedicated to covering wildlife, science, geography, and adventure for a lay audience. Features of 2,000 to 5,000 words earn $1,500 to $3,500 on acceptance – more paid for photos; Nexus pieces earn $250. "*Equinox* reaches more than half a million well-informed, well-educated readers, most of whom are 25 to 49 years old. Always query in writing rather than by phone. Often, untried contributors are assigned shorter pieces before being given a full feature. We do *not* secure electronic rights." Guidelines available.

Eyetalian
901 Lawrence Avenue W., Suite A201, Toronto, ON M6A 1C3
Phone: (416) 787-9598 Fax: (416) 787-9911
E-mail: eyetalian@magic.ca
Web site: www.total.net/~eyetalia
Contact: John Montesano, editor
Circulation: 10,000
Published quarterly

An English-language quarterly that explores the many aspects of Italian culture in Canada. Readers include second- and third-generation Canadians of Italian descent and Italiaphiles. Pays 10¢/word on publication for 800 to 1,500 words.

Our Family
P.O. Box 249, Battleford, SK SOM 0E0
Phone: (306) 937-7771 Fax: (306) 937-7644
E-mail: Gregmaryomi@sk.sympatico.ca
Contact: Nestor Gregoire, editor
Circulation: 10,000
Published monthly

A Christian general interest magazine. Buys photo stories on personalities, events, and issues, mostly with religious themes. Pays 7¢ to 11¢/word on acceptance for 1,000 to 3,000 words. Guidelines available.

Que Pasa Magazine
P.O. Box 65097, Toronto, ON M4K 3Z2
Phone: (416) 423-1340 Fax: (416) 423-1340
E-mail: qpasa@pathcom.com
Contact: Carmen Téllez O'Mahony, editor-in-chief
Circulation: 10,000
Published quarterly

A general interest magazine addressing all aspects of Hispanic culture. All articles should have Hispanic-related content. Preferred length 800 to 2,500 words. Fees are negotiated.

Reader's Digest

215 Redfern Avenue, Westmount, PQ H3Z 2V9
Phone: (514) 934-0751
Web site: www.readersdigest.ca
Contact: editorial department
Circulation: 1,226,000
Published monthly

This mass-interest magazine is among the freelancer's most lucrative potential markets. Carries articles on everything from nature, science, and politics to drama, self-improvement, and people, prominent or otherwise. All pieces contain advice, an experience, or a philosophical message of value to the magazine's more than 2 million readers. No fiction or poetry. Commissions original articles and adaptations of Canadian subjects of between 3,500 and 5,000 words, which earn $2,700. Also buys material previously published in books, magazines, or newspapers. Buys all rights and pays on acceptance for original articles, one-time rights for previously published "pickups." No unsolicited manuscripts. Send letter of inquiry with a two-page outline. Guidelines available.

Saturday Night

184 Front Street E., Suite 400, Toronto, ON M5A 4N3
Phone: (416) 368-7237 Fax: (416) 368-5112
Contact: Kenneth Whyte, editor
Circulation: 410,000
Published 10 times a year

A sophisticated, award-winning magazine with a long history – it was first published in 1887. Features profiles of the men, women, and institutions that shape and run Canadian society. Its insightful reporting goes far beyond explanations of events to focus on why things happen, who makes them happen, and how they may affect our future. Also publishes high-quality fiction. Boasts a list of contributing editors that reads like a who's who of Canadian literature. Pays about $1/word: $500 for one-page stories, $2,000 to $4,000 for features.

Up Here: Exploring the True North

P.O. Box 1350, Yellowknife, NT X1A 2N9
Phone: (867) 920-4343 Fax: (867) 873-2844
E-mail: outcrop@internorth.com

Contact: Cooper Langford, editor
Circulation: 40,000
Published bimonthly

A lively, informative magazine about Northern travel, wildlife, arts, culture, lifestyles, and especially the people who live in the region and cope with the harsh winters there. Articles 750 to 3,000 words. Pays 20¢ to 25¢/word on publication for articles and features, with a standard fee for columns and photos. Complete manuscripts with photos welcome. "We're looking for solid reporting and research, and top-notch photos. Always tell your story through the people involved." Written queries and sample photos strongly recommended. Guidelines available.

Western People
P.O. Box 2500, Saskatoon, SK S7K 2C4
Phone: (306) 665-9611 Fax: (306) 934-2401
E-mail: people@producer.com
Contacts: Sheila Robertson, features editor
Circulation: 90,000
Published weekly

A general interest, rural-oriented magazine featuring histories, memories, poetry, fiction, and contemporary profiles of Western Canadians. Especially interested in well-researched features, profiles, and Western history. Preferred length 700 to 2,000 words. Pays $100 to $300 on acceptance for articles, depending on length, less for poetry. "Eastern Canadian and U.S. writers have a hard time catching the flavour of this magazine. People profiles are seldom of big names, almost never politicians. We require photos for most articles." Guidelines available.

Home & Hobby

Build & Green
2922 West 6th Avenue, Vancouver, BC V6K 1X3
Phone: (604) 730-1940 Fax: (604) 730-7860
Contact: Leonard Wexler, publisher/editor
Circulation: 30,000
Published 9 times a year

A consumer-oriented magazine concerned with home building and renovating, gardening and landscaping. Detailed articles of 700 to 1,500 words should be relevant for Greater Vancouverites. Articles by contribution only. Submission inquiries welcome.

Canadian Coin News

103 Lakeshore Road, Suite 202, St. Catharines, ON L2N 2T6
Phone: (905) 646-7744 Fax: (905) 646-0995
E-mail: bret@trajan.com
Web site: www.trajan.com/coin
Contact: Bret Evans, editor
Circulation: 13,000
Published biweekly

A tabloid magazine for Canadian collectors of coins and paper money. Pays a month after publication. Fees negotiable. Prefers phone or fax queries.

Canadian Gardening

130 Spy Court, Markham, ON L3R 0W5
Phone: (905) 475-8440 Fax: (905) 475-9560
E-mail: cgeditorial@sympatico.ca
Contact: Liz Primeau, editor
Circulation: 130,000
Published 7 times a year

A magazine geared toward the avid home gardener. Carries people-oriented feature articles on home gardens, garden design, and tips and techniques on gardening in the Canadian climate. Pays on acceptance for 1,000 to 2,500 words – $400 to $700, depending on length and research required. "We prefer outlines suggesting story ideas to unsolicited finished stories." Guidelines available.

Canadian House & Home

511 King Street W., Suite 120, Toronto, ON M5V 2Z4
Phone: (416) 593-0204 Fax: (416) 591-1630
E-mail: mail@canhomepub.com
Web site: www.canadianhouseandhome.com
Contacts: Cobi Ladner, editor; Carolyn Kennedy, managing editor

Circulation: 130,000
Published 9 times a year

Focuses on creative home decoration and design. Inspires and teaches through pictorial essays and how-to articles, featuring Canadian artisans, designers, and architects. Articles between 300 and 1,000 words. Always include colour photos with written submissions as visual confirmation of descriptions. Pays on acceptance. Fees vary according to project.

Canadian Stamp News

202 – 103 Lakeshore Road, St. Catharines, ON L2N 2T6
Phone: (905) 646-7744 Fax: (905) 646-0995
E-mail: newsroom@trajan.com
Web site: www.trajan.com/trajan/stamp
Contact: Ellen Rodger, editor
Circulation: 9,500
Published semi-monthly

A tabloid magazine serving Canadian philatelists and enthusiasts around the world who collect Canadian stamps. Pays a month after publication. Fees negotiable. Query first. Guidelines available.

Canadian Workshop

340 Ferrier Street, Markham, ON L3R 2Z5
Phone: (905) 475-8440 Fax: (905) 475-9560
E-mail: letters@canadianworkshop.ca
Web site: www.canadianworkshop.ca
Contact: Doug Bennet, editor
Circulation: 100,000
Published monthly

Canada's leading magazine for woodworkers and do-it-yourself home-improvement enthusiasts. Elucidates a variety of home projects – from laying floors and cleaning furnaces to renovating basements and making kitchen cabinets. Rates negotiable. Pays $300 to $800 on acceptance for features of 800 to 2,000 words. "Freelancers should have a good grounding in the subjects they query. Our step-by-step and technical articles rely on detail – generalities will not do." Guidelines available.

Century Home

12 Mill Street South, Port Hope, ON L1A 2S5
Phone: (905) 885-2449 or 1-800-361-1957 Fax: (905) 885-5355
Contact: Joan Rumgay, publisher
Circulation: 50,000
Published 8 times a year

A magazine for lovers of vintage private homes. Carries articles
(1,000 to 1,800 words) about decorating, furnishings, art, crafts,
architecture, restoration, renovation, gardens, and country fare.
Fees vary according to project and are paid on publication. "Please
get to know the magazine before submitting. Articles require appropriate visual materials, or information on where materials are readily
obtained."

Collectibles Canada

103 Lakeshore Road, Suite 202, St. Catharines, ON L2N 2T6
Phone: (905) 646-7744 Fax: (905) 646-0995
E-mail: bret@trajan.com
Web site: www.trajan.com/trajan/collectibles/default.html
Contact: Bret Evans, editor
Circulation: 18,000
Published bimonthly

A magazine about art collecting, containing information on col-
lector plates, figurines, limited edition lithographs, new products,
and interviews with Canadian artists. Also publishes *Canadian
Collectibles Retailer*. Pays a month after publication for articles of 750
to 1,500 words. Fees negotiable. Phone or fax inquiries preferred.

Homes & Cottages

6557 Mississauga Road, Unit D, Mississauga, ON L5N 1A6
Phone: (905) 567-1440 Fax: (905) 567-1442
Contact: Jim Adair, editor-in-chief
E-mail: jimhc@pathcom.com
Web site: www.homesandcottages.com
Circulation: 63,000
Published 8 times a year

Canada's largest residential building magazine, for consumers as
well as builders, lumber retailers, and architects. Provides thought-
provoking and innovative ideas and technical information to help

Canadians build or renovate their homes and cottages. Articles 750 to 2,000 words. Fees vary according to complexity, but average is $600. All articles are assigned. Pays on acceptance. "We have consumer and trade editions. We write about architecture and design, but not decorating; hard landscaping, but not gardening; cottage renovation and construction, but not cottage lifestyles." Guidelines available.

Ontario Craft

Designers Walk, 170 Bedford Road, Suite 300, Toronto, ON M5R 2K9
Phone: (416) 925-4222 Fax: (416) 925-4223
Contact: Wendy Jacob, editor
Circulation: 4,000
Published quarterly

Multimedia publication of the contemporary craft movement. Profiles interesting craftspeople and reviews their work. Articles 600 to 2,000 words. Pays on publication. Fees vary. "Familiarize yourself with *Ontario Craft* by looking through back issues." Guidelines available.

Photo Life

Toronto-Dominion Bank Tower, 55 King Street W., Suite 2550,
    Box 77, Toronto, ON M5K 1E7
Phone: 1-800-905-7468 Fax: 1-800-664-2739
E-mail: editor@photolife.com
Web site: www.photolife.com
Contact: Jacques Thibault, editor
Circulation: 59,000
Published bimonthly

Established 1976. Delivers serious information to advanced photographers in a readable way. Articles 800 to 1,200 words. Pays $300 on publication for first-time articles; other fees are negotiated. "Our contributors are professional photographers who can write, or writers familiar with photography." Guidelines available.

Plant & Garden

1200 Markham Road, Suite 300, Scarborough, ON M1H 3C3
Phone: (416) 438-7777 Fax: (416) 438-5333
E-mail: plant@wheels.ca

Circulation: 45,000

Published bimonthly

An informative, practical national magazine for Canadian gardeners. Articles 500 to 1,200 words preferred. Pays about 20¢/word on publication, but rates vary according to project. First query with story outline.

Style at Home

25 Sheppard Avenue W., Suite 100, North York, ON M2N 6S7

Phone: (416) 733-7600 Fax: (416) 218-3632

E-mail: letters@styleathome.com

Contact: Laurie Grassi, managing editor

Circulation: 200,000

Published 8 times a year

A glossy magazine featuring home decor stories, news, products, and trends. Rates vary with project and writer, but pays up to $1/word on acceptance for stories of 300 to 800 words. Guidelines available.

Lifestyle

Alive: The Canadian Journal of Health and Nutrition

7436 Fraser Park Drive, Burnaby, BC V5J 5B9

Phone: (604) 435-1919 Fax: (604) 435-4888

Contact: Rhody Lake, managing editor

Published monthly

A national magazine for health-conscious Canadians featuring articles of 600 to 800 words by health professionals and personalities. Also carries short book reviews. Pays 15¢/word on publication.

Campus Canada

287 MacPherson Avenue, Toronto, ON M4V 1A4

Phone: (416) 928-2909 Fax: (416) 928-1357

E-mail: campus@idirect.com

Contact: Sarah Moore, managing editor

Circulation: 125,000

Published 4 times during school year

A student lifestyle magazine featuring sports, entertainment, issues on campus, travel, and other topics of interest to university and college students. Short articles of 500 to 1,200 words preferred. Pays an average of $100 for 800 words on acceptance. Query first with story idea, by e-mail, mail, or fax.

Canada WYDE

511 – 99 Dalhousie Street, Toronto, ON M5B 2N2
Phone: (416) 861-0217   Fax: (416) 861-1668
E-mail: cdawyde@interlog.com
Contact: Heléna Spring, publisher/editor-in-chief
Published twice a year

The lifestyle magazine for large Canadians and their admirers. Addresses positive body image and size acceptance, size discrimination, advocacy and medical issues for men and women. No diet or weight loss promotions. Length 100 to 1,000 words. Cannot pay but welcomes submission inquiries. Guidelines available.

Canadian Cowboy Country

355 Yellowhead Highway, Unit 316, Kamloops, BC V2H 1H1
Phone: (250) 314-1507   Fax: (250) 314-1508
E-mail: cowgirl@mail.netshop.net
Web site: www.canadiancowboy.com
Contact: Sherril Siebert, editor
Circulation: 9,000
Published bimonthly

Carries stories on working cowboys and cowgirls, ranch stories, and historical western stories. At the time of writing *CCC* has no editorial budget but welcomes submission inquiries. Guidelines available.

CARP News

27 Queen Street E., Suite 702, Toronto, ON M5C 2M6
Phone: (416) 363-5562   Fax: (416) 363-7394
E-mail: editor@fifty-plus.net
Contact: Bryan Dearsley, associate editor
Circulation: 152,000
Published 9 times a year

The official voice of the Canadian Association of Retired Persons, and a leading magazine for the over-50s. Accepts a limited number of freelance articles each year. A negotiated fee is paid on acceptance. First send a brief outline with clippings.

City Parent
467 Speers Road, Oakville, ON L6K 3S4
Phone: (905) 815-0017 Fax: (905) 815-0511
Contact: Jane Muller, editor-in-chief
Circulation: 160,000
Published monthly

A magazine to inform parents of news related to children and families. Also carries arts and entertainment news. Articles 500 to 750 words. Pays about 10¢/word, depending on research and quality. Welcomes submission inquiries.

Cottage Life
111 Queen Street E., Suite 408, Toronto, ON M5C 1S2
Phone: (416) 360-6880 Fax: (416) 360-6814
E-mail: clmag@cottagelife.com
Contact: David Zimmer, editor
Circulation: 70,000
Published bimonthly

An award-winning magazine directed toward those who own and spend time at cottages on Ontario's lakes. Examines and celebrates the history, personalities, and issues of cottaging. Also provides lots of practical advice to help readers keep their cottages, docks, and boats in working order. Pays on acceptance for articles of 150 to 3,000 words. Query all ideas before submission. Guidelines available with SASE.

The Cottage Magazine
4623 William Head Road, Victoria, BC V9C 3Y7
Phone: (604) 478-9209 Fax: (604) 478-1184
E-mail: chet@islandnet.com
Web site: www.cottageplan.com
Contact: Peter Chettleburgh, editor/publisher
Circulation: 12,000

Published bimonthly

Established 1992. For cottage owners in western Canada. Feature articles of 1,000 to 2,000 words include entertaining profiles of individuals and companies and analysis of issues that affect cottage owners. Regular columns and departments on small boats, solar power, and other practical topics. Pays on publication $200 to $500 for features, $150 to $200 for columns; news items up to 400 words are paid 20¢/word. Query editor by phone or with a brief written proposal. Guidelines available.

The Country Connection
691 Pinecrest Road, Boulter, ON K0L 1G0
Phone: (613) 332-3651 Fax: (613) 332-5183
Web site: www.cyberus.ca/~queenswood/pinecone
Contact: Gus Zylstra, editor
Circulation: 10,000
Published twice a year

A country magazine presenting informative, how-to, and historical pieces with rural themes and/or relating to Central and Eastern Ontario. Also humorous or light short fiction. Prefers articles and stories around 1,000 to 2,000 words. Submit article ideas and short fiction. Pays 10¢/word on disk, laser quality, 7¢/word handwritten and dot matrix, on publication. Guidelines available.

Fifty-Five Plus
95 Abbeyhill Drive, Kanata, ON K2L 3M3
Phone: (613) 592-3578 Fax: (613) 592-9033
E-mail: warrenty@compmore.net
Contact: Pat den Boer, editor-in-chief
Circulation: 40,000
Published bimonthly

Informs active retirees in Eastern Ontario of options and opportunities for a successful retirement. Pays $60 to $350, depending on project and length, on publication for 800 to 2,500 words. Fees for features may be negotiated. "This is a small operation, and writers should be prepared to wait up to six months for a response. Photos are necessary for most stories, and submissions are accepted only on IBM diskette or by e-mail." Guidelines available.

Good Times
5148 St. Laurent Boulevard, Montreal, PQ H2T 1R8
Phone: (514) 273-9773 Fax: (514) 273-3408
Contact: Denise Crawford, editor-in-chief
Published 11 times a year

Addresses the concerns of retired Canadians and those planning retirement. Topics include financial planning, health and fitness, personal rights, interpersonal relationships, profiles of celebrities, and leisure activities. Articles are assigned. Welcomes inquiries, noting areas of expertise and suggestions, with writing samples. Pays 40¢/word on publication. "No phone or fax queries; material must be supplied on disk."

Great Expectations
269 Richmond Street W., Toronto, ON M5V 1X1
Phone: (416) 596-8680 Fax: (416) 596-1991
Contact: Holly Bennett, editor
Circulation: 200,000
Published 3 times a year

Articles directed toward expectant and new parents, promoting healthy pregnancy and an active role in the birth and early care of the child. Encourages informed consumer choice, breastfeeding, and gentle parenting. Fees around $600 for departments, $600 to $1,200 for features, depending on level of research, medical complexity, and length, which should fall between 1,000 and 2,500 words. Pays 30 days after acceptance. "Most editorial is provided by our regular freelancers. We are especially interested in writers with background in childbirth issues." Guidelines available.

Health Naturally
P.O. Box 1165, 2255B Queen Street E., Toronto. ON M4E 1G3
Phone: (705) 746-7839 Fax: (705) 746-7893
Contact: Lorrie Imbert, editor
Circulation: 30,000
Published bimonthly

For people interested in using natural methods to build and maintain optimal health. Covers holistic nutrition, food supplements, alternatives to drugs and surgery, prevention, herbs, homeopathy, alternative therapies, organic farming, and health politics.

Pays on publication $250 for major article (800 to 1,200 words), $150 for feature therapy, $50 for book review, 25¢/word for short items. "Study our magazine before pitching story ideas or sending unsolicited manuscripts. We do not publish articles dealing with mainstream medicine."

Hi-Rise Magazine

95 Leeward Glenway, Unit 121, Don Mills, ON M3C 2Z6
Phone: (416) 424-1393 Fax: (416) 467-8262
Contact: Valerie Dunn, editor
Circulation: 45,000
Published 11 times a year

A magazine mirroring the concerns of high-rise dwellers. Carries self-help articles about tenants' rights and legal issues, issues of interest to condominium owners, plus regular features on food, travel, sports, hobbies, and business. Articles 400 to 600 words. Pays $25 for articles, $15 for short pieces. Guidelines available.

Leisure World

1253 Ouellette Avenue, Windsor, ON N8X 1J3
Phone: (519) 971-3208 Fax: (519) 977-1197
Contact: Doug O'Neil, editor
Circulation: 342,000
Published bimonthly

Circulated to CAA members, this lifestyle magazine features travel, leisure, and automotive stories and articles. Seeks dramatic narratives of real-life experiences involving compelling characters. Articles 1,200 to 1,600 words. Pays $300 to $500 for first-run feature; $200 to $300 for second serial rights. "We purchase second rights only when article hasn't appeared in same geographic market. Travel features accompanied by slides stand a greater chance of publication. Completed manuscripts should be sent to the attention of the editor-in-chief." Guidelines and editorial calendar available.

Lethbridge Living Magazine

P.O. Box 22005, Lethbridge, AB T1K 6X5
Phone: (403) 329-1008 Fax: (403) 329-0264
Contact: Martin Oordt, editor
Circulation: 15,000

Published quarterly

A lifestyle magazine focusing on the concerns and interests of the people of Lethbridge and Southern Alberta. Pays 15¢/word on publication for articles up to 1,200 words. "We have a group of regular freelancers. All writers must be screened/interviewed with a portfolio of sample writing."

MENZ

4150 St. Catherine Street W., Suite 610, Westmount, PQ H3Z 2Y5
Phone: (514) 937-3131 Fax: (514) 937-3515
E-mail: editor@menz.com
Web site: www.menz.com
Contact: Vanessa Berkling, editor
Circulation: 115,000
Published quarterly

Established 1994. An informative lifestyle quarterly carrying features on personalities, women we love, entertainment, fine food and spirits, cutting-edge technology, cars, sports, fashion and style, books, and travel, among many other topics of interest to its intelligent, success-driven male readers. Also includes fiction and humour. *Menz Online* enhances rather than merely duplicating the printed magazine. Pays 25¢/word on publication. Welcomes all ideas and submission inquiries. Guidelines available.

Model☆Talent

466 Bathurst Street, Toronto, ON M5T 2S6
Phone: (416) 323-9093 Fax: (416) 653-2291
E-mail: info@modeldbs.com
Web site: www.modeldbs.com
Contact: Peter Holub, editor-in-chief
Published twice a year

A magazine linked to the *MTTV* nightly interactive magazine-format television series, profiling models and talent, and carrying guest interviews, fashion, beauty, entertainment, travel, health and wellness, celebrities, behind-the-scenes features, and lifestyle. Sold on newsstands in North America and England. Pays a competitive rate for pieces of 500 to 750 words. Guidelines available.

The Rural Voice

P.O. Box 429, Blyth, ON NOM IHO
Phone: (519) 523-4311 Fax: (519) 523-9140
E-mail: norhuron@huron.net
Contact: Keith Roulston, editor/publisher
Circulation: 15,000
Published monthly

Established 1975. A regional periodical featuring agricultural news, profiles, and politics, with regular sections on marketing, the law, finances, and home life. Aimed at the agricultural heartland of Ontario. Pays 12¢/word on publication for articles of 1,000 to 2,000 words. Guidelines available.

The Senior Times

4077 Decarie Boulevard, Montreal, PQ H4A 3J8
Phone: (514) 484-5033 Fax: (514) 484-8254
Contact: Barbara Moser, managing editor/publisher
Circulation: 30,000
Published monthly

An informative news source targeting the English-speaking 50-plus community of Montreal and surrounding areas. Pays a variable fee on publication for 400 to 600 words.

Today's Parent

269 Richmond Street W., Toronto, ON M5V IXI
Phone: (416) 596-8680 Fax: (416) 596-1991
Web site: www.todaysparent.com
Contact: Linda Lewis, editor
Circulation: 160,000
Published 11 times a year

A parenting magazine for parents of children up to the age of 12. Editorial is positive, supportive, and offers a mixture of service and controversial/philosophical "issues" stories. Carries articles about child development, education, health, and family life. Pays $1,400 to $2,000 for features (1,500 to 2,500 words), $1,000 for Education, Health, and Behaviour columns (1,200 to 1,500 words), and $650 for humour column, Slice of Life (750 words), 30 days after acceptance. "Always query first and include samples of published work.

First read the magazine to become familiar with our editorial style. Send SASE for guidelines. Do not send manuscripts." Guidelines available.

The Upper Canadian

P.O. Box 653, Smiths Falls, ON K7A 4T6
Phone: (613) 283-1168 Fax: (613) 283-1345
Circulation: 5,000
Published bimonthly

Serves collectors and dealers of antiques and collectibles. Covers shows and auctions, providing insights into price trends. Articles 750 to 1,250 words. Fees negotiated for each project, paid on publication. Submissions should include good photos or illustrations with story. Guidelines available.

WEDDINGBELLS

50 Wellington Street E., 2nd Floor, Toronto, ON M5E 1C8
Phone: (416) 862-8479 Fax: (416) 862-2184
E-mail: editor@weddingbells.com
Web site: www.weddingbells.com
Contact: Crys Stewart, editor
Circulation: 120,000
Published twice a year

A fat glossy magazine with regional editions in Atlantic Canada, Saskatchewan, Calgary, Edmonton, Hamilton, London, Ottawa, Montreal, Toronto, Vancouver, and Winnipeg, and a national edition. Covers all aspects of wedding planning for engaged couples, their friends and families. Pays on acceptance for 1,000 to 2,000 words. Fees negotiable. Query by mail, but first read back issues.

Weddings & Honeymoons

65 Helena Avenue, Toronto, ON M6G 2H3
Phone: (416) 653-4986 Fax: (416) 653-2291
E-mail: barslow@to.org
Contact: Joyce Barslow, editor
Circulation: 50,000
Published twice a year

A glossy magazine featuring information for brides-to-be and tips, trends, and how-to pieces on second marriages, honeymoons, and travel. Stories range between 50 and 1,250 words. Pays a negotiated rate of $50 to $150. A free monthly tabloid supplement, *Weddings & Honeymoons newsPaper*, is distributed to various retail outlets. Include SASE for return of material.

Western Living
555 West 12th Avenue, Suite 300, East Tower, Vancouver, BC V5S 4LC
Phone: (604) 877-7732 Fax: (604) 877-4849
E-mail: westernliving@ican.net
Contact: Carolann Rule, editor
Circulation: 220,000
Published 10 times a year
A general interest and lifestyle magazine with a special emphasis on the home. The largest regional magazine in Canada. Regular features address personalities, trends, Western travel, fashion, recreation, decorating, and cuisine. All stories should have Western Canadian focus. Articles 1,500 to 2,000 words. Pays 50¢/word on acceptance to first-time writers, more to experienced contributors. Guidelines available.

Why Magazine
496 Champagne Drive, North York, ON M3J 2T9
Phone: (416) 630-1470 Fax: (416) 630-4601
E-mail: whymag@interlog.com
Contact: Diane Spivak, managing editor
Circulation: 65,000
Published quarterly
A lifestyle magazine about learning to balance our lives and make meaningful choices – at home and at work, about health, food, travel, relationships, and the products and services we use. Preferred length 1,200 to 2,000 words. Pays variable rate on acceptance.

Your Baby
269 Richmond Street W., Toronto, ON M5V 1X1
Phone: (416) 596-8680 Fax: (416) 596-1991
Contact: Holly Bennett, editor

Circulation: 190,000

Published 3 times a year

A digest-sized magazine for parents of babies and toddlers up to 24 months. Supportive articles focusing on baby care, health, fun and games, practical tips, and the experience of parenting promote a gentle, nurturing parenting style. Emphasis on developmental issues. Distributed with *Chatelaine* magazine; also published in French as *Mon Enfant*. Pays $400 to $1,000 on acceptance for 700 to 2,000 words, depending on length and research required. Query in advance with samples of published work. Guidelines available.

News, Opinions, & Issues

Adbusters Quarterly

1243 West 7th Avenue, Vancouver, BC V6H 1B7

Phone: (604) 736-9401 Fax: (604) 737-6021

E-mail: adbuster@adbuster.org

Web site: www.adbusters.org

Contact: Kalle Lasn, editor

Circulation: 40,000

Published quarterly

Established 1989. A combative, uncompromising commentator on the politics of media control and environmental strategy. Produced by the Media Foundation. Pays 50¢/word on publication for 100 to 1,500 words, though rates vary. Contact editor first if planning a lengthy submission. Guidelines available.

Alberta Sweetgrass

15001 – 112th Avenue N.W., Edmonton, AB T5M 2V6

Phone: (403) 455-2945 or 1-800-661-5469 Fax: (403) 455-7639

E-mail: edsweet@ammsa.com

Contact: Rob McKinley, editor

Circulation: 7,500

Published monthly

A community newspaper highlighting Aboriginal issues, programs, people, arts, culture, and advances in Alberta. Pays $3.00 to $3.60/column inch on publication for stories of 300 to 900 words (rate depends on sources, editing, photos, etc.). "Many Alberta connections can be found from outside of the province. Query first. Sometimes a good local story can be found by asking the right questions." Guidelines available.

Anglican Journal
600 Jarvis Street, Room 224, Toronto, ON M4Y 2J6
Phone: (416) 924-9192, ext. 304 Fax: (416) 921-4452
E-mail: dharris@national.anglican.ca
Contact: David Harris, editor (ext. 306), or Janet MacMaster, editorial assistant (ext. 304)
Circulation: 245,000
Published 10 times a year
Independently edited national publication of the Anglican Church of Canada, established in 1875. Contains news and features from across Canada and abroad. Subjects include news of all denominations and faiths, and articles on a range of social and ethical issues. Stories should be of interest to a national audience. Length 600 to 1,000 words maximum. Pays a base rate of 25¢/word, with a premium paid for major research articles; book reviews, $75 (plus the book). Initial inquiry recommended. Guidelines available.

Annals of Saint Anne de Beaupré
P.O. Box 1000, St. Anne de Beaupré, PQ G0A 3C0
Phone: (418) 827-4538 Fax: (418) 827-4530
Contact: Father Roch Achard, editor
Circulation: 50,000
Published 11 times a year
A general interest religious magazine, established in 1878. Buys fiction and articles with a Catholic dimension. Pays 3¢ to 4¢/word on acceptance for "educational, inspirational, objective, and uplifting" articles up to 1,500 words. Seeks analysis rather than reporting. No poetry. Send complete manuscript, and expect a reply in 3 to 4 weeks. Unsolicited submissions are put into an "article bank" and pulled as need arises, so it can take time. Guidelines available.

Behind the Headlines
5 Devonshire Place, Toronto, ON M5S 2C1
Phone: (416) 979-1851 Fax: (416) 979-8575
E-mail: copeland@CIIA.org

Web site: www.trinity.utoronto.ca/CIIA/intro.htm
Contact: Daryl Copeland, editor
Circulation: 2,250
Published quarterly

For CIIA members and all with an interest in foreign policy, global issues, and international affairs. Preferred length 1,500 to 3,500 words. Cannot pay contributors but welcomes submissions. "We're a non-partisan, not-for-profit NGO. Our hallmarks are insight, criticism, perspective, dissent."

bout de papier

47 Clarence Street, Suite 412, Ottawa, ON KIN 9KI
Phone: (613) 241-1391 Fax: (613) 241-5911
E-mail: boutdepapier@pafso.com
Web site: www.pafso.com
Contact: Debra Hulley, managing editor
Circulation: 2,500
Published quarterly

A bilingual journal that examines all aspects of Canadian foreign policy and life in the Foreign Service. Provides a unique first-hand insight into the conduct and evolution of Canadian diplomacy. Articles are published in the language of submission. Features articles, interviews, book reviews, and commentaries from 1,000 to 2,800 words. Contributors are not paid. Welcomes submission inquiries from qualified writers.

Briarpatch

2138 McIntyre Street, Regina, SK S4P 2R7
Phone: (306) 525-2949 Fax: (306) 565-3430
Contact: George Martin Manz, managing editor
Circulation: 2,000
Published 10 times a year

An award-winning regional magazine providing alternative views on issues concerning Saskatchewan and Canada. Carries short critical articles of 600 to 1,100 words on politics, the environment, agriculture, Aboriginal and women's rights, and labour. Specializes in investigative, activist journalism, its purpose "to publish articles that would not be published in the mainstream media." No poetry.

Contributors are paid in copies only, but submission inquiries, with short bio, welcome.

British Columbia Report
535 Thurlow Street, Suite 305, Vancouver, BC V6E 3L2
Phone: (604) 682-8202 Fax: (604) 682-0964
Contact: Steve Leguire, executive editor
Circulation: 29,000
Published weekly
   This weekly news magazine gives analysis and news of B.C. from a conservative perspective. Preferred length 700 to 1,200 words. Unsolicited freelance material should be "hard news" from B.C.'s regions. Pays a variable rate on publication.

Canadian Dimension
91 Albert Street, Suite 2B, Winnipeg, MB R3B 1G5
Phone: (204) 957-1519 Fax: (204) 943-4617
E-mail: info@canadiandimension.mb.ca
Web site: www.canadiandimension.mb.ca/cd/index.htm
Contact: Todd Scarth, office manager
Circulation: 3,000
Published bimonthly
   Fact and analysis that bring Canada and the world into focus. Carries alternative information on issues concerning women, the labour movement, peace politics, Aboriginal peoples, the environment, economics, and popular culture. "*CD* is a magazine for people who want to change the world. We debate issues, share ideas, recount our victories, and evaluate our strategies for social change." Articles 600 to 2,000 words. Can occasionally pay those whose sole income comes from writing. Guidelines available on web site.

The Canadian Forum
804 – 251 Laurier Avenue W., Ottawa, ON K1P 5J6
Phone: (613) 230-3078 Fax: (613) 233-1458
Contact: Duncan Cameron, editor
Circulation: 10,000
Published 10 times a year

Publishing for 75 years. Tackles a wide range of subjects, including politics, national and international affairs, the arts in Canada, economics, travel, civil liberties, the environment, film, and literature. Carries some high-quality fiction. Articles 2,500 to 3,000 words. Pays an honorarium of $100 per article and $50 per review on publication. Guidelines available.

Canadian Lawyer

240 Edward Street, Aurora, ON L4G 3S9
Phone: (905) 841-6480 Fax: (905) 841-5078
E-mail: canlawmag@canadalawbook.ca
Contact: Michael Fitz-James, executive editor
Circulation: 30,000
Published 11 times a year

Sent to practising lawyers, judges, and corporate counsel, this is the magazine Canada's legal professionals turn to for the news, events, and issues that continually shape the profession. Pay rates vary, depending on project. Guidelines available.

Companion Magazine

695 Coxwell Avenue, Suite 600, Toronto, ON M4C 5R6
Phone: (416) 690-5611 Fax: (416) 690-3320
E-mail: FranCentre@aol.com
Web site: www.cmpa.ca
Contact: Friar Richard Riccioli, editor
Circulation: 5,000
Published 11 times a year

A Catholic inspirational magazine whose purpose is to "build community, foster renewal, and provide hope for our readers" (mostly adult over-50s). Prefers strong human-interest feature articles that are "positive, upbeat, brief, and from a first-hand point of view." Pays 6¢/word on publication for 600 to 1,200 words. Guidelines available.

Education Forum

OSSTF, 60 Mobile Drive, Toronto, ON M4A 2P3
Phone: (416) 751-8300 Fax: (416) 751-3394
Contact: Neil Walker, editor

Circulation: 46,000
Published quarterly
A magazine of news, views, and personal experience. Published by the Ontario Secondary School Teachers' Federation and distributed to Ontario education workers. Buys articles of 2,000 to 3,000 words. Fees vary. Inquiries welcome. Guidelines available.

Education Today
439 University Avenue, 18th Floor, Toronto, ON M5G 1Y8
Phone: (416) 340-2540 Fax: (416) 340-7571
E-mail: admin@opsba.org
Web site: www.opsba.org
Contact: Elsa Moura, editor
Circulation: 3,500
Published 3 times a year
Delivers up-to-date information and interest pieces to people involved in or concerned about the education system. Articles 200 to 1,500 words. Rates vary with project, paid on publication. "Short factual pieces including statistics or national education trends are needed regularly." Guidelines available.

Emergency Librarian
101 – 1001 West Broadway, Suite 343, Vancouver, BC V5Z 4C9
Phone: (604) 925-0266 Fax: (604) 925-0566
E-mail: eml@rockland.com
Contact: Ken Haycock, editor
Circulation: 10,000
Published 5 times a year
Canada's independent library journal. Thought-provoking and challenging articles (1,000 to 4,000 words) address all aspects of library services for children and young adults. Regular review columns and critical analysis of management and programming issues. Designed for school and public librarians. Pays a small honorarium on publication. Guidelines available.

Highgrader Magazine
P.O. Box 714, Cobalt, ON P0J 1C0
Phone: (705) 679-5533 Fax: (705) 679-5234

E-mail: higrade@nt.net
Web site: www.nt.net/highgrader
Contact: Charlie Angus, editor
Circulation: 3,000
Published bimonthly

A magazine articulating culture in northern rural Canada, especially northern Ontario. We cover resource and land conflict, with some how-to's and historical pieces. Articles 500 to 2,000 words. Pays between $40 and $75; investigative, in-depth pieces $75 to $120. "Please read magazine before submitting." Guidelines available.

Humanist in Canada

P.O. Box 3769, Station C, Ottawa, ON K1Y 4J8
Phone: (613) 749-8929
E-mail: jepiercy@cyberus.ca
Contact: J.E. Piercy, president, Canadian Humanist Publications
Circulation: 1,500
Published quarterly

For non-believers with an interest in social issues, its aim "to print literature with a humanist content, reflecting the principle that human problems can best be solved by people relying on their own capabilities, without belief in the supernatural." Articles 1,000 to 2,500 words. Cannot pay but welcomes submission inquiries. Guidelines available.

Legion Magazine

359 Kent Street, Suite 407, Ottawa, ON K2P 0R6
Phone: (613) 235-8741 Fax: (613) 233-7159
Contact: Dan Black, managing editor
Circulation: 434,000
Published 5 times a year

A magazine for Canada's war veterans, RCMP members, forces personnel and their families, seniors, and the wider public. Carries news, views, and serious articles exploring Canada's military history, defence, veterans' affairs, health, and pensions. Offers humour and opinion columns, and also buys memoirs and nostalgia. Articles 600 to 2,500 words. Pays $150 to $1,200 on acceptance (fee determined after final edit). Query first. Sample copies available on request. Average assessment time is 6 months.

Maclean's

777 Bay Street, Toronto, ON M5W 1A7
Phone: (416) 596-5386 Fax: (416) 596-7730
E-mail: letters@macleans.ca
Web site: www.canoe.ca/macleans
Contact: Robert Lewis, editor
Circulation: 540,000
Published weekly

Canada's most widely read news magazine, with about 2.6 million readers. Examines news events, trends, and issues from a Canadian perspective. Has a broad network of bureaus, with correspondents in 5 Canadian cities and 35 other countries. Staff writers and freelancers contribute to weekly sections on politics, business, entertainment, sports, leisure, education, health, science, personal finance, justice, and technology. Pays a variable but competitive fee on acceptance.

McGill News Alumni Quarterly

3605, rue de la montagne, Montreal, PQ H3G 2M1
Phone: (514) 398-3552 Fax: (514) 398-7338
E-mail: janicep@martlet1.lan.mcgill.ca
Web site: www.mcgill.ca/alumni/news
Contact: Janice Paskey, editor
Circulation: 65,000

Sent to McGill graduates, donors to McGill, and all graduates in Quebec. Features articles about current affairs, entertainment, the humanities, medicine, and science with a McGill connection, and profiles of graduates. Pays $300 to $600, depending on complexity, on acceptance for features of 1,000 to 2,000 words. Also buys news stories of 200 to 600 words. Accepts both French and English queries – publishes in both languages. Prospective contributors may write for a sample copy.

New Internationalist

1011 Bloor Street W., Toronto, ON M6H 1M1
Phone: (416) 588-6478 Fax: (416) 537-6435
Contact: Richard Swift, co-editor
Circulation: 8,000 in Canada; 70,000 worldwide
Published 11 times a year

An uncompromising international periodical providing information and analysis on the major issues concerning international development. Exposes the politics of aid, militarism, and national and multinational exploitation of the developing countries, and discusses racial, gender, and social politics in the developed and developing worlds. Issues are thematic. Articles 500 to 1,800 words. Pays $400 on publication for full-length article. Guidelines available.

NeWest Review

P.O. Box 394, R.P.O. University, Saskatoon, SK S7N 4J8
Phone: (306) 934-1444 Fax: (306) 343-8579
E-mail: verne.clemence@sk.sympatico.ca
Contact: Verne Clemence, editor/manager
Circulation: 1,000
Published bimonthly

Carries news and opinion on Western Canadian cultural, social, and political issues. Reviews books and theatre, and carries some fiction and poetry. Articles/stories 1,500 to 2,500 words. Pays on publication $100 for 2,000 words; $25 for short reviews; $60 for gazette items (800 words). Prefers initial proposals. Guidelines available.

The Next City

225 Brunswick Avenue, Toronto, ON M5S 2M6
Phone: (416) 964-9223 Fax: (416) 964-8239
E-mail: letters@nextcity.com
Web site: www.nextcity.com
Contact: Lawrence Solomon, editor
Circulation: 3,000
Published quarterly

A solutions-oriented magazine that tackles issues confronting our new urban society. Features run from 3,000 to 8,000 words. Pays $1/word up to 1,000 words, 50¢ thereafter, on publication for features. Rates vary for non-features.

Our Schools/Our Selves

107 Earl Grey Road, Toronto, ON M4J 3L6
Phone: (416) 463-6978 Fax: (416) 463-6978
Contact: Satu Repo, executive editor

Circulation: 1,000
Published bimonthly

Offers a critical left perspective on education policy, curriculum, and classroom practices, and reports on activism among parents, teachers, and students. Articles 1,000 to 3,000 words. Cannot pay but welcomes submission inquiries.

Our Times

1209 King Street W., Suite 201A, Toronto, ON M6K 1G2
Phone: (416) 531-6877 Fax: (416) 531-7641
E-mail: ourtimes@web.net
Contact: Lorraine Endicott, editor
Circulation: 3,000
Published bimonthly

Published by a not-for-profit organization to promote workers' rights, unionization, and social justice. "Many articles are contributed by union activists. We pay between $200 and $400 for feature stories of 1,500 to 2,500 words from working writers." Guidelines available.

Peace Magazine

736 Bathurst Street, Toronto, ON M5S 2R4
Phone: (416) 533-7581 Fax: (416) 531-6214
E-mail: mspencer@web.net
Web site: www.peacemagazine.org
Contact: Metta Spencer, editor
Circulation: 3,000
Published bimonthly

Provides interviews, commentary, and topical features relating to multilateral disarmament and nonviolent conflict resolution. Covers domestic and world issues. Articles 1,500 to 3,000 words. Cannot pay but welcomes submission inquiries. "We prefer clearly focused, thoroughly researched material on topics the mainstream media ignore." Guidelines available.

Policy Options

1470, rue Peel, Bureau 200, Montreal, PQ H3A 1T1
Phone: (514) 985-2461 Fax: (514) 985-2559
E-mail: policyop@irpp.org

Contact: Alfred LeBlanc, editor
Circulation: 3,000
Published 10 times a year

Published by the Institute for Research on Public Policy, a national, independent, not-for-profit think-tank. Carries analyses of public policy so as to encourage wide debate on major policy issues. Articles 1,500 to 2,500 words. Contributors are unpaid, but submission inquiries by qualified writers welcome. Guidelines available.

Raven's Eye: The Aboriginal Newspaper of British Columbia

15001 – 112th Avenue, Edmonton, AB T5M 2V6
Phone: 1-800-661-5469 or (403) 455-2700 Fax: (403) 455-7639
E-mail: edraven@ammsa.com
Web site: www.ammsa.com
Contact: Paul Barnsley, editor
Circulation: 10,000
Published monthly

Spotlights Aboriginal people and/or issues in British Columbia. Pays a competitive set fee per column inch on publication for stories of 500 to 1,000 words. "We need writers/photographers located in all areas of B.C. – the further from Vancouver the better." Guidelines available.

Saskatchewan Sage

15001 – 112th Avenue, Edmonton, AB T5M 2V6
Phone: (403) 455-2700 Fax: (403) 455-7639
E-mail: edsage@ammsa.com
Web site: www.ammsa.com
Contact: Kenneth Williams, editor
Circulation: 7,500
Published monthly

A community newspaper featuring news, arts and entertainment, reviews, and feature articles about and by Aboriginal people of Saskatchewan. Pays $3.00 to $3.60/column inch on publication for 500 to 1,000 words. "Stories must be of provincial interest. Always query first, preferably by phone or e-mail. Guidelines available on Internet site."

The Social Worker

383 Parkdale Avenue, Suite 402, Ottawa, ON KIY 4R4
Phone: (613) 729-6668 Fax: (613) 729-9608
E-mail: casw@casw-acts.ca
Web site: www.intranet.ca/~casw-acts
Contact: Penny Sipkes, co-ordinator
Circulation: 14,500
Published 3 times a year

Publication of the Canadian Association of Social Workers. A bilingual forum for social work professionals in which social workers and others share their knowledge, skills, research, and information with each other and with the general public. Articles from 300 to 2,500 words. Cannot pay but welcomes submission inquiries. First preference given to CASW members. Guidelines available.

This Magazine

401 Richmond Street W., Suite 396, Toronto, ON M5V 3A8
Phone: (416) 979-8400 Fax: (416) 979-1143
E-mail: thismag@web.net
Contact: Andrea Curtis, editor
Circulation: 8,000
Published bimonthly

Canada's leading alternative news and opinion magazine carrying investigative features and researched commentary on culture, politics, labour, and other issues. Features of 2,000 to 4,000 words are paid a negotiated fee of between $200 and $350 on publication. "We prefer clearly focused, thoroughly researched, and sharply written investigative articles on topics the mainstream media ignore." Send a query letter. Guidelines available.

The United Church Observer

478 Huron Street, Toronto, ON M5R 2R3
Phone: (416) 960-8500 Fax: (416) 960-8477
E-mail: general@ucobserver.org
Web site: www.ucobserver.org
Contact: Muriel Duncan, editor
Circulation: 112,000
Published 11 times a year

The national magazine of the United Church of Canada. Provides news of the church, the nation, and the world, while maintaining an independent editorial policy. Prints serious articles on issues such as human rights, social justice, and Christian faith in action, and stories of personal courage – all with a Christian perspective. Also covers the religious dimensions of art, literature, and theatre. Articles 850 to 1,000 words. Uses freelancers infrequently. Fees negotiable, paid on publication. Personal stories are paid at lower rates. Guidelines available.

University Affairs
600 – 350 Albert Street, Ottawa, ON KIR IBI
Phone: (613) 563-1236, ext. 228 Fax: (613) 563-9745
E-mail: pberkowi@aucc.ca
Web site: www.aucc.ca
Contact: Peggy Berkowitz, managing editor
Circulation: 24,000
Published 10 times a year
  Canada's main source of information on university education, published by the Association of Universities and Colleges of Canada. Covers major issues and trends in higher education and other articles of interest to professors and administrators. Stories from 300 to 2,000 words. Fees are negotiated and paid on acceptance. "Please read the magazine and guidelines before submitting a story idea. Easy stories earn a lower per-word rate than complex features, which are generally assigned to writers we have worked with before." Guidelines available.

University of Toronto Magazine
21 King's College Circle, Toronto, ON M5S 3J3
Phone: (416) 978-2988 or 946-3192 Fax: (416) 978-7430 or 978-5102
E-mail: k.dahlin@utoronto.ca or karen.hanley@utoronto.ca
Contacts: Karina Dahlin or Karen Hanley, co-editors
Circulation: 215,000
Published quarterly
  Promotes the University of Toronto to its alumni by publishing articles on research, issues, campus news, alumni and faculty profiles, and more. U. of T. angle must be strong. Pays 50¢ to $1/word

on acceptance for articles of 1,000 to 3,000 words. Rates negotiated based on writer's experience and complexity of project.

Windspeaker

15001 – 112th Avenue, Edmonton, AB T5M 2V6
Phone: (403) 455-2700 Fax: (403) 455-7639
Contact: Debora Lockyer, editor
Circulation: 17,000–29,000
Published monthly

An Aboriginal newspaper focusing on national issues. Includes sports and entertainment, columns, and features of 300 to 800 words. Welcomes stories and profiles on issues of concern to Native peoples and those who work with them. Pays $3.00 to $3.60 per published column inch on publication for multi-source stories and profiles. Guidelines available.

Special Interest

Abilities

489 College Street, Suite 501, Toronto, ON M6G 1A5
Phone: (416) 923-1885 Fax: (416) 923-9829
E-mail: able@interlog.com
Web site: www.indie.ca/abilities/
Contact: Lisa Bendall, managing editor
Circulation: 50,000
Published quarterly

Canada's lifestyle magazine for people with disabilities. A source of information and inspiration. Articles/stories 500 to 2,000 words. A non-profit organization that pays honoraria to writers ranging from $50 to $300 on publication. "First-hand knowledge of disability is helpful. We are interested in new ideas, resources, or strategies that will empower our readers. Avoid telling them what they already know." Guidelines available.

Active Living Magazine

P.O. Box 237, Grimsby, ON L3M 9Z9
Phone: (905) 338-6894 Fax: (905) 338-1836
E-mail: activeliv@aol.com

Contact: Jeff Tiessen, editor
Circulation: 50,000
Published quarterly

Formerly *Disability Today*. An access and awareness magazine aimed at better informing readers about physical disabilities and opportunities that exist for this population. Directed particularly toward educators, employers, and advocates. Articles 1,000 to 3,000 words. Pays about $300 on publication. Guidelines available.

The Atlantic Co-operator
P.O. Box 1386, Antigonish, NS B2G 2L7
Phone: (902) 863-2776 Fax: (902) 863-8077
E-mail: rcdccomm@istar.ca
Contact: Brenda MacKinnon, editor
Circulation: 30,000
Published bimonthly

Established 1939. An informational resource for co-ops and credit unions and those involved in community ownership initiatives in Atlantic Canada. Pays about 20¢/word on publication for 400 to 600 words. Guidelines available.

Aviation Quarterly
72 Sunnyside Avenue, Ottawa, ON KIS ORI
Phone: (613) 730-9439 Fax: (613) 730-1321
E-mail: avq@cyberus.ca
Contact: Bob Baglow, publisher
Circulation: 16,000

Canada's only full-colour national aviation magazine, addressing recreational, general, and commercial aviation. Pays 10¢/word for articles between 1,800 and 4,500 words. "Pay rate is negotiable depending on expertise. Unsolicited material not accepted. All writing projects must have prior approval of publisher."

Boudoir Noir
P.O. Box 5, Station F, Toronto, ON M4Y 2L4
Phone: (416) 591-2387 Fax: (416) 591-1572
E-mail: boudoir@boudoir-noir.com
Web site: www.boudoir-noir.com

Contact: Robert Dante, editor
Circulation: 5,000
Published quarterly

A candid erotic magazine for people interested in the leather/fetish/consensual SM scene. Aims to "integrate psychosexuality into the larger context of the world as it is, bringing the kink out of the closet into the warm light of day. Query first. Editors will help with resources, contacts. We tend to use the same writers regularly. We are very approachable." Pays $25 to $100 on publication for 500 to 1,500 words. Guidelines available.

Cannabis Canada

21 Water Street, Unit 504, Vancouver, BC V6B IAI
Phone: (604) 669-9069 Fax: (604) 669-9038
E-mail: muggles@hempbc.com
Web site: www.hempbc.com
Contact: Dana Larsen, editor
Circulation: 30,000
Published bimonthly

For cannabis consumers and those interested in drugs and drug policy, featuring current drug news, growing advice, travel stories, and politics. Articles 300 to 2,500 words. Pays 4¢/word on publication, depending on quality and content. "We exist to bring an end to prohibition and censorship in Canada and everywhere else. Read us to see what we print."

The Computer Paper

425 Carrall Street, Suite 503, Vancouver, BC V6B 6E3
Phone: (604) 688-2120 Fax: (604) 688-4680
E-mail: david@tcp.ca
Web site: www.tcp.ca
Contact: David Tanaka, editor
Circulation: 365,000
Published monthly

Provides computer industry news and product reviews aimed at knowledgeable consumers and small business readers. Articles 500 to 3,000 words. Pays 17¢/word plus on publication for first Canadian periodical and first world electronic rights. "We're looking for articles that show a deep technical understanding but don't require an advanced degree in computer science to understand. Write for real people, not techies." Guidelines available.

Detective Files Group
1350 Sherbrooke Street W., Suite 600, Montreal, PQ H3G 2T4
Phone: (514) 849-7733 Fax: (514) 849-8330
Contact: Dominick Merle, editor-in-chief
Circulation: 100,000/month
Published bimonthly

A stable of six bimonthly true crime magazines. Stories from 3,000 to 6,000 words. Pays on acceptance $250 to $350 per article including photos. "Over 90 per cent of our readership is in the United States, but we welcome queries on Canadian cases as well." No phone queries. Guidelines available.

Dogs in Canada
89 Skyway Avenue, Suite 200, Etobicoke, ON M9W 6R4
Phone: (416) 798-9778 Fax: (416) 798-9671
E-mail: info@dogs-in-canada.com
Web site: www.dogs-in-canada.com
Contact: Allan Reznik, editor
Circulation: 30,000
Published monthly

Geared toward the dog breeder and exhibitor, and the serious purebred dog enthusiast. (A separate annual issue is broadened to appeal to new and prospective dog owners, with complete information on selecting, caring for, and training a pet.) Articles 750 to 2,500 words. Pays $150 and up for 1,000-plus words, on acceptance. "The monthly is quite specialized while the annual appeals to a broader readership. Query in detail before submitting. Written queries from new contributors should include outlines and tearsheets demonstrating particular expertise in purebred dogs." Guidelines available.

Drive
716 Gordon Baker Road, Unit 217, Toronto, ON M2H 3B4
Phone: (416) 492-9539 Fax: (416) 492-1596
E-mail: readers@drive.ca
Web site: www.drive.ca

Contact: Joe Duarte, editor
Circulation: 30,000
Published quarterly

Canada's luxury automotive and lifestyle magazine. Familiarize yourself with the magazine before you submit. Rates vary, depending on project.

Food & Drink
55 Lakeshore Boulevard E., Toronto, ON M5E 1A4
Phone: (416) 864-6630 Fax: (416) 365-5935
Contact: Jody Dunn, co-ordinator
Circulation: 300,000
Published quarterly

Established 1988. Published by the Liquor Control Board of Ontario and "dedicated to the art of entertaining in the home." Length from short, one-paragraph items to 2,000-word essays. Pays up to $1/word on publication.

Pets Magazine
10 Gateway Boulevard, Suite 490, North York, ON M3C 3T4
Phone: (416) 696-5488 Fax: (416) 696-7395
Contact: Edward Zapletal, editor
Circulation: 50,000
Published bimonthly

Offers advice and guidance to Canadian pet owners, including general pet care, human interest (working dogs), obedience and training, grooming, and breeding. Preferred length 500 to 1,500 words. No fiction or poetry. First send one-page outline. "No U.S. postage on SASEs – only international postage coupons." Pays 12¢ to 15¢/word on publication. Guidelines available.

Stitches: The Journal of Medical Humour
16787 Warden Avenue, R.R.3, Newmarket, ON L3Y 4W1
Phone: (905) 853-1884 Fax: (905) 853-6565
Contact: Simon Hally, editor
Circulation: 42,000
Published 11 times a year

A magazine of humour and travel for practising physicians. Pays 35¢/word on publication for 150 to 1,500 words. "Aspiring contributors are encouraged to request a free sample copy of the magazine. No story ideas, please; we need to see the story itself. We are eager to hear from genuinely funny writers."

Toronto Computes!

99 Atlantic Avenue, Suite 408, Toronto, ON M4V 1M7
Phone: (416) 588-6818 Fax: (416) 588-4110
E-mail: editor@tcpon.com
Contact: Mara Gulens, chief editor
Circulation: 110,000
Published monthly

Runs articles and features about the full spectrum of personal computers and related technologies, with regular software and hardware reviews and an emphasis on local events. Pays 30 days after publication for articles of 100 to 5,000 words. Fees negotiable. Query first, please. Guidelines available.

Winetidings

5165 Sherbrooke Street W., Suite 414, Montreal, PQ H4A 1T6
Phone: (514) 481-5892 Fax: (514) 481-9699
Contact: Tony Aspler, editor
Circulation: 16,000
Published 8 times a year

A magazine for discerning wine lovers. Reports on price trends and vintages, offers recipes, and profiles well-known wine cellars. Also compares wines and grape types, and reviews developments in the Canadian wine industry. Articles run from 500 to 1,500 words, the longer paying $200. Pays on publication. "Advanced knowledge of wine and wine tasting is a prerequisite."

World of Wheels

1200 Markham Road, Suite 300, Scarborough, ON M1H 3C3
Phone: (416) 438-7777 Fax: (416) 438-5333
E-mail: editor@wheels.ca
Web site: www.wheels.ca
Contact: Joe Knycha, editor
Circulation: 127,000
Published bimonthly

A magazine for auto enthusiasts, and for those interested in developments in the auto industry and their impact on Canada. Evaluates and compares the latest in cars, light pickup trucks, vans, and sport-utility vehicles. Pays 30¢/word on publication for 400 to 2,000 words. Guidelines available.

Sports & Outdoors

The Atlantic Salmon Journal
P.O. Box 429, St. Andrews, NB E0G 2X0
Phone: (506) 529-4581 Fax: (506) 529-4985
E-mail: asfpub@nbnet.nb.ca
Contact: Jim Gourlay, editor
Circulation: 10,000
Published quarterly

A full-colour magazine for serious anglers who fly-fish and Atlantic salmon conservationists. Carries articles on researching salmon and where to catch them, and focuses on angling adventures and conservation. Knowledgeable, lucid, and lively prose as well as superior photography and art. Pays $300 to $500 on publication for articles of 1,500 to 2,500 words, $50 to $100 for short items, including book reviews. "We normally expect writers to provide photos for their stories." Guidelines available.

B.C. Outdoors
780 Beatty Street, Suite 300, Vancouver, BC V6B 2M1
Phone: (604) 606-4644 Fax: (604) 687-1925
E-mail: oppubl@istar.ca
Contact: Karl Bruhn, editor
Circulation: 40,000
Published 8 times a year

Carries articles up to 2,000 words on fishing and hunting in British Columbia. Pays 27¢/word on publication for articles accompanied by photos. Guidelines available.

Camping Canada's RV Lifestyle Magazine
2585 Skymark Avenue, Suite 306, Mississauga, ON L4W 4L5
Phone: (905) 624-8218 Fax: (905) 624-6764
Contact: Peter Tasler, editorial director

Circulation: 50,000

Published 7 times a year

Focuses on recreational vehicle lifestyle articles featuring travel routes, destinations, and technical information on motor homes, wide-body vans, trailers, and trailer homes. Accepts articles of 1,500 to 3,000 words on RV camping in Canada. Destinations stories should have photos/slides with credits. Fees negotiable, paid on publication.

Canadian Biker

P.O. Box 4122, Victoria, BC v8x 3x4

Phone: (250) 384-0333   Fax: (250) 384-1832

E-mail: canbike@islandnet.com

Web site: www.canadianbiker.com

Contact: Kim Prinz, editor

Circulation: 20,000

Published 8 times a year

A family-oriented motorcycle magazine carrying a variety of articles and columns for sport and touring enthusiasts. Subjects include events, racing, maintenance, new models and products, vintage, custom, and off-road motorcycling. Preferred length 500 to 1,500 words. Pays $50 to $200 on publication. "Articles paid according to quality rather than quantity and based on topic, frequency of contributions, and originality. Preference given to work sent on disk with hard copy and a minimum of two photos (captioned)." Guidelines available.

Canadian Horseman

225 Industrial Parkway S., P.O. Box 670, Aurora, ON L4G 4J9

Phone: (905) 727-0107   Fax: (905) 841-1530

E-mail: horsepower@horsenet.com

Contact: Lee Benson, managing editor

Circulation: 10,000

Published bimonthly

Canadian-focus equine magazine that covers training and horse care. Interesting reading for horse enthusiasts of all disciplines, competitive and non-competitive. Preferred length 500 to 1,500 words. Pays a negotiated rate on publication. Guidelines available.

Canadian Rodeo News

2116 – 27th Avenue N.E., Suite 223, Calgary, AB T2E 7A6
Phone: (403) 250-7292 Fax: (403) 250-6926
E-mail: rodeonews@iul-ccs.com
Web site: www.rodeocanada.com
Contact: Kirby Meston, editor
Circulation: 48,000
Published monthly

A tabloid of news, views, and opinions from the Canadian and U.S. rodeo circuit. Also accepts articles related to the West or to Canada's Western heritage. Pays $50 on publication for stories of 1,000 to 1,200 words, $25 for 500 to 600 words, $10 for photos. Phone editor with ideas before submitting. Guidelines available.

Canadian Sportfishing Magazine

937 Centre Road, Dept. 2020, Waterdown, ON L0R 2H0
Phone: (905) 689-1112 Fax: (905) 689-2065
E-mail: mattn@globalserve.net
Contact: Matt Nicholls, editor
Circulation: 45,000
Published 6 times a year

Aimed at active readers engaged in a range of sportfishing techniques and issues in Canada. Accepts articles of 250 to 2,500 words. Pays 25¢/word on publication. Query for features/articles that interest you. Submit stories in hard copy and on disk (3½ inch, Word or ASCII). All stories should include photo support, preferably slides. Stories may be e-mailed to the editor. Guidelines available.

The Canadian Sportsman

P.O. Box 129, 25 Old Plank Road, Straffordville, ON N0J 1Y0
Phone: (519) 866-5558 Fax: (519) 866-5596
Contact: Dave Briggs, editor
Circulation: 5,500
Published biweekly

"The voice of harness racing since 1870." Carries features and news mostly about harness racing in Canada. Mail, phone, or fax inquiries welcome. Fees negotiable.

Canadian Thoroughbred

225 Industrial Parkway S., P.O. Box 670, Aurora, ON L4G 4J9
Phone: (905) 727-0107 Fax: (905) 841-1530
E-mail: horsepower@horsenet.com
Contact: Susan Jane Anstey, publisher
Circulation: 5,000
Published bimonthly

Canada's national journal on thoroughbred racing features news and information on horses and their owners – pedigrees and stable product updates. Fees negotiable. A very specialist market, so always inquire first. Guidelines available.

Canadian Yachting

395 Matheson Boulevard E., Mississauga, ON L4Z 2H2
Phone: (905) 890-1846 Fax: (905) 890-5769
E-mail: canyacht@kerrwil.com
Web site: www.canyacht.com
Contact: Heather Ormerod, editor
Circulation: 15,000
Published 6 times a year, in spring/summer/fall

Written for sailboat enthusiasts across Canada. Includes adventure, regattas, profiles, maintenance, boat reviews, news and gossip for cruisers, racers, keelboat and dinghy sailors. Features of 1,500 to 2,500 words earn $250 to $350; shorter pieces for departments (1,200 to 2,000 words) earn $200 to $250. Prefers to buy articles with photos. Pays 60 days after publication. Send initial query letter. Guidelines available.

Cycle Canada

411 Richmond Street E., Suite 301, Toronto, ON M5A 3S5
Phone: (416) 362-7966 Fax: (416) 362-3950
Contact: Bruce Reeve, editor
Circulation: 20,000
Published 10 times a year

A magazine written for Canadian motorcycle enthusiasts, with product tests and evaluations, technical information, and how-to maintenance articles, plus profiles from the world of biking. Pays on acceptance $50 for brief news items of approx. 100 words, $500 for a top feature up to 4,000 words plus photos.

Diver Magazine
P.O. Box 1312, Delta, BC V4M 3Y8
Phone: (604) 274-4333 Fax: (604) 274-4366
E-mail: divermag@axionet.com
Web site: www.medianetcom.com/divermag/
Contact: Stephanie Bold, editor
Circulation: 15,000
Published 9 times a year

For North American sport divers. Carries regular articles on travel destinations, snorkelling, and scuba and deep-water diving. Also covers marine life and underwater photography. Articles 500 to 1,000 words. Pays $3/column inch after publication. Check guidelines before submitting material.

Explore: Canada's Outdoor Adventure Magazine
301 – 14th Street N.W., Suite 420, Calgary, AB T2N 2A1
Phone: (403) 270-8890 Fax: (403) 270-7922
E-mail: explore@explore-mag.com
Web site: www.explore-mag.com
Contact: Marion Harrison, editor
Circulation: 35,000
Published bimonthly

For people who enjoy self-propelled outdoor recreational activities such as backpacking, cycling, paddling, and backcountry skiing. Articles of 1,500 to 2,500 words cover adventure, outdoor equipment evaluations, new products, and environmental issues. Pays $750 for 2,000 words on publication. Payment includes use of photos. Fees may in some cases be negotiated. "Published writers query first. Unpublished writers should send ms. and photos on spec. We're always in need of short destination articles with photos (Canada only); 300 to 800 words pays $125 to $250 – query first." Guidelines available.

Gam On Yachting
250 The Esplanade, Suite 202, Toronto, ON M5A 1J2
Phone: (416) 368-1559 Fax: (416) 368-2831
Contact: Karin Larson, publisher/editor
Circulation: 14,000
Published 8 times a year

A magazine for the racing and cruising sailor, with how-to articles, upcoming events, harbour profiles, book reviews, safety information, and humour. Special issues coincide with Canadian boat shows. "Exists as a medium of communication between Canadian sailors, and as such cannot pay for contributions."

Golf Canada

1333 Dorval Drive, Oakville, ON L6J 4Z3
Phone: (905) 849-9700 Fax: (905) 845-7040
E-mail: steinburg@rcga.org
Web site: www.rcga.org
Contact: Bill Steinburg, editor
Circulation: 120,000
Published quarterly

The official organ of the Royal Canadian Golf Association. Covers amateur championships and other golfing issues, including player profiles and related topics. Features are 750 to 2,000 words. Pays 25¢ to 50¢/word on acceptance. Fees are negotiated.

Horse Sport Magazine

225 Industrial Parkway S., P.O. Box 670, Aurora, ON L4G 4J9
Phone: (905) 727-0107 or 1-800-505-7428 Fax: (905) 841-1530
E-mail: horsepower@horsenet.com
Contact: Susan Stafford, managing editor
Circulation: 10,000
Published monthly

An authoritative equestrian periodical featuring articles on horse care, riding and training techniques, breeding, animal health, and the industry at large. Provides coverage of equestrian sporting events in Canada and abroad, profiles of top riders, and how-to articles. Preferred length 1,000 to 2,000 words. Pays 10¢ to 15¢/word on publication. Contact editor before submitting. Guidelines available.

Horsepower Magazine for Young Horse Lovers

P.O. Box 670, Aurora, ON L4G 4J9
Phone: (905) 727-0107 Fax: (905) 841-1530
E-mail: horsepower@horsenet.com

Contact: Susan Stafford, managing editor
Circulation: 20,000
Published bimonthly

Provides young riders and horse lovers with advice on horse care, feeding, and tips for riding and stable skills, plus profiles, puzzles, and contests. Pays $50 for 500 to 700 words, $75 for 1,000 words, on publication. "Our editorial focus is always on safety. Submissions must be horse-related (English or Western, all breeds), and suitable for pre-teens and young teens. Please contact editor in writing before submitting. We prefer how-to type articles to fiction." Guidelines available.

Hot Water

2585 Skymark Avenue, Unit 306, Mississauga, ON L4W 4L5
Phone: (905) 624-8218 Fax: (905) 624-6764
Contact: Yvan Marston, editor
Circulation: 15,000
Published quarterly

For personal watercraft owners. Carries features on newest PWC models and other jet-driven boats plus all accessories that contribute to their enjoyment. Also covers technical aspects of the sport, racing and other events, and destination stories. Preferred feature length 1,500 to 3,000 words. Pays from $200 on publication for articles plus photos. Writers should have a knowledge and interest in water sports.

Impact Magazine

2007 – 2nd Street S.W., Calgary, AB T2S 1S4
Phone: (403) 228-0605 Fax: (403) 228-0627
E-mail: impact@enernet.com
Contact: Robin Wheeler, editor
Circulation: 50,000
Published bimonthly

Features health, fitness, and sports for the active and physically fit of Calgary. All content focused on Calgary and surroundings. Articles 750 to 1,500 words. Query all ideas by phone or letter before submitting. "Our budget is very limited. We occasionally pay a negotiated fee to freelancers."

Kanawa: Canada's Canoeing and Kayaking Magazine

446 Main Street W., Merrickville, ON K0G 1N0
Phone: (613) 269-2910 Fax: (613) 269-2908
E-mail: staff@crca.ca
Web site: www.crca.ca
Contact: Joseph Agnew, editor
Circulation: 20,000
Published quarterly

Articles (1,500 to 2,500 words) on destinations, equipment, instruction, environment, heritage, and much more. Cannot pay but welcomes submission inquiries. Guidelines available.

Ontario Out of Doors

777 Bay Street, 6th Floor, Toronto, ON M5W 1A7
Phone: (416) 596-5908 Fax: (416) 596-2517
E-mail: 102677.1125@compuserve.com
Web site: www.fishontario.com
Contact: Burton Myers, editor
Circulation: 89,000
Published 10 times a year

Established 1969. A magazine for Ontario's hunters and anglers. Carries how-to and where-to articles on topics such as boating, firearms, archery, and backroad touring. Regular columns on hunting, fishing, wildlife, camp cooking, dogs, fly-fishing, scientific research, and new products. Pays on acceptance for articles of 500 to 1,500 words. Fees negotiated; average feature earns $350 to $700. Pays $500 to $750 for cover photo. Guidelines available.

Ontario Snowmobiler

18540 Centre Street, R.R.3, Mount Albert, ON L0G 1M0
Phone: (905) 473-7009 Fax: (905) 473-5217
Contact: Terrence Kehoe, publisher
Circulation: 80,000
Published monthly, September–January

Informs Ontario snowmobilers of industry developments, snowmobile people, clubs, programs, and travel. Pays $75 to $100 on acceptance for 400 to 800 words. Uses freelancers infrequently.

Outdoor Canada
703 Evans Avenue, Suite 202, Toronto, ON M9C 5E9
Phone: (416) 695-0311 Fax: (416) 695-0381
E-mail: ocanada@istar.ca
Contact: James Little, editor
Circulation: 90,000
Published 8 times a year
   A magazine dedicated to the use and conservation of Canada's outdoors. Carries articles on fishing, boating, hunting, cross-country skiing, snowmobiling, canoeing, hiking, outdoor photography, and camping. "Concentrates on destination and service stories that help readers get more out of their outdoor experiences. Canadian content only. Professional photos accompanying queries/articles improve chance of acceptance." Pays on publication $80 and up for short news pieces, $500 and up for features up to 3,000 words. Invites on-spec submissions. Guidelines available.

The Outdoor Edge
5829 – 97th Street, Edmonton, AB T6E 3J2
Phone: (403) 448-0381 Fax: (403) 438-3244
Contact: Mark Yelic, associate editor
Circulation: 60,000
Published bimonthly
   Targeting hunters and anglers, circulated among members of Western Canada's fish and game associations and wildlife federations. Interested in informative, how-to articles of 1,500 to 2,000 words. Pays $150 to $200 on publication. "Articles must be accompanied by a good selection of photos. Please submit completed manuscripts unless arranged ahead of time. All material returned." Guidelines available.

Pacific Golf Magazine
4180 Lougheed Highway, 4th Floor, Burnaby, BC V5C 6A7
Phone: (604) 299-7311 Fax: (604) 299-9188
Contact: Alison McMillan, associate editor
Circulation: 20,000
Published 7 times a year
   The West Coast's leading golf magazine serving the diverse

interests and needs of golf enthusiasts (both serious and beginners) throughout the Pacific Northwest. Pays 30¢ to 40¢/word on publication for 1,000 to 2,500 words. Pay rates vary with project. Query first; don't send completed articles on spec.

Pacific Yachting

780 Beatty Street, Suite 300, Vancouver, BC V6B 2MI
Phone: (604) 606-4644 Fax: (604) 687-1925
E-mail: oppubl@istor.ca
Web site: www.oppub.com
Contact: Duart Snow, editor
Circulation: 20,000
Published monthly

Stories written from personal experience relating to powerboating and sailing on Canada's West Coast, with an emphasis on cruising, destinations, local history, and personalities. Carries racing reports, adventure, and articles (800 to 2,500 words). "Writers must be familiar with our special-interest viewpoint, language, and orientation. First-hand experience of subject is essential." Buys photos and stories together at negotiated rates. Pays on publication. Guidelines available.

Parks & Recreation Canada

306 – 1600 James Naismith Drive, Gloucester, ON KIB 5N4
Phone: (613) 748-5651 Fax: (613) 748-5854
E-mail: cpra@activeliving.ca
Web site: www.activeliving.ca/activeliving/cpra.html
Contact: Mary-Lynn Charlton, editor
Circulation: 2,000
Published bimonthly

Focuses on issues, research, and trends relating to innovative leisure programs and facilities, the environment, arts and culture, active living, and healthy communities. Preferred length 1,000 to 1,500 words. Cannot pay but welcomes submissions. "We rely on volunteer writers who are usually professionals or volunteers in the parks, leisure, and recreation field."

Power Boating Canada

2585 Skymark Avenue, Suite 306, Mississauga, ON L4W 4L5
Phone: (905) 624-8218 Fax: (905) 624-6764
Web site: www.powerboating.com
Contact: Peter Tasler, editor
Circulation: 40,000
Published bimonthly
Carries stories on powerboat performance and evaluates new equipment and boating techniques. Also covers waterskiing. Pays around $350 on publication for a feature of 1,500 to 2,000 words with photos. Query first with ideas.

Score: Canada's Golf Magazine

287 MacPherson Avenue, Toronto, ON M4V 1A4
Phone: (416) 928-2909 Fax: (416) 928-1357
E-mail: weeksy@idirect.com
Web site: www.scoregolf.com
Contact: Bob Weeks, editor
Circulation: 140,000
Published bimonthly
A national golf magazine with regional inserts (Ontario and Western Canada). Profiles prominent golfers and golfing personalities, and reviews courses, clubs, and equipment. Also carries articles on travel and international competitions, and instructional pieces. Pays 50¢/word on acceptance for 750 to 1,500 words – sometimes more for detailed stories. Guidelines available.

Ski Canada

117 Indian Road, Toronto, ON M6R 2V5
Phone: (416) 538-2293 Fax: (416) 538-2475
E-mail: mac@skicanadamag.com
Web site: www.skicanadamag.com
Contact: Iain MacMillan, editor
Circulation: 57,000
Published bimonthly
Published during the ski season, with a balanced mix of entertainment and information for both the experienced and the novice-intermediate skier and snowboarder. "Published from early autumn

through winter (with one summer issue), *SC* covers equipment, travel, instruction, competition, fashion, and general skiing- and alpine-related news and stories. Query letters are preferred – no phone calls. Replies will take time. Note: yearly editorial schedules are set at least six months before commencement of publishing season." Articles 400 to 2,500 words. Pays (within 30 days of publication) between $100 (news) and $500 to $800 (features), depending on length, research necessary, and writer's experience.

Western Skier

P.O. Box 430, 1132 – 98th Street, North Battleford, SK S9A 2Y5
Phone: (306) 445-7477 Fax: (306) 445-1977
Contact: Rod McDonald, publisher
Circulation: 28,000
Published 5 times a year (November to March)

A magazine targeting ski enthusiasts from Manitoba to B.C. Articles to inform and entertain family-oriented skiers and junior and recreational racers. Covers resorts, equipment, and fashions, with fiction and racing features. Circulated to provincial alpine associations and by subscription. Pays 20¢/word on publication for articles of 1,500 to 2,500 words. Guidelines available.

Travel & Tourism

Above & Beyond

P.O. Box 2348, Yellowknife, NT X1A 2P7
Phone: (403) 873-2299 Fax: (403) 873-2295
E-mail: apool@internorth.com
Contact: Annelies Pool, editor
Circulation: 30,000
Published quarterly

Glossy, full-colour inflight magazine for First Air, NWT Air, and Air Inuit carrying articles pertaining to Arctic areas (mainly Northwest Territories, Arctic Quebec, and Greenland), its people, communities, lifestyles, tourist attractions, and commercial activities. Prefers articles 1,000 to 1,500 words. Pays $300 per article, $15 per published photo, on publication. "Assignments are not given to new freelancers. Commitment to publish provided only upon receipt of article with colour photos/slides." Guidelines available.

Atmosphere
3300 Bloor Street W., Suite 3120, Centre Tower, Toronto,
    ON M8X 2X3
Phone: (416) 233-4348 Fax: (416) 233-9367
E-mail: melaine@inforamp.net
Contact: Susan Melnyk, publisher/editor
Circulation: 150,000
Published twice a year
   On-board magazine for Canada 3000 Airlines. Spring/summer issue appears May 1; fall/winter November 1. Pays $700 for features of 2,500 words. Photos ($50/image) should accompany articles. Welcomes story submissions and assigns features based on destinations served by airline. Guidelines available.

Beautiful British Columbia
929 Ellery Street, Victoria, BC V9A 7B4
Phone: (250) 384-5456 Fax: (250) 384-2812
E-mail: ed@bbcmag.bc.ca
Web site: www.beautifulbc.com
Contact: Bryan McGill, editor-in-chief
Circulation: 240,000
Published quarterly
   Established 1959. Publishes non-fiction stories about British Columbia, focusing on geography and travel. No poetry or fiction. Articles 1,500 to 2,500 words. Pays 50¢/word on acceptance. "Almost all the freelance material we publish is by established B.C. writers." Guidelines available.

Beautiful British Columbia Traveller
929 Ellery Street, Victoria, BC V9A 7B4
Phone: (250) 384-5456 Fax: (250) 384-2812
Web site: www.beautifulbc.com
Contact: Anita Willis, editor
Circulation: 120,000
Published quarterly

A supplement to *Beautiful British Columbia* magazine, the *Traveller* provides vicarious travel experiences to places around B.C. Does *not* "promote" travel/tourism. Preferred length 1,000 to 2,500 words. Pays 50¢/word on acceptance. Most stories are purchased as text and photo packages. "We're interested in non-fiction stories about B.C. destinations only, but 99 per cent of the freelance material we publish is written by established professional B.C. writers. Please, no poetry or fiction." Guidelines available.

Canadian
2700 – 777 Bay Street, Toronto, ON M5G 2C8
Phone: (416) 340-8000 Fax: (416) 977-0566
Contact: Marianne Tefft, editor
Published monthly

An inflight magazine for Canadian Airlines International and its affiliates. Features travel, business, and technology-related stories targeted to its key audience of frequent business travellers. Travel stories must relate to destinations serviced by the airline or its affiliates. Welcomes high-quality contributions from writers and photographers. No armchair tourism. Articles 200 to 1,200 words. All material assigned only on basis of detailed queries. Clippings required from new contributors. Not a market for novice writers. Pays a standard fee of $500 for 800 words. Mail or fax inquiries. No phone approaches, please. Guidelines available.

enRoute
7 Bates Road, Outremont, PQ H2V 1A6
Phone: (514) 270-0688 Fax: (514) 270-4050
E-mail: info@enroute.quebecor.com
Contact: Lise Ravary, editor-in-chief
Circulation: 125,000
Published monthly

Air Canada's inflight magazine. Publishes strong Canadian pieces on business and technical trends, travel, successful personalities, fashion, and fine dining, aimed at the business flier. Pay rates vary depending on project. Uses published writers only. No unsolicited manuscripts; inquire first with ideas and enclose tearsheets. Guidelines available.

Journeywoman Online Ezine

50 Prince Arthur Avenue, Suite 1703, Toronto, ON M5R 1B5
Phone: (416) 929-7654
E-mail: editor@journeywoman.com
Web site: www.journeywoman.com
Contact: Evelyn Hannon, editor/publisher
Circulation: 25,000

An on-line international resource co-operative ("We don't charge for the information at our site, and we don't pay for articles") publishing women-centred travel stories and tips, focusing on the specific needs and interests of women travellers. Stories average 500 to 850 words. "We welcome submissions (by e-mail only), especially from women who are starting out as writers and looking for an avenue to publish their travel stories."

LeisureWays

2 Carlton Street, Suite 801, Toronto, ON M5B 1J3
Phone: (416) 595-5007   Fax: (416) 924-6308
Contact: Deborah Milton, editor
Circulation: 685,000
Published bimonthly

A Southern Ontario travel and leisure magazine financed by the CAA and circulated among Ontario members. Carries articles on personalities, interesting places, recipes, culture, current events, and ingenious entrepreneurs. Also automotive-related pieces. Articles (1,000 to 1,500 words) should be accompanied by suitable colour slides. Pays 50¢/word on acceptance. Line-ups for following year made in late September. Guidelines available.

Outpost

490 Adelaide Street W., Toronto, ON M5V 1T2
Phone: (416) 703-5394   Fax: (416) 504-3628
E-mail: outpost@echo-on.net
Web site: www.outpostmagazine.com
Contact: Kisha Ferguson, editor
Circulation: 20,000
Published quarterly

Spotlights adventure travel and world culture. Pays a negotiated fee on publication. Features 2,500 to 4,000 words. "*Outpost*'s goal is to be on the cutting edge of travel. We need writers to help us achieve this by feeding us current information about events, places, and trends in articles both big and small." Guidelines available.

Westworld Alberta / Westworld British Columbia / Going Places Manitoba / Westworld Saskatchewan

4180 Lougheed Highway, 4th Floor, Burnaby, BC V5C 6A7
Phone: (604) 299-7311 Fax: (604) 299-9188
Contact: Pat Price, editor
Circulations: 330,000 (*WA*), 485,000 (*WBC*), 102,000 (*GPM*), 108,000 (*WS*)
Published bimonthly (*WA* and *GPM*), quarterly (*WBC* and *WS*)

Distributed to members of the respective regional automobile association, these travel magazines feature local and international travel and automotive-related articles. Pay 50¢/word on publication for articles of 1,000 to 1,200 words, extra for good photos. Rates can vary depending on complexity of subject. "Please query first in writing (no phone queries accepted). Include previous writing samples. Familiarize yourself with editorial content of the magazine before submitting." Guidelines available.

Where Calgary

1 Palliser Square, 125 – 9th Avenue S.E., Suite 250, Calgary, AB T2G 0P6
Phone: (403) 299-1888 Fax: (403) 299-1899
Contact: Jill Sawyer, editor
Circulation: 26,000
Published monthly

News of events and attractions for visitors. Covers dining, entertainment, shopping, fine art, and weekend excursions in and around Calgary for vacationers and business travellers. Cover stories highlight things to do and see. Pays 35¢/word on acceptance for nonfiction of 500 to 800 words, but rates vary with project.

Where Halifax

5475 Spring Garden Road, Box 14, Suite 500, Halifax, NS B3J 3T2
Phone: (902) 420-9943 Fax: (902) 429-9058
Contact: Karen Janik, editor
Circulation: 25,000

Published 10 times a year

What to do and where to go in the Halifax area. Shopping, sightseeing, events – anything of interest to visitors. Welcomes written inquiries with story ideas. Articles/pieces 500 to 800 words. Fees average $150 for 800 words, paid on publication.

Where Vancouver
2208 Spruce Street, Vancouver, BC V6H 2P3
Phone: (604) 736-5586 Fax: (604) 736-3468
E-mail: louisep@istar.ca
Contact: Louise Phillips, editor
Circulation: 48,000
Published monthly

A visitors' guide incorporating entertainment listings, its aim to provide an intelligent city guide for the upscale traveller. Monthly events sections are popular features. Articles 1,200 to 1,500 words. Pay rates vary depending on project, but 1,200 words earns about $250. At press time, this magazine was not using freelancers. Writers should first contact editor, since all projects are assigned.

Women's

B.C. Woman
2061 Cape Horn Avenue, Coquitlam, BC V3K 1J2
Phone: (604) 540-8448 Fax: (604) 524-0041
Contact: Nikki Groocock, editor
Circulation: 33,000
Published monthly

Designed to inspire and celebrate the achievements of B.C. women, and to inform, entertain, and provide a forum for discussion of issues of importance to B.C. women. Pays 30 days after publication for 800 to 1,500 words. "We negotiate a flat fee for each story, based on length, research required, complexity of topic, and writer's skill level. Send written queries with writing samples. All stories must be targeted to the B.C. market. Spec manuscripts are welcome, though it sometimes takes several months to respond." Guidelines available.

Canadian Living

25 Sheppard Avenue W., North York, ON M2N 6S7
Phone: (416) 733-7600   Fax: (416) 733-3398
E-mail: canadianliving@sympatico.ca
Web site: www.canadian-living.com
Contact: Bonnie Cowan, editor-in-chief
Circulation: 600,000
Published monthly

A vastly popular mass-market magazine emphasizing practical information to help Canadian families better cope with today's changing world. Also carries articles on food, beauty, fashion, decorating, crafts, contemporary living, health, and fitness. Prefers original manuscripts of 800 to 2,000 words. Pays on acceptance. Fee depends on article and writer's experience. Guidelines available.

Chatelaine

777 Bay Street, 8th Floor, Toronto, ON M5W 1A7
Phone: (416) 596-5425   Fax: (416) 596-5516
E-mail: editors@chatelaine.com
Web site: www.chatelaine.com
Contact: Rona Maynard, editor
Circulation: 800,000
Published monthly

High-quality glossy magazine addressing the needs, interests, and preferences of Canadian women. Covers current issues, personalities, lifestyles, health, relationships, travel, and politics. Features of 1,000 to 2,500 words earn $1,250 and up; one-page columns start at $350. "For all serious articles, deep, accurate, and thorough research and rich details are required. Features on beauty, food, fashion, and home decorating are supplied by staff writers and editors only." Also accepts appropriate fiction submissions of up to 2,500 words. Buys first North American serial rights in English and French (to cover possible use in French-language edition). Fees are negotiated. Pays on acceptance. Query first with brief outline. Guidelines available.

Elm Street

655 Bay Street, Suite 1100, Toronto, ON M5G 2K4
Phone: (416) 595-9944   Fax: (416) 595-7217

E-mail: elmstreet@m-v-p.com
Contact: Stevie Cameron, editor-in-chief
Circulation: 730,000
Published 8 times a year

A glossy, upscale general interest magazine targeting urban, educated women. Rates vary with project. Pays a negotiated fee on acceptance. Send brief queries rather than unsolicited manuscripts. Guidelines available.

Focus on Women
1218 Langley Street, Suite 1, Victoria, BC v8w 1w2
Phone: (250) 388-7231 Fax: (250) 383-1140
E-mail: focus@octonet.com
Contact: Leslie Campbell, editor
Circulation: 30,000
Published monthly

A magazine serving women of the Greater Victoria area. Covers political, health, and social issues, local news and profiles, and relationships. Rates vary, depending on project, but average about 10¢/word on publication; $250 for features (2,000 to 2,500 words). "Articles should relate to Vancouver Island women and should include photos when possible. Photo fees negotiable. No queries, please – only articles on spec. Allow 4 to 6 weeks for response." Guidelines available.

Homemaker's Magazine
25 Sheppard Avenue W., Suite 100, North York, ON M2N 6s7
Phone: (416) 733-7600 Fax: (416) 733-8683
E-mail: homemakers@telemedia.ca
Contact: Sally Armstrong, editor-in-chief
Circulation: 1.3 million
Published 8 times a year

A national magazine of current affairs and service articles directed toward women aged 25 to 54. Feature articles, which average about 2,000 words, deal with issues of particular concern to women, their families, and communities. Also published in French as *Madame au Foyer*. Pays up to $1/word on acceptance for features, less for personal essays and pieces requiring less research. "We prefer queries in writing – 1 or 2 pages that outline the proposed article and the direction the writer intends to take it. Finished articles on spec are also welcome. We have a special need for dramatic first-person stories (Herstory)." Guidelines available.

Modern Woman

777 Bay Street, 8th Floor, Toronto, ON M5W 1A7
Phone: (416) 596-5061 Fax: (416) 593-3197
Contact: Judy Allen, editor
Circulation: 500,000
Published 10 times a year

A general interest glossy women's magazine. Pays $250 to $1,000 on acceptance for 650 to 1,200 words. Fees are usually negotiated. Guidelines available.

Today's Bride

37 Hanna Avenue, Suite 1, Toronto, ON M6K 1X1
Phone: (416) 537-2604 Fax: (416) 538-1794
Web site: www.todaysbride.ca
Contact: Tracy Hitchcock, assistant editor
Circulation: 150,000
Published twice a year

Complete how-to advice on planning and co-ordinating formal weddings. Pays $200 to $300 on acceptance for 500 to 1,000 words. "Articles may be anecdotal but must have informational value for brides-to-be. All travel and standard planning pieces are written in-house."

Woman newsmagazine

422 Parliament Street, P.O. Box 82510, Toronto, ON M5A 3A0
Phone: (416) 920-6849 Fax: (416) 920-8548
E-mail: woman@web.net
Web site: www.web.net/~woman
Contact: Elizabeth Scott, publisher/editor
Circulation: 10,000
Published quarterly

A national magazine directed toward urban women, mid-twenties to mid-fifties. Seeks to create a sense of women's inter-dependence within the larger community through exploration of common issues from a woman's perspective. Presents news items and feature stories on finance and business, health and wellness, women and technology, arts and creativity, parenting and education, plus humour pieces and inspiring profiles. Pays an honorarium on publication for 350 to 3,000 words (hopes to be able to pay more by mid-1998). "Query first in writing with SASE. Articles that provide insight, information, and inspiration, and are solution-oriented, are particularly appropriate." Guidelines available.

Youth & Children's

Chickadee

179 John Street, Suite 500, Toronto, ON M5T 3G5
Phone: (416) 340-2700 Fax: (416) 340-9769
E-mail: wiredowl@owl.on.ca
Web site: www.owlkids.com
Contact: Kat Motosune, editor
Circulation: 73,000
Published 9 times a year

A magazine focusing on science and nature that offers 6- to 9-year-olds a bright, lively look at the world. Designed to entertain and educate, each issue contains photographs, illustrations, fiction, poetry, an animal story, puzzles, a science experiment, and a pullout poster. Pays $250 on acceptance for stories of between 800 and 900 words. "Avoid anthropomorphic and religious material. Keep in mind the age range of readers, but do not talk down to them." Guidelines available.

Chirp

179 John Street, Suite 500, Toronto, ON M5T 3G5
Phone: (416) 340-2700 Fax: (416) 340-9769
E-mail: wiredowl@owl.on.ca
Web site: www.owlkids.com
Contact: Mary Beth Leatherdale, editor
Published 9 times a year

The "see and do" magazine for children aged 2 to 6. Publishes puzzles, games, rhymes, stories, and songs to entertain and teach preschoolers about animals, nature, letters, numbers, and more. Prefers complete manuscripts of 300 to 400 words (fees range between $100 and $250). Short poems (25 to 40 words) are paid $10 to $50. Query first.

Kidsworld Magazine

345 Danforth Avenue, Toronto, ON M4K 1N7
Phone: (416) 466-4956 Fax: (416) 466-5002
E-mail: lydia@kidsworld-online.com
Web site: www.kidsworld-online.com
Contact: Lydia Stone, editor
Circulation: 200,000
Published bimonthly

   A general interest magazine for children in grades 4, 5, and 6, distributed nationally through schools. Editorial concerns include Canadian curricula, popular culture, and media literacy. Articles 350 to 700 words preferred. Rates vary, paid on publication. "Most of our editorial is written in-house or assigned to teachers. We have limited resources and are unable to respond to submissions or return manuscripts."

OWL

179 John Street, Suite 500, Toronto, ON M5T 3G5
Phone: (416) 971-5275 Fax: (416) 971-5294
E-mail: wiredowl@owl.on.ca
Web site: www.owlkids.com
Contact: Maria Birmingham, assistant editor
Circulation: 75,000
Published 9 times a year

   A discovery magazine for 8- to 12-year-olds. Sparks children's curiosity about the world around them. Topics include science, technology, animals, and the environment. Pays around $200 and up on publication for 500 to 800 words. Prefers submission inquiries. Strongly recommends writers check back issues (available in libraries) for a sense of *OWL*'s approach.

Treehouse Canadian Family

655 Bay Street, Suite 1100, Toronto, ON M5G 2K4
Phone: (416) 595-9944 Fax: (416) 595-7217

E-mail: owlfamily@m-v-p.com
Contact: Kristin Jenkins, editor
Circulation: 100,000
Published bimonthly

A parenting magazine supplement sent to the parents of children who subscribe to *OWL*, *Chickadee*, and *Chirp* magazines (3- to 12-year-olds). Presents quick, practical information and ideas. Stories run from 500 to 1,500 words, including anecdotal, first-person, and short opinion pieces. Fees, paid on acceptance, range from $200 up to $1,000 for fully researched, usually issue-oriented feature articles. Send ideas by fax, e-mail, or mail (no phone submissions, please). First-time writers will need to supply clippings after first approach. Guidelines available.

Watch Magazine
401 Richmond Street W., Suite 245, Toronto, ON M5V 1X3
Phone: (416) 595-1313 Fax: (416) 595-1312
E-mail: watchmag@compuserve.com
Contact: Gary Butler, editor
Circulation: 125,000
Published monthly

Youth culture unleashed – *Watch* covers only what's cool and important to teens, from music to movies to fashion to life, and delivers it to them free in their high schools. Directed at, and written by, 14- to 20-year-olds, the magazine uses some adult freelancers as editors and writing tutors for its young writers. Prefers writers with a strong sense of humour. Pays 10¢/word on publication for 300 to 1,000 words.

What! A Magazine
108 – 93 Lombard Avenue, Winnipeg, MB R3B 3B1
Phone: (204) 985-8160 Fax: (204) 943-8991
E-mail: what@fox.nstn.ca
Contact: Stuart Slayen, editor
Circulation: 200,000
Published 5 times a year

A national magazine for high school students distributed through schools, covering a mix of news, social issues, entertainment, sports, and more. Designed to be empowering, interactive, and entertaining. Articles 700 to 2,000 words. Rates depend on length and complexity of story. Fees are paid on acceptance. "Query first. No fiction or poetry from professional writers considered. Avoid clichéd teen stuff; be unique and be respectful of this market's intelligence and spirit." Guidelines available.

2

LITERARY AND SCHOLARLY

It's ironic that literary and scholarly journals, among the most prestigious outlets for a writer's work, can usually afford to pay their contributors the least. Many journals rely on funding from arts councils, or academic or professional sources, and still run at a loss. They have relatively small subscription lists and perhaps two or three unpaid or part-time staff, and they attract little or no advertising support. The upshot is that they can rarely afford to pay their contributors much. In many cases, modest funding and low revenues preclude payment altogether, or limit it to small honoraria or free copies. Contributors to scholarly journals are frequently graduate students, salaried academics, or professionals, who draw on current areas of research. For graduate students, journal publication is often an essential element of their professional development: the successful applicant for a university teaching position, for instance, will usually have a substantial publishing history.

Writers would be unwise to look to this sector of publishing as a significant source of income. Qualified writers would be just as unwise to neglect it because of this. Publishing your work in a distinguished literary or scholarly journal can add immeasurably to your reputation, and may well open up other publishing opportunities. This chapter lists many of Canada's most notable journals and literary magazines. Use the information presented in each entry to help you choose the most appropriate publications to approach.

Before you make your submission, familiarize yourself thoroughly with the journal to which you hope to contribute. Editors take a dim view of submissions from writers who are demonstrably unfamiliar with their journal. Study several recent numbers, or better still, subscribe. Learn what you can of the editors' approaches and points of view and the kind of work they favour. Determine who their readers are. Again, if they have a web site, be sure to visit it. Always request writer's guidelines, and follow these closely to ensure you meet the editors' needs. (Remember to include an SASE whenever you expect a response.) Refereed journals will require several copies of your submission. Scholarly articles will need to be accompanied by full documentation. Fiction, poetry, reviews, and criticism must be carefully targeted and professionally presented. The extra care and attention will pay dividends.

Acadiensis: Journal of the History of the Atlantic Region

University of New Brunswick, P.O. Box 4400, Fredericton,
   NB E3B 5A3
Phone: (506) 453-4978 Fax: (506) 453-4599
E-mail: acadnsis@unb.ca
Contact: Gail Campbell, editor
Circulation: 850
Published twice a year

Includes original academic research, review articles, documents, notes, and a running bibliography compiled by librarians in the four Atlantic provinces. "Canada's most ambitious scholarly journal" – Michael Bliss, *Journal of Canadian Studies*. Articles published in English and in French. Cannot pay but welcomes submission inquiries. Guidelines available.

The Amethyst Review

23 Riverside Avenue, Truro, NS B2N 4G2
Phone: (902) 895-1345
E-mail: amethyst@col.auracom.com
Web site: www.col.auracom.com/~amethyst
Contact: Penny Ferguson, co-editor
Circulation: 190
Published twice a year

A literary journal of poetry and prose. Stories up to 5,000 words, poems to 200 lines. Pays in copies. "Don't try to shock us. Impress us with the quality of your work." Guidelines available.

The Antigonish Review

St. Francis Xavier University, P.O. Box 5000, Antigonish,
    NS B2G 2W5
Phone: (902) 867-3962 Fax: (902) 867-2448
E-mail: tar@stfx.ca
Contact: George Sanderson, editor
Circulation: 800
Published quarterly

A creative literary review featuring poetry, fiction, and critical articles from Canada and abroad. Preferred length 1,500 to 4,000 words. Pays up to $150 for articles, $50 for reviews, $25 for fiction, on publication; 2 copies for poetry. Rights remain with author. Guidelines available.

Arachnē: An Interdisciplinary Journal of Language and Literature

Laurentian University, Ramsey Lake Road, Sudbury, ON P3E 2C6
Phone: (705) 675-1151, ext. 4338 Fax: (705) 675-4870
E-mail: tgerry@nickel.laurentian.ca
Web site: www.laurentian.ca/engl/arachnē/Index.html
Contact: Dr. Tom Gerry, chief editor
Published twice a year

Established 1994. A scholarly journal that seeks to gauge the status quo of disciplines such as literature, film, philosophy, religion, art history, law, classics, history, and rhetoric, and to play an active role in bringing these disciplines into dialogue. Articles 5,000 to 7,500 words. Cannot pay but welcomes submission inquiries. No fiction. "Freelancers will always receive more than a form letter from *Arachnē*." Guidelines available.

ARC

P.O. Box 7368, Ottawa, ON K1L 8E4
Contact: Rita Donovan or John Barton, co-editors
Circulation: 750
Published twice a year

Publishes poetry from Canada and abroad, as well as reviews, interviews, and articles about aspects of Canadian poetry and Canada's poetry community. No fiction or drama. Poetry submissions must be typed and include up to 6 unpublished poems. Reviews, interviews, and other articles must be queried first. Pays $25/published page on publication. Guidelines available.

BC Studies: The British Columbian Quarterly

University of British Columbia, 161 – 1855 West Mall, Vancouver, BC V6T 1Z2
Phone: (604) 822-3727 Fax: (604) 822-9452
E-mail: bcstudie@unixg.ubc.ca
Web site: www.interchange.ubc.ca/bcstudie
Contact: Carlyn Craig, managing editor
Circulation: 650

Established in 1968. A small interdisciplinary academic journal that seeks to interpret B.C., past and present, for a wide readership. Aims to present good scholarship on important topics in an accessible form. Articles 7,000 to 8,000 words. Cannot pay for submissions, but welcomes inquiries. "A large part of our mandate is to publish the work of scholars who are writing as part of their academic careers, thus we retain all rights to the work." Guidelines available.

B&A New Fiction

P.O. Box 702, Station P, Toronto, ON M5S 2Y4
Phone: (416) 535-1233 Fax: (416) 535-1233
E-mail: fiction@interlog.com
Web site: www.interlog.com/~fiction
Contact: Michelle Alfano, fiction editor
Circulation: 2,000
Published quarterly

Formerly *Blood & Aphorisms*, established in 1990. A literary journal carrying new, emerging, and established writers along with reviews and interviews with emerging writers, from 200 to 7,500 words. A great market for innovative newcomers. Pays on publication $25 for reviews, etc., up to 400 words; $35/printed page for fiction. Guidelines available. "Support literary magazines by subscribing to them. If you don't, they disappear."

Border/Lines

400 Dovercourt Drive, Toronto, ON M6J 3E7
Phone: (416) 534-3224 Fax: (416) 534-2301
Contact: Julie Jenkinson, managing editor
Circulation: 2,000
Published quarterly

An interdisciplinary magazine exploring all aspects of culture. Features articles, reviews, and visual pieces on the theory and practice of popular culture, including film, art, music, the landscape, mass communications, and political culture. Articles are between 1,500 and 3,500 words. Pays $150 to $300 on publication for features. Guidelines available.

Canadian Children's Literature

Department of English, University of Guelph, Guelph,
ON N1G 2W1
Phone: (519) 824-4120, ext. 3189 Fax: (519) 837-1315
E-mail: ccl@uoguelph.ca
Web site: www.uoguelph.ca/englit/ccl
Contact: Gay Christofides, administrator
Circulation: 800
Published quarterly

Presents in-depth criticism and reviews of Canadian literature for children and young adults. Directed toward teachers, librarians, academics, and parents. Scholarly articles (2,000 to 8,000 words), interviews, profiles, and reviews are supplemented by illustrations and photographs. Now also covers film and electronic media. Cannot pay but welcomes submissions. Guidelines available.

Canadian Ethnic Studies

Research Unit for Canadian Ethnic Studies, University of
Calgary, 2500 University Drive N.W., Calgary, AB T2N 1N4
Phone: (403) 220-7257 Fax: (403) 284-5467
E-mail: jcleaver@acs.ucalgary.ca
Contact: Jo-Ann Cleaver, editorial assistant
Circulation: 800
Published 3 times a year

An interdisciplinary journal devoted to the study of ethnicity, immigration, inter-group relations, and the history and cultural life of ethnic groups in Canada. Also carries book reviews, opinions, memoirs, creative writing, and poetry, and has an ethnic voice section. All material should address Canadian ethnicity. "We accept short poetry, book review queries, and ethnic memoirs. Querying first is always helpful; we return unused manuscripts." Contributors are not paid. Guidelines available.

Canadian Fiction Magazine
P.O. Box 1061, 240 King Street E., Kingston, ON K7L 4Y5
Phone: (613) 548-8429 Fax: (613) 548-1556
Contact: managing editor, Quarry Press
Circulation: 1,200
Published quarterly
    Published in partnership with Quarry Press, through whom all inquiries should be made. Dedicated for 25 years to new Canadian fiction, including translations from Québécois and other languages spoken in Canada. Publishes short stories and novel excerpts, and is especially interested in innovative and experimental fiction. Cannot usually pay.

Canadian Historical Review
UTP Journals, 5201 Dufferin Street, North York, ON M3H 5T8
Phone: (416) 667-7994 Fax: (416) 667-7881
E-mail: chr@utpress.utoronto.ca
Web site: www.utpress.utoronto.ca/journal/depthome.htm
Contacts: Margaret Conrad and Keth Walden, co-editors
Circulation: 1,800
Published quarterly
    Publishes original research articles in all areas of Canadian history as well as research notes and book reviews. For historians, scholars, students of history, and general readers. Preferred length 40 to 45 pages. Cannot pay but welcomes submission inquiries.

Canadian Journal of Adlerian Psychology
Port Alberni Assessment and Referral Service, 201 – 4988 Argyle
    Street, Port Alberni, BC V9Y 1V7
Phone: (250) 724-2443 Fax: (250) 723-2387
E-mail: slavik@cedar.alberni.net
Contact: Steven Slavik, editor

Circulation: 500
Published twice a year
Interested in academic and popular treatments of theory and practice in Adlerian psychology. Also publishes humorous/satirical articles on psychology/therapy. Whether academic or popular, articles (2,000 to 5,000 words) must demonstrate accurate knowledge of subject. No e-mail submissions. Articles should be in APA format, submitted on disk (WordPerfect 5.1). No payment. Guidelines available.

Canadian Journal of Contemporary Literary Stuff
P.O. Box 53106, Ottawa, ON KIN IC5
Phone: (613) 592-9714 or (416) 463-0703
E-mail: grunge@achilles.net or fairchild@sympatico.ca
Contacts: Grant Wilkins or Tamara Fairchild, co-editors
Circulation: 1,000
Published quarterly
An irreverent new literary quarterly featuring prose and poetry from across the Canadian literary spectrum. Also includes reviews, interviews, cartoons, and articles about Canadian literature and the literary life. Length to 2,500 words. Welcomes submission inquiries – send a proposal and writing sample. Particularly looking for writers to take on regular columns. "While we hope eventually to be able to pay contributors, at present we can only promise them 3 courtesy copies." Guidelines available.

Canadian Literature
University of British Columbia, 1855 West Mall, Suite 167,
    Vancouver, BC V6T 1Z2
Phone: (604) 822-2780 Fax: (604) 822-5504
E-mail: orders@cdn-lit.ubc.ca
Contact: E.M. Kröller, editor
Circulation: 1,400
Published quarterly
Devoted to studying many aspects of Canadian literature and offering a literary critique of Canadian writers. For students and academics at all levels as well as general readers. Contributors are not paid. Articles 3,000 to 6,000 words. Guidelines available.

Canadian Modern Language Review

UTP Journals, 5201 Dufferin Street, North York, ON M3H 5T8
Phone: (416) 667-7994 Fax: (416) 667-7881
E-mail: cmlr@utpress.utoronto.ca
Web site: www.utpress.utoronto.ca/journal/depthome.htm
Contacts: Jill Sinclair Bell and Sharon Lapkin, co-editors
Circulation: 2,100
Published quarterly

Publishes literary, linguistic, and pedagogical articles, book reviews, current advertisements, and other material of interest to teachers of French, German, Italian, Russian, Spanish, and English as a second language, at all levels of instruction. Balance of theory and practice. All articles are voluntarily submitted rather than assigned, and are refereed. Length to 6,500 words. Contributors are not paid, but submissions are welcome. Consult "Guide to Authors" in each issue and write to editors for further information.

Canadian Poetry: Studies, Documents, Reviews

University of Western Ontario, Department of English, London,
   ON N6A 3K7
Phone: (519) 661-2111, ext. 3403 Fax: (519) 661-3776
Contact: D.M.R. Bentley, editor
Circulation: 400
Published twice a year

A scholarly and critical refereed journal devoted to the study of poetry from all periods and regions of Canada. Also prints articles, reviews, and documents – 500 to 5,000 words – directed toward university and college students and teachers. No original poetry. Cannot pay but welcomes submissions. Follow *MLA Handbook* for style.

Canadian Public Administration

1075 Bay Street, Suite 401, Toronto, ON M5S 2B1
Phone: (416) 924-8787 Fax: (416) 924-4992
E-mail: ntl@ipaciapc.ca
Web site: www.ipaciapc.ca
Contact: Paul Thomas, editor
Circulation: 3,000

Published quarterly
A refereed journal, written by public administrators and academics, that examines structures, processes, and outcomes of public policy and public management related to executive, legislative, judicial, and quasi-judicial functions in municipal, provincial, and federal spheres of government. Articles from 10 to 30 pages. Contributors are unpaid. Guidelines available.

Canadian Public Policy
c/o C.M. Beach, Room 409, School of Policy Studies, Queen's
    University, Kingston, ON K7L 3N6
Phone: (613) 545-6644 Fax: (613) 545-6960
E-mail: cpp@qsilver.queensu.ca
Web site: www.qsilver.queensu.ca/~cpp
Contact: Charles Beach, editor
Circulation: 1,200
Published quarterly
A bilingual, refereed journal directed toward academic and policy analysts, providing a forum for information about economic and social policy developments affecting all Canadians. Reviews books, articles, and government reports. Accepts submissions up to 5,000 words. Submission inquiries welcome, but no payment is made.

Canadian Woman Studies
212 Founders College, York University, 4700 Keele Street, North
    York, ON M3J 1P3
Phone: (416) 736-5356 Fax: (416) 736-5765
E-mail: cwscf@yorku.ca
Contact: Luciana Ricciutelli, managing editor
Circulation: 5,000
Published quarterly
A bilingual journal featuring current scholarly writing and research on a wide variety of feminist topics. Welcomes creative writing, poetry, experimental articles, and essays of 500 to 2,000 words, as well as book, art, and film reviews. Contributors are unpaid but receive a complimentary copy of the issue containing their work. Guidelines available.

The Capilano Review
2055 Purcell Way, North Vancouver, BC V7J 3H5
Phone: (604) 984-1712 Fax: (604) 983-7520
E-mail: mminiovi@capcollege.bc.ca
Web site: www.capcollege.bc.ca/dept/tcr/tcr.htm
Contact: Robert Sherrin, editor
Circulation: 1,000
Published 3 times a year

Established 1972. Features poetry, prose, and fine art by some of Canada's most innovative writers and artists before they become famous. Pays $50/page, to a maximum of $200, on publication. Carries stories up to 6,000 words. Guidelines available, but read the magazine before submitting.

The Challenger
441 Shepherd Avenue, Quesnel, BC V2J 4X1
Phone: (250) 991-5567
Contact: Dan Lukiv, editor
Circulation: 150
Published 3 times a year

This low-budget, high school-based literary journal publishes poetry and fiction by 13-year-olds through to seasoned Canadian authors. Encourages young writers, especially teenagers, to submit poetry. Experimental work welcome if it makes sense. Stories 1,000 to 3,000 words. No profanity or pornography. Include author details. Contributors paid in copies. Don't submit work in June, July, or August.

The Claremont Review
4980 Wesley Road, Victoria, BC V8Y 1Y9
Phone: (604) 658-5221 Fax: (604) 658-5387
E-mail: review@claremont.victoria.bc.ca
Web site: www.claremont.victoria.bc.ca
Contact: Terence Young, co-editor
Circulation: 500
Published twice a year

Dedicated to publishing the fiction, poetry, and short drama of emerging young writers aged 13 to 19. Introduces some of the best student writing in Canada. Includes an interview with a writer every second issue. Preferred length of stories 1,500 to 3,500 words. Honoraria only when grants are available. "Our editorial board responds to all submissions with a critical evaluation. Guidelines available on request, but the best way to find out what we publish is to pick up a copy."

Contemporary Verse 2

P.O. Box 3062, Winnipeg, MB R3C 4E5
Phone: (204) 949-1365
Contact: Janine Tschuncky, managing editor
Circulation: 650
Published quarterly

A feminist literary journal that publishes mainly poetry, prose, reviews, and artwork by emerging and established writers, both women and men. Prose 800 to 1,000 words. Pays $20 for poems, $40 for reviews, on publication. "Please send a short bio and an SASE with your submission. Do not submit more than 6 poems at a time." Guidelines available.

The Dalhousie Review

1456 Henry Street, Dalhousie University, Halifax, NS B3H 3J5
Phone: (902) 494-2541 Fax: (902) 494-3561
E-mail: Dalhousie.Review@is.dal.ca
Contact: Ron Huebert, editor
Circulation: 700
Published 3 times a year

Welcomes submissions of poetry, short fiction, and articles up to 5,000 words in such fields as history, literature, political science, sociology, and philosophy. Prefers poetry of fewer than 40 lines. Contributors to this distinguished quarterly, first published in 1921, are not usually paid. "Wherever possible we commission external referees to assess submissions. Please enclose SASE if you require the return of your manuscript." Guidelines available.

Descant

P.O. Box 314, Station P, Toronto, ON M5S 2S8
Phone: (416) 593-2557 Fax: (416) 293-2557
Contact: Mary Myers, managing editor
Circulation: 1,200

Published quarterly

Established 1970. A literary journal publishing poetry, prose, fiction, interviews, travel pieces, letters, photographs, engravings, art, and literary criticism. Pays an honorarium of $100 on publication to all contributors. "Our purpose is the critical reading of manuscripts of new and established writers. We ask for one-time publishing rights, and only use unpublished work. Turnaround time for manuscripts can be up to 4 months. Each manuscript is read three times before acceptance." Guidelines available.

Environments: A Journal of Interdisciplinary Studies

University of Waterloo, Heritage Resources Centre, Waterloo,
    ON N2L 3GI
Phone: (519) 888-4567, ext. 2072   Fax: (519) 746-2031
E-mail: hrc@fes.uwaterloo.ca
Web site: www.fes.uwaterloo.ca/research/HRC/environments.html
Contact: Ken Van Osch, managing editor
Circulation: 500
Published 3 times a year

A refereed journal for scholars and practitioners. Promotes greater understanding of environmental, economic, and social change through articles (2,000 to 5,000 words) that assess the implications of change and provide information for improved decision-making. Oriented to academics, students, professionals, and concerned citizens. For more information, check inside front cover. Cannot pay but welcomes submission inquiries. Guidelines available.

Essays on Canadian Writing

2120 Queen Street E., Suite 200, Toronto, ON M4E 1E2
Phone: (416) 694-3348   Fax: (416) 698-9906
E-mail: ecw@sympatico.ca
Web site: www.ecw.ca/Press
Contacts: Jack David and Robert Lecker, editors
Circulation: 1,000
Published 3 times a year

Devoted to criticism of Canadian writers and their works. Concentrates on essays featuring contemporary authors and current critical approaches. Publishes bibliographies, interviews, and full-length book reviews of fiction, poetry, and criticism. Pays $75 to $100 on publication for 4,000 to 11,000 words.

Event: The Douglas College Review

Douglas College, P.O. Box 2503, New Westminster, BC V3L 5B2
Phone: (604) 527-5293 Fax: (604) 527-5095
E-mail: Event_Mag@Douglas.BC.CA
Web site: www.douglas.bc.ca/Event/homepage.html
Contact: Bonnie Bauder, assistant editor
Circulation: 1,000
Published 3 times a year

Presents new and established Canadian and international writers through their fiction and poetry, and reviews of their work, as well as creative non-fiction and notes on writing. (Features an annual $500 Creative Non-Fiction Contest each spring – see page 296.) Stories and non-fiction up to 5,000 words or up to 8 poems per submission. Pays $22/page on publication. Guidelines available.

Exile

P.O. Box 67, Station B, Toronto, ON M5T 2CO
Phone: (416) 969-8877 Fax: (416) 966-9556
Contact: Barry Callaghan, publisher
Circulation: 1,200
Published quarterly

Devoted to fine fiction, poetry, and drama on the edge from Canada and abroad. Pays on publication. Mail typed inquiries. Study journal first.

The Fiddlehead

Campus House, University of New Brunswick, P.O. Box 4400,
    Fredericton, NB E3B 5A3
Phone: (506) 453-3501 Fax: (506) 453-4599
Contact: Ross Leckie, editor
Circulation: 900
Published quarterly

A highly respected literary journal, established in 1945, publishing poetry, short fiction, book reviews, and sometimes art. Focus on freshness and vitality. While retaining an interest in writers of

Atlantic Canada, it is open to outstanding work from all over the English-speaking world. Stories up to 4,000 words, poetry up to 10 poems. Pays $10/page on publication. "Do not fax or e-mail submissions, and include SASE for replies."

filling Station
P.O. Box 22135, Bankers Hall, Calgary, AB T2P 4J5
Phone: (403) 252-8185 Fax: (403) 253-2980
Web site: www.cadvision.com/tmvir/fsintro.htm
Contact: Rajinderpal S. Pal, managing editor
Circulation: 400
Published 3 times a year
  Publishes poetry, fiction, reviews, interviews, creative literary non-fiction, and artwork. Preferred length for prose 1,000 to 2,500 words. Pays a one-year subscription for accepted submissions. Guidelines available.

Grain
P.O. Box 1154, Regina, SK S4P 3B4
Phone: (306) 244-2828 Fax: (306) 244-0255
E-mail: grain.mag@sk.sympatico.ca
Web site: www.skwriter.com
Contact: J. Jill Robinson, editor
Circulation: 1,500
Published quarterly
  A literary journal of national and international scope published by the Saskatchewan Writers Guild. Prints previously unpublished, high-quality literary work, both traditional and experimental, with the aim of presenting new and challenging writing by established and emerging writers. Fiction, creative non-fiction, poetry, and sometimes drama considered. Pays $30 to $100 on publication. Use e-mail for queries only. Read back issues before submitting. Guidelines available.

Ink Magazine
P.O. Box 52558, 264 Bloor Street W., Toronto, ON M5S 1V0
Contact: John Degen, editor/publisher
Circulation: 500
Published quarterly

"*Ink* surveys the mess of creativity in Canada. Anything that can be reproduced in ink, we reproduce in *ink*. Lynn Crosbie, Al Purdy, Steven Heighton and more, all have *ink* on their fingers." Length up to 3,000 words. Welcomes submission inquiries. *Ink* assumes First Canadian Serial Rights, after which rights revert to writer. Payment is a one-year subscription to *ink*. Guidelines available.

Labour/Le travail
Memorial University, Department of History, St. John's,
   NF AIC 5S7
Phone: (709) 737-2144 Fax: (709) 737-4342
E-mail: cclh@plato.ucs.mun.ca
Web site: www.mun.ca/cclh
Contact: Bryan D. Palmer, editor
Circulation: 1,000
Published twice a year
   A bilingual, interdisciplinary historical journal concerned with work, workers, and the labour movement. Includes articles of 5,000 to 10,000 words, book notes, archival notes, and an annual bibliography of Canadian labour studies. Cannot pay but welcomes submission inquiries. Guidelines available.

The Literary Review of Canada
1400 CTTC, Carleton University, 1125 Colonel By Drive, Ottawa,
   ON KIS 5B6
Fax: (613) 520-7554 Fax: (613) 520-2893
E-mail: lit.rev@ccs.carleton.ca
Contact: John Flood, editor
Circulation: 2,000
Published 11 times a year
   A scholarly tabloid, in the style of *The New York Review of Books*, carrying substantive book reviews of Canadian non-fiction. Intriguing, incisively written, and informative, it attracts a highly educated readership. Reviews are 3,000 to 5,000 words. Warmly welcomes faxed or mailed proposals and outlines, but study review first.

The Malahat Review
University of Victoria, P.O. Box 1700, Victoria, BC V8W 2Y2
Phone: (250) 721-8524

E-mail: malahat@uvic.ca
Contact: Derk Wynand, editor
Circulation: 1,200
Published quarterly

A distinguished, award-winning literary journal publishing Canada's best poets and short-story writers. Pays $25 per estimated published page on acceptance. Use e-mail address for queries only. For poetry, submit 6 to 10 pages of poems; for fiction, send one complete story. Write for guidelines.

Matrix

1400 de Maisonneuve Street W., Suite 514-8, Montreal, PQ H3G
   1M8
Phone: (514) 848-2357 Fax: (514) 848-4501
Contact: Robert Allen, editor
Circulation: 1,800
Published 3 times a year

A literary/cultural magazine rooted in Quebec but open to writers from across Canada, the United States, and abroad. Seeks out the best contemporary fiction, non-fiction, articles, and artwork. Described by Bill Katz, in *Library Journal*, as "a northern combination of *The New Yorker* and *Atlantic Monthly*." Publishes original prose and poetry by new and established writers. Length 1,500 to 5,000 words. Articles/fiction receive $100 to $200; poetry $15 to $100. Pays on publication. Guidelines available.

Mosaic: A Journal for the Interdisciplinary Study
   of Literature

208 Tier Building, University of Manitoba, Winnipeg, MB R3T 2N2
Phone: (204) 474-9763 Fax: (204) 474-7584
E-mail: ejhinz@bldgarts.lanl.umanitoba.ca
Web site: www.umanitoba.ca/publications/mosaic
Contact: Dr. Evelyn J. Hinz, editor
Circulation: 900
Published quarterly

For scholars, educators, students, and the sophisticated general reader. Combining reader-friendly prose and current research, essays (5,000 to 6,000 words) use insights from a wide variety of disciplines to highlight the practical and cultural relevance of literary works. Contributors are unpaid. Submission inquiries welcome. "We strongly encourage potential contributors to subscribe to *Mosaic* in order to become familiar with our format, editorial mandate, and interdisciplinary requirements." Guidelines available.

The Muse Journal

226 Lisgar Street, Toronto, ON M6J 3G7
Phone: (416) 539-9517 Fax: (416) 539-0047
E-mail: mannyg@paradigm-x.com
Web site: www.paradigm-x.com/muse.htm
Contact: Emanuel Goncalves, editor

An on-line journal for writers, poets, and visual artists open to all topics, themes, and genres but emphasizing the metaphysical, philosophical, and humorous. Preferred length 1,000 to 2,000 words. Generally only pays for solicited works. The web site is divided into two sections: one provides an unmoderated site where poets, writers, and artists can post their work and communicate with each other freely; the other carries the on-line magazine, where selected submissions are collected in a more structured format. Both sections are accessible to all. "*The Muse Journal* serves, supports, and publishes poets, writers, and artists of exceptional talent, whether known or unknown." Guidelines available on web site.

The New Quarterly

University of Waterloo, English Language Proficiency Program,
PAS 2082, Waterloo, ON N2J 2N5
Phone: (519) 885-1211, ext. 2837
E-mail: mmerikle@watarts.uwaterloo.ca
Web site: www.watarts.uwaterloo.ca/~mmerikle/newquart.html
Contact: Mary Merikle, managing editor
Circulation: 500

Publishes poetry, novel excerpts, short fiction, interviews, and essays on the writer's craft. Prose should be 20 to 30 pages in length; very short fiction, 5 pages. Pays $125 for a short story or novel excerpt, $25 for very short fiction, and $25 for a poem, on publication. Guidelines available.

Ontario History

34 Parkview Avenue, Willowdale, ON M2N 3Y2
Phone: (416) 226-9011 Fax: (416) 226-2740
Contact: Terry Crowley, editor
Circulation: 1,200
Published quarterly

A regional journal of current scholarly writing on various aspects
of the province's past, directed toward academics, professional and
amateur historians, libraries, and universities. Articles 6,000 to
7,000 words. Cannot pay but welcomes submission inquiries.
Guidelines available.

Other Voices

Garneau P.O. Box 52059, 8210 – 109th Street, Edmonton,
    AB T6G 2T5
Contact: editorial collective
Circulation: 600
Published twice a year

A small literary journal, published in the spring and fall, seeks
submissions of fiction, poetry, black and white prints, and artwork.
Submission deadlines March 15 and September 15. Payment by
one-year subscription and small honorarium for up to 3,500 words.
Guidelines available.

Pacific Affairs

164 – 1855 West Mall, University of British Columbia, Vancouver,
    BC V6T 1Z2
Phone: (604) 822-6504 Fax: (604) 822-9452
E-mail: jgarnett@unixg.ubc.ca
Contact: Jacqueline Garnett, managing editor
Circulation: 2,800
Published quarterly

A source of scholarly insight into the current social, cultural,
political, and economic issues of Asia and the Pacific region,
directed toward universities, institutions, governments, embassies,
consulates, and, increasingly, the business sector. Runs articles and
review articles contributed by authors from around the world. Also
reviews about 50 books each issue. Preferred length 6,000 to 6,250

words. Contributors are not paid. Submission inquiries welcome. See inside back cover for guidelines.

paperplates

19 Kenwood Avenue, Toronto, ON M6C 2R8
Phone: (416) 651-2551
E-mail: beekelly@perkolator.com
Web site: www.perkolator.com
Contact: Bernard Kelly, publisher/editor
Circulation: 500
Published quarterly
   Established 1991. Publishes poetry, fiction, plays, travel pieces, essays, interviews, memoirs. Length 2,500 to 15,000 words. Contributors receive two copies. Inquiries welcome. Guidelines available.

Poetry Canada

P.O. Box 1061, Kingston, ON K7L 4Y5
Phone: (613) 548-8429 Fax: (613) 548-1556
Contact: the editor
Circulation: 1,500
Published quarterly
   The nation's only magazine devoted entirely to publishing poetry, criticism of poetry, and poetry news. Carries about 30 poems each issue, some by Canada's leading poets, others by new writers. Aims to discover the best new work by established and emerging poets in Canada. Includes essays and in-depth interviews of 1,750 to 3,500 words. "Please read the magazine first to get a sense of what we publish."

Pottersfield Portfolio

P.O. Box 27094, Halifax, NS B3H 4M8
Phone: (902) 443-7178 Fax: (902) 443-9178
E-mail: saundc@auracom.com
Web site: www.auracom.com/~saundc/potters.htm
Contact: Ian Colford, editor
Circulation: 500
Published 3 times a year
   A literary magazine publishing fiction, poetry, and essays up to

5,000 words. Pays $5/printed page, up to a maximum of $25, for all contributions. Submissions, accepted from across the country, may be on any topic and in any style, but it's advisable to read the magazine before submitting (sample copies $6). Guidelines available.

Prairie Fire

100 Arthur Street, Suite 423, Winnipeg, MB R3B 1H3
Phone: (204) 943-9066 Fax: (204) 942-1555
Contact: Andris Taskans, managing editor
Circulation: 1,500
Published quarterly

Publishes poetry, fiction, essays, interviews, reviews, commentary, satire, and literary and other arts criticism. Submissions may be from 200 to 5,000 words. Pays on publication: for fiction, $40/first page, $35 for each succeeding page (max. $200); for poems, $30/$25 (max. $150); for articles/essays, $35/$30 (max. $175); for reviews, $25/$20 (max. $125); for interviews, $20/$15 (max. $100). Guidelines and full payment schedule available.

Prairie Forum

Canadian Plains Research Center, University of Regina, Regina,
  SK S4S 0A2
Phone: (306) 585-4758 Fax: (306) 585-4699
E-mail: canadian.plains@uregina.ca
Web site: www.cprc.uregina.ca/journals.html
Contact: Patrick Douaud, editor-in-chief
Circulation: 300
Published twice a year

An interdisciplinary scholarly journal that publishes research articles dealing with the prairie region of Canada. Articles 3,000 to 7,500 words. Welcomes inquiries. No fees are paid. Guidelines available.

Prairie Journal

P.O. Box 61203, Brentwood P.O., Calgary, AB T2L 2K6
Contact: A. Burke, editor
Circulation: 500
Published twice a year

A literary journal, founded in 1983, featuring new and established writers of short fiction, poetry, drama, reviews, criticism, interviews, and bibliography. Pays an honorarium of $10 to $100 on publication, depending on length and genre. Guidelines available.

PRISM international

Department of Creative Writing, University of British Columbia,
    1866 Main Mall – Buch E462, Vancouver, BC V6T 1Z1
Phone: (604) 822-2514 Fax: (604) 822-3616
E-mail: prism@unixg.ubc.ca
Web site: www.arts.ubc.ca/prism/
Contacts: Sioux Browning and Melanie Little, co-editors
Circulation: 1,000
Published quarterly

Features innovative new fiction, poetry, drama, literary nonfiction, and translation from Canada and around the world. The oldest literary journal in the West. Welcomes submissions of 500 to 5,000 words from established and unknown writers. Pays $20/published page for prose, $40/published page for poetry, on publication. No multiple submissions. "We look for striking work of the highest quality. Show us originality of thought and attention to language. No genre fiction, please. Only unpublished work will be considered." Guidelines available.

Public

c/o Department of Fine Art, 100 St. George Street, 6th Floor,
    Toronto, ON M5S 3G3
Phone: (416) 978-7892 Fax: (416) 978-1491
Contact: Stella Kyriakakis, administrator
Circulation: 1,000
Published twice a year

An interdisciplinary journal combining scholarly and critical writing in cultural studies, focusing on the visual arts, performance, and literature. Dedicated to providing a forum in which artists, critics, and theorists exchange ideas on topics previously segregated by ideological boundaries of discipline. Can no longer pay for contributions. No unsolicited submissions.

Quarry

P.O. Box 1061, Kingston, ON K7L 4Y5
Phone: (613) 548-8429
Contact: Mary Cameron, editor
Circulation: 1,200
Published quarterly

For more than 45 years this literary magazine has been publishing new, innovative fiction, poetry, and essays by established and emerging Canadian writers. Also carries translations, travel writing, and reviews. Committed to discovering talented new writers. Cannot usually pay.

Queen Street Quarterly

P.O. Box 311, Station P, 704 Spadina Road, Toronto, ON M5S 2S8
Phone: (416) 657-1637
E-mail: zelazo@psych.utoronto.ca
Web site: www.psych.utoronto.ca/~zelazo/~qsq.htm
Contact: Suzanne Zelazo, editor
Circulation: 500

A literary and arts magazine with academic and non-academic readers. Publishes stories of 1,000 to 3,000 words, 1 to 3 pages of poetry. Pays in copies only. Welcomes submission inquiries. Where possible, submissions to be accompanied by a Mac-readable disk.

Queen's Quarterly

184 Union Street, Kingston, ON K7L 3N6
Phone: (613) 545-2667 Fax: (613) 545-6822
E-mail: qquartly@post.queensu.ca
Web site: http://info.queensu.ca/quarterly
Contact: Boris Castel, editor
Circulation: 3,000
Published quarterly

A distinctive and multidisciplinary university-based review with a Canadian focus and an international outlook. First published in 1893. Features scholarly articles (up to 3,000 words) of general interest on politics, history, science, the humanities, and arts and letters, plus regular music and science columns, original poetry, fiction, and extensive book reviews. Fees, paid on acceptance, vary and are sometimes negotiated. Guidelines available.

Raddle Moon

112 West Hastings Street, Suite 401, Vancouver, BC V6B 1G8
Phone: (604) 688-6001
Contact: Lisa Robertson, co-editor
Published twice a year

An international literary review featuring mostly Canadian and U.S. poetry and criticism as well as previously untranslated writing from many countries. Welcomes submission inquiries from those who have familiarized themselves with the journal.

Rampike

81 Thornloe Crescent, Sault Ste. Marie, ON P6A 4J4
Phone: (705) 949-6498 Fax: (705) 949-4734
E-mail: jirgens@tbird.auc.on.ca
Web site: www.auc.on.ca
Contact: Karl Jirgens, publisher/editor
Circulation: 4,000
Published twice a year

A journal of contemporary art and writing featuring poetry, fiction, one-act plays, and cinema and video scripts. Innovative work by writers, theorists, and artists from around the world. There's never a shortage of stimulating contributors to this visually arresting and highly regarded magazine. But feel free to e-mail or write to the editor to ask about upcoming themes. Preferred length 2,000 to 3,000 words. Funds are limited, so usually pays a nominal fee. Guidelines available.

Resources for Feminist Research

OISE, 252 Bloor Street W., Toronto, ON M5S 1V6
Phone: (416) 923-6641, ext. 2277 Fax: (416) 926-4725
E-mail: pmasters@oise.utoronto.ca
Web site: www.oise.utoronto.ca/rfr
Contact: Philinda Masters, co-ordinating editor
Circulation: 2,000
Published quarterly

A journal of feminist scholarship containing papers, abstracts, reviews, reports of work in progress, and bibliographies. Preferred length 3,000 to 5,000 words. Cannot pay but welcomes submissions. Guidelines are outlined on inside back cover.

Room of One's Own

P.O. Box 46160, Station D, Vancouver, BC v6J 5G5
Web site: www.islandnet.com/Room
Contact: the growing *Room* collective
Circulation: 900
Published quarterly

An irregular quarterly, established 1975. Solicits fine writing and editing from women authors in Canada and other countries, both well-known and unknown. Features original poetry, fiction, reviews, artwork, and, occasionally, creative non-fiction. Length 2,000 to 2,500 words. Pays $25 honorarium plus 2 copies of issue. Guidelines are available, but reading recent back issues will provide best guidance, including notice of forthcoming theme issues.

Rotunda

Royal Ontario Museum, 100 Queen's Park, Toronto, ON M5S 2C6
Phone: (416) 586-5590 Fax: (416) 586-5827
Contact: Sandra Shaul, executive editor
Circulation: 20,000
Published 3 times a year

A semi-scholarly magazine, published by the Royal Ontario Museum, carrying authoritative pieces on art, archaeology, the earth and life sciences, astronomy, and museology, addressing the research of ROM scholars and their associates worldwide. Preferred length 2,000 to 2,500 words. Occasionally buys articles from professional journalists. Academics receive honoraria.

Scholarly Publishing

UTP Press, 10 St. Mary Street, Suite 700, Toronto, ON M4Y 2W8
Phone: (416) 978-2239 Fax: (416) 978-4738
E-mail: hcameron@utpress.utoronto.ca
Contact: Hamish Cameron, editor
Circulation: 1,500
Published quarterly

Concerned with the "pleasure and perils" of publishing. Coverage ranges from the classic concerns of manuscript editing and list building to such contemporary issues as on-demand publishing and computer applications. Also explores the delicate balance of author-editor relations, and the intricacies of production and budgeting. Carries articles with a unique blend of philosophical analysis and practical advice. Contributors unpaid, but submission inquiries welcome. Guidelines available.

Smoke: A Journal of Literary Prose

c/o The Bathurst Street Press, P.O. Box 73587, 509 St. Clair
 Avenue W., Toronto, ON M6C 2K7
Phone: (416) 651-6679
E-mail: bsp@yesic.com
Web site: www.yesic.com/~gmurray
Contact: George Murray, managing editor
Published at least twice a year

Focuses mainly on prose fiction, micro-fiction, and prose poetry. Also reviews, interviews, and academia (query first on these). Length 500 to 3,500 words. Pays in copies on publication. "We look for intelligent use of language to build narrative or character, or innovative challenges to traditions: narrative over exposition, content over superfluous style. We try to publish established and developing writers in equal proportions." Guidelines available.

Studies in Canadian Literature

University of New Brunswick, English Department, Hut 5,
 P.O. Box 4400, Fredericton, NB E3B 5A3
Phone: (506) 453-3501 Fax: (506) 453-4599
E-mail: scl@unb.ca
Contact: John Clement Ball, editor
Circulation: 500
Published twice a year

A bilingual, refereed journal of Canadian literary criticism. Carries essays of 8,000 to 10,000 words. Contributors receive complimentary subscription. Guidelines in journal. Use *MLA Handbook* for style.

sub-TERRAIN Magazine

175 East Broadway, Suite 204-A, Vancouver, BC V5T IW2
Phone: (604) 876-8710 Fax: (604) 879-2667
E-mail: subter@pinc.com
Contact: Brian Kaufman, managing editor
Circulation: 3,000
Published quarterly

Publishes new and established writers from across North America. Interested in contemporary poetry, fiction, and commentary. Preferred length 1,000 to 4,000 words. Pays $20/page on publication for solicited work only; other accepted manuscripts are paid in copies. Read the magazine before submitting (sample copy $5). Send 4 to 6 poems at a time. Guidelines available.

Teak Roundup

9060 Tronson Road, Unit 5, Vernon, BC VIH IE7
Phone: (250) 545-4186 Fax: (250) 545-4194
Contact: Robert G. Anstey, editor

An international prose and poetry quarterly featuring mostly North American material but some work from other countries too. Preferred length 500 to 1,000 words. Only subscribers may contribute. Cannot pay but welcomes submission inquiries. Guidelines available.

Tessera

c/o Lianne Moyes, Dépt. d'études anglaises, Université de
Montréal, C.P. 6128, succ. Centre-Ville, Montréal, PQ H3C 3J7
Phone: (514) 343-2218 Fax: (514) 343-6443
E-mail: moyesl@ere.umontreal.ca
Contacts: Lianne Moyes, co-editor
Circulation: 250
Published twice a year

Established 1982. A bilingual journal of experimental writing, feminist theory, and cultural critique. "We encourage play along borders, especially crossings of the boundary between creative and theoretical texts. *Tessera* accepts submissions in response to our calls for papers/texts on specific topics; consult the back pages of the journal and the editors for forthcoming topics. The most common reason for rejection of texts is that they bear no relation to the upcoming topics. We're eager to read feminist interventions in writing and culture that address (however obliquely) the upcoming topics!" Length 250 to 3,000 words. Pays $10/page on publication for experimental prose, poetry, or visual art. Contributions, which should include a biographical note, must be supplied on disk. Guidelines available.

TickleAce
P.O. Box 5353, St. John's, NF A1C 5W2
Phone: (709) 754-6610 Fax: (709) 754-5579
E-mail: tickleace@nfld.com
Contact: Bruce Porter, managing editor
Circulation: 1,000
Published twice a year

Publishes poetry, fiction, book reviews, visual art, and literary interviews with a focus on (but not restricted to) Newfoundland and Labrador. Stories run from 500 to 6,000 words. Pays an average of $20/page to a maximum of $200, depending on availability of funds.

The Toronto Review of Contemporary Writing Abroad
P.O. Box 6996, Station A, Toronto, ON M5W 1X7
Contact: Ms. Nurjehan Aziz, editorial board
Published 3 times a year

Carries poetry, fiction, drama, criticism, and book reviews by writers who originate from the Indian subcontinent, Africa, and the Caribbean. A bias toward diasporic and Third World subjects. Prose 2,000 to 4,000 words. Cash payment for solicited material only; other contributors receive free subscriptions. Published in English and in translation.

Urban History Review
Becker Associates, P.O. Box 507, Station Q, Toronto, ON M4T 2M5
Phone: (416) 483-7282 Fax: (416) 489-1713
E-mail: jbecker@interlog.com
Contact: John Becker, managing editor
Circulation: 500
Published twice a year

A bilingual interdisciplinary and refereed journal presenting lively articles covering such topics as architecture, heritage,

urbanization, housing, and planning – all in a generously illustrated format. Regular features include in-depth articles, research
notes, two annual bibliographies covering Canadian and international publications, comprehensive book reviews, and notes and
comments on conferences, urban policy, and publications.
Contributors are unpaid.

West Coast Line

2027 East Annex, Simon Fraser University, Burnaby, BC V5A 1S6
Phone: (604) 291-4287 Fax: (604) 291-5737
Contact: Jacqueline Larson, managing editor
Circulation: 600
Published 3 times a year

A creative arts magazine featuring contemporary poetry, short
fiction, visual art, critical essays, and photography. Devoted to "contemporary writers who are experimenting with, or expanding the
boundaries of, conventional forms of poetry, fiction, and criticism.
. . . We encourage Western Canadian writers but also publish occasional international features. Read back issues (available at
$10/copy) for an idea of our interests." Fiction up to 7,000 words.
Pay rates vary but average $8/page, paid after publication. Query
first. Guidelines available.

Zygote Magazine

P.O. Box 219, Warren, MB ROC 3E0
E-mail: tschmidt@man.net
Contacts: Tom Schmidt and Brent Pahl, co-editors
Circulation: 1,000
Published quarterly

Zygote's mandate is to publish new writers, though well-known
authors are also included and used as guest editors. Features an
eclectic mix of poetry, short stories, book reviews, interviews, and
other pieces on literary topics. Preferred lengths: articles and interviews, 1,000 words; book reviews, 500 to 1,000 words; and 5 to 8
poems (50 lines max.). Rates vary depending on funds available.
Guidelines available.

3

TRADE, BUSINESS, FARM, & PROFESSIONAL PUBLICATIONS

Trade publications are a potentially lucrative sector of the writer's market that is often overlooked. Although most pay no more than $500 for a full-length article, and usually less, the writing may require considerably fewer sources than are needed for consumer magazine features. An article can often be completed in a day or two, sometimes after research and interviews conducted solely by telephone. In terms of hours spent, therefore, the pay is generally relatively good. What's more, trade editors are often keen to find competent new writers. Writers living in remote areas can find themselves at an unexpected advantage, as editors seek regional balance, and e-mail or fax submissions can be sent across the country as simply and as fast as they can across town.

The secret to making money from these publications is to work frequently for as many as possible, always bearing in mind that they may want a degree of technical detail that will inform readers already well acquainted with the specific fields they serve. Most trade periodicals, however, deliberately avoid becoming too technical, and aim to appeal to a wide readership. If you're not well informed on your subject, become so through research. It bears repeating that before submitting, you *must* familiarize yourself with the magazine thoroughly by reading back issues and related periodicals.

Magazines in each of the following categories carry pieces about new products and developments, unusual marketing and promotion ideas, innovative management techniques, and prominent people and events specific to the industry, trade, or profession they serve. The regional business journals are highly recommended for freelance writers with business knowledge, since they often pay top dollar for timely and well-informed contributions. Those writers who have found markets through the main business section in Chapter 1 may profitably pursue this specialty further in the business listing below.

In many cases, staff writers produce the bulk of the feature writing, and call on outside experts to provide specific material. But they will often utilize freelancers when there is an editorial shortfall. Some editors cultivate long-term relationships with regular free-lancers, who produce much of their copy. Often one editor is involved in several magazines, so that making yourself and your work known to him or her can lead to further commissions, especially if you show yourself to be reliable and adaptable. Chapter 11, Book Resources, lists some of the larger publishers of trade magazines in Canada, who can be contacted for a list of their publications. If you have an area of technical or specialist knowledge, you have a significant advantage. If not, you would do well to familiarize yourself with at least one trade or business area and the publications that serve it.

This chapter offers a broadly representative selection of trade publications across a wide range of industrial and professional areas, including many well-established, dependable employment sources, and provides a solid resource for the freelance writer looking to break into a new market. However, this is perhaps the most fluid sector in publishing: periodicals come and go, and reappear under a new masthead; editors move from job to job relatively often in response to industry and structural changes. For a monthly updated reference source, consult Maclean-Hunter's *CARD* directory, or refer to *Matthews Media Directory*, published three times a year by Canadian Corporate News, at your library. Check *CARD*, too, or the annual supplement *Publication Profiles*, for upcoming editorial themes, media profiles, circulation figures, and other useful information.

Advertising, Marketing, & Sales

Adnews Insight Magazine
80 Parklawn Road, Suite 212, Toronto, ON M8Y 3H8
Phone: (416) 252-9400 Fax: (416) 252-8002

Contact: Derek Winkler, editor
Published quarterly

Canadian Retailer
121 Bloor Street E., Suite 1210, Toronto, ON M4W 3M5
Phone: (416) 922-6678 Fax: (416) 922-8011
Contact: Randall Scotland, editor
Published bimonthly

Government Purchasing Guide
10 Gateway Boulevard, Suite 490, North York, ON M3C 3T4
Phone: (416) 696-5488 Fax: (416) 696-7395
Contact: John Dujay, editor
Published bimonthly

Marketing
777 Bay Street, Toronto, ON M5W 1A7
Phone: (416) 596-2680 Fax: (416) 593-3170
Contact: Stan Sutter, editor
Published weekly

Marketnews
364 Supertest Road, 2nd Floor, North York, ON M3J 2M2
Phone: (416) 667-9945 Fax: (416) 667-0609
Contact: Robert Franner, editor
Published monthly

Meetings Monthly
P.O. Box 365, Montreal, PQ H2Y 3H1
Phone: (514) 274-0004 Fax: (514) 274-5884
Contact: Guy Jonkman, publisher/editor
Published 10 times a year

Modern Purchasing
777 Bay Street, Toronto, ON M5W 1A7
Phone: (416) 596-5704 Fax: (416) 596-5866
Contact: Joe Terrett, editor
Published 10 times a year

Pool & Spa Marketing
270 Esna Park Drive, Unit 12, Markham, ON L3R 1H3
Phone: (905) 513-0090 Fax: (905) 513-1377
Contact: David Barnsley, editor
Published 7 times a year

Sales Promotion
3228 South Service Road, West Wing, Burlington, ON L7N 3H8
Phone: (905) 634-2100 Fax: (905) 634-2238
Contact: Jackie Roth, editorial director
Published quarterly

Spa Management
P.O. Box 365, Montreal, PQ H2Y 3HI
Phone: (514) 274-0004 Fax: (514) 274-5884
Contact: Guy Jonkman, editor
Published bimonthly

Strategy
366 Adelaide Street W., Suite 500, Toronto, ON M5V IR9
Phone: (416) 408-2300 Fax: (416) 408-0870
Contact: Patrick Allossery, editor
Published biweekly

Architecture, Building, Engineering, & Heavy Construction

Atlantic Construction Journal
900 Windmill Road, Unit 107, Dartmouth, NS B3B IP7
Phone: (902) 420-0437 Fax: (902) 468-2425
Contact: Ken Partridge, editor
Published quarterly

AWARD Magazine
4180 Lougheed Highway, Suite 401, Burnaby, BC V5C 6A7
Phone: (604) 299-7311 Fax: (604) 299-9188
Contact: Janet Collins, editor
Published bimonthly

Building Magazine
360 Dupont Street, Toronto, ON M5R 1B9
Phone: (416) 966-9944 Fax: (416) 966-9946
Contact: Albert Warson, editor
Published bimonthly

Canadian Architect
1450 Don Mills Road, Don Mills, ON M3B 2X7
Phone: (416) 445-6641 Fax: (416) 442-2214
Contact: Bronwen Ledger, managing editor
Published monthly

Canadian Consulting Engineer
1450 Don Mills Road, Don Mills, ON M3B 2X7
Phone: (416) 445-6641 Fax: (416) 442-2214
Contact: Sophie Kneisel, editor
Published 7 times a year

Canadian Homebuilder & Renovation Contractor
403 – 1230 Quayside Drive, New Westminster, BC V3M 6H1
Phone: (604) 522-6033 or 1-800-665-3566 Fax: (604) 522-3277
Contact: Mark Bowen, general manager
Published quarterly

Canadian Masonry Contractor
1735 Bayly Street, Suite 7A, Pickering, ON L1W 3G7
Phone: (905) 831-4711
Contact: Tanja Nowotny, editor
Published 3 times a year

Canadian Roofing Contractor
1735 Bayly Street, Suite 7A, Pickering, ON L1W 3G7
Phone: (905) 831-4711
Contact: Tanja Nowotny, editor
Published quarterly

Construction Alberta News
10536 – 106th Street, Edmonton, AB T5H 2X6
Phone: (403) 424-1146 Fax: (403) 425-5886

Contact: Don Coates, editor
Published twice a week

Construction Canada
316 Adelaide Street W., Toronto, ON M5V IRI
Phone: (416) 977-8104 Fax: (416) 598-0658
Contact: Jim Tobros, executive editor
Published bimonthly

Daily Commercial News & Construction Record
280 Yorkland Boulevard, North York, ON M2J 4Z6
Phone: (416) 494-4990 Fax: (416) 756-2767
Contact: Scott Button, editor

Design Engineering
777 Bay Street, Toronto, ON M5W IA7
Phone: (416) 596-5822 Fax: (416) 596-5881
Contact: James Barnes, editor
Published 8 times a year

Engineering Dimensions
25 Sheppard Avenue W., Suite 1000, North York, ON M2N 6S9
Phone: (416) 224-1100 Fax: (416) 224-8168
Contact: Stephen Pawlett, editor
Published bimonthly

Equipment Journal
5160 Explorer Drive, Unit 6, Mississauga, ON L4W 4T7
Phone: (905) 629-7500 Fax: (905) 629-7988
Contact: E.E. Abel, editor
Published 17 times a year

Heavy Construction News
777 Bay Street, Toronto, ON M5W IA7
Phone: (416) 596-5844 Fax: (416) 593-3193
Contact: Russ Noble, editor
Published monthly

Home Builder Magazine

4819 St. Charles Boulevard, Pierrefonds, PQ H9H 3C7
Phone: (514) 620-2200 Fax: (514) 620-6300
Contact: Frank O'Brien, editor
Published bimonthly

Innovation

4010 Regent Street, Suite 200, Burnaby, BC V5C 6N2
Phone: (604) 929-6733 Fax: (604) 929-6753
Contact: Wayne Gibson, editor
Published 10 times a year

Journal of Commerce

4285 Canada Way, Burnaby, BC V5G 1H2
Phone: (604) 433-8164 Fax: (604) 433-9549
Contact: Frank Lillquist, editor
Published twice a week

Ontario Home Builder

1455 Lakeshore Road, Suite 205S, Burlington, ON L7S 2J1
Phone: (905) 634-5770 Fax: (905) 634-8335
Contact: Jan Matthews, publisher
Published 5 times a year

The Pegg

10060 Jasper Avenue, 15th Floor, Tower One, Scotia Place,
    Edmonton, AB T5J 4A2
Phone: (403) 426-3990 Fax: (403) 426-1877
Contact: Trevor Maine, managing editor
Published 10 times a year

Perspectives

512 King Street E., Suite 300, Toronto, ON M5A 1M1
Phone: (416) 955-1550 or 1-800-644-0666 Fax: (416) 955-1391
Contact: Gordon Grice, editor
Published quarterly

Toronto Construction News
280 Yorkland Boulevard, North York, ON M2J 4Z6
Phone: (416) 494-4990 Fax: (416) 756-2767
Contact: Randy Threndyle, managing editor
Published quarterly

Yardstick
2020 Portage Avenue, Unit 3C, Winnipeg, MB R3J 0K4
Phone: (204) 985-9780 Fax: (204) 985-9795
Contact: Jim Watson, managing editor
Published bimonthly

Automotive (see also Transportation & Cargo)

Aftermarket Canada
2050 Speers Road, Unit 1, Oakville, ON L6L 2X8
Phone: (905) 847-0277 Fax: (905) 847-7752
Contact: Steve Manning, editor
Published 11 times a year

Automotive Parts & Technology
130 Belfield Road, Etobicoke, ON M9W 1G1
Phone: (416) 614-0955 Fax: (416) 614-2781
Contact: Allan Janssen, editor
Published 9 times a year

Automotive Retailer
8980 Fraserwood Court, Unit 1, Burnaby, BC V5J 5H7
Phone: (604) 432-7987 Fax: (604) 432-1756
Contact: Reg Romero, editor
Published bimonthly

Bodyshop
1450 Don Mills Road, Don Mills, ON M3B 2X7
Phone: (416) 445-6641 Fax: (416) 442-2213
Contact: Brian Harper, editor
Published bimonthly

Canadian Auto World
1200 Markham Road, Suite 300, Scarborough, ON MIH 3C3
Phone: (416) 438-7777 Fax: (416) 438-5333
Contact: Joe Knycha, editor
Published monthly

Canadian Automotive Fleet
95 Barber Greene Road, Suite 207, Don Mills, ON M3C 3E9
Phone: (416) 383-0302 Fax: (416) 383-0313
Contact: Kevin Sheehy, managing editor
Published bimonthly

Jobber News
1450 Don Mills Road, Don Mills, ON M3B 2X7
Phone: (416) 445-6641 Fax: (416) 442-2213
Contact: Andrew Ross, editor
Published monthly

Octane
101 – 6th Avenue S.W., Suite 2450, Calgary, AB T2P 3P4
Phone: (403) 266-8700 or 1-800-561-1294
    Fax: (403) 266-6634
Contact: Gordon Jaremko, editor
Published bimonthly

Service Station & Garage Management
1450 Don Mills Road, Don Mills, ON M3B 2X7
Phone: (416) 445-6641 Fax: (416) 442-2077
Contact: Gary Kenez, editor
Published monthly

Taxi News
38 Fairmount Crescent, Toronto, ON M4L 2H4
Phone: (416) 466-2328 Fax: (416) 466-4220
Contact: William McQuat, editor
Published monthly

Aviation & Aerospace

Airforce Magazine
100 Metcalfe Street, P.O. Box 2460, Station D, Ottawa, ON KIP 5W6
Phone: (613) 992-5184 Fax: (613) 995-2196
Contact: Vic Johnson, editor
Published quarterly

Airports Americas
203 – 2323 Boudary Road, Vancouver, BC V5M 4V8
Phone: (604) 298-3004 Fax: (604) 298-3966
Contact: Toni Dabbs, editor
Published quarterly

Canadian Flight
1001 – 75 Albert Street, Ottawa, ON KIP 5E7
Phone: (613) 565-0881 Fax: (613) 236-8646
Contact: Doris Ohlmann, managing editor
Published monthly

Helicopters
3115 – 12th Street N.E., Suite 320, Calgary, AB T2E 7J2
Phone: (403) 735-5000 Fax: (403) 735-0537
Contact: Paul Skinner, editor/publisher
Published quarterly

ICAO Journal
Published by the International Civil Aviation Organization,
    999 University Street, Montreal, PQ H3C 5H7
Phone: (514) 954-8222 Fax: (514) 954-6376
Contact: Eric MacBurnie, editor
Published 10 times a year

Wings Magazine
3115 – 12th Street N.E., Suite 320, Calgary, AB T2E 7J2
Phone: (403) 735-5000 Fax: (403) 735-0537
Contact: Paul Skinner, editor/publisher
Published bimonthly

Business, Commerce, Banking, Law, Insurance, & Pensions

Alberta Venture
17225 – 109 Avenue, Edmonton, AB T5S 1H7
Phone: (403) 486-4424 Fax: (403) 483-1327
Contact: Ruth Kelly, publisher/editor
Published 10 times a year

Atlantic Progress
1660 Hollis Street, Suite 603, Halifax, NS B3J 1V7
Phone: (902) 494-0999 Fax: (902) 494-0998
Contact: David Holt, editor

Benefits & Pensions Monitor
245 Fairview Mall Drive, Suite 501, North York, ON M2J 4T1
Phone: (416) 494-1066 Fax: (416) 494-2536
Contact: Patricia McCullagh, managing editor
Published bimonthly

Benefits Canada
777 Bay Street, Toronto, ON M5W 1A7
Phone: (416) 596-5958 Fax: (416) 596-5071
Contact: Lori Bak, editor
Published 11 times a year

BIZ Hamilton/Halton Business Report
875 Main Street W., Hamilton, ON L8S 4R1
Phone: (905) 522-6117 Fax: (905) 529-2242
Contact: Arthur Kelly, editor
Published quarterly

The Bottom Line
75 Clegg Road, Suite 200, Markham, ON L6G 1A1
Phone: (905) 479-2665 Fax: (905) 479-3758
Contact: Michael Lewis, editor
Published monthly

The Business Advocate
244 Pall Mall Street, Box 3295, London, ON N6A 5P6
Phone: (519) 432-7551 Fax: (519) 432-8063
Contact: John Redmond, editor/publisher
Published monthly

Business & Professional Woman
95 Leeward Glenway, Unit 121, Don Mills, ON M3C 2Z6
Phone: (416) 424-1393 Fax: (416) 467-8262
Contact: Valerie Dunn, editor
Published quarterly

Business Careers Canada
299 Perth Avenue, Suite 200, Toronto, ON M6P 3X9
Phone: (416) 537-7700 Fax: (416) 537-7722
Contact: Paul Macygyn, publisher
Published twice a year

Business in Calgary
237 – 8th Avenue S.E., Suite 600, Calgary, AB T2G 5C3
Phone: (403) 264-3270, ext. 226 Fax: (403) 264-3276
Contact: Richard Bronstein, editor
Published monthly

Business in Vancouver
1155 West Pender Street, Suite 500, Vancouver, BC V6E 2P4
Phone: (604) 688-2398 Fax: (604) 688-1963
Contact: Peter Ladner, editor/publisher
Published weekly

Business People Magazine
232 Henderson Highway, Winnipeg, MB R2L 1L9
Phone: (204) 982-4000 Fax: (204) 982-4001
Contact: Al Davies, editor/associate publisher
Published quarterly

The Business Times
244 Adelaide Street S., London, ON N5Z 3L2
Phone: (519) 685-1624 Fax: (519) 649-0908

Contact: Katherine Wiggett, publisher
Published monthly

Business Today
266 Assiniboine Drive, Saskatoon, SK S7K 3KI
Phone: (306) 242-3641 Fax: (306) 242-3641
Contact: Eileen Rekve, editor
Published monthly

CA Magazine
Published by the Canadian Institute of Chartered Accountants,
    277 Wellington Street W., Toronto, ON M5V 3H2
Phone: (416) 977-3222 Fax: (416) 204-3409
Contact: Christian Bellavance, editor-in-chief
Published 10 times a year

CGA Magazine
Published by the Certified General Accountants' Association
    of Canada, 1188 West Georgia Street, Suite 700, Vancouver,
    BC V6E 4E2
Phone: (604) 669-3555 Fax: (604) 689-5845
Contact: Lesley Wood, publisher/editor
Published monthly

CMA Magazine
Published by the Society of Management Accountants of Canada,
    P.O. Box 176, Hamilton, ON L8N 3C3
Phone: (905) 525-4100 Fax: (905) 525-4533
Contact: Dan Hicks, publisher/editor
Published 10 times a year

Canada Japan Journal
220 Cambie Street, Suite 370, Vancouver, BC V6B 2M9
Phone: (604) 688-2486 Fax: (604) 688-1487
Contact: Taka Aoki, editor
Published monthly

Canadian Banker
Commerce Court West, 199 Bay Street, Suite 3000, Toronto,
ON M5L IG2
Phone: (416) 362-6092 Fax: (416) 362-8465
Contact: Simon Hally, editor/publisher
Published bimonthly

Canadian Bar Review
50 O'Connor Street, Suite 902, Ottawa, ON KIP 6L2
Phone: (613) 237-2925 Fax: (613) 237-0185
Contact: A.J. McClean, editor
Published twice a year

Canadian Insurance
III Peter Street, Suite 202, Toronto, ON M5V 2HI
Phone: (416) 599-0772 Fax: (416) 599-0867
Contact: Craig Harris, editor
Published monthly

Canadian Investment Review
777 Bay Street, Toronto, ON M5W IA7
Phone: (416) 596-5959 Fax: (416) 596-5071
Contact: Paul Williams, editor/publisher
Published quarterly

The Canadian Manager
2175 Sheppard Avenue E., Suite 310, North York, ON M2J IW8
Phone: (416) 493-0155 Fax: (416) 491-1670
Contact: Ruth Max, editor
Published quarterly

Canadian Underwriter
1450 Don Mills Road, Don Mills, ON M5B 2X7
Phone: (416) 445-6641 Fax: (416) 442-2213
Contact: Larry Welsh, managing editor
Published monthly

Church Business
4040 Creditview Road, Unit 11, P.O. Box 1800, Mississauga,
ON L5C 3Y8
Phone: (905) 813-7100 Fax: (905) 813-7117
Contact: Jay Barwell, editor
Published bimonthly

Commerce & Industry
1839 Inkster Boulevard, Winnipeg, MB R2X IR3
Phone: (204) 697-0835 Fax: (204) 633-7784
Contact: Kelly Gray, editor
Published bimonthly

Commerce News
10123 – 99th Street, Suite 600, Edmonton, AB T5J 3G9
Phone: (403) 426-4620 Fax: (403) 424-7946
Contact: Gary Slywchuk, editor
Published 11 times a year

Government Business
4040 Creditview Road, Unit 11, P.O. Box 1800, Mississauga,
ON L5C 3Y8
Phone: (905) 813-7100 Fax: (905) 813-7117
Contact: Jay Barwell, editor
Published bimonthly

Head Office at Home
44 Carleton Road, Unionville, ON L3R IZ5
Phone: (905) 477-4349
Contact: Elizabeth Harris, publisher/editor
Published 5 times a year

Human Resources Professional
920 Yonge Street, 6th Floor, Toronto, ON M4W 3C7
Phone: (416) 923-2324 Fax: (416) 924-4408
Contact: Lori Knowles, editor
Published bimonthly

Huronia Business Times
24 Dunlop Street E., 2nd Floor, Barrie, ON L4M 1A3
Phone: (705) 721-1450 Fax: (705) 721-1449
Contact: Bruce Hain, editor
Published 10 times a year

IE: Money
90 Richmond Street E., Suite 400, Toronto, ON M5C 1P1
Phone: (416) 366-4200 Fax: (416) 366-7846
Contact: Tessa Wilmott, editor
Published 5 times a year

In Business Windsor
1614 Lesperance Road, Tecumseh, ON N8N 1Y3
Phone: (519) 735-2080 Fax: (519) 735-2082
Contact: Mike Petrovich, editor
Published monthly

Journal of Commerce
4285 Canada Way, Burnaby, BC V5G 1H2
Phone: (604) 433-8164 Fax: (604) 433-9549
Contact: Frank Lillquist, editor
Published twice a week

Kootenay Business Magazine
1510 – 2nd Street N., Cranbrook, BC V1C 3L2
Phone: (250) 426-7253 Fax: (250) 426-4125
Contact: Stacey Curry, editor
Published monthly

LUAC Forum
Published by the Life Underwriters' Association of Canada,
   41 Lesmill Road, Don Mills, ON M3B 2T3
Phone: (416) 444-5251 Fax: (416) 444-8031
Contact: Valarie Osborne, editor
Published 10 times a year

Law Times
240 Edward Street, Aurora, ON L4G 3S9
Phone: (905) 841-6481 Fax: (905) 841-5078
Contact: Beth Marlin, managing editor
Published weekly

The Lawyers Weekly
75 Clegg Road, Markham, ON L6G 1A1
Phone: (905) 415-5804 Fax: (905) 479-3758
Contact: Jordan Furlong, editor

Mississauga Business Times
1606 Sedlescomb Drive, Unit 8, Mississauga, ON L4X 1M6
Phone: (905) 625-7070 Fax: (905) 625-4856
Contact: Rosalind Stefanac, editor
Published 10 times a year

Montreal Business Magazine
275 St. Jacques Street W., Suite 43, Montreal, PQ H2Y 1M9
Phone: (514) 286-8038 Fax: (514) 287-7346
Contact: Mike Carin, editor
Published quarterly

National (The Canadian Bar Foundation)
777 Bay Street, 5th Floor, Toronto, ON M5W 1A7
Phone: (416) 596-2538 Fax: (416) 593-5871
Contact: J. Stuart Langford, editor
Published 8 times a year

Northern Ontario Business
158 Elgin Street, Sudbury, ON P3E 3N5
Phone: (705) 673-5705 or 1-800-757-2766 Fax: (705) 673-9542
Contact: Mark Sandford, publisher/editor
Published monthly

Northwest Business
2915 – 19th Street N.E., Suite 201, Calgary, AB T2E 7A2
Phone: (403) 250-1128 Fax: (403) 250-1194

Contact: Donald Sylvester, publisher/editor
Published bimonthly

Nova Scotia Business Journal
900 Windmill Road, Unit 107, Dartmouth, NS B3B 1P7
Phone: (902) 468-8027 Fax: (902) 468-2425
Contact: Ken Partridge, editor
Published monthly

Okanagan Business Magazine
P.O. Box 1479, Station A, Kelowna, BC V1Y 7V8
Phone: (604) 861-5399 Fax: (604) 868-3040
Contact: J. Paul Byrne, publisher/managing editor
Published 8 times a year

Ottawa Business Journal
319 – 126 York Street, Ottawa, ON K1N 5T5
Phone: (613) 789-0403 Fax: (613) 789-0227
Contact: Mark Sutcliffe, editor-in-chief
Published weekly

Profiles
Published by York University, Suite 280, York Lanes, 4700 Keele
    Street, North York, ON M3J 1P3
Phone: (416) 736-2100, ext. 33160 Fax: (416) 736-5681
Contact: Michael Todd, managing editor
Published quarterly

Sounding Board
999 Canada Place, Suite 400, Vancouver, BC V6C 3C1
Phone: (604) 681-2111 Fax: (604) 681-0437
Contact: Ron Stanaitis, editor
Published 10 times a year

Sports Business
3883 Highway 7, Suite 214, Woodbridge, ON L4L 6C1
Phone: (905) 856-2600 Fax: (416) 856-2667
Contact: Steve Silva, editor
Published 5 times a year

Today's Woman in Business

Grandview Industrial Park, 185 Old Black River Road,
   P.O. Box 1291, Saint John, NB E2L 4H8
Phone: (506) 658-0754 Fax: (506) 633-0868
Contact: Carol Maber, publisher/editor
Published quarterly

Toronto Business Magazine

Zanny Ltd., 11966 Woodbine Avenue, Gormley, ON L0H 1G0
Phone: (905) 887-5048 Fax: (905) 887-0764
Contact: Kate Fleming, editor
Published bimonthly

Upwardly Mobile

P.O. Box 72611, 345 Bloor Street E., Toronto, ON M4W 3S9
Phone: (416) 920-0533 Fax: (416) 920-0702
Contact: Linda Darmanie, editor
Published quarterly

Computers & Data Processing

CAD Systems

395 Matheson Boulevard E., Mississauga, ON L4Z 2H2
Phone: (905) 890-1846 Fax: (905) 890-5769
Contact: Karen Dalton, editor
Published bimonthly

CIO Canada

501 Oakdale Road, North York, ON M3N 1W7
Phone: (416) 746-7360 Fax: (416) 746-1421
Contact: John Pickett, editor-in-chief
Published 10 times a year

Canadian Computer Reseller

777 Bay Street, Toronto, ON M5W 1A7
Phone: (416) 596-2640 Fax: (416) 593-3166
Contact: Alison Eastwood, editor
Published twice a month

Computer & Entertainment Retailing
2005 Sheppard Avenue E., Willowdale, ON M2J 5B1
Phone: (416) 497-9562 Fax: (416) 497-9427
Contact: Pamela Addo, managing editor
Published monthly

Computer Dealer News
2005 Sheppard Avenue E., 4th Floor, Willowdale, ON M2J 5B1
Phone: (416) 497-9562, ext. 367 Fax: (416) 497-5022
Contact: Ian Johnston, editor
Published twice a month

The Computer Paper
408 – 99 Atlantic Avenue, Toronto, ON M6K 3J8
Phone: (416) 588-1580 Fax: (416) 588-8574
Contact: J. David Ritter, publisher
Published monthly

The Computer Post
660 – 125 Garry Street, Winnipeg, MB R3C 3P2
Phone: (204) 947-9766 Fax: (204) 947-9767
Contact: Brenna Douglas, editorial assistant
Published monthly

ComputerWorld Canada
501 Oakdale Road, North York, ON M3N 1W7
Phone: (416) 746-7360 Fax: (416) 746-1421
Contact: John Pickett, editor-in-chief
Published twice a month

Computing Canada
2005 Sheppard Avenue E., 4th Floor, Willowdale, ON M2J 5B1
Phone: (416) 497-9562 Fax: (416) 497-5022
Contact: Martin Slofstra, editor
Published twice a month

Government Computer
408 – 99 Atlantic Avenue, Toronto, ON M6K 3J8
Phone: (416) 588-1580 Fax: (416) 588-8574

Contact: Lee Hunter, editor
Published 11 times a year

Government Computing Digest
132 Adrian Crescent, Markham, ON L3P 7B3
Phone: (905) 472-2801 Fax: (905) 472-3091
Contact: Nicholas Stephens, editor
Published bimonthly

InfoWorld Canada
501 Oakdale Road, North York, ON M3N 1W7
Phone: (416) 746-7360 Fax: (416) 746-1421
Contact: John Pickett, editor-in-chief
Published monthly

Network World Canada
501 Oakdale Road, North York, ON M3N 1W7
Phone: (416) 746-7360 Fax: (416) 746-1421
Contact: John Pickett, editor-in-chief
Published biweekly

Toronto Computes!
408 – 99 Atlantic Avenue, Toronto, ON M6K 3J8
Phone: (416) 588-6818 Fax: (416) 588-4110
Contact: Mara Gulens, editor
Published monthly

Education & School Management

Educational Digest
11966 Woodbine Avenue, Gormley, ON L0H 1G0
Phone: (905) 887-5048 Fax: (905) 887-0764
Contact: Amy Margaret, editor
Published quarterly

Quebec Home & School News
3285 Cavendish Boulevard, Suite 562, Montreal, PQ H4B 2L9
Phone: (514) 481-5619 Fax: (514) 481-5610

Contact: Dorothy Nixon, editor
Published 5 times a year

The Reporter
65 St. Clair Avenue E., Toronto, ON M4T 2Y8
Phone: (416) 925-2493 Fax: (416) 925-7764
Contact: Aleda O'Connor, editor
Published 3 times a year

School Business
4040 Creditview Road, Unit 11, P.O. Box 1800, Mississauga,
    ON L5C 3Y8
Phone: (905) 813-7100 Fax: (905) 813-7117
Contact: Jay Barwell, editor
Published bimonthly

TEACH Magazine
258 Wallace Avenue, Suite 206, Toronto, ON M6P 3M9
Phone: (416) 537-2103 Fax: (416) 537-3491
Contact: Wili Liberman, publisher/editor
Published 5 times a year

University Manager
388 Donald Street, Suite 200, Winnipeg, MB R3B 2J4
Phone: (204) 957-0265 Fax: (204) 957-0217
Contact: Andrea Kuch, editor
Published quarterly

Electronics & Electrical

Canadian Electronics
135 Spy Court, Markham, ON L3R 5H6
Phone: (905) 477-3222 Fax: (905) 477-4320
Contact: Tim Gouldson, editor
Published 7 times a year

Electrical Business
395 Matheson Boulevard E., Mississauga, ON L4Z 2H2
Phone: (905) 890-1846 Fax: (905) 890-5769
Contact: Roger Burford Mason, editor
Published monthly

Electrical Equipment News
1450 Don Mills Road, Don Mills, ON M3B 2X7
Phone: (416) 445-6641 Fax: (416) 442-2214
Contact: Olga Markovich, editor/associate publisher
Published twice a year

Electricity Today
345 Kingston Road, Suite 101, Pickering, ON L1V 1A1
Phone: (905) 509-4448 Fax: (905) 509-4451
Contact: Michael MacMillan, editor
Published 10 times a year

Electronic Products & Technology
1200 Aerowood Drive, Unit 27, Mississauga, ON L4W 2S7
Phone: (905) 624-8100 Fax: (905) 624-1760
Contact: David Kerfoot, editor
Published 8 times a year

Energy, Mining, Forestry, Lumber, Pulp & Paper, & Fisheries

Atlantic Fisherman
3695 Barrington Street N., Unit 30, Halifax, NS B3K 2Y3
Phone: (902) 422-4990 Fax: (902) 422-4728
Contact: Karen Fulton, editor
Published monthly

Canadian Forest Industries
1, rue Pacifique, Ste.-Anne-de-Bellevue, PQ H9X 1C5
Phone: (514) 457-2211 Fax: (514) 457-2558
Contact: Scott Jamieson, editor
Published 8 times a year

Canadian Mining Journal
1450 Don Mills Road, Don Mills, ON M3B 2X7
Phone: (416) 445-2094 Fax: (416) 442-2175
Contact: Patrick Whiteway, editor
Published bimonthly

Canadian Wood Products
1, rue Pacifique, Ste.-Anne-de-Bellevue, PQ H9X 1C5
Phone: (514) 457-2211 Fax: (514) 457-2558
Contact: Scott Jamieson, editor
Published bimonthly

Energy Processing/Canada
900 – 6th Avenue S.W., 5th Floor, Calgary, AB T2P 3K2
Phone: (403) 263-6881 Fax: (403) 263-6886
Contact: Alister Thomas, managing editor
Published bimonthly

The Fisherman
111 Victoria Drive, Suite 160, Vancouver, BC V5L 4C4
Phone: (604) 255-1366 Fax: (604) 255-3162
Contact: Sean Griffin, editor
Published monthly

The Forestry Chronicle
151 Slater Street, Suite 606, Ottawa, ON K1P 5H3
Phone: (613) 234-2242 Fax: (613) 234-6181
Contacts: V.J. Nordin and D. Burgess, editors
Published bimonthly

Hiballer Forest Magazine
P.O. Box 54239, 1562 Lonsdale Avenue, North Vancouver, BC V7M 3L5
Phone: (604) 984-2002 Fax: (604) 984-2820
Contact: Paul Young, managing editor/publisher
Published bimonthly

Logging & Sawmilling Journal
P.O. Box 86670, North Vancouver, BC V74 4L2
Phone: (604) 944-6146 Fax: (604) 990-9971

Contact: Norm Poole, editor
Published 10 times a year

Mining Review
100 Sutherland Avenue, Winnipeg, MB R2W 3C7
Phone: (204) 947-0222 Fax: (204) 947-2047
Contact: Janis Connolly, editor
Published quarterly

The Northern Miner
1450 Don Mills Road, Don Mills, ON M3B 2X7
Phone: (416) 445-6641 Fax: (416) 442-2175
Contact: Vivian Danielson, editor
Published weekly

Oil Patch Magazine
17420 – 106th Avenue, Suite 200, Edmonton, AB T5S 1E6
Phone: (403) 486-1295 Fax: (403) 484-0884
Contact: Lucille Hyman, publisher
Published bimonthly

Oilweek
101 – 6th Avenue S.W., Suite 2450, Calgary, AB T2P 3P4
Phone: (403) 266-8700 Fax: (403) 266-6634
Contact: Phil Boyd, executive publisher
Published monthly

Propane/Canada
900 – 6th Avenue S.W., Calgary, AB T2P 3K2
Phone: (403) 263-6881 Fax: (403) 263-6886
Contact: Alister Thomas, managing editor
Published bimonthly

Pulp & Paper Canada
3300 Côte Vertu, Suite 410, St. Laurent, PQ H4R 2B7
Phone: (514) 339-1399 Fax: (514) 339-1396
Contact: Graeme Rodden, editor
Published monthly

The Roughneck
900 – 6th Avenue S.W., Calgary, AB T2P 3K2
Phone: (403) 263-6881 Fax: (403) 263-6886
Contact: Scott Jeffrey, publisher
Published monthly

The Sou'Wester
P.O. Box 128, Yarmouth, NS B5A 4B1
Phone: (902) 742-7111 Fax: (902) 742-2311
Contact: Alain Meuse, editor
Published biweekly

Truck Logger Magazine
815 West Hastings Street, Suite 725, Vancouver, BC V6C 1B4
Phone: (604) 682-4080 Fax: (604) 682-3775
Contact: David Webster, editor/publisher
Published bimonthly

The Westcoast Fisherman
1496 West 72nd Avenue, Vancouver, BC V6P 3C8
Phone: (604) 266-7433 Fax: (604) 263-8620
Contact: David Rahn, publisher
Published monthly

Environmental Science & Management

Canadian Environmental Protection
201 – 2323 Boundary Road, Vancouver, BC V5M 4V8
Phone: (604) 291-9900 Fax: (604) 291-1906
Contact: Dan Kennedy, editor
Published 9 times a year

Environmental Science & Engineering
220 Industrial Parkway, Unit 30, Aurora, ON L4G 3V6
Phone: (905) 727-4666 Fax: (905) 841-7271
Contact: Tom Davey, publisher/editor
Published bimonthly

Hazardous Materials Management
951 Denison Street, Unit 4, Markham, ON L3R 3W9
Phone: (905) 305-6155 Fax: (905) 305-6255
Contact: Guy Crittenden, editor
Published bimonthly

Recycling Product News
201 – 2323 Boundary Road, Vancouver, BC V5M 4V8
Phone: (604) 291-9900 Fax: (604) 291-1906
Contact: Dan Kennedy, editor
Published 9 times a year

Water & Pollution Control
11966 Woodbine Avenue, Gormley, ON L0H 1G0
Phone: (905) 887-5048 Fax: (905) 887-0764
Contact: Amy Margaret, editor
Published quarterly

Farming

Canada Poultryman
222 Argyle Avenue, Delhi, ON N4B 2Y2
Phone: (519) 582-2513 Fax: (519) 582-4040
Contact: Tony Greaves, editor/manager
Published monthly

Canadian Fruitgrower
222 Argyle Avenue, Delhi, ON N4B 2Y2
Phone: (519) 582-2513 Fax: (519) 582-4040
Contact: Dan Wilkens, editor
Published 9 times a year

Canadian Guernsey Journal
368 Woolwich Street, Guelph, ON N1H 3W6
Phone: (519) 836-2141
Contact: V. Macdonald, editor
Published quarterly

Canadian Hereford Digest
5160 Skyline Way N.E., Calgary, AB T2E 6V1
Phone: (403) 274-1734
Contact: Kurt Gilmore, editor
Published 9 times a year

Canadian Jersey Breeder
350 Speedvale Avenue W., Unit 9, Guelph, ON N1H 7M7
Phone: (519) 821-9150 Fax: (519) 821-2723
Contact: Betty Clements, editor
Published 10 times a year

Canola Guide
P.O. Box 6600, Winnipeg, MB R3C 3A7
Phone: (204) 944-5761 Fax: (204) 942-8463
Contact: Bill Strautman, editor
Published 8 times a year

Cattlemen
P.O. Box 6600, Winnipeg, MB R3C 3A7
Phone: (204) 944-5760 Fax: (204) 942-8463
Contact: Gren Winslow, editor
Published monthly

Country Guide
P.O. Box 6600, Winnipeg, MB R3C 3A7
Phone: (204) 944-5761 Fax: (204) 942-8463
Contact: Dave Wreford, editor
Published 11 times a year

Country Life in BC
3308 King George Highway, Surrey, BC V4P 1A8
Phone: (604) 536-7622 Fax: (604) 536-5677
Contact: D.M. Young, publisher/editor
Published monthly

Dairy Contact
P.O. Box 549, 4917 – 50th Street, Onoway, AB T0E 1V0
Phone: (403) 967-2929 Fax: (403) 967-2930

Contact: Allen F. Parr, publisher/editor
Published monthly

Dairy Guide
P.O. Box 6600, Winnipeg, MB R3C 3A7
Phone: (204) 944-5761 Fax: (204) 942-8463
Contact: Gren Winslow, editor
Published 11 times a year

Farm & Country
1 Yonge Street, Suite 1504, Toronto, ON M5E 1E5
Phone: (416) 364-5324 Fax: (416) 364-5857
Contact: John Muggeridge, managing editor
Published 15 times a year

Farm Focus
P.O. Box 128, Yarmouth, NS B5A 4B1
Phone: (902) 742-7111 Fax: (902) 742-2311
Contact: Heather Jones, editor
Published biweekly

The Farm Gate
15 King Street, Elmira, ON N3B 2R1
Phone: (519) 669-5155
Contact: Bob Verdun, editor/publisher
Published monthly

Farm Light & Power
2352 Smith Street, Regina, SK S4P 2P6
Phone: 1-800-668-3300 Fax: 1-888-213-9999
Contact: Tom Bradley, publisher
Published 10 times a year

Farmers' Choice
2950 Bremner Avenue, Bag 5200, Red Deer, AB T4N 5G3
Phone: (403) 343-2400 Fax: (403) 342-4051
Contact: Howard Janzen, publisher
Published monthly

Grainews
P.O. Box 6600, Winnipeg, MB R3C 3A7
Phone: (204) 944-5569 Fax: (204) 944-5416
Contact: Andy Sirski, editor
Published 16 times a year

The Grower
355 Elmira Road, Suite 103, Guelph, ON N1K 1S5
Phone: (519) 763-8728 Fax: (519) 763-6604
Contact: Gayle Anderson, editor
Published monthly

Holstein Journal
9120 Leslie Street, Unit 105, Richmond Hill, ON L4B 3S9
Phone: (905) 886-4222 Fax: (905) 886-0037
Contact: Bonnie Cooper, editor
Published monthly

The Manitoba Co-operator
P.O. Box 9800, Winnipeg, MB R3C 3K7
Phone: (204) 934-0401 Fax: (204) 934-0480
Contact: John Morriss, publisher/editor
Published weekly

Niagara Farmers' Monthly
P.O. Box 52, Smithville, ON L0R 2A0
Phone: (905) 957-3751 Fax: (905) 957-0088
Contact: Steve Ecker, publisher
Published 11 times a year

Ontario Corn Producer
90 Woodlawn Road W., Guelph, ON N1H 1B2
Phone: (519) 837-1660 Fax: (519) 837-1674
Contact: Terry Boland, editor-in-chief
Published 10 times a year

Ontario Dairy Farmer
P.O. Box 7400, London, ON N5Y 4X3
Phone: (519) 473-0010 Fax: (519) 473-2256

Contact: Paul Mahon, editor
Published bimonthly

Ontario Farmer

P.O. Box 7400, London, ON N5Y 4X3
Phone: (519) 473-0010 Fax: (519) 473-2256
Contact: Paul Mahon, editor
Published weekly

Ontario Milk Producer

6780 Campobello Road, Mississauga, ON L5N 2L8
Phone: (905) 821-8970 Fax: (905) 821-3160
Contact: Bill Dimmick, editor
Published monthly

Quebec Farmers' Advocate

P.O. Box 80, Ste.-Anne-de-Bellevue, PQ H9X 3L4
Phone: (514) 457-2010 Fax: (514) 398-7972
Contact: Hugh Maynard, editor
Published 11 times a year

Rural Roots

30 – 10th Street E., P.O. Box 550, Prince Albert, SK S6V 5R9
Phone: (306) 764-4276 Fax: (306) 922-4237
Contact: Ruth Griffiths, editor
Published weekly

Saskatchewan Farm Life

4 – 75 Lenore Drive, Saskatoon, SK S7K 7Y1
Phone: (306) 242-5723 Fax: (306) 668-6164
Contact: Larry Hiatt, manager
Published biweekly

Simmental Country

13, 4101 – 19th Street N.E., Calgary, AB T2E 7C4
Phone: (403) 250-5255 Fax: (403) 250-5279
Contact: Ted Pritchett, publisher/editor
Published monthly

Western Hog Journal
10319 Princess Elizabeth Avenue, Edmonton, AB T5G 0Y5
Phone: (403) 474-8288 Fax: (403) 471-8065
Contact: Ed Schultz, editor
Published quarterly

The Western Producer
P.O. Box 2500, Saskatoon, SK S7K 2C4
Phone: (306) 665-3500 Fax: (306) 653-8750
Contact: Garry Fairbairn, editor
Published weekly

Food, Drink, Hostelry, & Hotel & Restaurant Supplies

Bakers Journal
222 Argyle Avenue, Delhi, ON N4B 2Y2
Phone: (519) 582-2513 Fax: (519) 582-4040
Contact: Blair Adams, editor
Published 10 times a year

Canadian Grocer
777 Bay Street, Toronto, ON M5W 1A7
Phone: (416) 596-5772 Fax: (416) 593-3162
Contact: G.H. Condon, editor
Published 10 times a year

Canadian Pizza Magazine
222 Argyle Avenue, Delhi, ON N4B 2Y2
Phone: (519) 582-2513 Fax: (519) 582-4040
Contact: Blair Adams, editor
Published bimonthly

Centre Magazine
1450 Don Mills Road, Don Mills, ON M3B 2X7
Phone: (416) 442-2069 Fax: (416) 442-2213
Contact: Elena Opasini, editor
Published 8 times a year

Food in Canada
777 Bay Street, Toronto, ON M5W 1A7
Phone: (416) 596-5477 Fax: (416) 593-3189
Contact: Catherine Wilson, editor
Published 9 times a year

Foodservice & Hospitality
23 Lesmill Road, Suite 101, Don Mills, ON M3B 3P6
Phone: (416) 447-0888 Fax: (416) 447-5333
Contact: Rosanna Caira, editor
Published monthly

Grocer Today
401 – 4180 Lougheed Highway, Burnaby, BC V5C 6A7
Phone: (604) 299-7311 Fax: (604) 299-9188
Contact: Marisa Paterson, editor
Published 10 times a year

Hardware Merchandizing
777 Bay Street, Toronto, ON M5W 1A7
Phone: (416) 596-5258 Fax: (416) 596-2642
Contact: Robert Gerlsbeck, editor
Published 9 times a year

Home Improvement Retailing
245 Fairview Mall Drive, 5th Floor, North York, ON M2J 4T1
Phone: (416) 494-1066 Fax: (416) 494-2536
Contact: Peter White, managing editor
Published bimonthly

Hotelier
23 Lesmill Road, Suite 101, Don Mills, ON M3B 3P6
Phone: (416) 447-0888 Fax: (416) 447-5333
Contact: Rosanna Caira, editor
Published bimonthly

Inn Business
65 St. John Side Road E., Aurora, ON L4G 3G8
Phone: (905) 841-8753 Fax: (905) 841-7416

Contact: Amy Margaret, managing editor
Published quarterly

Ontario Restaurant News
2065 Dundas Street E., Suite 201, Mississauga, ON L4X 2WI
Phone: (905) 206-0150 Fax: (905) 206-9972
Contact: Mike Deibert, editor
Published monthly

Western Grocer
1839 Inkster Boulevard, Winnipeg, MB R2X IR3
Phone: (204) 697-0835 Fax: (204) 633-7784
Contact: Kelly Gray, editor
Published bimonthly

Health, Dentistry, Medicine, Pharmacy, & Nursing

Alberta Doctors' Digest
122230 – 106th Avenue N.W., Edmonton, AB T5N 3ZI
Phone: (403) 482-2626 Fax: (403) 482-5445
Contact: Dr. G.L. Higgins, editor
Published 9 times a year

British Columbia Medical Journal
115 – 1665 West Broadway, Vancouver, BC V6J 5A4
Phone: (604) 736-5551 Fax: (604) 733-7317
Contact: Dr. James A. Wilson, editor
Published monthly

Canadian Family Physician
2630 Skymark Avenue, Mississauga, ON L4W 5A4
Phone: (905) 629-0900 Fax: (905) 629-0893
Contact: Dr. Calvin Gutkin, editorial director
Published monthly

Canadian Healthcare Manager
777 Bay Street, Toronto, ON M5W IA7
Phone: (416) 596-5794 Fax: (416) 596-5901

Contact: Celia Milne, editor
Published bimonthly

Canadian Journal of Continuing Medical Education
955, boulevard St.-Jean, Suite 306, Pointe Claire, PQ H9R 5K3
Phone: (514) 695-7623 Fax: (514) 695-8554
Contact: Paul Brand, executive editor
Published monthly

Canadian Journal of Hospital Pharmacy
1145 Hunt Club Road, Suite 350, Ottawa, ON KIV OY3
Phone: (613) 736-9733 Fax: (613) 736-5660
Contact: Scott Walker, editor
Published bimonthly

Canadian Journal of Public Health
1565 Carling Avenue, Suite 400, Ottawa, ON KIZ 8RI
Phone: (613) 725-3769 Fax: (613) 725-9826
Contact: Gerald H. Dafoe, managing editor
Published bimonthly

Canadian Medical Association Journal
1867 Alta Vista Drive, Ottawa, ON KIG 3Y6
Phone: (613) 731-8610 Fax: (613) 523-0824
Contact: Patrick Sullivan, news and features editor
Published biweekly

The Canadian Nurse
50 The Driveway, Ottawa, ON K2P IE2
Phone: (613) 237-2133 Fax: (613) 237-3520
Contact: Judith Haines, editor-in-chief
Published 10 times a year

Canadian Pharmaceutical Journal
1382 Hurontario Street, Mississauga, ON L5G 3H4
Phone: (905) 278-6700 Fax: (905) 278-4850
Contact: Andrew Reinboldt, editor
Published 10 times a year

The Care Connection
Published by the Ontario Association of Registered Nursing
    Assistants, 5025 Orbitor Drive, Building 4, Suite 200,
    Mississauga, ON L4W 4Y5
Phone: (905) 602-4664 Fax: (905) 602-4666
Contact: Barbara Thomber, editor
Published quarterly

Dental Practice Management
1450 Don Mills Road, Don Mills, ON M3B 2X7
Phone: (416) 442-2046 Fax: (416) 442-2214
Contact: Erla Kay, editor
Published quarterly

Doctor's Review
400 McGill Street, 3rd Floor, Montreal, PQ H2Y 2G1
Phone: (514) 397-8833 Fax: (514) 397-0228
Contact: Madeleine Partous, editor
Published monthly

Family Practice
777 Bay Street, Toronto, ON M5W 1A7
Phone: (416) 596-3483 Fax: (416) 596-3498
Contact: John Shaughnessy, editor
Published 32 times a year

Healthcare Management Forum
350 Sparks Street, Suite 402, Ottawa, ON K1R 7S8
Phone: (613) 235-7218 Fax: (613) 235-5451
Contact: Marilyn Laidlaw, editor
Published quarterly

Healthcare Product News
201 – 2323 Boundary Road, Vancouver, BC V5M 4V8
Phone: (604) 291-9900 Fax: (604) 291-1906
Contact: Len Webster, editor
Published bimonthly

Hospital Business
4040 Creditview Road, Unit 11, P.O. Box 1800, Mississauga,
    ON L5C 3Y8
Phone: (905) 813-7100 Fax: (905) 813-7117
Contact: Jay Barwell, editor
Published bimonthly

Hospital News
23 Apex Road, Toronto, ON M6A 2V6
Phone: (416) 781-5516 Fax: (416) 781-5499
Contact: Cindy Woods, editor
Published monthly

The Journal
Published by the Addiction Research Foundation, 33 Russell Street,
    Toronto, ON M5S 2S1
Phone: (416) 595-6059 Fax: (416) 593-4694
Contact: Anita Dubey, editor
Published bimonthly

Journal of the Canadian Dental Association
1815 Alta Vista Drive, Ottawa, ON K1G 3Y6
Phone: (613) 523-1770 Fax: (613) 523-7736
Contact: Terence Davis, managing editor
Published 11 times a year

Journal of the Canadian Dietetic Association
480 University Avenue, Suite 604, Toronto, ON M5G 1V2
Phone: (416) 596-0857 Fax: (416) 596-0603
Contact: Eunice Chao, editor
Published quarterly

The Medical Post
777 Bay Street, Toronto, ON M5W 1A7
Phone: (416) 596-5771 Fax: (416) 593-3177
Contact: Pat Rich, editor
Published 42 times a year

Medicine North America
400 McGill Street, 3rd Floor, Montreal, PQ H2Y 2GI
Phone: (514) 397-9393 Fax: (514) 397-0228
Contact: Dr. Ian R. Hart, editor
Published monthly

Nursing BC
2855 Arbutus Street, Vancouver, BC V6J 3Y8
Phone: (604) 736-7331 Fax: (604) 738-2272
Contact: Bruce Wells, editor
Published 5 times a year

The Nutrition Post
777 Bay Street, Toronto, ON M5W 1A7
Phone: (416) 596-6099 Fax: (416) 593-3177
Contact: Diana Swift, editor
Published quarterly

Ontario Dentist
4 New Street, Toronto, ON M5R 1P6
Phone: (416) 922-3900 Fax: (416) 922-9005
Contact: Jim Shosenberg, editor
Published 10 times a year

Ontario Medical Review
525 University Avenue, Suite 300, Toronto, ON M5G 2K7
Phone: (416) 599-2580 Fax: (416) 599-9309
Contact: Jeff Henry, managing editor
Published monthly

Oral Health
1450 Don Mills Road, Don Mills, ON M3B 2X7
Phone: (416) 442-2046 Fax: (416) 442-2214
Contact: Erla Kay, publisher
Published monthly

Patient Care
777 Bay Street, Toronto, ON M5W 1A7
Phone: (416) 596-3483 Fax: (416) 596-3498

Contact: Vil Meere, editor
Published monthly

Pharmacy Practice
777 Bay Street, Toronto, ON M5W 1A7
Phone: (416) 596-5000 Fax: (416) 596-3499
Contact: Anne Bokma, editor
Published monthly

Rehab and Community Care Management
101 Thorncliffe Park Drive, Toronto, ON M4H 1M2
Phone: (416) 421-7944 Fax: (416) 421-0966
Contact: Helmut Dostal, managing editor
Published quarterly

Rural Medicine
1867 Alta Vista Drive, Ottawa, ON K1G 3Y6
Phone: (613) 731-8610 Fax: (613) 523-0824
Contact: Dr. John Wootton, editor
Published quarterly

Industrial

Accident Prevention
250 Yonge Street, 28th Floor, Toronto, ON M5B 2N4
Phone: (416) 506-8888
Contact: Susan Stanton, editor
Published bimonthly

Canadian Chemical News
130 Slater Street, Suite 550, Ottawa, ON K1P 6E2
Phone: (613) 232-6252
Contact: Nola Haddadian, editor
Published 10 times a year

Canadian Facility Management & Design
62 Olsen Drive, Don Mills, ON M3A 3J3
Phone: (416) 447-3417 Fax: (416) 447-4410

Contact: Victor von Buchstab, editor
Published bimonthly

Canadian Industrial Equipment News
1450 Don Mills Road, Don Mills, ON M3B 2X7
Phone: (416) 445-6641 Fax: (416) 442-2214
Contact: Olga Markovich, editor/associate publisher
Published monthly

Canadian Machinery & Metalworking
777 Bay Street, Toronto, ON M5W 1A7
Phone: (416) 596-5833 Fax: (416) 596-5881
Contact: Jim Barnes, editor
Published 7 times a year

Canadian Occupational Safety
3228 South Service Road, West Wing, 2nd Floor, Burlington,
    ON L7N 3H8
Phone: (905) 634-2100 Fax: (905) 634-2238
Contact: Jackie Roth, editor
Published bimonthly

Canadian Packaging
777 Bay Street, Toronto, ON M5W 1A7
Phone: (416) 596-5746 Fax: (416) 596-5554
Contact: Douglas Faulkner, editor
Published 11 times a year

Canadian Plastics
1450 Don Mills Road, Don Mills, ON M3B 2X7
Phone: (416) 422-2290 Fax: (416) 442-2213
Contact: Michael LeGault, editor
Published 8 times a year

Canadian Process Equipment & Control News
343 Eglinton Avenue E., Toronto, ON M4P 1L7
Phone: (416) 481-6483 Fax: (416) 481-6436
Contact: Vince Sharp, editor
Published bimonthly

Canadian Textile Journal
1, rue Pacifique, Ste.-Anne-de-Bellevue, PQ H9X 1C5
Phone: (514) 457-2347 Fax: (514) 457-2147
Contact: Douglas Cariou, managing editor
Published bimonthly

Heating–Plumbing–Air Conditioning
1370 Don Mills Road, Suite 300, Don Mills, ON M3B 3N7
Phone: (416) 759-2500 Fax: (416) 759-6979
Contact: Lynne Erskine-Chelo, editor
Published 7 times a year

Laboratory Product News
1450 Don Mills Road, Don Mills, ON M3B 2X7
Phone: (416) 442-2052 Fax: (416) 442-2213
Contact: Rita Tate, publisher/editor
Published 7 times a year

Machinery & Equipment MRO
1450 Don Mills Road, Don Mills, ON M3B 2X7
Phone: (416) 442-2089 Fax: (416) 442-2214
Contact: William Roebuck, editor
Published bimonthly

Metalworking Production & Purchasing
135 Spy Court, Markham, ON L3R 5H6
Phone: (905) 477-3222 Fax: (905) 477-4320
Contact: Jerry Cook, editor
Published bimonthly

National Industrial Magazine
801 York Mills Road, Suite 201, Don Mills, ON M3B 1X7
Phone: (416) 446-1401 Fax: (416) 446-0502
Contact: W.R. Bryson, editor/publisher
Published bimonthly

New Equipment News
2 Carlton Street, Suite 1511, Toronto, ON M3B 1J3
Phone: (416) 599-3737 Fax: (416) 599-3730

Contact: Barrie Lehman, editor
Published monthly

OH&S Canada
1450 Don Mills Road, Don Mills, ON M3B 2X7
Phone: (416) 442-2288 Fax: (416) 442-2200
Contact: David Dehaas, editor
Published 7 times a year

Plant
777 Bay Street, Toronto, ON M5W 1A7
Phone: (416) 596-5761 Fax: (416) 596-5552
Contact: Wayne Karl, editor
Published 18 times a year

Plant Engineering & Maintenance
3228 South Service Road, West Wing, 2nd Floor, Burlington,
   ON L7N 3H8
Phone: (905) 634-2100 Fax: (905) 634-2238
Contact: Todd Phillips, editor
Published bimonthly

Landscaping & Horticulture

Canadian Florist, Greenhouse & Nursery
1090 Aerowood Drive, Unit 1, Mississauga, ON L4W 1Y5
Phone: (905) 625-2730 Fax: (905) 625-1355
Contact: Peter Heywood, editor/publisher
Published monthly

Greenhouse Canada
222 Argyle Avenue, Delhi, ON N4B 2Y2
Phone: (519) 582-2513 Fax: (519) 582-4040
Contact: Dave Harrison, editor
Published monthly

GreenMaster

27 West Beaver Creek, Suite 201, Richmond Hill, ON L4B 1M8
Phone: (905) 771-7333 Fax: (905) 771-7336
Contact: Nicholas Stephens, editor
Published bimonthly

Hortwest

5830 – 176A Street, Suite 101, Surrey, BC V3S 4E3
Phone: (604) 574-7772 Fax: (604) 574-7773
Contact: Jane Stock, managing editor
Published 7 times a year

Landmark

1000 – 1777 Victoria Avenue, Regina, SK S4P 4K5
Phone: (306) 584-1000 Fax: (306) 584-2824
Contact: Tom Steve, editor
Published bimonthly

Landscape Trades

7856 Fifth Line South, R.R.4, Milton, ON L9T 2X8
Phone: (905) 875-1805 Fax: (905) 875-0183
Contact: Linda Erskine, editor
Published 9 times a year

Prairie Landscape Magazine

237 – 8th Avenue, Unit 600, Calgary, AB T2G 5C3
Phone: (403) 264-3270 Fax: (403) 264-3276
Contact: Nigel Bowles, editor
Published bimonthly

Turf & Recreation

123B King Street, Delhi, ON N4B 1X9
Phone: (519) 582-8873 Fax: (519) 582-8877
Contact: Mike Jiggens, editor
Published 7 times a year

Media, Music, & Communications

Broadcast Technology
264 Queen's Quay W., P.O. Box 803, Toronto, ON M5J 1B5
Phone: (416) 260-9364 Fax: (416) 260-9372
Contact: Lee Noel Rickwood, editor
Published 10 times a year

Broadcaster
1450 Don Mills Road, Don Mills, ON M3B 2X7
Phone: (416) 445-6641 Fax: (416) 442-2213
Contact: John Bugailiskis, editor
Published 10 times a year

Cablecaster
1450 Don Mills Road, Don Mills, ON M3B 2X7
Phone: (416) 445-6641 Fax: (416) 442-2213
Contact: Steve Pawlett, editor
Published 8 times a year

Canada on Location
366 Adelaide Street W., Suite 500, Toronto, ON M5V 1R9
Phone: (416) 408-2300 Fax: (416) 408-0870
Contact: Mary Maddever, editor
Published twice a year

Canadian Music Trade
23 Hannover Drive, Unit 7, St. Catharines, ON L2W 1A3
Phone: (905) 641-1512 Fax: (905) 641-1648
Contact: Carolyn Heinze, editor
Published bimonthly

Masthead: The Magazine about Magazines
1606 Sedlescomb Drive, Unit 8, Mississauga, ON L4X 1M6
Phone: (905) 625-7070 Fax: (905) 625-4856
Contact: Patrick Walsh, editor
Published 10 times a year

Media

Carleton University, St. Patrick's Building, Room 316B, 1125
    Colonel By Drive, Ottawa, ON K1S 5B6
Phone: (613) 526-8061 Fax: (613) 521-3904
Contact: David McKie, editor
Published quarterly

News Canada

366 Adelaide Street W., Suite 606, Toronto, ON M5V 1R9
Phone: (416) 599-9900 Fax: (416) 599-9700
Contact: Linda Kroboth, editor
Published monthly

Press Review

P.O. Box 368, Station A, Toronto, ON M5W 1C2
Phone: (416) 368-0512 Fax: (416) 366-0104
Contact: Bryan Michael Cassidy, editor/publisher
Published quarterly

Playback

366 Adelaide Street W., Suite 500, Toronto, ON M5V 1R9
Phone: (416) 408-2300 Fax: (416) 408-0870
Contact: Mary Maddever, editor
Published biweekly

RealScreen

366 Adelaide Street W., Suite 500, Toronto, ON M5V 1R9
Phone: (416) 408-2300 Fax: (416) 408-0870
Contact: Mary Maddever, editor
Published monthly

Premiere Video Magazine

1314 Britannia Road E., Mississauga, ON L4W 1C8
Phone: (905) 564-1033 Fax: (905) 564-3398
Contact: Salah Bachir, editor
Published monthly

Professional Sound
23 Hannover Drive, Unit 7, St. Catharines, ON L2W 1A3
Phone: (905) 641-1512 Fax: (905) 641-1648
Contact: Shauna Kennedy, editor
Published bimonthly

The Publisher
90 Eglinton Avenue E., Suite 206, Toronto, ON M4P 2Y3
Phone: (416) 482-1090 Fax: (416) 482-1908
Contact: Robert MacKenzie, editor
Published 10 times a year

RPM Weekly
6 Brentcliffe Road, Toronto, ON M4G 3Y2
Phone: (416) 425-0257 Fax: (416) 425-8629
Contact: Walter Grealis, publisher

Miscellaneous Trade & Professional

Blue Line Magazine
12A – 4981 Suite 254, Highway 7E, Markham, ON L3R 1N1
Phone: (905) 640-3048 Fax: (905) 640-7547
Contact: Morley Lymburner, editor
Published 10 times a year

CM Condominium Manager
191 West Mall, Suite 1105, Etobicoke, ON M9C 5K8
Phone: (416) 626-7895 Fax: (416) 620-5392
Contact: Stephanie Cox, executive editor
Published quarterly

Campground & Cottage Resort Management
Target Publications, R.R.1, Elgin, ON K0G 1E0
Phone: (888) 219-5225 Fax: 613) 359-6456
Contact: James Barton, publisher/editor
Published bimonthly

Canadian Apparel Manufacturer Magazine
555 Chabanel W., Suite 801, Montreal, PQ H2N 2H8
Phone: (514) 382-4243 Fax: (514) 382-4612
Contact: Gillian Crosby, publisher/editor
Published bimonthly

Canadian Defence Review
132 Adrian Crescent, Markham, ON L3P 7B3
Phone: (905) 472-2801 Fax: (905) 472-3091
Contact: Nick Stephens, managing editor
Published quarterly

The Canadian Firefighter
P.O. Box 95, Station D, Etobicoke, ON M9A 4X1
Phone: (416) 233-2516 Fax: (416) 233-2051
Contact: Lorne Campbell, editor/publisher
Published bimonthly

Canadian Footwear Journal
1, rue Pacifique, Ste.-Anne-de-Bellevue, PQ H9X 1C5
Phone: (514) 457-2423 Fax: (514) 457-2577
Contact: Barbara McLeish, managing editor
Published 8 times a year

The Canadian Funeral Director Magazine
174 Harwood Avenue S., Suite 206, Ajax, ON L1S 2H7
Phone: (905) 427-6121 Fax: (905) 427-1660
Contact: Scott Hillier, editor
Published monthly

Canadian Funeral News
237 – 8th Avenue S.E., Suite 600, Calgary, AB T2G 5C3
Phone: (403) 264-3270 Fax: (403) 264-3276
Contact: Natika Sunstrom, editor
Published monthly

Canadian HR Reporter
133 Richmond Street W., Suite 700, Toronto, ON M5H 3M8
Phone: (416) 869-1177 Fax: (416) 869-3288

Contact: Chris Knight, managing editor
Published 22 times a year

Canadian Home Economics Journal
151 Slater Street, Suite 307, Ottawa, ON KIP 5H3
Phone: (613) 238-8817 Fax: (613) 238-8972
Contact: J. Estelle Reddin, editor
Published quarterly

Canadian Home Style Magazine
598 Stillwater Court, Burlington, ON L7T 4G7
Phone: (905) 681-7932 Fax: (905) 681-2141
Contact: Laurie O'Halloran, publisher/editorial director
Published 7 times a year

Canadian Interiors
360 Dupont Street, Toronto, ON M5R 1V9
Phone: (416) 966-9944 Fax: (416) 966-9946
Contact: Sheri Craig, publisher/editor
Published bimonthly

Canadian Jeweller
1448 Lawrence Avenue W., Suite 302, Toronto, ON M4A 2V6
Phone: (416) 755-5199 Fax: (416) 755-9123
Contact: Carol Besler, editor
Published 7 times a year

Canadian Property Management
5255 Yonge Street, Suite 1000, North York, ON M2N 6P4
Phone: (416) 512-8186 Fax: (416) 512-8344
Contact: Angela Atlass, editor
Published 8 times a year

Canadian Realtor News
344 Slater Street, Suite 1600, Ottawa, ON KIR 7Y3
Phone: (613) 237-7111 Fax: (613) 234-2567
Contact: Jim McCarthy, editor
Published 10 times a year

Canadian Rental Service
145 Thames Road W., Exeter, ON N0M 1S3
Phone: (519) 235-2400 Fax: (519) 235-0798
Contact: Peter Darbishire, managing editor
Published 8 times a year

Canadian Security
46 Crockford Boulevard, Scarborough, ON M1R 3C3
Phone: (416) 755-4343 Fax: (416) 755-7487
Contact: Richard Skinulis, editor
Published 7 times a year

Canadian Veterinary Journal
339 Booth Street, Ottawa, ON K1R 7K1
Phone: (613) 236-1162 Fax: (613) 236-9681
Contact: Dr. Doug Hare, editor
Published monthly

Condominium Magazine
5255 Yonge Street, Suite 1000, North York, ON M2N 6P4
Phone: (416) 512-8186 Fax: (416) 512-8344
Contact: Kim Morningstar, managing editor
Published monthly

Cosmetics
777 Bay Street, 5th Floor, Toronto, ON M5W 1A7
Phone: (416) 596-5817 Fax: (416) 596-5179
Contact: Ron Wood, editor
Published bimonthly

Fire Fighting in Canada
222 Argyle Avenue, Delhi, ON N4B 2Y2
Phone: (519) 582-2513 Fax: (519) 582-4040
Contact: James Knisley, editor
Published 10 times a year

Focus
1025 Richmond Road, Suite 107, Ottawa, ON K2B 8G8
Phone: (613) 820-3272 Fax: (613) 820-3646

Contact: Richard Newport, editor
Published 8 times a year

Footwear Forum
1448 Lawrence Avenue E., Suite 302, Toronto, ON M4A 2V6
Phone: (416) 755-5199 Fax: (416) 755-9123
Contact: Victoria Curran, editor
Published 7 times a year

Gifts & Tablewares
1450 Don Mills Road, Don Mills, ON M3B 2X7
Phone: (416) 442-2996 Fax: (416) 442-2213
Contact: Dawn Dickinson, editor
Published 7 times a year

Glass Canada
145 Thames Road W., Exeter, ON NOM 1S3
Phone: (519) 235-2400 Fax: (519) 235-0798
Contact: Peter Darbishire, managing editor
Published bimonthly

The Hill Times
69 Sparks Street, Ottawa, ON KIP 5A5
Phone: (613) 232-5952 Fax: (613) 232-9055
Contact: Kate Malloy, managing editor
Published weekly

Lighting Magazine
395 Matheson Boulevard E., Mississauga, ON L4Z 2H2
Phone: (905) 890-1846 Fax: (905) 890-5769
Contact: Bryan Rogers, editor
Published bimonthly

Luggage, Leathergoods & Accessories
501 Oakdale Road, Downsview, ON M3N 1W7
Phone: (416) 746-7360 Fax: (416) 746-1421
Contact: Tammy Mang, publisher/editor
Published quarterly

Materials Management & Distribution
777 Bay Street, 6th Floor, Toronto, ON M5W 1A7
Phone: (416) 596-5708 Fax: (416) 596-5554
Contact: Rob Robertson, editor
Published monthly

Municipal World
P.O. Box 399, St. Thomas, ON N5P 3V3
Phone: (519) 633-0031 Fax: (519) 633-1001
Contact: Michael Smither, editor
Published monthly

News & Views
180 Yorkland Boulevard, North York, ON M2J 1R5
Phone: (416) 491-4301 Fax: (416) 494-4948
Contact: Elizabeth Alexander, editor
Published monthly

Optical Prism
31 Hastings Drive, Unionville, ON L3R 4Y5
Phone: (905) 475-9343 Fax: (905) 477-2821
Contact: Allan Vezina, editor/publisher
Published 9 times a year

Salon Magazine
411 Richmond Street E., Suite 300, Toronto, ON M5A 3S5
Phone: (416) 869-3131 Fax: (416) 869-3008
Contact: Alison Wood, editor
Published 8 times a year

Style
1448 Lawrence Avenue E., Suite 302, Toronto, ON M4A 2V6
Phone: (416) 755-5199 Fax: (416) 755-9123
Contact: Doris Montanero, editor
Published 14 times a year

Toys & Games
364 Supertest Road, Suite 203, North York, ON M3J 2M2
Phone: (416) 665-4666 Fax: (416) 665-2775

Contact: Lynn Winston, editor
Published bimonthly

Woodworking
135 Spy Court, Markham, ON L3R 5H6
Phone: (905) 477-3222 Fax: (905) 477-4320
Contact: Maurice Holtham, editor
Published 7 times a year

Printing & Photography

Canadian Printer
777 Bay Street, Toronto, ON M5W 1A7
Phone: (416) 596-5898 Fax: (416) 596-5965
Contact: Stephen Forbes, editor
Published 10 times a year

EC&I (Electronic Composition & Imaging)
2240 Midland Avenue, Suite 201, Scarborough, ON M1P 4R8
Phone: (416) 299-6007 Fax: (416) 299-6674
Contact: Rusell Keziere, editor
Published bimonthly

Graphic Monthly
1606 Sedlescomb Drive, Unit 8, Mississauga, ON L4X 1M6
Phone: (905) 625-7070 Fax: (905) 625-4856
Contact: Nancy Clark, managing editor
Published bimonthly

Photo Retailer
55 King Street W., Suite 2550, P.O. Box 77, Toronto, ON M5K 1E7
Phone: (416) 692-2110 Fax: (416) 692-3392
Contact: Don Long, editor
Published 3 times a year

Photonews & Electronic Imaging
101 Thorncliffe Park Drive, Toronto, ON M4H 1M2
Phone: (416) 421-7944 Fax: (416) 421-0966

Contact: Gunter Ott, editor
Published 3 times a year

PrintAction
2240 Midland Avenue, Suite 201, Scarborough, ON M1P 4R8
Phone: (416) 299-6007 Fax: (416) 299-6674
Contact: Vincent de Franco, editor
Published monthly

Second Impressions
35 Mill Drive, St. Albert, AB T8N 1J5
Phone: (403) 458-9889 Fax: (403) 458-9839
Contact: Loretta Puckrin, publisher
Published bimonthly

Transportation & Cargo

Atlantic Transportation Journal
900 Windmill Road, Unit 107, Dartmouth, NS B3B 1P7
Phone: (902) 468-8027 Fax: (902) 468-2425
Contact: Ken Partridge, managing editor
Published quarterly

Canadian Shipper
777 Bay Street, Toronto, ON M5W 1A7
Phone: (416) 596-5708 Fax: (416) 596-5554
Contact: Robert Robertson, editor
Published bimonthly

Canadian Transportation & Logistics
1450 Don Mills Road, Don Mills, ON M3B 2X7
Phone: (416) 442-2228 Fax: (416) 442-2214
Contact: Paul Briggs, editor
Published monthly

Harbour & Shipping
1865 Marine Drive, Suite 200, West Vancouver, BC V7V 1J7
Phone: (604) 922-6717 Fax: (604) 922-1739

Contact: Liz Bennett, editor
Published monthly

Motor Truck
1450 Don Mills Road, Don Mills, ON M3B 2X7
Phone: (416) 445-2062 Fax: (416) 442-2213
Contact: Lou Smyrlis, editor
Published bimonthly

Today's Trucking
130 Belfield Road, Etobicoke, ON M9W 1G1
Phone: (416) 614-2200 Fax: (416) 614-8861
Contact: Rolf Lockwood, editor
Published 10 times a year

Truck News
1450 Don Mills Road, Don Mills, ON M3B 2X7
Phone: (416) 442-2062 Fax: (416) 442-2092
Contact: John G. Smith, editor
Published monthly

Travel

Canadian Travel Press
310 Dupont Street, Toronto, ON M5R 1V9
Phone: (416) 968-7252 Fax: (416) 968-2377
Contact: Edith Baxter, editor-in-chief
Published weekly

Canadian Traveller
780 Beatty Street, Suite 300, Vancouver, BC V6B 2M1
Phone: (604) 606-4644 Fax: (604) 606-4612
Contacts: Eldrid and Ursula Retief, editors
Published monthly

Meetings & Incentive Travel
777 Bay Street, 5th Floor, Toronto, ON M5W 1A7
Phone: (416) 596-2697 Fax: (416) 596-5810

Contact: Julie Charles, editor
Published 7 times a year

Tours on Motorcoach
C.P. 365, Montreal, PQ H2Y 3H1
Phone: (514) 274-0004 Fax: (514) 274-5884
Contact: Guy Jonkman, publisher/editor
Published monthly

Travel Courier
310 Dupont Street, Toronto, ON M5R 1V9
Phone: (416) 968-7252 Fax: (416) 968-2377
Contact: Edith Baxter, editor-in-chief
Published weekly

Travelweek Bulletin
282 Richmond Street E., Suite 100, Toronto, ON M5A 1P4
Phone: (416) 365-1500 Fax: (416) 365-1504
Contact: Patrick Dineen, editor
Published twice a week

4

DAILY NEWSPAPERS

Many a successful writing career began in the pages of a small community newspaper or local daily. High-profile, high-circulation magazines are alluring, but top-quality magazine pieces are among the most difficult of literary forms, and many editors are disinclined to try out inexperienced writers. Discouragement mounts with each rejection slip, often to the point where a promising writing career is abandoned. A planned approach to becoming a published writer is the surest road to success.

Weekly community newspapers are a good starting point. With small staffs and low budgets (and no wire services to rely on), their editors are often happy to accept outside contributions, particularly feature articles that cover the local scene. And since payment is modest, there is little competition from more experienced writers. Many established writers began by writing for no pay for their local paper. (Phone or speak to the editors directly, since they have neither the time nor the resources to respond to written queries.)

Always remember that news loses its value as quickly as it changes, and it is therefore usually gathered hurriedly – on large papers and small – by staff reporters. Therefore, it is to your advantage to concentrate on background stories about ongoing issues, or to write profiles of prominent, interesting, or unusual local citizens and institutions. Stories about travel, hobbies, lifestyles, personal finance, and business are particularly welcome. So are strong human-interest pieces – always among the best-read articles in any newspaper. Most editors like to build up a resource of timely articles that do not have to be used immediately.

Writers do not propose ideas to daily newspapers in the same way as they do for magazines. On newspapers, time is a much more crucial factor. So, again, rather than craft a written proposal, it is perfectly acceptable to solicit a go-ahead decision from the editor of one of the paper's sections with a quick telephone call. Initially, however, they will probably want to see tearsheets of published work. If they have published your letters, it may be worth including clippings of these, too.

If you are considering this market, your best preparation is to read critically several issues of the newspaper. Note the paper's editorial approach, the style, the story lengths preferred, the use of photographs, and the difference in content, construction, and tone of news stories and feature articles. If you have never studied journalism, you might need a reference book, such as *News Reporting and Writing*, by Melvin Mencher, a professor at Columbia University's School of Journalism (see Chapter 11, Book Resources).

Naturally, it will take more experience to sell to large, well-staffed metropolitan dailies like the *Toronto Star* or the *Winnipeg Free Press*. But even here, the outside contributor has a chance, provided he or she has some specialized knowledge, can handle human-interest material deftly, and can write full-bodied issue stories with conviction and authority. For a well-written, well-researched article on an important or intriguing subject, many of the bigger city dailies pay as much as or more than the average consumer magazine. And they settle faster: most pay at the end of the month, some even on acceptance.

Freelance writers submit their manuscripts to newspapers in much the same way as they do for magazines, and many write successfully for both. They meet deadlines even when it means losing sleep. They are always aware that for the daily press, accuracy and reliability are two virtues worth cultivating, even under pressure. While the news story is essentially factual and must have a strong sense of immediacy, the feature article needs body and strength as well as originality and freshness. Timing is a key element. Keep a calendar of dates for seasonal stories – Hallowe'en, Thanksgiving, Chinese New Year, Canada Day, and so on – and read behind the news for feature ideas.

Besides writing for your city paper, look for opportunities to act as a correspondent, or stringer, for one published elsewhere. The full listing of English-language Canadian daily newspapers that follows will prove useful. For suburban weeklies, check the *CARD* directory. Canadian newspapers are also listed in *Matthews Media Directory* and annual publications such as the *Canadian Almanac & Directory* and *Corpus Almanac and Canadian Sourcebook* (see Chapter 11, Book Resources).

Alberta

Calgary Herald
215 – 16th Street S.E., Calgary, AB T2P 0W8
Phone: (403) 235-7396 Fax: (403) 235-7189

Calgary Sun
2615 – 12th Street N.E., Calgary, AB T2E 7W9
Phone: (403) 250-4200 Fax: (403) 250-4258

Daily Herald Tribune
10604 – 100th Street, Grande Prairie, AB T8V 2M5
Phone: (403) 532-1110 Fax: (403) 532-2120

Edmonton Journal
10006 – 101st Street, P.O. Box 2421, Edmonton, AB T5J 2S6
Phone: (403) 429-5400 Fax: (403) 498-5604

Edmonton Sun
4990 – 92nd Avenue, Suite 250, Edmonton, AB T6B 3A1
Phone: (403) 468-0154 Fax: (403) 468-0128

Fort McMurray Today
8550 Franklin Avenue, Bag 4008, Fort McMurray, AB T9H 3G1
Phone: (403) 743-8186 Fax: (403) 790-1006

Lethbridge Herald
504 – 7th Street S., Lethbridge, AB T1J 3Z7
Phone: (403) 328-4411 Fax: (403) 329-8089

Medicine Hat News
3257 Dunmore Road S.E., P.O. Box 10, Medicine Hat, AB T1A 7E6
Phone: (403) 527-1101 Fax: (403) 527-6029

Red Deer Advocate
2950 Bremner Avenue, Bag 5200, P.O. Box 250, Red Deer,
    AB T4N 5G3
Phone: (403) 343-2400 Fax: (403) 342-4051

British Columbia

Alaska Highway News
9916 – 98th Street, Fort St. John, BC V1J 3T8
Phone: (604) 785-5631 Fax: (604) 785-3522

Alberni Valley Times
4918 Napier Street, P.O. Box 400, Port Alberni, BC V9Y 7N1
Phone: (250) 723-8171 Fax: (250) 723-0586

Cranbrook Daily Townsman
822 Cranbrook Street N., Cranbrook, BC V1C 3R9
Phone: (604) 426-5201 Fax: (604) 426-5003

Kamloops Daily News
393 Seymour Street, Kamloops, BC V2C 6P6
Phone: (604) 372-2331 Fax: (604) 372-0823

Kelowna Daily Courier
550 Doyle Avenue, Kelowna, BC V1Y 7V1
Phone: (604) 762-4445 Fax: (604) 762-3866

Kimberley Daily Bulletin
335 Spokane Street, Kimberley, BC V1A 1Y9
Phone: (250) 427-5333

Nanaimo Daily News
2575 McCullough Road, Nanaimo, BC V9S 5W5
Phone: (250) 758-4917 Fax: (250) 758-4513

Nelson Daily News
266 Baker Street, Nelson, BC VIL 4H3
Phone: (604) 352-3552 Fax: (604) 352-2418

Peace River Block News
901 – 100th Avenue, P.O. Box 180, Dawson Creek, BC VIG 4G6
Phone: (250) 782-4888 Fax: (250) 782-6770

Penticton Herald
186 Nanaimo Avenue W., Penticton, BC V2A 1N4
Phone: (250) 492-4002 Fax: (250) 492-2403

Prince George Citizen
150 Brunswick Street, P.O. Box 5700, Prince George, BC V2L 5K9
Phone: (250) 562-2441 Fax: (250) 562-9201

Prince Rupert Daily News
801 – 2nd Avenue W., Prince Rupert, BC V8J 1H6
Phone: (604) 624-6781 Fax: (604) 624-2851

Trail Times
1163 Cedar Avenue, Trail, BC VIR 4B8
Phone: (250) 364-1416 Fax: (250) 368-8550

Vancouver Sun Province
200 Granville Street, Suite 1, Vancouver, BC V6C 3N3
Phone: (604) 732-2478 Fax: (604) 732-2704

Victoria Times–Colonist
2621 Douglas Street, P.O. Box 300, Victoria, BC V8W 2N4
Phone: (604) 380-5211 Fax: (604) 380-5353

Manitoba

Brandon Sun
501 Rosser Avenue, Brandon, MB R7A 5Z6
Phone: (204) 727-2451 Fax: (204) 725-0976

Daily Graphic
1941 Saskatchewan Avenue W., P.O. Box 130, Portage La Prairie,
  MB RIN 3B4
Phone: (204) 857-3427 Fax: (204) 239-1270

The Reminder
P.O. Box 727, 10 North Avenue, Flin Flon, MB R8A IN5
Phone: (204) 687-3454 Fax: (204) 687-4473

Winnipeg Free Press
1355 Mountain Avenue, Winnipeg, MB R2X 3B6
Phone: (204) 697-7000 Fax: (204) 697-7370

Winnipeg Sun
1700 Church Avenue, Winnipeg, MB R2X 3A2
Phone: (204) 694-2022 Fax: (204) 632-8709

New Brunswick

Fredericton Daily Gleaner
Prospect Street at Smythe, P.O. Box 3370, Fredericton, NB E3B 5A2
Phone: (506) 452-6671 Fax: (506) 452-7405

Moncton Times–Transcript
939 Main Street, P.O. Box 1001, Moncton, NB E1C 8P3
Phone: (506) 859-4900 Fax: 859-4899

Telegraph Journal/Times Globe
210 Crown Street, P.O. Box 2350, Saint John, NB E2L 3V8
Phone: (506) 632-8888 Fax: (506) 648-2661

Newfoundland

Evening Telegram
P.O. Box 5970, St. John's, NF AIC 5X7
Phone: (709) 364-6300 Fax: (709) 364-9333

Western Star
West Street, P.O. Box 460, Corner Brook, NF A2H 6E7
Phone: (709) 634-4348 Fax: (709) 634-9824

Nova Scotia

Amherst Daily News
P.O. Box 280, Amherst, NS B4H 3Z2
Phone: (902) 667-5102 Fax: (902) 667-0419

Cape Breton Post
255 George Street, Box 1500, Sydney, NS B1P 6K6
Phone: (902) 564-5451 Fax: (902) 562-7077

Chronicle–Herald & Mail-Star
1650 Argyle Street, Halifax, NS B3J 2T2
Phone: (902) 426-2898 Fax: (902) 426-3382

Daily News
P.O. Box 8330, Station A, Halifax, NS B3K 5M1
Phone: (902) 468-2288 Fax: (902) 468-3609

Evening News
352 East River Road, New Glasgow, NS B2H 5E2
Phone: (902) 752-3000 Fax: (902) 752-1945

Truro Daily News
6 Louise Street, P.O. Box 220, Truro, NS B2N 5C3
Phone: (902) 893-9405 Fax: (902) 893-0518

Ontario

Barrie Examiner
16 Bayfield Street, Barrie, ON L4M 4T6
Phone: (705) 728-2414 Fax: (705) 726-7706

The Beacon-Herald
108 Ontario Street, P.O. Box 430, Stratford, ON N5A 6T6
Phone: (519) 271-2220   Fax: (519) 271-1026

Brockville Recorder & Times
23 King Street W., Box 10, Brockville, ON K6V 5T8
Phone: (613) 342-4441   Fax: (613) 342-4456

Cambridge Reporter
26 Ainslie Street S., Cambridge, ON N1R 3K1
Phone: (519) 621-3810   Fax: (519) 621-8239

Chatham Daily News
45 – 4th Street, Box 2007, Chatham, ON N7M 2G4
Phone: (519) 354-2000   Fax: (519) 436-0949

Cobourg Daily Star
415 King Street W., Box 400, Cobourg, ON K9A 4L1
Phone: (905) 372-0131   Fax: (905) 372-4966

Cornwall Standard–Freeholder
44 Pitt Street, Cornwall, ON K6J 3P3
Phone: (613) 933-3160   Fax: (613) 933-7521

Daily Miner & News
33 Main Street S., P.O. Box 1620, Kenora, ON P9N 3X7
Phone: (807) 468-5555   Fax: (807) 468-4318

Daily Observer
186 Alexander Street, Pembroke, ON K8A 4L9
Phone: (613) 732-3691   Fax: (613) 732-2645

The Examiner
400 Water Street, P.O. Box 3890, Peterborough, ON K9J 8L4
Phone: (705) 745-4641   Fax: (705) 741-3217

The Expositor
53 Dalhousie Street, Brantford, ON N3T 5S8
Phone: (519) 756-2020   Fax: (519) 756-4911

Financial Post
333 King Street E., Toronto, ON M5A 4N2
Phone: (416) 350-6000 Fax: (416) 350-6031

Fort Frances Daily Bulletin
P.O. Box 339, Fort Frances, ON P9A 3M7
Phone: (807) 274-5373 Fax: (807) 274-7286

Globe and Mail
444 Front Street W., Toronto, ON M5V 2S9
Phone: (416) 585-5600 Fax: (416) 585-5275

Guelph Mercury
14 Macdonell Street, Suite 8, Guelph, ON N1H 6P7
Phone: (519) 822-4310 Fax: (519) 767-1681

Hamilton Spectator
44 Frid Street, Hamilton, ON L8N 3G3
Phone: (416) 526-3333 Fax: (416) 522-1696

The Intelligencer
45 Bridge Street E., Belleville, ON K8N 1L5
Phone: (613) 962-9171 Fax: (613) 962-9652

Kingston Whig–Standard
P.O. Box 2300, 6 Cataraqui Street, Kingston, ON K7L 4Z7
Phone: (613) 544-5000 Fax: (613) 530-4122

Kitchener–Waterloo Record
225 Fairway Road, Kitchener, ON N2G 4E5
Phone: (519) 894-2231 Fax: (519) 894-0292

Lindsay Daily Post
15 William Street N., Lindsay, ON K9V 3Z8
Phone: (705) 324-2114 Fax: (705) 324-0174

London Free Press
369 York Street, Box 2280, London, ON N6A 4G1
Phone: (519) 679-6666 Fax: (519) 667-4523

Niagara Falls Review
4801 Valley Way, Box 270, Niagara Falls, ON L2E 6T6
Phone: (905) 358-5711 Fax: (905) 356-0785

North Bay Nugget
259 Worthington Street W., P.O. Box 570, North Bay, ON P1B 8J6
Phone: (705) 472-3200 Fax: (705) 472-1438

Northern Daily News
8 Duncan Avenue, Kirkland Lake, ON P2N 3L4
Phone: (705) 567-5321 Fax: (705) 567-6162

Orillia Packet & Times
31 Colborne Street E., Orillia, ON L3V 1T4
Phone: (705) 325-1355 Fax: (705) 325-7691

Ottawa Citizen
1101 Baxter Road, Box 5020, Ottawa, ON K2C 3M4
Phone: (613) 829-9100 Fax: (613) 726-1198

Ottawa Sun
380 Hunt Club Road, Ottawa, ON K1G 5H7
Phone: (613) 739-7100

Pembroke Daily News
86 Pembroke Street W., Box 10, Pembroke, ON K8A 6X1
Phone: (613) 735-3141 Fax: (613) 732-7214

Port Hope Evening Guide
415 King Street W., Box 400, Cobourg, ON K9A 4L1
Phone: (905) 372-0131 Fax: (905) 372-4966

St. Catharines Standard
17 Queen Street, St. Catharines, ON L2R 5G5
Phone: (905) 684-7251 Fax: (905) 684-8011

St. Thomas Times–Journal
16 Hincks Street, St. Thomas, ON N5P 3W6
Phone: (519) 631-2790 Fax: (519) 631-5653

Sarnia Observer
140 South Front Street, Sarnia, ON N7T 7M8
Phone: (519) 344-3641 Fax: (519) 332-2951

Sault Ste. Marie Star
145 Old Garden River Road, Sault Ste. Marie, ON P6A 5M5
Phone: (705) 759-3030 Fax: (705) 942-8690

The Sentinel Review
16 Brock Street, Woodstock, ON N4S 8A5
Phone: (519) 537-2341 Fax: (519) 537-3049

Simcoe Reformer
105 Donly Drive, Simcoe, ON N3Y 4L2
Phone: (519) 426-5710 Fax: (519) 426-9255

Sudbury Star
33 Mackenzie Street, Sudbury, ON P3C 4Y1
Phone: (705) 674-5271 Fax: (705) 674-0624

The Sun–Times
290 – 9th Street E., Owen Sound, ON N4K 5P2
Phone: (519) 376-2250 Fax: (519) 376-7190

Thunder Bay Chronical–Journal
75 South Cumberland Street, Thunder Bay, ON P7B 1A3
Phone: (807) 343-6200 Fax: (807) 345-3582

Timmins Daily Press
187 Cedar Street S., Timmins, ON P4N 2G9
Phone: (705) 268-5050 Fax: (705) 268-7373

Toronto Star
1 Yonge Street, Suite 300, Toronto, ON M5E 1E6
Phone: (416) 869-4321 Fax: (416) 869-4416

Toronto Sun
333 King Street E., Toronto, ON M5A 3X5
Phone: (416) 947-2333 Fax: (416) 361-1205

Welland–Port Colborne Tribune
228 East Main Street, Welland, ON L3B 3W8
Phone: (416) 732-2411 Fax: (416) 732-4883

Windsor Star
167 Ferry Street, Windsor, ON N9A 4M5
Phone: (519) 255-5711 Fax: (519) 255-5778

Prince Edward Island

The Guardian
165 Prince Street, Charlottetown, PE C1A 4R7
Phone: (902) 629-6000 Fax: (902) 566-3808

Journal Pioneer
4 Queen Street, Box 2480, Summerside, PE C1N 4K5
Phone: (902) 436-2121 Fax: (902) 436-3027

Quebec

The Gazette
250 St. Antoine Street W., Montreal, PQ H2Y 3R7
Phone: (514) 987-2399 Fax: (514) 987-2323

The Record
2850 Delorme Street, Sherbrooke, PQ J1K 1A1
Phone: (819) 569-9525 Fax: (819) 569-3945

Saskatchewan

Daily Herald
30 – 10th Street E., Prince Albert, SK S6V 5R9
Phone: (306) 764-4276 Fax: (306) 763-3119

Daily Times
4828 – 44th Street, Lloydminster, SK S9V 0G8
Phone: (306) 825-5522 Fax: (306) 825-3207

LeaderPost
1964 Park Street, Regina, SK S4P 3G4
Phone: (306) 565-8211 Fax: (306) 565-8350

The StarPhoenix
204 – 5th Avenue N., Saskatoon, SK S7K 2P1
Phone: (306) 664-8340 Fax: (306) 664-8208

Times–Herald
44 Fairford Street W., Moose Jaw, SK S6H 6E4
Phone: (306) 692-6441 Fax: (306) 694-1216

Yukon

Whitehorse Star
2149 – 2nd Avenue, Whitehorse, YT Y1A 1C5
Phone: (403) 668-2060 Fax: (403) 668-7130

5

BOOK PUBLISHERS

Unless they are crafting novels or writing on subjects deeply personal to them, professional writers rarely produce books on spec. The hard work involved – research and revisions stretched over months or years – is better invested in a firm commitment from a publisher. This follows a full proposal on how the book will be shaped, what each chapter will include, and how it will be written. Where an unpublished writer is concerned, however, most publishers will not make a final commitment until they have read the finished manuscript.

The first-time author should be under no illusions about the difficulties of breaking into the book publishing market – still less, unless you are phenomenally talented or hit on that rare winning formula, of making a living from the often slender proceeds. Nonetheless, every year brings a new success story – another brilliant unknown author takes the publishing world by storm. Every writer must be a realist, *and* an optimist.

Professional writers will attest that writing books is a little easier after having consistently fed well-tailored articles to top magazines. As opposed to a long newspaper story, the magazine piece, in design, content, tone, and colour, conforms more closely to a short book, and can be a logical stepping-stone to longer, more substantial works. On the other hand, some publishers put greater trust in the newcomer than the journalist-turned-author. Certainly the disciplines are very different, though there are plenty of professional writers who have successfully crossed these boundaries. Many experienced Canadian authors supplement their royalty cheques with earnings from their magazine contributions.

Canada has all kinds of book publishers – from small presses producing a couple of titles a year to large houses that turn out as many as a hundred or more. Most larger houses can offer authors an advance against royalties on acceptance of their proposal, though this is seldom the case with small and scholarly presses. Depending on the author's record and the book's potential in the marketplace, an advance can range from a couple of thousand to underwrite the cost of a laptop computer to tens of thousands. After publication, and once the advance has been earned, the author receives a royalty cheque every six or twelve months for the life of his or her book. An average royalty on a hardcover book is 10 per cent of the selling price. At this rate, a 3,000-copy sale of a $25 book could eventually yield the writer $7,500, although book club and other discount sales will often reduce this sum. Usually, authors can expect an 8 per cent royalty on the paperback version, but because it is cheaper than a hardcover, the paperback is likely to sell through in larger quantities so may be a bigger money-spinner. Some small presses offer royalties in copies, usually 10 per cent of the print run for adult books.

Small presses are more likely to take an interest in an unpublished writer, and are generally more receptive to unsolicited manuscripts. They also may be more accessible, offer more personal attention to their authors, and be more willing to take a risk. Nino Ricci's prize-winning first novel, *Lives of the Saints*, was published by Cormorant Books, having been rejected by a raft of the larger players. But he had no difficulty placing his eagerly awaited second novel with McClelland & Stewart. Small presses almost always work with unagented writers. On the down side, small publishers can rarely offer an advance, their print runs tend to be low, and their distribution systems cannot match those of the big houses.

While editors are always on the lookout for high-quality fiction, non-fiction books are far easier to market. Books are normally bought well in advance of publication. Manuscripts for fall books are usually required to be on an editor's desk by January or February. The contract for each book will usually have been signed a year or eighteen months prior to publication. Occasionally a title rejected by a publisher one year will be bought a couple of years later, when it fits better with the publisher's current needs. A book may be turned down because the publisher has a similar one under way. If you study a big trade publisher's list for one season, you'll notice that it does not publish a random selection of books so much as an editorial program of releases likely to satisfy a range of tastes.

You can save yourself much wasted time and dashed hopes by undertaking a little research into the Canadian publishing scene *before* you submit your proposal or manuscript. Use this chapter to draw up a shortlist of publishers whose programs seem most compatible with your own work, then check out some of their books at a good bookstore. If this is not practical, write to their publicity departments, including a large SASE, to request current catalogues. Better still, visit their web site, if they have one. Familiarity with the programs of several houses can help you develop an attractive proposal as well as target the most appropriate potential publishers.

Given how difficult it is to place a manuscript, it's worth re-emphasizing the importance of an attractive, interesting, well-presented proposal. Editors simply do not have the time to unravel an ill-prepared proposal or to sift through unwieldy, indifferently written manuscripts that arrive unannounced. It's always best to know the name of the editor or publisher to whom you are submitting. Manuscripts addressed to "The Editor" often end up in the slush pile, where they can languish indefinitely. The sad truth is that most of the unsolicited material that crosses editors' desks is unpublishable. Your aim must be to present a submission that will stand out dramatically from the rest. Generally, a detailed outline together with a sample chapter and a covering letter will be received best. *Always* include an SASE if you want your material returned, and prepare for a wait of up to two or three months for the editor's response. What the editor will be looking for is originality, a strong, timely central idea, intelligent organization, clarity, an engaging writing style, and, of course, "saleability." Marketing information is always useful. Enclose a list of recent books on similar subjects with your submission (check *Books in Print* at the library). Think about your audience and how the publisher might best reach it.

It is a truism that would-be authors must learn to cope with rejection. First-timers might draw comfort from the knowledge of how many great writers could paper their walls with publishers' rejection letters received early in their careers. (Faulkner's great work *The*

Sound and the Fury was rejected thirteen times before finding a publisher, as, coincidentally, was William Kennedy's Pulitzer Prize-winning *Ironweed*. On an altogether different scale, big-selling English crime writer John Creasey is said to have received no fewer than 744 rejections during his career!) Since editors usually don't have time to issue more than a standard rejection note, take heart if the rejection is sugared with qualified praise or, better still, specific constructive criticism. Chances are the editor is not simply letting you down gently but genuinely sees value in your work. Be open to suggestions, and consider reworking your manuscript if the advice seems sensible. You may even be able to resubmit to the same editor.

Writing is an isolating occupation, and it is good for morale as well as immensely practical to tap into one or more of the many writers' groups that exist in the community – a list of provincial associations is provided in Chapter 10. For professional writers with at least one published book behind them, valuable support is available from the Writers' Union of Canada (with offices in Toronto and Vancouver), which offers members an impressive array of services and resources, from assistance with contracts and grievances with publishers to a manuscript evaluation service, and a range of practical publications, along with other benefits. Some of the union's professional guides that may be ordered by non-members for a small cost are *Anthology Rates and Contracts, Income Tax Guide for Writers, Author and Literary Agent, Author and Editor, Writers' Guide to Canadian Publishers, Ghost Writing, Libel: A Handbook for Canadian Publishers, Editors and Writers,* and *Contracts Self-Help Package* (including *Model Trade Book Contract, Help Yourself to a Better Contract,* and *Writers' Guide to Electronic Publishing Rights*). Above all, the Writers' Union of Canada gives its members the opportunity to share their concerns and experiences with fellow writers, providing a forum for collective action to support their interests.

Many of these services are also available to members of the Canadian Authors Association, which has branches across the country. Founded in Montreal in 1921, the CAA has represented the interests of Canadian writers on many fronts, from championing improved copyright protection and the Public Lending Right to helping individual writers improve their contracts with publishers. (The Public Lending Right provides published writers with income from books held in libraries by compensating them according to how often their books are borrowed. In 1993, according to *Masthead* magazine, 8,393 authors received an average of $821 each. It may come as no surprise that federal cuts have since reduced this benefit.) The CAA publish the quarterly magazine *Canadian Author* and *The Canadian Writer's Guide*, a handbook for freelance writers. They also administer several major literary awards (see Chapter 7), and local branches hold writing classes, workshops, and literary competitions, and organize author tours.

The Writers' Development Trust is another national non-profit service organization mandated to advance and nurture Canadian writers and writing, and for more than twenty years, working with an ever-changing pool of corporate partners, they have done just that in a number of practical and creative ways. Here are some of them:

- Writers in Electronic Residence (WIER) links professional writers with school students via the Internet in a kind of virtual writers' workshop. Each year the Trust, in partnership with York University, employs fifteen authors to work on this project. In 1997 WIER participated in a total of 111 classes from 79 schools (eight provinces and both territories were represented).
- They help to organize public readings and bring authors into high-school classrooms across the country.
- They sponsor no fewer than six major writing awards (see Chapter 7).
- They support the Woodcock Fund to provide bridge funding for established writers facing financial crisis, and they support the Canadian Writers' Foundation, a body that helps impecunious senior writers in financial need.
- They help raise the profile of Canadian writers and writing through public manifestations such as Canada Book Day and the annual Great Literary Dinner Party.

Specialist writers' organizations, too, offer resources and support to writers in their field. The Canadian Society of Children's Authors, Illustrators and Performers (CANSCAIP), through its newsletter, regular meetings, and other organized activities, offers practical advice, moral support, and useful contacts to writers of children's books. The Canadian Children's Book Centre in Toronto also offers writers and illustrators of children's books a range of resources and services. The centre has a comprehensive reference library of children's books and promotes children's writers and titles through author tours and book readings. Their publication *Get Published: The Writing for Children Kit* is particularly useful for aspiring children's authors.

Before outlining what we do cover in this chapter, perhaps it's worth clarifying what we don't. Educational publishers are not listed unless they have a significant trade publishing arm. Today more than ever, educational publishers are commissioning their books in close collaboration with schools and colleges to meet specific curricular needs. These texts are nearly always written by specialists in the field. Very few educational publishers consider unsolicited manuscripts or proposals, and fewer still are likely to look favourably upon them unless their author has a proven track record in the area.

Neither, with a few exceptions, have we included publishers that specialize in poetry. For a comprehensive listing, consult *Poetry Markets for Canadians* (6th edition), published by the League of Canadian Poets. Also, as mentioned in the Introduction, we have again focused on English-language publishing houses only. On the other hand, we have included a selection of hitherto unrepresented small presses interested in receiving manuscripts.

The inventory that follows, then, includes almost all the major (a couple begged off for fear of an inundation of unwanted submissions) and mid-range and many of the smaller English-language trade publishers currently operating in Canada. Some have large general interest lists; others are more specialized, either in their subject areas or in their regional concerns; all offer market opportunities for your work. Wherever possible, we have included e-mail addresses and web sites in this edition. It is well worth checking out a publisher's web page before approaching them with a submission, since it will offer an overview of the house's publishing program and interests, usually including abstracts of and/or excerpts from current titles. Often it will also include guidelines for author submissions.

The Anglican Book Centre
600 Jarvis Street, Toronto, ON M4Y 2J6
Phone: (416) 924-9192 Fax: (416) 924-2760

Contact: Robert Maclennan, publisher

Publishes manuscripts by Canadians on religious and contemporary issues, such as theology, spirituality, life issues, peace, justice, and feminism. Produced 15 new titles in 1997. No unsolicited manuscripts. Accepts written inquiries, with outline and sample chapter, in the stated areas of interest.

Notable 1997 title: *Mansions of the Spirit*, Michael Ingham.

Annick Press

15 Patricia Avenue, North York, ON M2M 1H9
Phone: (416) 221-4802 Fax: (416) 221-8400
E-mail: annickpress@powerwindows.ca
Contact: the editor

Established 1975. Publishes children's literature, mainly picture books with some non-fiction and pre-teen novels. Annick titles "project supportive and positive messages to young readers while also entertaining and enthralling them." Released 29 new titles in 1997. Accepts unsolicited manuscripts, but first send outline and sample chapters. "Be sure your submission is appropriate to our list and that you include an SASE." No faxed or e-mailed submissions accepted. Guidelines available.

Notable 1997 title: *Ogre Fun*, Loris Lesynski.

Anvil Press

175 East Broadway, Suite 204A, Vancouver, BC V5T 1W2
Phone: (604) 876-8710 Fax: (604) 879-2667
E-mail: subter@pinc.com
Contact: Brian Kaufman, managing editor

A small literary press interested in work from new and established writers. Publishes contemporary work in all genres. Releases 4 books a year. Accepts unsolicited manuscripts. Send synopsis with sample chapter or two. Expect a wait of 3 to 4 months for reply. Send #10 SASE for reply without manuscript. Guidelines available.

Notable 1997 title: *Salvage King, Ya!*, Mark Anthony Jarman.

Arsenal Pulp Press

103 – 1014 Homer Street, Vancouver, BC V6B 2W9
Phone: (604) 687-4233 Fax: (604) 669-8250
E-mail: arsenal@pinc.com

Contact: Linda Field, editor

Established 1971. Publishes literary fiction, cultural and gender studies, Native studies, politics, regional, humour, and popular culture. Released 12 new titles in 1997. "Our mandate is to publish provocative books that challenge the status quo, regardless of the subject matter." Accepts unsolicited manuscripts, but first send inquiry, outline, and sample chapters. Does not accept submissions by phone, fax, or e-mail. Guidelines available.

Notable 1997 title: *American Whiskey Bar*, Michael Turner.

Bantam Books Canada
105 Bond Street, 4th Floor, Toronto, ON M5B 1Y3
Phone: (416) 340-0777 Fax: (416) 340-1069
Contact: editorial department

Publishes mass-market fiction and non-fiction. Will not accept unsolicited manuscripts.

Beach Holme Publishers
2040 West 12th Avenue, Suite 226, Vancouver, BC V6J 2G2
Phone: (604) 733-4868 Fax: (604) 733-4860
E-mail: bhp@beachholme.bc.ca
Web site: www.beachholme.bc.ca
Contact: Joy Gugeler, managing editor

Formerly Press Porcepic, established 1971. Exclusively a fiction and poetry house. Historical young adult fiction with teacher's guides under the Sandcastle imprint; literary fiction and poetry under the Porcepic imprint. Publishes 8 to 10 titles a year. Accepts unsolicited manuscripts, but first send an inquiry with sample chapter(s) (up to 30 pages). Response time two months. Canadian citizens only. Guidelines available.

Notable 1997 title: *The Lion of Venice*, Mark Frutkin.

Between the Lines
720 Bathurst Street, Suite 404, Toronto, ON M5S 2R4
Phone: (416) 535-9914 Fax: (416) 535-1484
E-mail: mamorris@web.net
Contact: Marg Anne Morrison, managing editor

Established 1977. Publishes non-fiction books on Canadian social and political issues, culture, Third World development, gender politics, and the media. Produced 6 new titles in 1997. Send full proposal with outline. No unsolicited manuscripts.

Notable 1997 title: *We Lived a Life and Then Some: The Life, Death, and Life of a Mining Town*, Charlie Angus and Brit Griffin.

Blizzard Publishing
73 Furby Street, Winnipeg, MB R3C 2A2
Phone: (204) 775-2923 Fax: (204) 775-2947
E-mail: cfoster@blizzard.mb.ca
Web site: www.blizzard.mb.ca/catalog
Contact: Clarise Foster, assistant to managing editor

Established 1985. A literary publisher specializing in contemporary drama, dramatic criticism, and theatre-related books. The Bain & Cox imprint publishes prose and non-fiction (but no fiction, poetry, or children's literature). Blizzard's publish-on-demand company, International Readers Theatre, produces scripts in chapbook form. Publishes 4 to 6 new titles a year. No unsolicited manuscripts. Send an inquiry with a brief sample. Guidelines for IRT available.

Notable 1997 title: *Peregrinations*, Robert Enright.

Borealis Press
9 Ashburn Drive, Nepean, ON K2E 6N4
Phone: (613) 224-6837 Fax: (613) 829-7783
Contact: Glenn Clever, editor

Established 1972. Publishes poetry, fiction, and general trade with Canadian authorship or interest. Releases about 10 new books each year. "We do not consider multiple submissions or unsolicited material. Query first, including synopsis and a sample chapter or equivalent, together with return postage or international postal coupons and adequate-sized envelope." Guidelines available.

Notable 1997 title: *Hungarian & Transylvanian Folk Tales*, Emoke de Papp Severo.

The Boston Mills Press
132 Main Street, Erin, ON N0B 1T0
Phone: (519) 833-2407 Fax: (519) 833-2195
E-mail: books@boston-mills.on.ca
Web site: www.boston-mills.on.ca

Contact: John Denison, publisher

Established 1974. Specializes in historical works. Publishes local or regional history, guidebooks, and large-format pictorials. Releases about 20 new titles a year. Accepts unsolicited manuscripts, but first send an inquiry with outline and sample chapter. Send SASE for catalogue.

Notable 1997 title: *Lines of Country*, Chris Andreae.

Breakwater Books

100 Water Street, St. John's, NF AIC 6E6
Phone: (709) 722-6680 or 1-800-563-3333 Fax: (709) 753-0708
E-mail: breakwater@nfld.com
Web site: www.nfld.com/~krosebreakw.htm
Contact: Michele Cable, executive assistant

Established 1973. Publishes educational materials and a wide selection of manuscripts about Atlantic Canada, including plays, poetry, satire, biography, songbooks, cookbooks, and fiction. Main areas of interest include environmental science, enterprise education, and language arts. Publishes about 10 new books a year. "We are especially interested in Canadian writers with experience in writing for the school market." No unsolicited manuscripts. Send outline and writing sample.

Notable 1997 title: *Hibernia: Promise of Rock and Sea*, Lara Maynard.

Breton Books

Wreck Cove, NS BOC IHO
Phone: (902) 539-5140 Fax: (902) 539-9117
E-mail: speclink@atcon.com
Contact: Ronald Caplan, publisher

A small press publishing fiction and non-fiction, poetry and children's books, with a focus on Cape Breton and Maritimes writers and subjects. Accepts unsolicited manuscripts. "Breton Books publishes local books that read well anywhere" – *Halifax Herald*.

Notable 1997 title: *The Story So Far*, Sheldon Currie.

Brick Books

431 Boler Road, P.O. Box 20081, London, ON N6K 4G6
Phone: (519) 657-8579 Fax: (519) 657-8579

E-mail: brick.books@sympatico.ca
Contact: Kitty Lewis, general manager
   Established 1975. Publishes Canadian poetry only. Reads manuscripts January through April every year. Released 5 new titles during 1997. Accepts unsolicited manuscripts. First send inquiry. Guidelines available.
   Notable 1997 title: *A Broken Bowl*, Patrick Friesen.

Broadview Press
P.O. Box 1243, Peterborough, ON K9J 7H5
Phone: (705) 743-8990 Fax: (705) 743-8353
E-mail: 75322.44@compuserve.com
Web site: www.broadviewpress.com
Contact: Michael Harrison, vice-president
   Established 1985. Publishes university and college texts, specializing in the arts and social sciences, and some general trade non-fiction. Subject areas include anthropology, politics, history, philosophy, sociology, English literature, and medieval studies. Covers a broad range of political and philosophical viewpoints. About 30 new titles a year. Catalogues available on request. No unsolicited manuscripts. Send an outline and sample chapters.
   Notable 1997 title: *We Are Not You: First Nations and Canadian Modernity*, Claude Denis.

Brown Bear Press
122A Felbrigg Avenue, Toronto, ON M5M 2M5
E-mail: ruthbear@istar.ca
Contact: Ruth Bradley-St-Cyr, publisher
   A small press publishing non-fiction trade paperback originals by Canadian authors only (Canadian social, political, and family issues) and reprints of Canadian classics. Produces 4 titles a year. Reports in two months on proposals. Offers a small advance. Send SASE for submission guidelines.

Butterworths Canada
75 Clegg Road, Markham, ON L6G 1A1
Phone: (905) 479-2665 Fax: (905) 479-6266
E-mail: repstein@butterworths.ca
Web site: www.butterworths.ca:80

Contact: Ruth Epstein, publishing director

Established 1912. Specializes mainly in legal works; also business and accounting materials for the professional market. Publishes about 30 new titles a year, as well as ongoing looseleaf and electronic materials. Welcomes inquiries within these designated areas. Send an outline and sample chapters.

Notable 1997 title: *Financial & Estate Planning for the Mature Client in Ontario*, gen. ed. Belle Wong.

The Caitlin Press

P.O. Box 2387, Station B, Prince George, BC V2N 2S6

Phone: (604) 964-4953 Fax: (604) 964-4970

Contact: Cynthia Wilson, managing editor

Established 1977. A small regional publisher specializing in trade books by B.C. Interior authors. Some literary titles by B.C. authors. Publishes about 7 new titles each year. "We are interested primarily in Canada's North – and more particularly, Northern British Columbia." Accepts unsolicited manuscripts that meet these criteria. Send outline and sample chapters. Guidelines available.

Canadian Arctic Resources Committee

1 Nicholas Street, Suite 1100, Ottawa, ON K1P 7B7

Phone: (613) 241-7379 Fax: (613) 241-2244

E-mail: ay385@freenet.carleton.ca

Contact: C.A. Samhaber, office manager

Established 1971. Publishes mostly scholarly non-fiction, usually related to Canada's North: its people, environment, and resource development. Particularly concerned with environmental issues. Also Aboriginal rights, self-government, and international matters pertaining to northern Canada and the circumpolar world. Produces 4 to 6 new titles a year. Accepts unsolicited manuscripts.

Canadian Stage and Arts Publications

104 Glenrose Avenue, Toronto, ON M4T 1K8

Phone: (416) 484-4534 Fax: (416) 484-6214

E-mail: kbell@interlog.ca

Contact: Karen Bell, editor

Established 1975. Publishes an average of 4 new arts, Canadiana, and children's books each year. No unsolicited manuscripts.

Notable 1997 title: *Mickey, Taggy, Puppo & Cica Visit Greece*, Kati Rekai.

Carleton University Press

1125 Colonel By Drive, Suite 1400, CTTC, Ottawa, ON K1S 5B6
Phone: (613) 520-3740 Fax: (613) 520-2893
E-mail: cu_press@ccs.carleton.ca
Web site: www.carleton.ca/cupress
Contact: John Flood, director and general editor
Established 1963. Publishes scholarly and trade books focusing on Canadian studies. Subject areas include women's studies, geography, history, sociology, anthropology and Aboriginal peoples, media studies, political science, law, business, economics, public administration, international affairs, literature, art, philosophy, biography, and the classics. Published 26 new books in 1997. Accepts manuscripts in declared areas of interest, but first send an outline or proposal. Guidelines available.
Notable 1997 title: *Resistance and Revolution*, Rob McRae.

Cormorant Books

R.R.1, Dunvegan, ON K0C 1J0
Phone: (613) 527-3348 Fax: (613) 527-2262
Contact: Jan Geddes, publisher
Established 1986. Publishes long and short literary fiction for the adult market, and some non-fiction on literary themes. The focus is on a unique voice. Released 6 new titles in 1997. Accepts unsolicited manuscripts (send sample chapters or short stories). Generally, there's a 4- to 6-month response delay for submissions after acknowledgement.
Notable 1997 title: *Fox's Nose*, Sally Ireland.

Coteau Books

2206 Dewdney Avenue, Suite 401, Regina, SK S4R 1H3
Phone: (306) 777-0170 Fax: (306) 522-5152
E-mail: coteau@coteau.unibase.com
Web site: www: http://coteau.unibase.com
Contact: Nik L. Burton, managing editor
Established 1975. Publishes fiction, poetry, juvenile literature, drama, women's issues, and quality and popular non-fiction.

Averages 12 to 14 new titles a year. Internet users can sample some of the work published by Coteau on the Web. Reviews unsolicited manuscripts by Canadian writers. "We will not accept multiple/simultaneous submissions. We consider children's manuscripts only by Prairie authors."

Notable 1997 title: *Banjo Lessons*, David Carpenter.

Crabtree Publishing Co.
360 York Road, R.R.4, Niagara-on-the-Lake, ON L0S 1J0
Phone: (905) 682-5221 Fax: (905) 262-5890
E-mail: editor@crabtree-pub.com
Contact: Lynda Hale, managing editor

Established 1978. Publishes children's illustrated non-fiction series written at a specific reading level to meet educational demands for the children's library market. Main subjects are social studies and science. Releases 50 to 100 new titles a year. "We do not accept unsolicited manuscripts and discourage fiction, as it is not our market. Ideas for series that are accompanied by photos are considered."

Notable 1997 title: *Victorian Home*, Bobbie Kalman.

Creative Publishers
P.O. Box 8660, St. John's, NF A1B 3T7
Phone: (709) 722-8500 Fax: (709) 722-2228
Contact: Donald Morgan, manager

Established 1983. Publishes mainly local history and biography by Newfoundland writers. The Killick Press imprint specializes in literary books: novels, short stories, poetry, creative non-fiction, and drama. Tuckamore Books is a children's/YA imprint. Released 10 new titles in 1997. Query first. Guidelines available.

Notable 1997 title: *The Night Season*, Paul Bowdring.

Harry Cuff Publications
94 LeMarchant Road, St. John's, NF A1C 2H2
Phone: (709) 726-6590 Fax: (709) 726-0902
E-mail: bob@cuff.com (print inquiries), jeff@cuff.com
    (electronic inquiries)
Web sites: www.zyqote.com (for creative work); www.cuff.com
    (corporate homepage, with submission guidelines, etc.)

Contact: Robert Cuff, managing editor

Established 1981. Publishes an average of 8 books a year on Newfoundland and/or by Newfoundlanders. Also publishes electronic works in hypertext; interested in collaborative work with writers in hypertext. Accepts unsolicited manuscripts but prefers initial inquiry with outline. Guidelines available.

Notable 1997 title: *The Encyclopedia of Newfoundland and Labrador* (CD-ROM).

Robert Davies/Multimedia

330 – 4999 Ste. Catherine Street W., Westmount, PQ H3Z 1T3
Phone: (514) 481-2440 Fax: (514) 481-9973
E-mail: rdpub@vir.com
Contact: R. Davies, president

Publishes trade fiction and non-fiction, how-to, and children's books. Produces about 24 new titles each year. Accepts unsolicited manuscripts.

Notable 1997 title: *Some of Skippy's Blues*, Margie Taylor.

Detselig Enterprises

1220 Kensington Road N.W., Unit 210, Calgary, AB T2N 3P5
Phone: (403) 283-0900 Fax: (403) 283-6947
E-mail: temeron@telusplanet.net
Contact: T.E. Giles, president

Established 1975. Publishes academic, professional, and trade books. Half the list is academic/scholarly, the other half general interest non-fiction. No poetry, fiction, children's, or cookbooks. Averages 14 new books each year. Accepts unsolicited manuscripts, but first send inquiry letter with outline and sample chapters.

Notable 1997 title: *Passion and Scandal*, Barbara Smith.

Doubleday Canada

105 Bond Street, Toronto, ON M5B 1Y3
Phone: (416) 340-0777 Fax: (416) 977-8488
Web site: www.bdd.com
Contact: Kathryn Exner, assistant editor

Established 1944. Publishes non-fiction on politics, Canadiana, sports, and business, as well as fiction. Also interested in history, biography, children's picture books, travel, nature/outdoors, religion, and the performing arts. Publishes 50 new titles each year. No unsolicited manuscripts. Inquiries only. Guidelines available.

Notable 1997 title: *1967*, Pierre Berton.

Douglas & McIntyre

1615 Venables Street, Vancouver, BC V5L 2H1
Phone: (604) 254-7191 Fax: (604) 254-9099
E-mail: dm@douglas-mcintyre.com
Contact: editorial department
Toronto office: 585 Bloor Street W., 2nd Floor, Toronto,
    ON M6G 1K5
Phone: (416) 537-2501 Fax: (416) 537-4647
Contact: Lucy Fraser, editor

Established 1964. Publishes general trade books but specializes in history, biography, art, outdoors and recreation, and Native subjects. Imprints are Greystone Books and Groundwood Books. Produces 50 new titles annually. Toronto office handles all children's books. Submit an outline with two or three sample chapters.

Dundurn Press

8 Market Street, Suite 200, Toronto, ON M5E 1M6
Phone: (416) 214-5544 Fax: (416) 214-5544
E-mail: info@dundurn.com
Contact: Kirk Howard, publisher

Established 1973. Publishes Canadian history (notably of Ontario), biography, art, and literary criticism. Encompasses Dundurn (serious non-fiction), Hounslow (popular non-fiction), Simon & Pierre (literary), and Boardwalk (children's). Averages 50 new titles annually. Accepts unsolicited manuscripts, but first send outline and sample chapters, and identify your prospective market. Allow 4 to 12 weeks for reply.

Notable 1997 title: *Heartbreak & Heroism: Stories from Canadian Search & Rescue*, John Melady.

ECW Press

2120 Queen Street E., Suite 200, Toronto, ON M4E 1E2
Phone: (416) 694-3348 Fax: (416) 698-9906
E-mail: ecw@sympatico.ca
Web site: www.ecw.ca/Press

Contact: Jack David, president

Established 1974. Traditionally a publisher of reference books and literary criticism on Canadian writers and their works, ECW has now been transformed into a vigorous literary and trade house focusing on poetry, fiction, biography, and sports books. Released 42 titles in 1997. Accepts unsolicited manuscripts, but send a query first. Guidelines available.

Notable 1997 titles: *Scribes and Scoundrels*, George Galt. *Muddy Waters: The Mojo Man*, Sandra B. Tooze.

Ekstasis Editions

P.O. Box 8474, Main Postal Outlet, Victoria, BC V8W 3S1
Phone: (250) 361-9941 Fax: (250) 385-3378
E-mail: ekstasis@ampsc.com
Contact: Richard Olafson, publisher

Established 1982. A literary press publishing elegant editions of poetry, novels, short story collections, children's stories (under the Cherubim imprint), and criticism, along with general environmental and New Age trade books. Released 18 new books in 1997. Accepts written inquiries with outlines or sample chapters. "Please study our books (send $3 for a catalogue) and submit appropriate material." Guidelines available.

Notable 1997 title: *Shanghai Alley*, Jim Christy.

Exile Editions

P.O. Box 67, Station B, Toronto, ON M5T 2C0
Phone: (416) 969-8877 Fax: (416) 966-9556
Contact: Barry Callaghan, president

Established 1976. Publishes fiction, drama, poetry, and fiction and poetry in translation. Produces about 10 new titles a year. Rarely accepts unsolicited manuscripts. Be sure to study both *Exile* quarterly and the Exile Editions list before deciding to submit.

Fenn Publishing Company

34 Nixon Road, Bolton, ON L7E 1W2
Phone: (905) 951-6600 Fax: (905) 951-6601
E-mail: fenn@interhop.net
Contact: C. Jordan Fenn, publisher

Publishes primarily distinctive juvenile books – around 70 titles a year. Interested in Canadian and juvenile and works with potential for continued series. Accepts unsolicited manuscripts, but first send outline and sample chapters.

Notable 1997 title: *Taking Care of Business*, Heather Robertson.

Firefly Books

3680 Victoria Park Avenue, Willowdale, ON M2H 3K1
Phone: (416) 499-8412 Fax: (416) 499-1142
Contact: Michael Worek, associate publisher

Publishes practical how-to and illustrated books, with a special interest in gardening, cooking, astronomy, and nature, for the Canadian and U.S. markets. No fiction and very few children's books. No unsolicited full manuscripts. Send an outline and sample chapter in the designated area of interest.

Notable 1997 titles: *For the Love of Hockey*, Chris McDonell; *Painting and Decorating Furniture*, Sheila McGraw; *Splendors of the Universe*, Terence Dickinson.

Fifth House Publishers

6125 – 11th Street S.E., Unit 9, Calgary, AB T2H 2L6
Phone: (403) 571-5230 Fax: (403) 571-5235
Contact: Charlene Dobmeier, managing editor

Established 1982. Publishes general trade non-fiction (especially Western Canadiana), emphasizing history and biography, with some children's books and a strong Native list. Releases 14 to 16 books a year. No unsolicited manuscripts. Send an outline, sample chapter, and author background. No phone calls, please.

Notable 1997 title: *Loyal till Death: Indians and the North-West Rebellion*, Stonechild and Waiser.

Fitzhenry & Whiteside Co.

195 Allstate Parkway, Markham, ON L3R 4T8
Phone: (905) 477-9700 Fax: (905) 477-9179
E-mail: godwit@fitzhenry.ca
Web site: www.fitzhenry.ca
Contact: Richard Dionne, editor

Established 1966. Publishes a wide selection of general trade and education books, especially adult non-fiction. Specializes in reference, natural history, children's, and Canadiana. Canadian authors only. No adult fiction. Released 35 new titles in 1997. Accepts unsolicited manuscripts.

Notable 1997 title: *Sea Otter Inlet,* Celia Godkin.

Formac Publishing Co.

5502 Atlantic Street, Halifax, NS B3H 1G4
Phone: (902) 421-7022 Fax: (902) 425-0166
Contact: Carolyn MacGregor, co-publisher

Established 1977. Publishes regional titles, including history, folklore, cookbooks, and guidebooks, Canadian biography, and children's books. Accepts unsolicited manuscripts, but first send an outline or sample chapter.

Notable 1997 title: *The First Nova Scotian,* Mark Finnan.

The Frederick Harris Music Co.

5865 McLaughlin Road, Mississauga, ON L5R 1B8
Phone: (905) 501-1595, ext. 230 Fax: (905) 501-0929
E-mail: FHMC@inforamp.net
Contact: Trish Sauerbrei, publishing manager

Established 1904. A not-for-profit publisher of music education materials, particularly curriculum material for the Royal Conservatory of Music. Released 50 new titles in 1997. Accepts unsolicited manuscripts. Guidelines available.

Notable 1997 title: *The Royal Conservatory of Music Guitar Series.*

Garamond Press

67 Mowat Avenue, Suite 144, Toronto, ON M6K 3E3
Phone: (416) 516-2709 Fax: (416) 516-0571
E-mail: garamon@web.net
Web site: www.garamond.ca/garamond
Contact: Peter Saunders, director

Established 1981. Publishes academic monographs and university texts offering a critical perspective. Subject areas include women's studies, cultural and labour studies, education, Third World topics, and ethnicity. Releases 6 to 8 new titles a year. No unsolicited manuscripts. Written inquiries only. Very specific submission guidelines available.

Notable 1997 title: *Unequal Freedoms: The Global Market as an Ethical System,* John McMurtry.

Gaspereau Press

P.O. Box 143, Wolfville, NS B0P 1X0
Phone: (902) 681-0492
E-mail: editor@gaspereau.com
Contact: Andrew Steeves, general editor

Publishes smaller runs of Canadian fiction, poetry, and history books, as well as the literary quarterly *The Gaspereau Review*. Generally but not exclusively interested in work from Atlantic Canada. Releases about 10 new titles a year. Accepts unsolicited manuscripts. First send an inquiry.

Notable 1997 title: *The Haliburton Bi-Centenary Chaplet*, ed. Richard A. Davies.

General Store Publishing House

1 Main Street, Burnstown, ON K0J 1G0
Phone: (800) 465-6072   Fax: (613) 432-7184
E-mail: publisher@gsph.com
Web site: www.gsph.com
Contact: Tim Gordon, publisher

Established 1980. Publishes history, military, cookbooks, regional titles pertaining to the Ottawa Valley, and sports books. Released 13 titles in 1997. Accepts unsolicited manuscripts, but first send an outline and sample chapters. Guidelines available.

Notable 1997 title: *Down the Unmarked Roads*, Joan Finnigan.

Goose Lane Editions/Fiddlehead Poetry Books

469 King Street, Fredericton, NB E3B 1E5
Phone: (506) 450-4251   Fax: (506) 459-4991
Contact: Laurel Boone, acquisitions editor

Established 1958. Publishes Canadian adult literary fiction, non-fiction, and poetry. Produces about 12 new titles each year. Considers unsolicited manuscripts. "Query first for poetry, story collections, and non-fiction. Send outline or synopsis and 30- to 50-page sample for novels. No electronic queries or submissions, please." Guidelines available with SASE.

Notable 1997 title: *Homer in Flight*, Rabindranath Maharaj.

Guernica Editions

P.O. Box 117, Station P, Toronto, ON M5S 2S6
Phone: (416) 658-9888   Fax: (416) 657-8885
Contact: Antonio D'Alfonso, editor

Established 1978. Specializes in prose and poetry addressing the Italian/North American experience. Also translates Québécois authors. Published 26 new titles in 1997. No unsolicited manuscripts. Inquiries welcome. "A publisher is not just an outlet. It is the home of common thoughts. We want writers with a global world vision."

Notable 1997 title: *Devils in Paradise*, Pasquale Verdicchio.

Gutter Press

P.O. Box 600, Station Q, Toronto, ON M4T 2N4
Phone: (416) 822-8708   Fax: (416) 822-8709
E-mail: gutter@comnet.ca
Contact: Sam Hiyate, publisher

Specializes in pop culture, literary fiction, and avant-garde writing. "We want nothing less than to rewrite the literary canon. And we want your best work. Check out the literary magazine *B&A New Fiction* plus our backlist for an idea of what we might like." Produces 4 to 8 titles a year. Welcomes work by new writers, but first send a query plus sample chapters.

Notable 1997 title: *The Reluctant Pornographer*, Bruce La Bruce.

Hancock House Publishers

19313 Zero Avenue, Surrey, BC V4P 1M7
Phone: (604) 538-1114   Fax: (604) 538-2262
Contact: David Hancock, editor

Established 1970. Specializes in Pacific Northwest history and biography, Native culture, nature guides, and natural history. A second division focuses on international nature and conservation books. Publishes about 25 titles a year. No unsolicited manuscripts. Send a one- or two-page synopsis, a sample chapter, and biographical/marketing support material. Guidelines available.

Notable 1997 title: *Yukon Riverboat Days*, Joyce Yardley.

Harbour Publishing

P.O. Box 219, Madeira Park, BC V0N 2H0
Phone: (604) 883-2730   Fax: (604) 883-9451

E-mail: harbour@sunshine.net
Contact: Howard White, president

Established 1974. Publishes books on West Coast regional history and culture, both literary and non-fiction, as well as poetry and guides. Specializes in B.C. authors and women's issues. Published 22 titles in 1997. Accepts unsolicited manuscripts, but send letter of inquiry first. Guidelines available.

Notable 1997 title: *To Paris Never Again*, Al Purdy.

Harlequin Enterprises

225 Duncan Mill Road, Don Mills, ON M3B 3K9
Phone: (416) 445-5860 Fax: (416) 445-8655
Web site: www.romance.net
Contact: Candy Lee, executive vice-president and publisher

Established 1949. Each year publishes more than 700 mass-market paperback series romances (Harlequin and Silhouette imprints), single title women's fiction (Mira Books), and mystery and action adventure (Gold Eagle and Worldwide Library imprints). Interested in receiving manuscript outlines, particularly those with series potential, in either fiction or non-fiction. Accepts unsolicited manuscripts, but initial inquiry preferred. Tip sheets available. New authors are contracted only on full manuscript.

HarperCollins Publishers

55 Avenue Road, Suite 2900, West Tower at Hazelton Lanes,
    Toronto, ON M5R 3L2
Phone: (416) 975-9334 Fax: (416) 975-9884
E-mail: hccanada@harpercollins.com
Web site: www.harpercollins.com/canada
Contact: Harold Hill, acquisitions editor

Publishes a wide range of fiction, non-fiction, business, young adult and children's books. Produces over 50 new titles each year. No unsolicited manuscripts. Send query letter and SASE.

Notable 1997 title: *Any Known Blood*, Lawrence Hill.

Hartley & Marks Publishers

3661 West Broadway, Vancouver, BC V6R 2B8
Phone: (604) 739-1771 Fax: (604) 738-1913

E-mail: hartmark@direct.ca
Contact: Susan Juby, managing editor

Established 1973. Publishes self-help and how-to books, specializing in health, well-being, and family; building, crafts, and gardening; and typography. Produces about 16 titles each year. Accepts unsolicited manuscripts, but first send an inquiry, outline, sample chapters, and include author résumé. Guidelines available.

Heritage House Publishing Co.

17921 – 55th Avenue, Suite 8, Surrey, BC V3C 6C4
Phone: (604) 574-7067 Fax: (604) 574-7067
E-mail: herhouse@island.net
Web site: www.islandnet.com/herhouse
Contact: Rodger Touchie, publisher/managing editor

Established 1969. Emphasizes Western Canadian history, pioneer biographies, recreational guides, and Canadian themes. Averages 10 to 12 new books a year. Send an outline and sample chapters. "Our authors are often new writers with specialized knowledge and/or a unique personal history. No fiction, juvenile, or inspirational. We only consider children's books when writer and illustrator co-submit their work."

Notable 1997 title: *The Mountie Makers*, Robert G. Teether.

Highway Book Shop

R.R.1, Cobalt, ON POJ 1CO
Phone: (705) 679-8375 Fax: (705) 679-8511
E-mail: bookshop@nt.net
Contact: Lois Pollard, assistant manager

Began its serious publishing program in 1970. Publishes adult trade – mainly by Canadian authors and with Northern themes. Priority given to local, northeastern Ontario history. Also interested in Native Canadian works, and adult and young adult fiction accepted on Northern and Native themes, although sometimes strays from these priorities. Released 7 new titles in 1997. Accepts unsolicited manuscripts, but first send inquiry with outline and/or sample chapters. Guidelines available.

Notable 1997 title: *Echoes & Images*, Peter Koens.

Hinterland Publishers

P.O. Box 198, Sandy Hook, MB ROC 2WO
Phone: (204) 389-3842
E-mail: donkp@hinterland.mb.ca
Contact: Norma Norton, managing director

A small press publishing contemporary realistic fiction with a focus on First Nations people. No unsolicited manuscripts. Send an inquiry.

Notable 1997 title: *The Moons of Goose Island*, Don K. Philpot.

Horned Owl Publishing

3906 Cadboro Bay Road, Victoria, BC V8N 4G6
Phone: (250) 477-8488 Fax: (250) 721-1029
E-mail: hornowl@islandnet.com
Contact: Rob Von Rudloff, project manager

A small press specializing in quality books (children's and adult) on Earth-centred spirituality, particularly Aboriginal European religions and the Western Mystery Tradition, including Pagan religions such as Witchcraft/Wicca. Releases 2 or 3 titles a year. Accepts unsolicited manuscripts, but first send inquiry with outline and sample chapters. Guidelines available.

Notable 1997 title: *Journey of the Bard*, Yvonne Owens.

Horsdal & Schubart Publishers

425 Simcoe Street, Suite 623, Victoria, BC V8V 4T3
Phone: (250) 360-2031 Fax: (250) 360-0829
Contact: Marlyn Horsdal, editor

Established 1985. Specializes in Canadian non-fiction, with an emphasis on the North, Western history, and biography; also the occasional work of fiction. Publishes 5 to 8 titles a year. Accepts unsolicited manuscripts, but phone or send letter of inquiry first.

Notable 1997 title: *Moonrakers*, Beth Hill.

House of Anansi Press

1800 Steeles Avenue W., Concord, ON L4K 2P3
Phone: (905) 660-0611 Fax: (905) 660-0676
E-mail: anansi@irwin-pub.com
Web site: www.the-wire.com/irwin/anansi

Contact: Martha Sharpe, editor

A literary press that publishes fiction, poetry, criticism, and belles-lettres. Averages 10 to 15 new books a year – perhaps 3 or 4 poetry, 3 to 5 fiction, and 3 to 5 non-fiction titles. Accepts sample chapters/poems of unsolicited manuscripts. Send letter of inquiry with outline. Decisions on the year's list are usually made before July the previous year.

Notable 1997 title: *These Festive Nights*, Marie-Claire Blais.

Hyperion Press

300 Wales Avenue, Winnipeg, MB R2M 2S9

Phone: (204) 256-9204 Fax: (204) 255-7845

Contact: Dr. Marvis Tutiah, president

Established 1978. Specializes in craft and how-to books for all ages, and children's picture books for under-12s. Averages 8 to 10 new titles a year. Accepts unsolicited manuscripts.

Notable 1997 title: *The Wise Washerman*, Deborah Froese.

IHS/Micromedia

20 Victoria Street, Toronto, ON M5C 2N8

Phone: (416) 362-5211 Fax: (416) 362-6161

E-mail: info@micromedia.on.ca

Contact: Louise Fast, director, news/periodicals and government information

Electronic database publisher specializing in Canadian serials, government documents, and corporate information for libraries, information centres, and research departments. Products available on CD-ROM, WWW, print, and microform. Frequently offers employment to indexers and abstracters. No unsolicited manuscripts.

Insomniac Press

378 Delaware Avenue, Toronto, ON M6H 2T8

Phone: (416) 536-4308 Fax: (416) 588-4198

E-mail: mike@insomniacpress.com

Contact: Mike O'Connor, publisher

Established 1993. A vigorous new house concentrating on edgy, provocative, experimental work, primarily novels and short stories, but beginning to move into non-fiction too. Released 12 new titles in 1997. No unsolicited manuscripts. Send an outline with sample chapters.

Notable 1997 title: *Paul's Case*, Lynn Crosbie.

Irwin Publishing

1800 Steeles Avenue W., Concord, ON L4K 2P3
Phone: (905) 660-0611 Fax: (905) 660-0676
E-mail: norma@irwin.pub.com
Contact: Norma Pettit, managing editor

Established 1945. Specializes in texts and teacher-support materials for elementary and high schools, some college, and professional books. Also, with sister company Stoddart Publishing, young adult novels. Released 40 titles in 1996. Accepts unsolicited manuscripts, but first query with outline.

Island Scholastic Press

441 Shepherd Avenue, Quesnel, BC V2J 4X1
Phone: (250) 991-5567
Contact: Dan Lukiv, editor

Established 1997. Publishes chapbooks of poetry only by authors published in *The Challenger* literary journal (see page 138). Plans to release 5 titles in 1998. Accepts unsolicited manuscripts.

Notable 1998 title: *At the Water*, Kerry Randall.

Jesperson Publishing

39 James Lane, St. John's, NF A1E 3H3
Phone: (709) 753-0633 Fax: (709) 753-5507
Contact: John Symonds, editor

Established 1977. Publishes trade and educational books featuring Newfoundland content and/or authors, fiction and non-fiction. Produces about 8 new titles a year. Accepts unsolicited manuscripts, but send a sample chapter first. Guidelines available.

Notable 1997 title: *Newfoundland and Labrador Days*, Maxwell Harvey.

Kalobon

2339 Dufferin Street, Suite 1405, Toronto, ON M6E 4Z5
Phone: (416) 789-2423 Fax: (416) 781-8382
Contact: Ervin Bonkalo, director

Specializes in English and French scholarly works dealing with medieval art, architecture, and literature. German and Hungarian manuscripts accepted for translation into English. A special interest in the Greek Catholic Church in Hungary, 1650 to 1992. Two new titles in 1997. No unsolicited manuscripts. Query first.

Key Porter Books

70 The Esplanade, 3rd Floor, Toronto, ON M5E 1R2
Phone: (416) 862-7777 Fax: (416) 862-2304
E-mail: srenouf@keyporter.com
Contact: Susan Renouf, president and editor-in-chief

Established 1980. Specializes in high-profile non-fiction, business, biography, celebrity books, cookbooks, natural history, and the environment. Publishes 40 to 50 new titles a year. No unsolicited manuscripts.

Notable 1997 title: *Fear, Greed and the End of the Rainbow*, Andrew Sarlos.

Kids Can Press

29 Birch Avenue, Toronto, ON M4V 1E2
Phone: (416) 925-5437 Fax: (416) 960-5437
E-mail: info@kidscan.com
Contact: Valerie Hussey, publisher

Established 1973. Publishes quality books for children of all ages, including picture books, poetry, non-fiction, fiction, crafts, and activity books. Averages 40 new titles each year. "Please familiarize yourself with our list before sending a manuscript. Request a catalogue if you're having trouble getting a good sense of the entire publishing program." Accepts unsolicited manuscripts. Send outline and sample chapters of longer fiction. Guidelines available.

Notable 1997 title: *The Kids Book of Canada*, Barbara Greenwood.

Lone Pine Publishing

10426 – 81st Avenue, Suite 206, Edmonton, AB T6E 1X5
Phone: (403) 433-9333 Fax: (403) 433-9646
E-mail: 75667.2070@compuserve.com
Web site: www.ourworld.compuserve.com/homepages/
   LonePinePublishing
Contact: Nancy J. Foulds, senior editor

Established 1980. Specializes in natural history, outdoor recreation, and popular history. Most books have a regional focus. Has offices in Vancouver, Edmonton, and Washington State. Publishes 15 to 20 new titles each year. Accepts unsolicited manuscripts, but first send an inquiry by mail (after familiarizing yourself with Lone Pine's current titles). Guidelines available.

Notable 1997 title: *Best Hikes and Walks of Southwestern British Columbia*, Dawn Hanna.

James Lorimer & Co.

35 Britain Street, Toronto, ON M5A 1R7
Phone: (416) 362-4762 Fax: (416) 362-3939
E-mail: jlc@sympatico.ca
Contact: Diane Young, editor-in-chief

Established 1971. Specializes in books on Canadian politics, economics, and urban and social issues for the university and trade markets. Also children's/young adult (age 8 to 15) fiction addressing Canadian social issues. No picture books, fantasy, horror, or science fiction. Averages 25 new titles a year. Accepts unsolicited manuscripts. Ask for guidelines before submitting. Then send inquiry with outline and sample chapters.

Notable 1997 title: *Cabbagetown: The Story of a Victorian Neighbourhood*, Penina Coopersmith.

Lost Moose, the Yukon Publisher

58 Kluane Crescent, Whitehorse, YT Y1A 3G7
Phone: (867) 668-5076 Fax: (867) 668-6223
E-mail: lmoose@yknet.yk.ca
Web site: www.yukonweb.wis.net/business/lostmoose
Contact: Wynne Krangle, director

A small press publishing books – history, photography, humour – reflecting life in Canada's North. No unsolicited manuscripts. Send an inquiry. Guidelines available.

Notable 1997 title: *Great Northern Lost Moose Catalogue*.

Macfarlane, Walter & Ross

37A Hazelton Avenue, Toronto, ON M5R 2E3
Phone: (416) 924-7595 Fax: (416) 924-4254
E-mail: mwandr@interlog.com

Contact: Jan Walter, president

Established 1988. Publishes high-quality, popular non-fiction aimed at Canadian and international audiences, primarily in the fields of politics, business, history, biography, and popular culture. Produced 7 new titles in 1997. Accepts unsolicited manuscripts but first send query with outline and one sample chapter. Guidelines available.

Notable 1997 title: *Wrestling with the Elephant: The Inside Story of the Canada–U.S. Trade Wars*, Gordon Ritchie.

Macmillan Canada

29 Birch Avenue, Toronto, ON M4V 1E2

Phone: (416) 963-8830 Fax: (416) 923-4821

Contact: editorial assistant

Publishes a variety of general trade non-fiction, primarily for and by Canadians. Specializes in cookbooks, sports, business, health, and nutrition. Averages 50 new books each year. No unsolicited manuscripts. Accepts inquiries with an outline and sample chapters.

Notable 1997 title: *Fitzgerald's Storm*, Dr. Joseph MacInnis.

McClelland & Stewart

481 University Avenue, Suite 900, Toronto, ON M5G 2E9

Phone: (416) 598-1114 Fax: (416) 598-7764

Web sites: www.tceplus.com/mcclelland/home.htm (main page),
    www.tceplus.com/mcclelland/guidelin.htm (for guidelines)

Contact: editorial department

Established 1906. Publishes a wide selection of fiction, and non-fiction books on biography, history, natural history, politics, art, religion, and sports. Also publishes poetry, reference books, and *The Canadian Encyclopedia* on CD-ROM. Releases about 80 titles a year. "We are 'The Canadian Publishers' and take our role to publish the best in Canadian fiction, non-fiction, and poetry very seriously. With a stable of authors ranging from Margaret Atwood through Peter Gzowski on to Leonard Cohen and then to Alice Munro and Pierre Trudeau, this house is not a good point of entry for the beginning author." No unsolicited manuscripts. Send an inquiry for fiction, an outline for non-fiction.

Notable 1997 title: *The Underpainter*, Jane Urquhart.

McGill–Queen's University Press

McGill University, 3430 McTavish Street, Montreal, PQ H3A 1X9
Phone: (514) 398-3750 Fax: (514) 398-4333
Contact: Philip Cercone, editor
Queen's University office: Queen's University, Kingston,
   ON K7L 3N6
Phone: (613) 545-2155 Fax: (613) 545-6822
Contact: Professor Donald Akenson, editor

Established 1969. Publishes scholarly books on Arctic and Northern studies and history; political science with special emphasis on Canadian urban life; Commonwealth and Canadian literature; and books on architecture, philosophy and religion, North American Native peoples, anthropology, and sociology. Averages 70 new titles a year, a third of which are destined for the trade market. Accepts unsolicited manuscripts, but first send query letter. Guidelines available.

Notable 1997 title: *Mad Cows and Mother's Milk*, Doug Powell and William Leiss.

McGraw-Hill Ryerson

300 Water Street, Whitby, ON L1N 9B6
Phone: (905) 430-5000 Fax: (905) 430-5020
Web site: www.mcgrawhill.ca
Contact: Joan Homewood, publisher, consumer and trade division

Established 1944. Publishes adult non-fiction consumer and reference books, notably in the areas of business and personal finance, and to a lesser extent military history. Averages 20 trade titles a year. No fiction or children's manuscripts. Accepts unsolicited manuscripts. Query letter and outline with sample chapter must be submitted first. Allow 2 months for response to unsolicited submissions.

Notable 1997 title: *Canadian Snowbird Guide*, Douglas Gray.

Moonstone Press

167 Delaware Street, London, ON N5Z 2N6
Phone: (519) 659-5784
E-mail: pbaltens@odyssey.on.ca
Web site: www.mirror.org/commerce/hmspress/moon.html
Contact: Peter Baltensperger, publisher

Established 1984. Publishes adult literary fiction, poetry, and creative non-fiction. Special areas of interest include mysticism, spirituality, symbolism, and surrealism. Averages 5 new titles a year. Accepts unsolicited manuscripts, but first send outline and sample chapters. No multiple submissions. "We look for literary excellence; no social issues or moralistic topics." Guidelines available.

Notable 1997 title: *Travels on the Road Not Taken*, Martin Samuel Cohen.

Morgaine House

80 Mount Pleasant, Pointe Claire, PQ H9R 2T5
Phone: (514) 695-1624
E-mail: morgaine@videotron.ca
Contact: Mary Gurekas, editor

Established 1994. A small literary press interested in well-crafted manuscripts of poetry, short stories, and novels representing a cross-section of contemporary writing, not bound by a particular style or aesthetic. Produces a chapbook series for poets developing their work. Accepts unsolicited manuscripts. First send outline, synopsis, and sample chapters for novels. Guidelines available.

Notable 1997 title: *I Should Know & Other Stories*, Claudia Morrison.

New Star Books

2504 York Avenue, Vancouver, BC V6K 1E3
Phone: (604) 738-9429 Fax: (604) 738-9332
Contact: Rolf Maurer, publisher
E-mail: newstar@pinc.com

Publishes progressive books that challenge the status quo and fill a void left by the mainstream media. Subject areas include social issues, politics, the environment, along with literary fiction and non-fiction, and poetry. Averages 6 to 8 new titles a year. Accepts unsolicited manuscripts, but first send inquiry with outline. Guidelines available.

Notable 1997 title: *Autobiography of a Tattoo*, Stan Persky.

NeWest Publishers

8540 – 109th Street, Suite 201, Edmonton, AB T6G 1E6
Phone: (403) 432-9427 Fax: (403) 433-3179
E-mail: newest@planet.con.net

Contact: Liz Grieve, general manager

Established 1977. Publishes literary fiction by Western Canadian authors and non-fiction on Western Canada, including books on the history and social concerns of Western Canadians, play anthologies, first novels, and short story collections. Averages 8 new titles a year. No poetry. Accepts unsolicited manuscripts. Send outline and sample chapter. No editorial commentary given on rejected manuscripts. Guidelines available.

Notable 1997 title: *Mothertalk*, Roy Kiyoaka.

Nimbus Publishing

P.O. Box 9301, Station A, Halifax, NS B3K 5N5
Phone: (902) 455-4286 Fax: (902) 455-3652
Contact: Dorothy Blythe, managing editor

Established 1978. Publishes general trade books on all aspects of Atlantic Canada, including politics, social, cultural, and natural history, folklore and myth, biography, the environment, nautical books, cookbooks, children's, and photographic books. Most books are by first-time authors who have in-depth knowledge of their subject. Releases about 25 new titles each year. Accepts unsolicited manuscripts. Guidelines available.

Notable 1997 title: *Wilderness Nova Scotia*, Irwin Barrett.

Oberon Press

350 Sparks Street, Suite 400, Ottawa, ON K1R 7S8
Phone: (613) 238-3275 Fax: (613) 238-3275
Contact: Nicholas Macklem, general manager

Established 1966. Publishes Canadian literary fiction, poetry, and non-fiction (biographies, memoirs, literary criticism, and essays). No genre fiction. Averages 12 new books a year. Accepts unsolicited manuscripts, but first send outline and sample chapters. Multiple submissions not considered. Guidelines available.

Notable 1997 title: *97: Best Canadian Stories*, ed. Douglas Glover.

Oolichan Books

P.O. Box 10, Lantzville, BC V0R 2H0
Phone: (250) 390-4839 Fax: (250) 390-4839
E-mail: oolichan@mail.island.net
Contact: Ron Smith, publisher

Established 1974. Publishes literary fiction and poetry. Released 5 new titles in 1997. Considers unsolicited manuscripts, but send initial letter of inquiry and sample. Guidelines available.

Notable 1997 title: *Laterna Magika*, Ven Begamudré.

Orca Book Publishers

P.O. Box 5626, Station B, Victoria, BC V8R 6S4
Phone: (250) 380-1229 Fax: (250) 380-1892
E-mail: orca@pinc.com
Web site: www.swifty.com/orca
Contacts: Bob Tyrrell (adult and young adult); Ann Featherstone
(children's and older juvenile)

Established 1984. Adult titles comprise about half the list and include general non-fiction, guidebooks, outdoor adventure, and history. Released 20 new titles in 1997. A West Coast regional bias. Children's titles include picture books, older juvenile, and young adult novels on universal themes. Historical and sports stories considered. No poetry, sci-fi, or fantasy. No adult unsolicited manuscripts. Send a query with outline and sample chapters. Unsolicited manuscripts accepted for children's picture books; for novels, send a query with first three chapters and outline. Guidelines available.

Notable 1997 title: *Prairie Born*, David Bouchard.

Owl Books

179 John Street, 5th Floor, Toronto, ON M5T 3G5
Phone: (416) 340-2700 Fax: (416) 340-9769
Contact: submissions editor

Sister company to *OWL*, *Chirp*, and *Chickadee* magazines. Publishes high-quality, innovative information books, activity books, and picture books, with an emphasis on animals, nature, science, and children's activities such as crafts. Averages 8 to 10 new titles a year. Accepts unsolicited manuscripts, but first send query and outline for longer non-fiction works, the full manuscript for picture books. Before submitting, spend an hour or two familiarizing yourself with Owl books in the library. No response without SASE. Does not currently publish novels.

Notable 1997 title: *Crime Science*, Vivien Bowers.

Oxford University Press

70 Wynford Drive, Don Mills, ON M3C 1J9

Phone: (416) 441-2941 Fax: (416) 441-0345

E-mail: custserv@oupcan.com

Web site: www.oupcan.com

Contact: Anne Erickson, director, trade, medical, and professional division

Established in Canada in 1904. Publishes general trade and reference, university textbooks, and junior and senior high school textbooks. Averages 60 new titles each year. Accepts unsolicited manuscripts, but first send a query with outline and sample chapters. Guidelines available.

Notable 1997 title: *Oxford Companion to Canadian Literature* (2nd ed.), eds. W.E. Toye and Eugene Benson.

Pedlar Press

P.O. Box 26, Station P, Toronto, ON M5S 2S6

Phone: (416) 926-8110 Fax: (416) 926-8110

Contact: Beth Follett, managing editor

Publishes experimental work or work of cultural or community value that, despite its merits, may not be acceptable to other publishing houses. Releases 2 to 6 new titles each year. Accepts unsolicited manuscripts, but first send an outline and sample chapters. Guidelines available.

Notable 1997 title: *The Only-Good Heart*, Beth Goobie.

Pemmican Publications

1635 Burrows Avenue, Unit 2, Winnipeg, MB R2X 0T1

Phone: (204) 589-6346 Fax: (204) 589-2063

Contact: Sue MacLean, managing editor

Established 1980. Specializes in children's picture books. Committed to publishing books that depict Métis and Aboriginal cultures and lifestyles positively and accurately. Releases about 5 new titles each year. Accepts unsolicited manuscripts, but first send sample chapters. Guidelines available.

Notable 1997 title: *Chubby Champ*, Peter Eyvindson.

Penguin Books Canada

10 Alcorn Avenue, Suite 300, Toronto, ON M4V 3B2
Phone: (416) 925-2249 Fax: (416) 925-0068
Web site: www.penguin.ca
Contact: editorial department

Established in Canada in 1974. Publishes a wide selection of trade fiction and non-fiction. Released 36 new titles and a total of about 90 books in 1997. No unsolicited manuscripts.

Notable 1997 title: *Reflections of a Siamese Twin*, John Ralston Saul.

Periwinkle Books

P.O. Box 8052, Victoria, BC V8W 3R7
Phone: (250) 382-5868
E-mail: Hannah@islandnet.com
Contact: Tanya Yaremchuk, editor

A small press publishing mainstream as well as gay, lesbian, feminist, and alternative fiction and poetry. Also considers youth fiction. Accepts queries or full manuscripts in designated areas. Guidelines available.

Playwrights Canada Press

54 Wolseley Street, 2nd Floor, Toronto, ON M5T 1A5
Phone: (416) 703-0201 Fax: (416) 703-0059
E-mail: cdplays@interlog.com
Web site: www.puc.ca/pcp/pcp.html
Contact: Angela Rebeiro, publisher/managing editor

Established 1972. Publishes Canadian plays in single editions, anthologies, and collections. All plays must have had professional theatre production. Query first.

Polestar Press

P.O. Box 5238, Station B, Victoria, BC V8R 6N4
Phone: (250) 361-9718 Fax: (250) 361-9738
E-mail: pstarvic@direct.ca
Web site: www.mypage.direct.ca/p/polestar
Contact: Michelle Benjamin, publisher

Established 1980. Publishes fiction and poetry, children's fiction and non-fiction, sports books, and general trade non-fiction. (No longer publishes illustrated children's books.) Released 12 new titles in 1997. Accepts unsolicited manuscripts, but prefers initial query with sample chapters. Guidelines available with SASE.

Notable 1997 title: *Love Medicine and One Song*, Greg Scofield.

The Porcupine's Quill
68 Main Street, Erin, ON NOB 1TO
Phone: (519) 833-9158 Fax: (519) 833-9158
E-mail: pql@sentex.net
Contact: Elke Inkster, office manager
Established 1974. Specializes in Canadian literary fiction. Published 8 new titles in 1997. Does not accept unsolicited manuscripts. Send a query letter.

Notable 1997 title: *The Hidden Room*, P.K. Page.

Pottersfield Press
83 Leslie Road, East Lawrencetown, NS B2Z 1P8
Contact: Lesley Choyce, editor
Established 1979. Publishes general non-fiction, novels, and books of interest to Atlantic Canada. Particularly interested in biography proposals. Averages 5 new titles a year. Accepts proposals and/or full manuscripts. No phone calls, please.

Prentice-Hall Canada
1870 Birchmount Road, Scarborough, ON M1P 2J7
Phone: (416) 299-2500 Fax: (416) 299-2540
Web site: www.phcanada.com
Contact: Robert Harris, director, trade group
Established 1960. Though it is primarily an educational publisher, Prentice-Hall's PTR (professional, trade, and reference) division publishes non-fiction primarily for the Canadian consumer. Specialties include personal finance, business, new technology, health, self-help, and Canadiana. Published 31 new trade titles in 1997. Accepts unsolicited manuscripts, but first send outline and sample chapters. "We do not consider fiction manuscripts. Manuscripts that appeal to corporate consumers are given high priority. Please allow 4 to 6 weeks for a response to your proposal." Guidelines available.

Notable 1997 title: *1998 Buyer's Guide to Mutual Funds*, Gordon Pape.

Press Gang Publishers

225 East 17th Avenue, Suite 101, Vancouver, BC V5V 1A6
Phone: (604) 876-7787 Fax: (604) 876-7892
E-mail: pgangpub@portal.ca
Contact: Barbara Kuhne, managing editor

Established 1974. "Press Gang Publishers Feminist Co-operative is committed to producing quality books with social and literary merit. We prioritize Canadian women's work and include writing by lesbians and by women from diverse cultural and class backgrounds. Our purpose is to represent the diversity of women's voices not represented by mainstream publishers. Our list features vital and provocative fiction and non-fiction." Published 6 new books in 1997. Send initial inquiry with sample chapter (fiction) or outline (non-fiction).

Notable 1997 title: *Storm Clouds over Party Shoes*, Sheila Norgate.

Quarry Press

P.O. Box 1061, Kingston, ON K7L 4Y5
Phone: (613) 548-8429 Fax: (613) 548-1556
Contact: Bob Hilderley, president

Established 1965. Publishes literature, art history, popular culture, folklore, photography, local history. Averages 25 new titles a year. No unsolicited manuscripts. "Call or write for a catalogue of our books to determine the kind of work we publish. Don't inquire or submit blindly." Guidelines available.

Ragweed Press/gynergy books

P.O. Box 2023, Charlottetown, PE C1A 7N7
Phone: (902) 566-5750 Fax: (902) 566-4473
E-mail: editor@ragweed.com and editor@gynergy.com
Contact: Sibyl Frei, managing editor

Established 1974. Publishes regional fiction and non-fiction, and children's and young adult fiction under Ragweed Press. Also feminist and lesbian fiction and non-fiction under gynergy books. Releases an average of 8 to 10 new titles a year. Accepts unsolicited manuscripts. Send complete manuscript, or outline and sample chapters for non-fiction, plus SASE. No e-mail submissions.

Notable 1997 title: *Mothering Teens: Understanding the Adolescent Years*, ed. Miriam Kaufman.

Raincoast Books
8680 Cambie Street, Vancouver, BC V6P 6M9
Phone: (604) 323-7100 Fax: (604) 323-2600
E-mail: info@raincoast.com
Contact: Brian Scrivener, editorial director

Publishes regional, national, and international titles on the environment/nature, sports, travel (guides), and cooking, as well as children's fiction, non-fiction, and picture books. Accepts unsolicited manuscripts, but first send an inquiry or an outline and one sample chapter, including colour photocopies or duplicate slides of artwork for illustrated work or books with photographs. Guidelines available.

Notable 1997 title: *Haida Gwai: Journeys through the Queen Charlotte Islands*, Ian Gill.

Red Deer College Press
P.O. Box 5005, 56th Avenue and 32nd Street, Red Deer,
AB T4N 5H5
Phone: (403) 342-3321 Fax: (403) 357-3639
E-mail: umix@admin.rdc.ab.ca
Contacts: Dennis Johnson, managing editor; Peter Carver,
children's editor; Joyce Doolittle, drama editor

Established 1975. Publishes fiction and non-fiction (including some gardening and cookbooks) for adults and children, illustrated children's books, young adult fiction, poetry, and drama. Produces 14 to 18 books a year. Accepts unsolicited manuscripts. Query first with outline and sample chapters. "Submissions to children's illustrated list should come from established writers only please. Children's list is usually booked up two years in advance. Reports in 3 to 6 months."

Notable 1997 title: *Fern Hill*, Dylan Thomas (illust. Murray Kimber).

Reidmore Books
1200 Energy Square, 10109 – 106th Street, Edmonton, AB T5J 3L7
Phone: (403) 424-4420 Fax: (403) 441-9919
E-mail: reidmore@compusmart.ab.ca
Contact: Leah-Ann Lymer, editor-in-chief
    Established 1979. Produced 10 new titles in 1997. Publishes non-fiction, and specializes in educational titles developed to match a particular curriculum topic in social studies. Some trade titles. No children's picture books. Accepts unsolicited manuscripts, but first send outline (include market research). Guidelines available.
    Notable 1997 title: *Century of Change*, Alyn Mitchner and Joanne Tuffs.

Rocky Mountain Books
4 Spruce Centre S.W., Calgary, AB T3C 3B3
Phone: (403) 249-9490 Fax: (403) 249-2968
E-mail: tonyd@rmbooks.com
Contact: Gillean Daffern, editor
    Established 1976. Specializes in outdoor recreation (including skiing, hiking, climbing, biking, and whitewater), guidebooks, history pertaining to the Canadian Rockies, and the natural history of Alberta, British Columbia, and the Yukon. Averages 6 new titles a year. Accepts book proposals with outlines and writing samples. No complete unsolicited manuscripts. Guidelines available.
    Notable 1997 title: *Planning a Wilderness Trip in Canada and Alaska*, Keith Marton.

Ronsdale Press
3350 West 21st Avenue, Vancouver, BC V6S 1G7
Phone: (604) 738-1195 Fax: (604) 731-4548
E-mail: ronhatch@pinc.com
Web site: ronsdalepress.com
Contact: R.B. Hatch, director
    Established in 1988. A literary press specializing in fiction, poetry, biography, regional literature, and books on ideas. Also children's literature, but not picture books. Interested in quality and experimental literature. Released 10 new titles in 1997. Accepts unsolicited manuscripts. "Ronsdale Press is not interested in pulp fiction or

mass-market throwaways. Poets should already have published six poems in magazines. Please send the entire manuscript, or at least the first half – odd pages are of little value – and include a short bio. The best sales engine we have is a dynamic author who can help promote the title." Guidelines available with SASE.

Notable 1997 title: *Brave Soldiers, Proud Regiments: Canada's Military History*, Allen Andrews.

Royal British Columbia Museum
Publishing Services, 675 Belleville Street, Victoria, BC V8W 9W2
Phone: (250) 387-2478 Fax: (250) 952-6825
E-mail: gtruscott@rbml.01.rbmc.gov.bc.ca
Web site: www.rbmc/rbmc.gov.bc.ca
Contact: Gerry Truscott, publisher
Established 1891. Publishes scholarly and popular non-fiction concerning the human and natural histories of British Columbia and the museum's activities. All manuscripts must be sponsored by an RBCM curator or department. Produces about 3 new titles a year. No unsolicited manuscripts. Written inquiries only.

Notable 1997 title: *Food Plants of Interior First Peoples*, Nancy J. Turner.

Royal Ontario Museum
Publications, 100 Queen's Park, Toronto, ON M5S 2C6
Phone: (416) 586-5581 Fax: (416) 586-5827
Contact: Glen Ellis, managing editor
Publishes manuscripts relating to the museum's collection, with some general-readership and children's books. Averages 10 new titles each year. No unsolicited manuscripts; inquiries only. Priority is given to (1) ROM authors, (2) research associates, (3) others.

Notable 1997 title: *The Star-Man and Other Tales*, Basil Johnston.

Scholastic Canada
123 Newkirk Road, Richmond Hill, ON L4C 3G5
Phone: (905) 883-5300 Fax: (905) 731-3482
Web site: www.scholastic.ca
Contact: Sandra Bogart Johnston, senior editor
Established in Canada in 1957. Specializes in children's books,

both fiction and non-fiction, from preschool to young adult. Averages 50 titles a year. Also publishes professional materials for teachers. Query letters only.

Notable 1997 title: *The Party*, Barbara Reid (auth. and illust.).

Seal Books

105 Bond Street, Toronto, ON M5B 1Y3
Phone: (416) 340-0777 Fax: (416) 977-8488
Contact: Maya Mavjee, editor

Established 1977. Publishes mass market reprints and original titles, focusing on the following areas: adult fiction, current affairs, politics, and business. Averages 28 new titles a year. Accepts unsolicited manuscripts, but first send an outline.

Notable 1997 title: *Alias Grace* (mm), Margaret Atwood.

Second Story Press

720 Bathurst Street, Suite 301, Toronto, ON M5S 2R4
Phone: (416) 537-7850 Fax: (416) 537-0588
E-mail: secstory@fox.nstn.ca
Web site: www.coolbooks.com/~outpost/pubs/second/index.html
Contact: Lois Pike or Margie Wolfe, editorial

A women's press specializing in quality fiction and non-fiction (women's health and social issues are of particular interest), children's picture books, and juvenile novels. Averages 12 titles a year. Accepts unsolicited manuscripts, but first send outline. Guidelines available.

Notable 1997 title: *The Other Side*, Cynthia Holz.

Self-Counsel Press

1481 Charlotte Road, North Vancouver, BC V7J 1H1
Phone: (604) 986-3366 Fax: (604) 986-3947
E-mail: editorial@self-counsel.com
Web site: www.swifty.com/scp
Contact: Lori Ledingham, managing editor

Established 1971. Specializes in self-help titles covering legal issues (divorce, wills, incorporation) and business, written by experts in their fields. Also a new writing series. Produces 15 to 20 new titles each year. Accepts unsolicited manuscripts, but send an initial outline and sample chapters. "Ask for our catalogue to be sure your idea fits into Self-Counsel's publishing program." Guidelines available.

Notable 1997 title: *Writing Romance,* Vanessa Grant.

Somerville House Books

3080 Yonge Street, Suite 5000, Toronto, ON M4N 3N1
Phone: (416) 488-5938 Fax: (416) 488-5506
Web site: www.sombooks.com
Contacts: Patrick Crean, editorial director; Jane Somerville, publisher

Established 1983. Publishes general trade books, focusing on children's non-fiction/educational packages, with a small part of the program devoted to works of adult literary fiction and non-fiction of the highest calibre. Published 12 new titles in 1997. Send letter of inquiry (including outline and one sample chapter) before submitting unsolicited manuscripts.

Notable 1997 title: *Connected Intelligence: The Arrival of the Web Society*, Derrick de Kerckhove.

Sono Nis Press

1725 Blanshard Street, Victoria, BC V8W 2J8
Phone: (250) 382-1024 Fax: (250) 382-0775
E-mail: sononis@islandnet.com
Web site: www.islandnet.com/~sononis
Contact: Ann West, editor

Established 1968. Publishes history, especially historical biography, maritime history, transportation history, and regional history, as well as poetry and some juvenile fiction. Produced 9 new titles in 1997. Accepts unsolicited manuscripts, but send inquiry first. Guidelines available.

Notable 1997 title: *Unseen Dimensions: Musings on Art and Life*, John Koerner.

Sound & Vision Publishing

359 Riverdale Avenue, Toronto, ON M4J 1A4
Phone: (416) 465-2828 Fax: (416) 465-0755
E-mail: musicbooks@soundandvision.com

Web site: www.soundandvision.com
Contact: Geoff Savage, publisher
   A small specialist press featuring books on musical humour. "Writers should check out our web site to see the kind of books we publish." Send queries with outlines and sample chapters.
   Notable 1997 title: *Tenors, Tantrums & Trills*, David W. Barber.

Stoddart Publishing Co.

34 Lesmill Road, North York, ON M3B 2T6
Phone: (416) 445-3333   Fax: (416) 445-5967
Web site: www.genpub.com:80/stoddart
Contact: Don Bastian, managing editor (adult list); Kathryn Cole, publisher, Stoddart Kids (children's)
   Established 1964. Publishes timely, innovative, and original works across a broad range of non-fiction subjects, as well as fiction for adults, young adults, and children, and picture books. Produces about 60 adult new titles and 25 for Stoddart Kids each year. Accepts unsolicited manuscripts, but first send an outline and sample chapter. Guidelines available.
   Notable 1997 title: *Marshall McLuhan: Escape into Understanding*, W. Terrence Gordon.

Talon Books

3100 Production Way, Suite 104, Burnaby, BC V5A 4R4
Phone: (604) 444-4889   Fax: (604) 444-4119
E-mail: talon@pinc.com
Contact: Karl Siegler, editor
   Established 1967. Specializes in drama, serious fiction, poetry, popular non-fiction, women's literature, social issues, and ethnography. Published 12 new titles in 1997. No unsolicited poetry or children's literature. For the rest, first send an inquiry with an outline.
   Notable 1997 title: *loving without being vulnrabul*, bill bissett.

Thistledown Press

633 Main Street, Saskatoon, SK S7H 0J8
Phone: (306) 244-1722   Fax: (306) 244-1762
E-mail: thistle@sk.sympatico.ca
Contact: Patrick O'Rourke, editor-in-chief

Established 1975. Specializes in Canadian poetry, short fiction, and young adult fiction. Publishes 10 to 12 new titles a year. The New Leaf Editions series is devoted to books of 64 pages by previously unpublished writers. No unsolicited manuscripts. Submit an inquiry with a sample and writing/publishing history. Guidelines available.

Notable 1997 title: *The Crying Jesus*, R.P. MacIntyre.

Tundra Books
481 University Avenue, Suite 900, Toronto, ON M5G 2E9
Phone: (416) 598-4786 Fax: (416) 598-0247
Contact: Sue Tate, associate editor

Established 1967. Specializes in children's books as works of art; high-quality children's books with lasting value. Averages 15 new titles a year. Does not accept unsolicited manuscripts. Guidelines available. Artists, call for appointment.

Notable 1997 title: *Dippers*, written by Barbara Nichol, illustrated by Barry Moser.

Turnstone Press
100 Arthur Street, Suite 607, Winnipeg, MB R3B 1H3
Phone: (204) 947-1555 Fax: (204) 942-1555
E-mail: Editor@TurnstonePress.mb.ca
Contact: Manuela Dias, managing editor

Established 1976. A literary press publishing poetry, fiction, non-fiction, and literary criticism. Interested in non-formula genre fiction. Released 9 new titles in 1997. Accepts unsolicited manuscripts. Send an outline and sample chapters first. Guidelines available.

Notable 1997 title: *Bread, Wine and Angels*, Anna Zurzolo.

UBC Press
6344 Memorial Road, Vancouver, BC V6T 1Z2
Phone: (604) 822-3259 Fax: (604) 822-6083
Web site: www.ubcpress.ubc.ca
Contact: Jean Wilson, senior editor

Established 1971. Publishes non-fiction for scholarly, educational, and general audiences in the humanities, social sciences, and natural sciences. Subject areas include history, political science, law, anthropology, sociology, geography, art history, natural resources, the environment, and sustainable development. Releases about 30 new titles each year. No unsolicited manuscripts. Send an inquiry with outline and sample chapters. Guidelines available.

Notable 1997 title: *Sinews of Survival: The Living Legacy of Inuit Clothing*, Betty Kobayashi Issenman.

United Church Publishing House

3250 Bloor Street W., 4th Floor, Etobicoke, ON M8X 2Y4
Phone: (416) 231-7680, ext. 4086 Fax: (416) 232-6004
E-mail: bookpub@uccan.org
Contact: Ruth Bradley-St-Cyr, managing editor

Established in 1829 as Ryerson Press. Publishing program is not limited to "religious" matters, but rather reflects the broader interests of church members. Subjects include spirituality, creative worship, social justice, and ethics. Averages 12 new titles a year. No unsolicited manuscripts. Send a letter of inquiry with a brief outline of material. Guidelines available.

Notable 1997 title: *Sin Boldly*, Chris Levan.

University of Alberta Press

141 Athabasca Hall, University of Alberta, Edmonton,
   AB T6G 2E8
Phone: (403) 492-3662 Fax: (403) 492-0719
E-mail: uap@gpu.srv.ualberta.ca
Web site: www.ualberta.ca/~press
Contact: Glenn Rollans, director

Established 1969. Specializes in scholarly non-fiction and university-level textbooks, history, politics, natural sciences, Native studies, literary criticism, Slavic and Eastern European studies, Middle Eastern studies, anthropology, and archaeology. Mainly publishes original research with a strong Western Canadian interest. Published 8 new titles in 1997. No unsolicited manuscripts. Inquiries accepted. Guidelines available.

Notable 1997 title: *Shredding the Public Interest*, Kevin Taft.

University of Calgary Press

2500 University Drive N.W., Calgary, AB T2N 1N4
Phone: (403) 220-7578 Fax: (403) 282-0085
E-mail: 75001@aoss.ucalgary.ca

Web site: www.ucalgary.ca/UCPress
Contact: Joan Barton, editorial secretary

Established 1981. Publishes scholarly and trade books in a wide variety of subject areas. Will consider any innovative scholarly manuscript. Released 12 new titles in 1997. A complete manuscript, with prospectus, will be considered if it satisfies scholarly criteria but also appeals to a larger audience. Guidelines available.

Notable 1997 title: *Mendel's Children: A Family Chronicle*, Cherie Smith.

University of Manitoba Press

244 – 15 Gillson Street, University of Manitoba, Winnipeg,
     MB R3T 5V6
Phone: (204) 474-9495 Fax: (204) 474-7511
E-mail: www.umanitoba.ca/publications/uofmpress
Contact: David Carr, director

Established 1967. Publishes books for both scholarly and general audiences in Native studies, Western Canadian history, women's studies, and Icelandic studies. Averages 4 to 6 new titles each year. Unsolicited manuscripts are accepted, but prefers initial inquiry. Guidelines available.

Notable 1997 title: *Night Spirits: The Story of the Relocation of the Sayisi Dene*.

University of Toronto Press

10 St. Mary Street, Suite 700, Toronto, ON M4Y 2W8
Phone: (416) 978-2239 Fax: (416) 978-4738
Web site: www.library.utoronto.ca/www/utpress/publish/
     publish.htm
Contact: Bill Harnum, senior vice-president, scholarly publishing

Established 1901. A large university press publishing scholarly and general works, and many academic journals. Editorial program includes classical, medieval, Renaissance, and Victorian studies, modern languages, English and Canadian literature, literary theory and criticism, women's studies, social sciences, Native studies, philosophy, law, religion, music, education, modern history, geography, and political science. Averages 125 to 130 new titles each year. Accepts unsolicited manuscripts, but first send inquiry with outline and sample chapter. Use *Chicago* or *MLA* for style, though internal consistency is the most important.

Notable 1997 title: *Idleness, Water and a Canoe,* Jamie Benedickson.

Vanwell Publishing
1 Northrup Crescent, P.O. Box 2131, St. Catharines, ON L2R 7S2
Phone: (905) 937-3100 Fax: (905) 937-1760
Contact: Angela Dobler, general editor

Established 1983. Canada's leading publisher of military, naval, and aviation books. Also publishes children's fiction and non-fiction. Averages 9 new titles a year. Reviews unsolicited manuscripts. Guidelines available.

Notable 1997 title: *Wings of a Hero: Canadian Pioneer Flying Ace Wop May,* Sheila Reid.

Véhicule Press
P.O. Box 125, Place du Parc Station, Montreal, PQ H2W 2M9
Phone: (514) 844-6073 Fax: (514) 844-7543
E-mail: vpress@cam.org
Web site: www.cam.org/~vpress
Contact: Simon Dardick, publisher/general editor

Established 1973. Publishes fiction, non-fiction, and poetry within the context of social history. Released 14 titles in 1997. Accepts unsolicited manuscripts, but first send sample chapters with cover letter. No poetry at present.

Notable 1997 title: *Fuzzy Logic: Dispatches from the Information Revolution,* Matthew Friedman.

Whitecap Books
351 Lynn Avenue, North Vancouver, BC V7J 2C4
Phone: (604) 980-9852 Fax: (604) 980-8197
E-mail: whitecap@pinc.com
Contact: Robin Rivers, editorial director

Established 1977. Specializes in innovative cookbooks, gardening guides, colour scenics, and Canadian travel guides. Now publishes children's picture books as well as non-fiction. Releases about 20 books a year. Welcomes proposals and inquiries. Few unsolicited manuscripts are accepted, so check the list first. "Spend time researching what is already on the market before beginning a manuscript." Guidelines available.

Notable 1997 title: *Daxwin Wiggett Photographs Canada*, Daxwin Wiggett.

John Wiley & Sons Canada

22 Worcester Road, Etobicoke, ON M9W 1L1
Phone: (416) 236-4433 Fax: (416) 236-4448
E-mail: lmccurdy@Wiley.com
Web site: www.wiley.com
Contact: Elizabeth McCurdy, assistant editor, trade

Established 1968. The Professional, Reference, and Trade Division publishes non-fiction books for the business and general interest markets. Primary fields of interest are business (management, general business, human resources, careers, not-for-profit), small business and entrepreneurship, personal finance, and self-help law and reference books. Averages 13 new titles a year. Send written inquiries with outline and sample chapters.

Notable 1997 title: *You Can't Take It with You: The Common-Sense Guide to Estate Planning for Canadians* (2nd ed.), Sandra Foster.

Wilfrid Laurier University Press

75 University Avenue W., Waterloo, ON N2L 3C5
Phone: (519) 884-0710, ext. 6124 Fax: (519) 725-1399
E-mail: press@mach1.wlu.ca
Web site: www.info.wlu.ca/~wwwpress/home.html
Contact: Sandra Woolfrey, director

Established 1974. Publishes scholarly books (and academic journals) in the humanities and social sciences, and general interest titles based on sound research. Subject areas include film, the environment, literary criticism, religious studies, Canadian studies, life writing, philosophy, history, and women's studies. Produces 12 to 15 new books a year. Accepts unsolicited manuscripts, but first send outline and sample chapter. Guidelines available.

Notable 1997 title: *And Peace Never Came*, Elisabeth M. Raab.

Wolsak and Wynn Publishers

P.O. Box 316, Don Mills P.O., Don Mills, ON M3C 2S7
Phone: (416) 222-4690 Fax: (416) 237-0291

Contact: Maria Jacobs, publisher/editor

Publishes poetry only – about 5 new books a year. Will consider unsolicited material after an initial written inquiry along with a sample of 12 poems. Guidelines available.

Notable 1997 title: *The Photographer of Wolves*, John O'Neill.

Women's Press

517 College Street, Suite 302, Toronto, ON M6G 4A2
Phone: (416) 921-2425 Fax: (416) 921-4428
E-mail: wompress@web.net
Contact: Martha Ayim, managing editor

Established 1972. A feminist publishing collective committed to anti-racist/anti-classist publishing and to the development of feminism in Canada and internationally. Strongly interested in access to print for lesbians, disabled writers, and writers of colour. Publishes non-fiction, fiction, poetry, and plays. Released 6 new titles in 1997. No unsolicited manuscripts. Send a letter of inquiry and outline. Guidelines available.

Notable 1997 title: *The New Midwifery: Reflections on Renaissance and Regulation*, ed. Farah M. Shroff.

Wood Lake Books

10162 Newene Road, Winfield, BC V4V 1R2
Phone: (250) 766-2778 Fax: (250) 766-2736
E-mail: info@woodlake.com
Contact: Rhonda Pigott, publicist

Focuses on Christianity (mainstream Protestant), with an emphasis on social justice, the family, and resources for clergy and lay people. Produced 4 new books in 1997. No unsolicited manuscripts. Send letter of inquiry, outline, and sample chapter.

Notable 1997 title: *Future Faith Churches*, Don Posterski and Gary Nelson.

York Press

77 Carlton Street, Suite 305, Toronto, ON M5B 2J7
Phone: (416) 599-6652 Fax: (416) 599-2675
Contact: Dr. Saad Elkhadem, editor

Established 1975. Produces scholarly publications, reference books, and manuscripts on literary criticism and comparative literature. Strong emphasis on high-quality creative writing and Arabic/Egyptian literature and scholarship. Also translations of literary masterpieces. Released 8 new titles in 1997. No unsolicited manuscripts or author guidelines. Query first. Scholarly manuscripts are prepared according to *The York Press Style Manual* ($2.50 plus postage).

Notable 1997 title: *Robertson Davies: Life, Work, and Criticism*, Lynne Diamond-Nigh.

6

LITERARY AGENTS

In the United States most writers, established or not, place their books through an agent; even magazine writers often sell their work this way. Literary agents have played a lesser role in Canadian publishing. The pool of agents has always been small here, and Canadian publishers have traditionally acted as agents for their authors when it comes to selling their works to foreign markets.

Like publishers, most agents are very circumspect about taking on unpublished writers, though publication in journals or high-quality magazines can help. Plenty of published writers don't use an agent. Some seek the advice of a lawyer when it comes to contract signing. Don't use the family solicitor for this, though, and bear in mind that very few lawyers in Canada specialize in publishing law. Far better to consult your regional branch of the Canadian Authors Association or the Writers' Union of Canada, who have access to all the necessary expertise and experience to help you pick through the minefield of subsidiary rights and other arcane aspects of the publisher's contract.

There are, however, many advantages to securing a good agent. Most large publishers prefer to contract agented authors (some insist on it). A manuscript recommended by an agent will invariably be taken more seriously than one submitted by an unknown writer. And it will probably be read and acted on sooner because the publisher can be confident that it has merit and is in a relatively publishable condition. Indeed, books are occasionally contracted purely on the basis of a good proposal and a convincing pitch by the agent.

Established authors tend to use agents more, and may seek their counsel long before they actually begin writing a particular book. Because fiction is considerably harder to sell than non-fiction, fiction writers depend heavily on agents. Many literary agents, however, put a higher priority on maintaining a stable of proven non-fiction authors, because non-fiction sells in greater quantities than fiction, and since most agents work on commission, they will earn more from representing these clients.

Good agents deserve every penny they earn. Remember, they are not working for a salary; the efforts they expend hinge almost entirely on the promise of your future success. When you, the author, make money, the agent does too, so he or she will work hard to secure the best terms for you. Agents develop long-term relationships with publishers and editors, with whom they exchange ideas, learning their needs and interests, and they keep in close touch with what is sought after in the publishing marketplace. In so doing, they become expert at gauging the commercial possibilities of an author's proposal.

For new clients, it is on the strength of the agent's "first read" of the manuscript or proposal that he or she will agree to work with the writer. At contract-signing time, the agent can advise the writer on clauses that stipulate what rights the author should sell, or can negotiate every detail of a publisher's contract on the writer's behalf. The agent who fully understands the marketplace, publishing contracts, copyright law, and the broader sales possibilities of a book can negotiate a better publishing contract, often with a bigger advance against royalties.

Agents in Canada usually charge 15 or 20 per cent of the value of all rights sold. An agent today may evaluate a manuscript, suggest structural changes, sell the revised work to a publisher, negotiate the contract, secure an advance, and participate in designing a marketing program. He or she then often works closely with the author over the long term, helping the client to develop a career. Some agents are now, rather controversially, charging supplementary "handling" fees, which may cover the costs of everything from reading, evaluation, and editorial work to the agent's office expenses. But beware of agents who make more money from you, the author, than from the sale of your work. Insist on a strict accounting of fees and an upper limit to expenses.

This chapter lists most of the active literary agencies in Canada. Several others chose not to be included. Well-established agencies usually have a full slate of clients and consequently don't go out of their way to promote their services. As you will discover, agents tend to have very specific requirements and are becoming more and more selective. Below, you will find some advice on their subject interests and specialties; for further insights, ask the agent to send you a client list. Finding an agent, some claim, can be harder than finding a publisher. But every writer should consider the effort, since, in most cases, the relationship between agent and author is to great mutual advantage.

Acacia House Publishing Services Ltd.

51 Acacia Road, Toronto, ON M4S 2K6
Phone: (416) 484-8356 Fax: (416) 484-8356
Contact: Frances Hanna

Subject interests: Fiction with international potential. No horror, occult, science fiction, or adult fantasy. For non-fiction, no self-help, fitness, true crime, or business books.

Comments: Queries only, with writing sample (up to 50 pages). For evaluation, charges $1 per double-spaced page over 50 pages. Evaluates only complete manuscripts. All queries and submissions must be accompanied by SASE.

Aurora Artists

19 Wroxeter Avenue, Toronto, ON M4K 1J5
Phone: (416) 463-4634 Fax: (416) 463-4889
Contact: Janine Cheeseman or Leah Silverman (assistant)

Subject interests: Reality-based stories, unusual plots, unique characters.

Comments: Represents mostly film and television writers. No evaluation fee. No unsolicited manuscripts or unpublished writers. Query only. Include SASE to ensure response.

Author Author Literary Agency

P.O. Box 34051, 1200 – 37th Street S.W., Calgary, AB T3C 3W2
Phone: (403) 242-0226

Contact: Joan Rickard

Subject interests: Prefers adult fiction and non-fiction. Also handles juvenile, academic books, and New Age. No poetry or screenplays.

Comments: Welcomes unpublished writers. There is no reading or handling fee. Accepts unsolicited queries and submissions. Returns collect long-distance phone calls. Requires hard copy (no faxed or disk) submissions. Reports within about one month on sample manuscripts, about two months on complete manuscripts.

"Study your chosen genre thoroughly to learn technique and what publishers are buying. Ensure manuscripts are properly formatted. Always enclose SASE, IRCS, or certified cheque or money order for response to inquiries and/or return of manuscripts from agents and publishers. We offer *A Crash Course Kit in Business Letters, Basic Punctuation/Information Guidelines and Manuscript Formatting* for $8.95, including s/h."

Authors Marketing Services

200 Simpson Avenue, Toronto, ON M4K 1A6
Phone: (416) 463-7200 Fax: (416) 469-4444
E-mail: authors_lhoffman@_compuserve.com
Contact: Larry Hoffman

Subject interests: Adult fiction and non-fiction.

Comments: No unsolicited manuscripts. Unpublished writers are charged evaluation/handling fees. Query only.

Authors Only

55 Capella Starway, Willowdale, ON M2J 1N3
Phone: (416) 491-9511 Fax: (416) 491-9240
Contact: James McRae

Subject interests: No poetry, screenplays, scripts, or children's books. Otherwise all inclusive.

Comments: Specializes in helping unpublished authors and providing international representation. Commission rate 15 per cent. Charges handling fee: 299 pages and under, $75; over 300 pages, $100. Service includes reading, minor editing, and in-depth analysis of full manuscript.

Berry & Associates
P.O. Box 61178, Kensington Postal Outlet, Calgary, AB T2N 4S6
Phone: (403) 270-8411
Contact: Linda Berry
Subject interests: Long fiction; trade (history, Canadiana, self-help, New Age, art, humour, and general); academic (education, humanities, art, social sciences).
Comments: Accepts unsolicited manuscripts and unpublished writers. A reading fee for unsolicited material of $1 per typed, double-spaced page (minimum submission 50 pages) must be prepaid with submission.

The Bukowski Agency
86 Bloor Street W., Suite 602, Toronto, ON M5S 1M5
Phone: (416) 928-6728 Fax: (416) 963-9978
E-mail: Bukowski@interlog.com
Contact: Denise Bukowski
Subject interests: General adult trade books. Prefers literary fiction and non-fiction. No genre fiction (science fiction, romance, westerns); no children's or sports books; no scriptwriters or play-wrights. Specializes in projects with international potential and suitability for other media.
Comments: No unsolicited manuscripts or unpublished writers. Does not charge evaluation or other handling fees. Query first, by mail only, with writing samples and credentials. "What future projects do you have planned? Before making an investment in a little-known writer, I need to be convinced that you are not only talented but ambitious and driven as a writer." No phone or e-mail queries, please.

Canadian Speakers' & Writers' Service
44 Douglas Crescent, Toronto, ON M4W 2E7
Phone: (416) 921-4443 Fax: (416) 922-9691
Contacts: Matie Molinaro, Paul Molinaro, Julius Molinaro
Subject interests: Non-fiction, children's subjects, dramatic works.
Comments: Sometimes reads unpublished writers. "If an unpublished writer presents an interesting project, we do charge an evaluation fee, as working on manuscripts and promoting new writers is becoming more and more costly." No unsolicited manuscripts.

Charlene Kay Agency

901 Beaudry Street, Suite 6, St.-Jean-sur-Richelieu, PQ J3A 1C6
Phone: (514) 348-5296
Contact: Louise Meyers

Subject interests: TV scripts for episodic dramas or comedies, TV movie and film scripts; science fiction, real-life stories, family dramas, etc. No action-adventures or thrillers.

Comments: Accepts unsolicited manuscripts and reads unpublished writers. No handling fees charged. "We do not handle book manuscripts, only teleplays or screenplays. We won't look at any scripts that contain barbaric violence or graphic sex scenes."

Great North Artists Management Inc.

350 Dupont Street, Toronto, ON M5R 1V9
Phone: (416) 925-2051 Fax: (416) 925-3904
Contact: Shain Jaffe

Subject interests: Plays and film and television properties.

Comments: No evaluation or other handling fees. Reads some unpublished writers. No unsolicited manuscripts.

The Helen Heller Agency Inc.

892 Avenue Road, Toronto, ON M5P 2K6
Phone: (416) 481-5430 Fax: (416) 486-1505
Contact: Helen Heller or Daphne Hart

Comments: No evaluation or other handling fees. No unpublished writers. No unsolicited manuscripts. Query by mail only.

J. Kellock & Associates

11017 – 80th Avenue, Edmonton, AB T6G 0R2
Phone: (403) 433-0274
Contact: Joanne Kellock

Subject interests: Adult commercial and literary fiction; adult and children's non-fiction; all works for children, including picture books, first readers, middle readers, and young adult.

Comments: No unsolicited manuscripts. Written queries accepted. Reads unpublished writers. Evaluation and editorial fees charged. "There are two kinds of novels selling today: extraordinarily well-written commercial genre; and brilliantly written, stylistically innovative literature. Children's picture books are toughest to place, thus any first picture book must be unique, universal, and altogether wonderful. Do not supply illustrations with story unless the illustrator has a Fine Arts degree or has previously illustrated a published book for children."

Livingston Cooke

200 First Avenue, Toronto, ON M4M 1X1
Phone: (416) 406-3390 Fax: (416) 406-3389
E-mail: 104631.3230@compuserve.com
Contact: Dean Cooke
  Subject interests: Non-fiction.
  Comments: Accepts inquiries, but no unsolicited manuscripts and no unpublished writers. At present, no evaluation or other handling fees are charged.

Northwest Literary Services

2699 Decca Road, R.R.1, Shawnigan Lake, BC V0R 2W0
Phone: (250) 743-8236
Contact: Brent Laughren
  Subject interests: Literary and genre adult fiction; young adult and children's fiction. No poetry, scripts, or screenplays.
  Comments: No unsolicited manuscripts. Accepts inquiries and reads unpublished writers. Charges a reading fee for unpublished authors: children's picture books, $50; fiction and non-fiction synopsis and first three chapters, $75. Reading fee includes a short evaluation.

Pamela Paul Agency

253A High Park Avenue, Toronto, ON M6P 2S5
Phone: (416) 769-0540 Fax: (416) 769-0540
Contact: Sue Munro
  Subject interests: Film and television (writers and directors); literary fiction and non-fiction.
  Comments: No unsolicited manuscripts. Reads unpublished writers. No evaluation/handling fees. Written queries only (include SASE). "A deliberately small agency with a quality list and special emphasis on selling literary properties for film and television."

Beverley Slopen Literary Agency
131 Bloor Street W., Suite 711, Toronto, ON M5S 1S3
Phone: (416) 964-9598 Fax: (416) 921-7726
E-mail: slopen@inforamp.net
Web site: slopenagency.on.ca
Contact: Beverley Slopen
  Subject interests: General fiction and non-fiction. No poetry, short stories, children's, or illustrated books.
  Comments: No unsolicited manuscripts. Only occasionally reads unpublished writers. Does not charge evaluation/handling fees. This agent offers an "Ask an Agent" service on her web site and writes a column, The Insider, on book publishing on the Web.

Carolyn Swayze Literary Agency
W.R.P.S. Box 39588, White Rock, BC V4A 9P3
Phone: (604) 538-3478 Fax: (604) 531-3022
E-mail: cswayze@direct.ca
Contact: Carolyn N. Swayze
  Subject interests: Literary and commercial adult fiction, book-length non-fiction, young adult novels. No science fiction, poetry, or screenplays, please.
  Comments: Reads unpublished writers. Reads unsolicited manuscripts (first please send a brief synopsis, the first three chapters, biographical details, and SASE). Does not charge evaluation/handling fees, but authors with no publishing history may be asked for a deposit against major courier and photocopying disbursements. Also provides legal services to authors.

Westwood Creative Artists
94 Harbord Street, Toronto, ON M5S 1G6
Phone: (416) 964-3302 Fax: (416) 975-9209
Contact: Hilary Stanley
  Subject interests: General and literary fiction and non-fiction. No poetry.
  Comments: A busy agency that responds only to inquiries of current interest. No unsolicited manuscripts or unpublished writers.

7

WRITING AWARDS AND COMPETITIONS

This chapter surveys a broad range of the literary prizes and competitions open to Canadian writers. Most of the prizes and competitions may be applied for directly. Among a number of high-profile exceptions are the Harbourfront Festival Prize, conferred each year on a celebrated writer in mid-career, and McClelland & Stewart's Journey Prize, for the best short fiction from Canada's literary journals. In some cases, the judges prefer to receive submissions from publishers, but usually, so long as the application criteria are met, individual applications are also accepted.

Please note that application deadlines and details are subject to change, and that the following entries do not include full eligibility criteria or entry conditions. Many awards, for instance, require the provision of several copies of the work so that they can be circulated among the nominating jury. Applicants should always write for full guidelines before making a submission.

Canadian writers are also eligible for a range of overseas-sourced awards, and you'll find many of these listed in standard international reference books such as *Literary Market Place*. New Canadian awards are usually advertised in such industry publications as *Books in Canada*, *Canadian Author*, and *Quill & Quire*, and in some literary journals.

Acorn-Rukeyser Chapbook Contest

Unfinished Monument Press, 237 Prospect Street S., Hamilton,
    ON L8M 2Z6

Deadline: October 31

Named in honour of Milton Acorn and Muriel Rukeyser. The best poetry manuscript (published or unpublished) of up to 30 pages in the People's Poetry tradition receives a cash prize of $100 plus publication. Entry fee $10. Annual.

Alberta Writing for Youth Competition

Writers Guild of Alberta, 11759 Groat Road, 3rd Floor,
    Edmonton, AB T5M 3K6

Phone: (403) 422-8174 Fax: (403) 422-2663

E-mail: writers@compusmart.ab.ca

Deadline: December 31, 1998

A biennial competition offering Alberta writers a cash prize of $4,500. Manuscripts should be 40,000 words. Write for guidelines.

John Alexander Media Awards

Public Education Department, Multiple Sclerosis Society of
    Canada, 250 Bloor Street E., Suite 1000, Toronto, ON M4W 3P9

Deadline: September 30

An annual cash prize of $500 is awarded to the author of the best English or French newspaper or magazine article (and to the creator of the best television or radio broadcast) about some aspect of multiple sclerosis.

The Amethyst Review Writing Contest

Penny Ferguson, *The Amethyst Review*, 23 Riverside Avenue,
    Truro, NS B2N 4G2

Phone: (902) 895-1345

E-mail: amethyst@col.auracom.com

Deadlines: January 31 and August 31

The Amethyst Review administers two writing contests each year, corresponding to the semi-annual issues of the journal: January 31 is the deadline for the contest featured in the May issue, August 31 for that in the November issue. Entrants are invited to submit one short story (to 5,000 words) or up to five poems (to 200 lines per poem) on a proposed theme, which changes each year. Winners in each category receive a cash prize of $50 plus publication in the *Review*. Entry fee $12.

Atlantic Journalism Awards

University of King's College, School of Journalism, 6350 Coburg
   Road, Halifax, NS B3H 2A1
Phone: (902) 422-1271 Fax: (902) 425-8183
Deadline: January 31

A $300 cash prize is awarded to the winners in eight categories.
Only print and broadcast journalists working in the Atlantic region
eligible. Entry fee $20.

B&A Fiction Contest

P.O. Box 702, Station P, Toronto, ON M5S 2Y4
Phone: (416) 535-1233
Deadline: March 11

Five prizes valued at a total of $4,250 are awarded each year for
the best unpublished short stories in any genre. They are:
   The Random House/Knopf/Vintage Canada Prize (books, $1,000)
   The Humber School for Writers Prize (writing course, max. $1,000)
   The Chapters Prize (gift certificates, $1,000)
   The B&A Prize (cash, $750)
The Marketron Notebooks Plus Prize (Sharp PC3000, $500)
Entry fee $20 per story. Each entrant receives a one-year subscrip-
tion to *B&A New Fiction* (see page 132); each winning story is pub-
lished in the magazine.

B.C. Book Prizes

Ian Chunn, 1033 Davie Street, Suite 700, Vancouver, BC V6E 1M7
Phone: (604) 687-2405 Fax: (604) 687-2405
Deadline: December

A $2,000 prize is awarded annually in each category for the
year's most outstanding achievement in fiction, non-fiction, children's literature, and poetry by a British Columbia writer. An
equivalent prize is also conferred on the local book that "contributes most to an understanding of British Columbia." Governed
by the West Coast Book Prize Society but now administered by *B.C.
Book World*.

B.C. Gas Lifetime Achievement Award

c/o *B.C. BookWorld*, 3516 West 13th Avenue (rear), Vancouver,
   BC V6R 2S3
Phone: (604) 736-4011

A $5,000 prize is awarded annually for an exemplary literary career by a British Columbia resident. Administered by *B.C. BookWorld*.

B.C. Historical Federation Writing Competition

c/o P. McGeachie, 7953 Rosewood Street, Burnaby, BC V5E 2H4
Phone: (604) 522-2062
Deadline: December 31

The Lieutenant-Governor's Medal for Historical Writing, together with a monetary prize ($100 to $300), is awarded each year to the author of the most significant book on any facet of British Columbia's history. Also, to encourage amateur historians and students, an annual monetary prize is awarded for the best article (to 3,000 words) published in the *B.C. Historical News* magazine. Send articles to: The Editor, *B.C. Historical News*, P.O. Box 105, Wasa, BC V0B 2K0.

Herb Barrett Award

Hamilton Haiku Press, 237 Prospect Street S., Hamilton,
   ON L8M 2Z6
Deadline: November 30

The Hamilton branch of the Canadian Poetry Association offers cash prizes of $75, $50, and $25 for short poetry in the haiku tradition. The winning haiku and runners-up will be published in an anthology. Entry fee $10 for 1–2 poems, $15 for 3 or more. Annual.

Shaunt Basmajian Chapbook Award

Canadian Poetry Association, P.O. Box 22571, St. George Postal
   Outlet, Toronto, ON M5S 1V0
Deadline: November 30

The national CPA offers a cash prize of $100 plus publication to the winner of the best poetry manuscript of up to 24 pages (published or unpublished, in any style or tradition). Entry fee $10. Annual.

Geoffrey Bilson Award for Historical Fiction for Young People

Jeffrey Canton, Canadian Children's Book Centre, 35 Spadina
  Road, Toronto, ON M5R 2S9
Phone: (416) 975-0010 Fax: (416) 975-1839
E-mail: ccbc@sympatico.ca
Web site: www3.sympatico.ca/ccbc

  The Canadian Children's Book Centre awards an annual prize of $1,000 to the author of an outstanding work of historical fiction for young people. The author must be Canadian, and the book must have been published in the previous calendar year. To be considered, a book must first have been selected for inclusion in the CCBC's Our Choice list. The winner is chosen by a jury appointed by the CCBC.

Ann Connor Brimer Award

Heather MacKenzie, Halifax Regional Library,
  5381 Spring Garden Road, Halifax, NS B3J 1E9
Phone: (902) 490-5822 Fax: (902) 490-5743
E-mail: mahm1@tonyx.nsh.library.ns.ca
Deadline: April 30

  A $1,000 prize is awarded annually to the author of a fiction or non-fiction children's book published in the previous 12 months. The author must be a resident of Atlantic Canada.

Burnaby Writers' Society Competition

Eileen Kernaghan, Burnaby Writers' Society,
  6584 Deer Lake Avenue, Burnaby, BC V5T 3T7
Phone: (604) 435-6500
Deadline: May 31

  Annual cash prizes of $200, $100, and $50 are given to the top three entries in the competition. Categories and themes change from year to year (poetry in 1998, prose in 1999). Open to B.C. residents only. Entry fee $5. Write for guidelines.

Canada–Japan Book Award

Josiane Polidori, Writing and Publishing Section, Canada Council
  for the Arts, P.O. Box 1047, 350 Albert Street, Ottawa, ON K1P 5V8
Phone: 1-800-263-5588 or (613) 566-4414, ext. 5576
  Fax: (613) 566-4410

E-mail: josiane.polidori@canadacouncil.ca
Web site: www.canadacouncil.ca

A cash prize of $10,000 is awarded each year for an outstanding book by a Canadian author about Japan, by a Japanese author translated by a Canadian, or by a Japanese-Canadian writer. Publishers of eligible books may nominate titles for this award.

Canadian Association of Journalists Awards

Carleton University, Room 316B, St. Patrick's Building, Ottawa, ON KIS 5B6
Phone: (613) 526-8061   Fax: (613) 521-3904
Deadline: January 31

Cash prizes of $1,000 are awarded in the following categories: open newspaper/wire service; community newspaper; magazine; open TV (under 5 minutes); open TV (over 5 minutes); regional TV; radio news (under 10 minutes); radio news (over 10 minutes); photojournalism; conflict analysis. Entry fee $25 (CAJ members), $50 (non-members). One category is also open to students (no entry fee for CAJ members, $20 for non-members; deadline February 28). Annual.

Canadian Authors Association Awards

Alec McEachern, P.O. Box 419, Campbellford, ON KOL ILO
Phone: (705) 653-0323   Fax: (705) 653-0593
E-mail: canauth@redden.on.ca
Web site: www.CanAuthors.org/national.html

Air Canada Award

Deadline: March 31

A prize comprising two return tickets to any destination served by Air Canada is awarded to the most promising young writer under 30. Contenders are nominated by the Canadian Authors Association (to whom recommendations should be sent) and other writers' associations. Annual.

CAA Jubilee Award

Deadline: December 15

A prize of $2,500 and a silver medal is awarded for an outstanding collection of short stories by a Canadian author. Annual.

CAA Lela Common Award
Deadline: December 15

A prize of $2,500 goes to the best work of Canadian history written in English by a Canadian author. Annual.

CAA Literary Awards
Deadline: December 15

A prize of $2,500 and a sterling-silver medal is awarded in recognition of the year's outstanding books in the categories of fiction, poetry, and drama by Canadian writers. Entries should manifest "literary excellence without sacrifice of popular appeal." Nominations from author, publisher, individual, or group eligible. Annual.

The Vicky Metcalf Body of Work Award
Deadline: December 31

A prize of $10,000 is awarded annually to the author of the best body of work by a Canadian, whether fiction, non-fiction, poetry, or picture books.

The Vicky Metcalf Short Story Awards
Deadline: December 31

A prize of $3,000 is conferred on the writer of the best short story published in an English-language Canadian magazine or anthology during the previous year; the editor of this work receives a further $1,000. Annual.

Student Writing Contest
Deadline: March 31

Cash prizes of $500 are awarded annually for the best poem (up to 30 lines) and the best short story (up to 2,000 words) in any genre by a Canadian student.

Canadian Historical Association Awards
Joanne Mineault, 395 Wellington Street, Ottawa, ON K1A 0N3
Phone: (613) 233-7885 Fax: (613) 567-3110
E-mail: jmineault@archives.ca

John Bullen Prize
Deadline: November 30

A prize of $500 is awarded, in alternate years, for the best doctoral dissertation in Canadian history (1998) and the best doctoral dissertation in a field of history other than Canadian (1999).

The Wallace K. Ferguson Award
Deadline: December 15

A $1,000 prize is awarded annually for the best work of history by a Canadian writer on a non-Canadian subject.

Sir John A. Macdonald Prize
Deadline: December 15

A prize of $1,000 is awarded in recognition of the non-fiction work of history "judged to have made the most significant contribution to an understanding of the Canadian past." Annual.

The Hilda Neatby Prize in Women's History
Deadline: February 1

A non-cash prize is awarded for an academic article, published in a Canadian journal or book during the previous year, deemed to have made an original and scholarly contribution to the field of women's history. Annual.

Canadian Letters Award

Janette Hatcher, Periodical Marketers of Canada, 175 Bloor Street
    E., Suite 1007, South Tower, Toronto, ON M4W 2R8
Phone: (416) 968-7218 Fax: (416) 968-6182

Awarded to an individual who has made an outstanding contribution to literacy as a writer, publisher, or teacher. The award comprises a $5,000 grant to an educational or literary charity of the winner's choice plus a statuette. No call for entries. Annual.

Canadian Library Association Book Awards

Brenda Shields, CLA Membership Services, 200 Elgin Street, Suite
    602, Ottawa, ON K2P 1L5
Phone: (613) 232-9625, ext. 318 Fax: (613) 563-9895
Web site: www.cla.amlibs.ca

Book of the Year for Children Award

A commemorative medal is presented annually to the author of an outstanding book suitable for children up to the age of 14 published in Canada during the previous calendar year. Any creative work (fiction, poetry, anthologies, etc.) will be deemed eligible. Author must be a Canadian citizen or permanent resident. Nominations invited from CLA members and publishers.

Young Adult Canadian Book Award

This non-cash award recognizes the author of an outstanding English-language book written in the preceding calendar year that appeals to young adults between the ages of 13 and 18. The book must be a work of fiction published in Canada, and the author should be a Canadian citizen or landed immigrant. Annual.

Canadian Literary Awards
Robert Weaver, CBC Radio Performance, P.O. Box 500, Station A,
  Toronto, ON M5W 1E6
Phone: (416) 205-6016 (dedicated information line)
Deadline: September 30

One prize of $10,000 is awarded annually in each category to the writers of the year's most outstanding short stories, poetry, and personal essays (which may be memoirs, autobiographical sketches, or travel sketches). Required length: 2,000 to 3,500 words (prose); 1,500 to 2,500 words (poetry). Entry fee $10 per manuscript. Winning entries are published in *Saturday Night* and broadcast on CBC Radio. Sponsored by CBC Radio, *Saturday Night*, and the Canada Council for the Arts.

CNA Media Awards for Excellence in Health Reporting
Canadian Nurses Association, 50 Driveway, Ottawa, ON K2P 1E2
Phone: (613) 237-2133 Fax: (613) 237-3520
Web site: www.cna-nurses.ca
Contact: Carole Presseault, Senior Advisor,
  Government Relations
Deadline: January 30

Awarded annually to promote a greater understanding of the Canadian health system. Open to Canadian print and broadcast media, wire services, news syndicates, and affiliated reporters as well as freelance journalists whose work has been published or broadcast in Canada. Winners in print, radio, and television categories receive a trophy. For entry form and further information, check CNA's web site.

The Chalmers Awards
Chalmers Awards Office, Ontario Arts Council, 151 Bloor Street
   W., Toronto, ON M5S 1T6
Phone: (416) 961-1660 or 1-800-387-0058 Fax: (416) 961-7796

The Floyd S. Chalmers Canadian Play Awards
   To honour the creation of original Canadian plays, four awards of $25,000 go to the writers of distinguished plays receiving their Metro Toronto premiere by any professional Canadian theatre group. Translations, adaptations, and collective creations are eligible. Each play is assessed in production and judged on the basis of the playwright's contribution rather than on its production values. Winners are chosen by a jury drawn from the Toronto chapter of the Canadian Critics Association and the Toronto theatre community. Administered by the Ontario Arts Council. Annual.

The Chalmers Canadian Play Awards: Theatre for Young Audiences
   Two annual awards of $25,000 honour Canadian playwrights of original plays for young audiences, defined as of school age from primary to Ontario Academic Credit levels. The plays must have been performed at least four times within a 50-kilometre radius of Metro Toronto. Other conditions match those of the previous entry.

Chapters/Books in Canada First Novel Award
Gerald Owen, *Books in Canada*, 427 Mount Pleasant Road,
   Toronto, ON M4S 2L8
Phone: (416) 489-4755 Fax: (416) 489-6045
E-mail: binc@istar.ca
Deadline: December 1
   A $5,000 prize is awarded annually for the best first novel published in English by a Canadian.

The Lina Chartrand Poetry Award

CV2 Collective, P.O. Box 3062, Winnipeg, MB R3C 4E5

Administered by *Contemporary Verse 2* magazine. A cash prize of $400 recognizes a distinguished contribution by an emerging writer to *Contemporary Verse 2*'s promotion of women's writing. The winning entry, which is chosen from the poetry by women published in the magazine during the year, also receives republication in a future issue of *CV2*. Annual.

Mr. Christie's Book Awards

Marlene Yustin, c/o Christie Brown and Co.,
  2150 Lakeshore Boulevard W., Toronto, ON M8V 1A3
Phone: (416) 503-6050 Fax: (416) 503-6034
Deadline: January 31

Annual awards of $7,500 each are presented in three categories, in English and in French: the best children's book (7 years and under), the best children's book (8 to 11 years), and the best children's book (12 to 16 years). The winners are chosen by an expert panel, which judges entries on their ability to inspire the imagination of the reader, to recognize the importance of play, to bring delight and edification, and to help children understand the world, both intellectually and emotionally. Open to Canadian citizens or landed immigrants at the time of the book's publication.

City of Regina Writing Award

Paul Wilson, Saskatchewan Writers Guild, P.O. Box 3986,
  Regina, SK S4P 3R9
Phone: (306) 757-6310 Fax: (306) 565-8554
E-mail: swg@sk.sympatico.ca
Deadline: March

Each year this award provides $4,000 to enable a Regina writer to work on a specific project. Administered by the Saskatchewan Writers Guild, funded by the city.

City of Toronto Book Award

Richard Frank, c/o Corporate Communications, 22nd Floor,
  East Tower, City Hall, Toronto, ON M5H 2N2
Phone: (416) 392-0468 Fax: (416) 392-7999

Deadline: January 31

Each year prize money totalling $15,000 is apportioned in recognition of works of literary merit in all genres that are evocative of Toronto. Fiction and non-fiction, adult and children's are eligible. Each shortlisted writer (usually four to six) receives $1,000, the balance going to the winner (usually $9,000 to $11,000).

City of Vancouver Book Award

Alan Twigg, *B.C. Book World*, 3516 West 13th Avenue (rear),
   Vancouver, BC V6R 2S3
Phone: (604) 736-4011 Fax: (604) 736-4011
Deadline: June

An annual $2,000 cash prize is awarded in October at the opening of the Vancouver International Writers' Festival. Entered books must be primarily set in or about Vancouver, though the author's place of residence is not restricted and the book may be written/published anywhere in the world. Books may be fiction, non-fiction, poetry, or drama, written for children or adults, and may deal with any aspects of the city, including its history, geography, current affairs, or the arts. Apply for guidelines.

Connaught Medal for Excellence in Health Research Journalism

Canadians for Health Research, P.O. Box 126, Westmount,
   PQ H3Z 2T1
Phone: (514) 398-7478 Fax: (514) 398-8361
Deadline: February 27

This annual national award recognizes the role of journalists in raising public awareness of the importance of health research in Canada. The award consists of a medal and a $1,500 bursary. The winning article must have been published in a Canadian newspaper or magazine during the previous calendar year.

Contemporary Verse 2 Literary Contests

CV2 Collective, P.O. Box 3062, Winnipeg, MB R3C 4E5
Deadlines: December 15, May 30, and September 30

CV2 sponsors three literary contests over its publishing year – for poetry and prose, and an open writing competition. Usually each contest is given a theme. Awards are $200 for first prize, $150 for second, and $50 for third. The entry fee of $19 covers a one-year sub-scription to the magazine. Guidelines and themes available on request. *CV2* also administers The Lina Chartrand Poetry Award.

Dafoe Book Prize
J.E. Rea, Department of History, University of Manitoba,
    500 Dysart Road, Winnipeg, MB R3T 2M8
    An annual cash prize of $5,000 is awarded for a distinguished work of non-fiction by a Canadian, or an author resident in Canada, that "contributes to the understanding of Canada and/or its place in the world."

Dartmouth Book & Writing Awards
Sara Brodie, Adult Services Librarian, Halifax Regional Library,
    Alderney Gate Branch, 60 Alderney Drive, Dartmouth,
    NS B2Y 4P8
Phone: (902) 490-5887 Fax: (902) 490-5889
E-mail: agsb1@nsh.library.ns.ca
Deadline: December
    Two prizes of $1,000 each are awarded to honour the fiction and non-fiction books in any genre that have contributed most to the enjoyment and understanding of Nova Scotia and Nova Scotians. The winning titles best celebrate "the spirit of Nova Scotia and its people." Open to any Canadian citizen or landed immigrant. Annual.

Arthur Ellis Awards
Secretary/Treasurer, Crime Writers of Canada, P.O. Box 113, 3007
    Kingston Road, Scarborough, ON M1P 1P1
Fax: (416) 406-6141
Deadline: December 31
    Prizes are awarded annually in the following categories in the crime genre: the best novel, the best first novel, the best short story, and the best non-fiction. Cash prizes awarded depending on avail-ability. Open to any writer resident in Canada or any Canadian living abroad. Setting and imprint immaterial.

The Marian Engel Award
c/o The Writers' Development Trust, 24 Ryerson Avenue, Suite
    201, Toronto, ON M5T 2P3

Phone: (416) 504-8222 Fax: (416) 504-9090

An annual award of $10,000 is conferred on a Canadian woman writer in mid-career, recognizing her collective works and the promise of her future contribution to Canadian literature. Canada's premier literary award for women.

Event, The Douglas College Review Creative Non-Fiction Contest

P.O. Box 2503, New Westminster, BC V3L 5B2
Phone: (604) 527-5293
Deadline: April 15

An annual contest exploring the creative non-fiction form. Accepts previously unpublished submissions up to 5,000 words. Three winners each receive $500 plus publication payment, with their entries published in *Event*. Other entries may also be published. Entry fee $16.

The Lionel Gelber Prize

Prize Manager, Lionel Gelber Prize, c/o Meisner Publicity and
    Promotion, 112 Braemore Gardens, Toronto, ON M6G 2C8
E-mail: meisner@interlog.com
Deadline: May 31

Presented in October, an annual award of $50,000 goes to the year's most outstanding work of non-fiction in the field of international relations written in English or in English translation and appealing both to the scholarly and the general reader. The winner is selected by a panel of five people knowledgeable in the field of international relations. Applicants may be of any nationality, but the book must be available in Canada. Books must be published between September 1 of the previous year and August 31 of the award year. Bound manuscripts are also accepted. No entry fee.

The Giller Prize

Kelly Duffin, 21 Steepleview Crescent, Richmond Hill,
    ON L4C 9RI
Phone: (905) 508-5146 Fax: (905) 508-4469
Deadline: mid-August

The Giller Prize each year awards $25,000 to the author of the best Canadian novel or short story collection in English, according to a professional jury panel. The author must be a Canadian citizen or permanent resident, and the book must have been published by a professional publisher in Canada.

John Glassco Translation Prize

Charlotte Melançon, Literary Translators' Association,
    5782 Côte St.-Antoine, Montréal, PQ H4A 1S2
Phone: (514) 489-9027
E-mail: melancon@ere.umontreal.ca
Deadline: February 15

A $500 prize is awarded for an outstanding book-length published work of literary translation. Eligible genres include short and long fiction, poetry, drama, essays, children's literature, and works of history, biography, and philosophy. The target language must be English or French (there are no restrictions on the source language). The work must be the first published book-length translation by the entrant, who must be a Canadian citizen or landed immigrant. Annual.

Government of Newfoundland & Labrador Arts & Letters Competition

Regina Best, Arts and Letters Competition, P.O. Box 1854, St.
    John's, NF A1C 5P9
Phone: (709) 729-5253
Deadline: March 6

Three prizes are normally awarded each year in each category in recognition of outstanding original, unpublished fiction, non-fiction, poetry, and drama by residents of Newfoundland. First prize $600; second prize $300; third prize $150. There is also a junior division (age 12 to 18) in the categories of prose and poetry (first prize $300; second prize $200; third prize $100). No entry fees. Write or phone for application forms.

Governor General's Literary Awards

Josiane Polidori, Writing and Publishing Section, Canada Council
    for the Arts, P.O. Box 1047, 350 Albert Street, Ottawa,
    ON K1P 5V8
Phone: 1-800-263-5588 or (613) 566-4414, ext. 5576
    Fax: (613) 566-4410

E-mail: josiane.polidori@canadacouncil.ca
Web site: www.canadacouncil.ca
Deadlines: April 15 and August 1

Seven annual awards of $10,000 are conferred in recognition of the best books of the year in English and in French in the following categories: fiction, literary non-fiction, poetry, drama, children's literature (text), children's literature (illustration), and translation. Books must be first-edition trade books and be written, translated, or illustrated by Canadian citizens or permanent residents. For translations, the original work must also be written by a Canadian. Administered by the Canada Council. Write for eligibility criteria and other guidelines.

Grand Prix du livre de Montréal

Normand Biron, Service de la culture, Ville de Montréal,
   5650, rue d'Iberville, 4e étage, Montréal, PQ H2G 3E4
Phone: (514) 872-1160 Fax: (514) 872-1153
Web site: www.ville.montreal.qc.ca/culture/sectsout/
   gplmform.htm
Deadline: May 2

A $10,000 award is bestowed on a Montreal author or publisher of an outstanding book of exceptional originality written in English or French. Works of creative fiction, analysis, criticism, and social history are eligible. Annual.

Harbourfront Festival Prize

Greg Gatenby, Harbourfront, 410 Queen's Quay W., Toronto,
   ON M5V 2Z3
Phone: (416) 973-4760

Awarded each year to a Canadian writer in mid-career who has made a substantial contribution to Canadian letters through his or her writing and his or her efforts on behalf of other Canadian writers or writing. The winner, chosen by jury, receives a $5,000 cash prize. No submissions.

Hawthorne Poetry Prize

Guy Chadsey, The Hawthorne Society of Arts and Letters, 1051
   Roslyn Road, Victoria, BC V8S 4R4

Phone: (250) 592-4703 Fax: (250) 370-7722
Deadline: April 30

A cash prize of $500, plus publication in the Hawthorne Chapbook Series, is awarded for the best submission of 12 to 20 poems by a Canadian resident. Entry fee $15. All submissions and queries must includes a SASE. Annual.

Robert C. Hayes StoryBook Playwriting Competition

Paul Stanton, StoryBook Theatre, 2011 – 10th Avenue S.W.,
    Calgary, AB T3C OK4
Phone: (403) 216-0812 Fax: (403) 216-0810
Deadline: September 15

For playwrights of original stories or adaptations of classic children's stories designed for children aged 3 to 7 (ideal scripts will appeal to parents as well). Plays should be about 60 minutes long, and may be a single play or a connected series of playettes. The winning script, which should not have been previously produced, earns the writer a $100 cash prize and will be workshopped for possible production as a StoryBook Cabaret. Entry fee $5. Annual.

Harold Adams Innes Prize

Michelle Legault, HSSFC Scholarly Book Prizes, 151 Slater Street,
    Suite 410, Ottawa, ON K1P 5H3
Phone: (613) 234-1269, ext. 352 Fax: (613) 236-4853
E-mail: secaspp@aspp.hssfc.ca
Web site: http://aspp.hssfc.ca

A $1,000 prize is awarded for the best English-language book-length work of advanced scholarship published in the field of social sciences and funded by the ASPP in that fiscal year. Annual.

International 3-Day Novel Contest

Anvil Press, 175 East Broadway, Suite 204A, Vancouver,
    BC V5T 1W2
Phone: (604) 876-8710 Fax: (604) 879-2667
Brian Kaufman, sub-TERRAIN Magazine, P.O. Box 1575, Bentall
    Centre, Vancouver, BC V6C 2P7
Phone: (604) 876-8710 Fax: (604) 879-2667

Research and outlines prior to the contest are permissible, but the actual writing must take place over the long weekend. Entries are judged by the editorial staff of Anvil Press and *sub-TERRAIN Magazine*. The winner receives a publishing offer from Anvil Press. "The world's most notorious literary marathon" is held during Labour Day weekend in September. Annual.

IODE National Book Award
Marty Dalton, 40 Orchard View Boulevard, Suite 254, Toronto,
　ON M4R 1B9
Phone: (416) 487-4416　Fax: (416) 487-4417
Deadline: January 31
　A $3,000 prize is awarded each year in recognition of the year's best children's book of at least 500 words. Must have been written by a Canadian, and have been published in the past year. Fairy tales, anthologies, and books adapted from other sources ineligible.

IODE Toronto Book Award
Education Officer, Municipal Chapter of Toronto IODE,
　40 St. Clair Avenue E., Suite 205, Toronto, ON M4T 1M9
Phone: (416) 925-5078
Deadline: December 1
　A $1,000 prize is conferred on the author or illustrator of the best children's book of the year written or illustrated by a Toronto-area resident. Annual.

Island Literary Awards
Judy Macdonald, P.E.I. Council of the Arts, 115 Richmond Street,
　Charlottetown, PE C1A 1H7
Phone: (902) 368-4410　Fax: (902) 368-4418
　The Island Literary Awards are sponsored by the P.E.I. Council of the Arts.

Milton Acorn Poetry Award
Deadline: February 15
　Awarded annually to the author of a maximum of 10 pages of poetry. First prize: a trip for two between any two points in North America (excluding Boston). Open to residents of P.E.I. Authors of one or more books published in the past five years not eligible.

Cavendish Tourist Association Children's Literature Award
Deadline: February 15

Prizes of $75, $50, and $25 are awarded to P.E.I. students at elementary, junior, and senior high levels. Students may write five pages of poetry or a five-page short story on the topic of their choice. Annual.

Feature Article Award
Deadline: February 15

The Guardian/Patriot Prize ($500) along with a $200 second prize and a $100 third prize are awarded to the authors of the best feature articles either unpublished or published within the last 12 months. Open to P.E.I. residents. Annual.

L.M. Montgomery P.E.I. Children's Literature Award
Deadline: February 15

Three prizes (first $500, second $200, third $100) are awarded annually to the authors of the three best manuscripts (maximum length 60 pages) written for children between ages 5 and 12. Must be original and unpublished. Authors must be Island residents.

New Voices Playwriting Competition Full Length Play
Deadline: February 15

For original plays (minimum playing time 1 hour 30 minutes) not previously produced. First prize is $1,000. Open to any professional or non-professional in P.E.I. Annual.

New Voices Playwriting Competition One Act Play
Deadline: February 15

For original short plays (playing time 25 to 45 minutes) not previously produced. First prize $400, second prize $200, third prize $100. Open to any professional or non-professional in P.E.I. Annual.

Carl Sentner Short Story Award
Deadline: February 15

Annual awards of $500 (first prize), $200 (second prize), and $100 (third prize) go to the authors of the best short stories. Authors must be Island residents. Not open to writers with one or more books published in the last five years.

The Laura Jamieson Prize

CRIAW/ICREF, 151 Slater Street, Suite 408, Ottawa, ON KIP 5H3
Phone: (613) 563-0681 Fax: (613) 563-0682
E-mail: criaw@sympatico.ca
Web site: www3.sympatico.ca/criaw
Deadline: June 1

To encourage the recognition and celebration of the growing body of feminist research in book form, the Canadian Research Institute for the Advancement of Women offers an annual prize to a non-fiction feminist book by a Canadian author that advances the knowledge and/or understanding of women's experience. The prize is awarded for work in Canada's official languages in alternate years: in 1998 for a book written in French (published in 1996 or 1997); in 1999 for a book written in English (published in 1997 or 1998).

Jewish Book Awards

Diane Uslaner, Director of Cultural Programming, Koffler Centre
   of the Arts, 4588 Bathurst Street, North York, ON M2R 1W6
Phone: (416) 636-1880, ext. 352 Fax: (416) 636-5813
E-mail: bjc@interlog.com
Deadline: February 14

For Canadian authors, published in Canada in the previous two years, writing on subjects of Jewish interest in the following categories: fiction, poetry, biblical/rabbinic scholarship, history, literature for young readers, scholarship on a Canadian Jewish subject, original translation from Yiddish or Hebrew, Yiddish writing, Holocaust history or literature. Annual awards vary with donor between $250 and $1,000.

The Journey Prize

Rudy Mezzetta, McClelland & Stewart Inc.,
   481 University Avenue, Suite 900, Toronto, ON M5G 2E9
Phone: (416) 598-1114, ext. 235 Fax: (416) 598-7764
Deadline: January 15

The $10,000 annual Journey Prize is awarded to a new and developing writer of distinction. A selection of the best short fiction or novel excerpts published during the previous year in Canadian literary journals is collected in *The Journey Prize Anthology*, published by McClelland & Stewart. The prizewinner is drawn from this collection. McClelland & Stewart makes its own donation of $2,000 to the journal that first published the winning entry. Submissions accepted from journal editors only.

Kingston Literary Awards

Patricia MacAulay, 417 Glencastle Road, Kingston, ON K7M 5V3
Phone: (613) 389-8486 Fax: (613) 389-8486
Deadline: March 31

Prize money of $1,000, donated by Quarry Press, is awarded for the best original, previously unpublished short stories, written in English, of no more than 2,000 words. Judges select one or more (usually three) winning entries, which are published in *Kingston This Week*. Residents of the counties of Frontenac, Lennox and Addington, and Leeds–Grenville are eligible. Entry fee $5.

The Raymond Klibansky Prize

Michelle Legault, HSSFC Scholarly Book Prizes, 151 Slater Street,
    Suite 410, Ottawa, ON KIP 5H3
Phone: (613) 234-1269, ext. 352 Fax: (613) 236-4853
E-mail: secaspp@aspp.hssfc.ca
Web site: http://aspp.hssfc.ca

A $1,000 prize is awarded for the best English-language book-length work of advanced scholarship published in the field of the humanities and funded by the ASPP in that fiscal year. Annual.

The Last Poems Poetry Contest

Brian Kaufman, *sub-TERRAIN Magazine*, 204A – 175 East
    Broadway, Vancouver, BC V5T IW2
Phone: (604) 876-8710 Fax: (604) 879-2667
Deadline: January 31

Sponsored by *sub-TERRAIN Magazine*. For "poetry that encapsulates the North American experience at the close of the twentieth century." The winner receives a $250 cash prize plus publication in the spring issue of *sub-TERRAIN*. All entrants receive a four-issue subscription to the magazine. Annual.

Stephen Leacock Memorial Medal for Humour

Jean Bradley Dickson, P.O. Box 854, Orillia, ON L3V 6K8
Phone: (705) 329-1908

Deadline: December 31

A sterling-silver medal together with the Laurentian Bank of Canada Cash Award of $5,000 is awarded for the year's best humorous book written by a Canadian in prose, verse, or as drama. Send 10 copies of book, $25 entry fee, plus author bio and photo. Annual.

Stephen Leacock Poetry & Limerick Awards

The Registrar, Orillia International Poetry Festival,
   P.O. Box 2307, Orillia, ON L3V 6S2
Phone: (705) 329-1908 Fax: (705) 326-5578
E-mail: poetry@bconnex.net
Web site: www. bconnex.net/~poetry
Deadline: April 30

Annual cash prizes of $5,000 (first place), $1,000 (second), and $500 (third) are awarded for the best unpublished English-language poetry of any description not exceeding 50 lines. Prizes of $1,000 (first), $500 (second), and $200 (third) go to the best unpublished English-language limerick of any subject, theme, or content. Entry fee $5 per poem, $10 for three limericks. Multiple entries welcome.

Ontario Student Poetry Awards

Deadlines: October 2 and April 30

Fifteen $100 cash prizes are awarded in junior (K to grade 4), intermediate (grades 5 to 9), and senior (grade 10 to OAC) categories for original poems on set topics by Ontario students. Entry fee $10. Annual.

League of Canadian Poets Awards

Sandra Drzewiecki, 54 Wolseley Street, Suite 204, Toronto,
   ON M5T 1A5
Phone: (416) 504-1657 Fax: (416) 703-0059
E-mail: league@ican.net
Web site: www.swifty.com/lc

Gerald Lampert Memorial Award

Deadline: December 31

A $1,000 cash award is given each year in recognition of the best first book of poetry by a Canadian.

Pat Lowther Memorial Award
Deadline: December 31
   An annual $1,000 prize recognizes the best book of poetry written by a Canadian woman and published in Canada.

National Poetry Contest
Deadline: January 31
   Three prizes – of $1,000, $750, and $500 – are awarded annually for the best unpublished poems not exceeding 75 written lines. Fifty of the submitted poems, including the three winners, will be published in an anthology.

For entry fees and conditions for the above awards, contact the League or check their web site. Send SASE for submission forms for these and for the following new contests:
The Canadian Poetry Chapbook Competition
Deadline: March 1. Annual.
The Canadian Youth Poetry Competition
Deadline: March 1. Annual.

Literary Writes Competition

Federation of B.C. Writers, P.O. Box 2206 MPO, Vancouver,
   BC V6B 3W2
Phone: (604) 683-2057 Fax: (604) 683-8269
E-mail: fedbcwrt@pinc.com
   Open to B.C. writers only. Topic/theme changes each year. Up to 2,000 words of unpublished work. Cash prize, deadline, and genre undecided at time of writing. Write or phone for details. Annual.

The Macpherson Prize

The Canadian Political Science Association, 1 Stewart Street,
   Suite 205, University of Ottawa, Ottawa, ON K1N 6H7
Phone: (613) 564-4025 Fax: (613) 230-2746
Deadline: December
   A biennial award of $750 is made to the author of the best book published in English or French in the field of political theory. No textbooks, edited texts, collections of essays, or multiple-authored works will be considered. The deadline for the 2000 prize is

December 1999 and applies to books published in 1998 and 1999. The author must be a Canadian citizen or permanent resident.

Magazine and Newspaper Travel Writing Contest

Periodical Writers Association of Canada, 54 Wolseley Street,
  Suite 203, Toronto, ON M5T 1A5
Phone: (416) 504-1645 Fax: (416) 703-0059
E-mail: pwac@web.net
Web site: www.cycor.ca/PWAC
Contact: Ruth Biderman
Deadline: November 9

A cash prize of $2,000 is awarded each year for the best unpublished travel-related non-fiction article (1,200 to 2,500 words), written in English by a Canadian citizen or landed immigrant. The winning article is published in *Outpost* magazine (see p. 119). The Blue Pencil Option offers a critique of your entry by a professional writer. Entry fee $15, $45 for Blue Pencil Option.

The Malahat Review Long Poem Prize

Marlene Cookshaw, *The Malahat Review*, University of Victoria,
  P.O. Box 1700 MS 8524, Victoria, BC V8W 2Y2
Phone: (250) 721-8524
E-mail: malahat@uvic.ca
Deadline: March 1, 1999

Two prizes of $400, plus payment for publication, are awarded biennially for the best original, unpublished long poems or cycle of poems of 5 to 15 pages. Entry fee covers one subscription to *Malahat*.

The Malahat Review Novella Prize

Marlene Cookshaw, *The Malahat Review*, University of Victoria,
  P.O. Box 1700 MS 8524, Victoria, BC V8W 2Y2
Phone: (250) 721-8524
E-mail: malahat@uvic.ca
Deadline: March 1, 1998

A prize of $400, plus payment for publication, is awarded biennially for the best original, unpublished prose work no longer than 60,000 words. Entry fee covers one subscription to *Malahat*.

Manitoba Literary Awards

Robyn Maharaj, Manitoba Writers' Guild, 100 Arthur Street,
   Suite 206, Winnipeg, MB R3B 1H3
Phone: (204) 942-6134 or toll free (888) 637-5802
   Fax: (204) 942-5754
E-mail: mbwriter@mb.ca
Web site: www.mbwriter.mb.ca
Deadline: Spring (for all awards)

The Heaven Chapbook Prize
   A biennial cash prize of $250 is awarded for the best literary
chapbook by a Manitoba writer. Entries may be books of drama,
fiction, memoirs, or poetry, and must be under 100 pages and
written in English. Self-published books are conditionally eligible.
Sponsored by Heaven Art & Book Café.

The John Hirsch Award for Most Promising Manitoba Writer
   A cash prize of $2,500, donated by the estate of the late John
Hirsch, co-founder of the Manitoba Theatre Centre, is awarded
annually to the most promising Manitoba writer. Authors of poetry,
fiction, creative non-fiction, and drama are eligible.

The McNally Robinson Book for Young People Award
   An annual cash prize of $1,000, donated by McNally Robinson
Booksellers, is awarded for the best young person's book written by
a Manitoba author. Books submitted for this award are also eligible for the previous award.

The McNally Robinson Book of the Year Award
   An annual cash prize of $2,500, donated by McNally Robinson
Booksellers, is awarded for an outstanding book in any genre written
by a Manitoba resident. The title must be non-academic and written
in English. Fiction, poetry, creative non-fiction, and plays eligible.

W.O. Mitchell Literary Prize

c/o The Writers' Development Trust, 24 Ryerson Avenue,
   Suite 201, Toronto, ON M5T 2P3
Phone: (416) 504-8222 Fax: (416) 504-9090
Deadline: December 31

A $15,000 prize is awarded annually to a Canadian writer who has produced an outstanding body of work, has acted during his/her career as a "caring mentor" for writers, and has published a work of fiction or had a new stage play produced during the three-year period specified for each competition.

The Gordon Montador Award

c/o The Writers' Development Trust, 24 Ryerson Avenue,
    Suite 201, Toronto, ON M5T 2P3
Phone: (416) 504-8222 Fax: (416) 504-9090

An annual $2,000 joint prize goes to the author and publisher of the year's best Canadian book of non-fiction on contemporary social issues.

Morguard Literary Awards

Marlene A. Gamble, Manager, REIC Member and Chapter
    Services, 5407 Eglinton Avenue W., Suite 208, Etobicoke,
    ON M9C 5K6
Phone: (416) 695-9000 or 1-800-542-7230 Fax: (416) 695-7230
E-mail: marlene_gamble.reic.com
Deadline: March 31

Recognizes outstanding articles or speeches relevant to the Canadian real estate industry. Sponsored by the Real Estate Institute of Canada and Morguard Investments Ltd., a $2,000 prize goes to the winner in each of two categories: practising industry lay writers and academic writers. Submissions must be original, unpublished articles or speeches, 3,000 to 6,000 words long, given in the past 12 months. Annual.

{m}Öthêr Tøñgué Press Annual Poetry Chapbook Contest

Mona Fertig, {m}Öthêr Tøñgué Press, 290 Fulford-Ganges Road,
    Salt Spring Island, BC V8K 2K6
Fax: (604) 537-4725
Deadline: November 30

A first prize of $400 and second prize of $200 will be awarded to the two best Canadian manuscripts of unpublished poetry (10 to 15 pages). The winning manuscripts will also be published as beautifully designed limited-edition chapbooks. Annual.

National Business Book Awards

Faye Mattachione, Coopers & Lybrand, 145 King Street W.,
Toronto, ON M5H 1V8
Phone: (416) 869-1130
Deadline: mid-December

An annual award of $10,000 recognizes excellence in business writing. When more than one entry excels, a second prize of $5,000 is sometimes conferred. Coopers & Lybrand and Bank of Montreal are co-sponsors of this award. Media sponsors are *Maclean's* and *Canadian Business* magazine. Annual.

National Canadian One-Act Playwriting Competition

George Stonyk, Ottawa Little Theatre, 400 King Edward Avenue,
Ottawa, ON KIN 7M7
Phone: (613) 233-8948   Fax: (613) 233-8027
Deadline: May 31

With the object of encouraging literary and dramatic talent in Canada, the competition, for an unproduced original one-act play in English (playing time 25 to 49 minutes) is open to professional and non-professional Canadian playwrights resident in Canada including landed immigrants. First prize, the Solange Karsh Award, consists of $1,000 and a gold medal; second prize, the Dorothy White Award, is $700; third prize, the Gladys Cameron Watt Award, is $500. Annual.

National Magazine Awards

Pat Kendall, National Magazine Awards Foundation, 109
Vanderhoof Avenue, Suite 207, Toronto, ON M4G 2H7
Phone: (416) 422-1358   Fax: (416) 422-3762
E-mail: nmaf@interlog.com
Deadline: mid-January

The written categories are as follows: one-of-a-kind articles (any hard-to-classify non-fiction article); humour; business; science, health, and medicine; public issues – politics; public issues – social affairs; reporting; fiction (commissioned by the magazine); poetry (commissioned by the magazine); arts and entertainment; sports and recreation; columns (three columns by the same writer in the same magazine); travel; service (presenting practical and useful information); how-to (any article that presents practical how-to information); essays; personal journalism; profiles; editorial package (a theme issue reflecting collaboration between editors and writers); words and pictures (an article relying for its impact on text and visuals).

Canadian staff or freelance contributors are eligible. Magazine publishers or editors or freelancers may submit. Gold awards are $1,500, silver awards $500. As well, the President's Medal, worth $3,000, is awarded to an article considered the "Best of Show." The winner of the Alexander Ross Award for Best New Magazine Writer receives a cash prize of $1,500. Editors are encouraged to make submissions on behalf of new writers. The Foundation also awards winners in the categories Outstanding Achievement, Best New Magazine, and Magazine of the Year. Annual.

Nepean Public Library Annual Short Story Contest
Marlene McCausland, Communications Office, Nepean Public
  Library, 101 Centrepointe Drive, Nepean, ON K2G 5K7
Phone: (613) 727-6646 Fax: (613) 727-6677
Deadline: March 31
For an original, unpublished, English-language story (approximately 2,500 words or less) written by an adult (18 years and over) Ontario resident in the National Capital Region. First prize $500; second prize $250; third prize $100. Winners are announced at the Ottawa Valley Book Festival Literary Awards in May. Entry fee $5. Annual.

The bpNichol Chapbook Award
The Phoenix Community Works Foundation, 316 Dupont Street,
  Toronto, ON M5R 1V9
Phone: (416) 964-7919
Deadline: March 30
A prize of $1,000 is offered each year for the best poetry chapbook published in English in Canada. The chapbook should be between 10 and 48 pages long.

The Alden Nowlan Award
Arts Branch, New Brunswick Department of Municipalities,
  Culture & Housing, P.O. Box 6000, Fredericton, NB E3B 5H1
Phone: (506) 453-2555 Fax: (506) 453-2416

Deadline: October 1

Designed to recognize excellence in English-language literary arts, this award offers a cash prize of $5,000 for the outstanding achievements and contribution to literature of a New Brunswick writer. Nominees must have been born in the province or have lived there for at least five years. No self-nominations considered. Annual.

Ottawa-Carleton Book Award

Arts Office, Regional Municipality of Ottawa-Carleton, Ottawa-
    Carleton Centre, 111 Lisgar Street, Ottawa, ON K2P 2L7

Phone: (613) 560-1239 Fax: (613) 560-1380

Deadline: January 20

A $2,000 award is presented each year to both an English and a French author of a book of literary merit published within the previous two calendar years. Alternating annually between the categories of fiction and non-fiction, the 1998 award is for non-fiction, 1999 for fiction. The authors must reside in the Regional Municipality of Ottawa-Carleton and be Canadian citizens or landed immigrants. Entries are reviewed by professional juries. Awards are presented at the Ottawa Valley Book Festival in May.

Ottawa Citizen Award for Non-Fiction

For further information: Marsha Skuce, *The Ottawa Citizen*,
    Liaison for the *Ottawa Citizen* Book Award

Phone: (613) 596-3722 Fax: (613) 596-8455

E-mail: mskuce@the citizen.southam.ca

For submissions: Co-ordinator, The *Ottawa Citizen* Award for
    Non-Fiction, Ottawa Valley Book Festival, 305 St. Patrick
    Street, Ottawa, ON KIN 5K4

Deadline: second Friday in February

An annual prize of $1,000 is awarded for the best professionally published book of non-fiction, written in English, by a resident of the *Ottawa Citizen* circulation area.

Ottawa Valley Reading Council Children's Book Award

Sonja Karsh, President, Ottawa Valley Reading Council, P.O. Box
    8073, Station T, Ottawa, ON KIG 3H6

A cash prize of $250 is awarded for an outstanding children's book by an Ottawa Valley resident. Each year the award alternates between a book published in English and in French. Write for deadlines and conditions.

Prairie Fire Writing Contests

Prairie Fire Press Inc., 423 – 100 Arthur Street, Winnipeg,
 MB R3B IH3
Phone: (204) 943-9066 Fax: (204) 942-1555

Bliss Carman Poetry Award
Deadline: June 30

Cash prizes of $500, $200, and $100 are awarded for the best three submissions of up to three original, unpublished poems (no more than 30 lines each). The work must not have been submitted or accepted elsewhere, nor entered simultaneously in any other competition. Winning entries will be published in *Prairie Fire*, the authors paid for publication. The entry fee of $24 covers a one-year subscription to *Prairie Fire* magazine. Annual.

Prairie Fire*'s Writing Contests*

In each of the following annual contests, the entry fee of $24 covers a one-year subscription to *Prairie Fire* magazine, and each winning entry is published in *Prairie Fire*, the authors paid for publication. All entries must be original, unpublished, and not have been submitted elsewhere either for publication or broadcast or for another competition.
SHORT FICTION
Deadline: November 30

Cash prizes of $300, $200, and $100 are awarded for the three winning entries. One story per entry – maximum 3,000 words.
LONG SHORT STORY
Deadline: December 31

One prize of $500 is awarded to the author of the best short story to a maximum of 20,000 words.
LONG POEM
Deadline: February 28

Prizes of $350, $250, and $150 are awarded for the top three entries in this new annual contest. Contact *Prairie Fire* for details.
CREATIVE NON-FICTION
Deadline: April 30

Cash prizes of $300, $200, and $100 are awarded for the three best entries (to a maximum of 3,000 words).

Two Minute Tales or Asap's Fables
Deadline: September 30
A postcard fiction/prose poetry contest. Five $100 prizes are awarded to the winning pieces. Up to three pieces of no more than 500 words each may be entered. Each must be original, unpublished, and not have been submitted elsewhere. Winning entries will be published in *Prairie Fire*, the authors paid for publication. The entry fee of $24 covers a one-year subscription to *Prairie Fire* magazine. Annual.

PRISM international Short Fiction Contest

PRISM international, Creative Writing Program, University of
   British Columbia, Buch E-462, 1866 Main Mall, Vancouver,
   BC V6T IZI
Phone: (604) 822-2514 Fax: (604) 822-3616
E-mail: prism@unixg.ubc.ca
Web site: www.arts.ubc.ca/prism
Deadline: December 15
A $2,000 prize is awarded annually for the best original, unpublished short story (up to 25 double-spaced pages). Five runner-up prizes of $200 are also conferred. There is no limit on the number of stories that may be entered. Works of translation are eligible. All entrants receive a one-year subscription to *PRISM international*, who buy first North American serial rights for all works accepted for publication.

QSPELL Book Awards
Diana McNeill, QSPELL, 1200 Atwater Avenue, Montreal,
   PQ H3Z IX4
Phone: (514) 933-0878 Fax: (514) 933-0878
E-mail: qspell@total.net
Deadlines: May 31
   All entry fees $10.

A.M. Klein Prize for Poetry
An annual cash prize of $2,000 is awarded for the best work of poetry written in English by a writer who has lived in Quebec for at least three of the past five years.

Hugh MacLennan Prize for Fiction
An annual cash prize of $2,000 goes to the author of an outstanding work of fiction written in English by a Quebec writer.

QSPELL Prize for Non-Fiction
An annual cash prize of $2,000 is awarded to the writer of the best book of literary non-fiction written in English by a resident of Quebec.

QSPELL/FEWQ First Book Award
An annual cash prize of $500 honours the author of the best first book written in English by a Quebec resident.

Rogers Communications Writers' Trust Prize for Canadian Fiction
c/o The Writers' Development Trust, 24 Ryerson Avenue, Suite 201, Toronto, ON M5T 2P3
Phone: (416) 504-8222 Fax: (416) 504-9090
Deadline: April 30 or September 2, depending on publishing date
A $10,000 prize is awarded to the author of the year's outstanding novel or short story collection written in English by a Canadian citizen or landed immigrant. Annual.

Room of One's Own Literary Competition
Room of One's Own, P.O. Box 46160, Station D, Vancouver, BC V6J 5G5
Web site: www.islandnet.com/Room
Two competitions for women writers only are run through the journal each year. Cash prizes (first $300, second $150, third $75) are awarded for outstanding poetry (4 to 5 pieces, up to 70 lines per poem) and short fiction and creative non-fiction (up to 3,000 words). Winners and runners-up are published in a special issue of the journal. Check web site or journal for details.

Gabrielle Roy Prize for Canadian Literary Criticism

Lorna Knight, 2B Kroch Library, Cornell University, Ithaca,
NY 15853-5302
Phone: (607) 255-3530   Fax: (607) 255-9524
E-mail: lmk22@cornell.edu

A medal and a $150 cash award are presented each year to the authors of the English- and French-language books deemed to be the best works of literary criticism published in the previous year. The competition is open to works published anywhere in the world, but the subject must be Canadian or Quebec writing, and submissions must be made by the publishers. Sponsored and administered by the Association of Canadian and Quebec Literatures.

Sandburg–Livesay Anthology Contest

Unfinished Monument Press, 237 Prospect Street S., Hamilton,
ON L8M 2Z6
Deadline: October 31

Named in honour of Carl Sandburg and Dorothy Livesay. The winner of the best poem (published or unpublished) of up to 80 lines in the People's Poetry tradition exemplified by these poets receives a cash prize of $100 (U.S.) and U.S anthology publication. Entry fee $10 for up to 10 poems. Annual.

The Ruth Schwartz Children's Book Award

The Literature Office, Ontario Arts Council, 151 Bloor Street W.,
Toronto, ON M5S 1T6
Phone: (416) 969-7438   Fax: (416) 961-7796

A panel of children's booksellers selects two shortlists of five young adult and five picture books in February; two juries of children then select a winner in each category. There is no application process; all Canadian-authored/illustrated children's trade books published in the previous year are eligible. The annual awards ($3,000 for the picture book category, shared between author and illustrator; $2,000 for the YA category) are presented by the OAC at the annual CBA convention in June or July.

Science in Society Journalism Awards

Canadian Science Writers' Association, P.O. Box 75, Station A,
Toronto, ON M5W 1A2

Phone: (416) 928-9624 Fax: (416) 924-6715
E-mail: cswa@interlog.com
Web site: www.interlog.com/~cswa

Herb Lampert Student Writing Award
   An annual cash prize of $750 is awarded to the student science
writer of the best original material in either Print or TV and Radio
categories. Any student writer who has a science article published
in a student or other newspaper or magazine, or aired on a radio or
TV station, in Canada is eligible.

Science Journalism Competition
   Annual cash prizes of $1,000 are awarded to honour outstand-
ing original contributions to science journalism in Canada in the
following categories: newspapers, magazines, radio, television, trade
publications. Competitors must be Canadian citizens or residents.
Write for submission criteria.

SIS Book Awards
   Two $1,000 cash prizes are awarded annually to the authors of
books that make outstanding contributions to science writing for
the general public and for children. Entries may address aspects of
basic or applied science or technology, historical or current, in any
area including health, science, or environmental issues, regulatory
trends, etc. Books are judged on literary excellence and scientific
content. The writer must be a Canadian citizen or resident.

Short Grain Writing Contest
Business Manager, P.O. Box 1154, Regina, SK E4P 3B4
Phone: (306) 244-2828
E-mail: grain.mag@sk.sympatico.ca
Web site: www.skwriter.com
Deadline: January 31
   Offers $3,000 in prizes each year for original, unpublished works
in three categories: dramatic monologue (a self-contained speech
given by a single character in 500 words or less), postcard story (a
work of narrative fiction in 500 words or less), and prose poem (a
lyric poem written as a prose paragraph or paragraphs in 500 words

or less). In each category, first prize is $500, second prize $300, third prize $200. Winners and Honourable Mentions will be published in *Grain*. Entry fee $20.

Edna Staebler Award for Creative Non-Fiction

Kathryn Wardropper, Administrator, Wilfrid Laurier University,
    75 University Avenue W., Waterloo, ON N2L 3C5
Phone: (519) 884-0710, ext. 3109 Fax: (519) 884-8202
E-mail: kwardrop@mach1.wlu.ca
Deadline: March 31

A $3,000 prize is awarded annually for an outstanding work of creative non-fiction, which must be written by a Canadian and have a Canadian location and significance. To be eligible, an entry must be the writer's first or second published book. Established to give recognition and encouragement to new writers. Administered by Wilfrid Laurier University.

The sub-TERRAIN Short Story Contest

Brian Kaufman, *sub-TERRAIN Magazine*, 204A – 175 East
    Broadway, Vancouver, BC V5T 1W2
Phone: (604) 876-8710 Fax: (604) 879-2667
Deadline: May 15

Sponsored by *sub-TERRAIN Magazine*. The winner receives a $500 cash prize plus publication in the summer issue of *sub-TERRAIN*. All entrants receive a four-issue subscription. Any unpublished fiction of 2,000 words or less is eligible. Carries a $15 one-time, one-story entry fee; additional stories may be submitted with a supplementary fee of $5/story. Annual.

Theatre BC's Annual Canadian National Playwriting Competition

c/o 1005 Broad Street, Suite 307, Victoria, BC V8W 2A1
Phone: (250) 381-2443 Fax: (250) 381-4419
E-mail: theatrebc@pacificcoast.net (inquiries only)
Web site: www.culturenet.ca/theatrebc
Deadline: third Monday in June

For original, unproduced full-length and one-act stage plays submitted by resident Canadian professional and non-professional playwrights. Cash awards are $1,500 (full-length), $1,000 (one-act), and $750 (special merit), plus professional dramaturgy and public reading at Theatre BC's New Play Workshops in October/ November. Submissions should be made under a pseudonym. Send SASE or check out web site for guidelines. Entry fee $35 per play. Annual.

Trillium Book Award

Terry Smith, Ministry of Citizenship, Culture and Tourism,
  Cultural Programs Branch, 77 Bloor Street W., 2nd Floor,
  Toronto, ON M7A 2R9
Phone: (416) 314-7122 Fax: (416) 314-7091
Deadline: November/December

To honour outstanding achievement in writing by Ontario authors, a $12,000 prize is presented to the author of the winning English-language and the winning French-language books. A further $2,500 goes to the publishers. The works may be in any genre – fiction, non-fiction, children's, poetry, drama. Entrants must have been resident in Ontario for at least 3 of the last 5 years. Annual.

VanCity Book Prize

c/o *B.C. BookWorld*, 3516 West 13th Avenue (rear), Vancouver,
  BC V6R 2S3
Phone: (604) 736-4011
Deadline: May 15

A $4,000 prize is awarded annually for the best British Columbia book of fiction or non-fiction pertaining to women's issues. Author should be a B.C. resident. Publishers are invited to submit eligible titles. Administered by *B.C. BookWorld*.

Viacom Canada Writers' Trust Prize for Canadian Non-Fiction

c/o The Writers' Development Trust, 24 Ryerson Avenue,
  Suite 201, Toronto, ON M5T 2P3
Phone: (416) 504-8222 Fax: (416) 504-9090
Deadline: April 30 or September 2, depending on publishing date

A $10,000 prize is awarded annually to the Canadian author of the work of non-fiction, written in English, that in the opinion of the judges shows the highest literary merit. Up to four runner-up prizes of $1,000 will be awarded to other shortlisted authors.

Herman Voaden National Playwriting Competition

Maurice Breslow, Drama Department, Queen's University,
   Kingston, ON K7L 3N6
Phone: (613) 545-2104 Fax: (613) 545-6268
Deadline: January 31

Three prizes (first $3,000, second $2,000, third $1,000) honour the year's outstanding full-length plays (not previously produced or published) written in English by Canadians or landed immigrants. The first and second prize winning plays will receive a one-week workshop and public reading by a professional director and cast in affiliation with the Thousand Islands Playhouse, Gananoque. The two authors will be playwrights-in-residence for the rehearsal and reading period. Entry fee $30. Annual.

The Bronwen Wallace Award

c/o The Writers' Development Trust, 24 Ryerson Avenue,
   Suite 201, Toronto, ON M5T 2P3
Phone: (416) 504-8222 Fax: (416) 504-9090
Deadline: January 15

An award of $1,000 is presented, in alternate years, to a Canadian poet or a Canadian short fiction writer under the age of 35 who is unpublished in book form but whose work has appeared in at least one independently edited magazine or anthology. Applicants should submit 5–10 pages of unpublished poetry in English (1998) or up to 2,500 words of unpublished prose fiction in English (1999).

Western Magazine Awards

Western Magazine Awards Foundation, Main Post Office, Box
   2131, Vancouver, BC V6B 3T8
Phone: (604) 669-3717 Fax: (604) 669-2844
Deadline: January 31

Awards of $500 are offered in nine categories: business, science, technology, and medicine; arts, culture, and entertainment (includes spectator sports); travel and leisure (includes participatory sports and lifestyle articles); regular column; fiction; human experience;

public issues (includes environmental issues); and Gold Award for Best Articles in Alberta, B.C., Manitoba, Saskatchewan. Send SASE for complete guidelines and application forms. Submissions accepted from magazine editors and individual writers (who must be Canadian citizens, landed immigrants, or full-time residents).

Jon Whyte Memorial Essay Prize

Writers Guild of Alberta, 11759 Groat Road, 3rd Floor,
   Edmonton, AB T5M 3K6
Deadline: January 31

Alberta writers are invited to submit essays of up to 3,500 words on any subject. The winning essay will earn a $2,000 prize from the Alberta Foundation for the Arts. Annual.

The Kenneth Wilson Awards

Judy Johnson, Canadian Business Press, 40 Shields Court,
   Suite 201, Markham, ON L3R 0M5
Phone: (905) 946-8889 Fax: (905) 479-1711
Deadline: March

Recognizing excellence in writing and graphic design in specialized business/professional publications, the competition is open to all Canadian business publications. Eleven categories cover editorial, marketing, profiles, departments, features, news stories, and graphic design. Editorial staff or freelance contributors may enter. Winners of gold and silver awards receive cash prizes of $1,000 and $500 respectively. Annual.

Winners' Circle Short Story Contest

Bill Belfontaine, Canadian Authors Association, Metropolitan
   Toronto Branch, 33 Springbank Avenue, Scarborough,
   ON M1N 1G2
Phone: (416) 698-8687 Fax: (416) 698-8687
Deadline: November 30

A cash prize of $500 and four runners-up of $125 are awarded annually for the best new short stories (2,500 to 3,500 words) by Canadian authors. Ten more entrants receive honourable mentions. Entries are evaluated for $10. All 15 stories are published in the *Winners' Circle Anthology*. Opens July 1 each year. Multiple submissions encouraged. Send SASE for guidelines.

Writers' Federation of New Brunswick Literary Competition

Anna Mae Snider, Writers' Federation of New Brunswick, 404
  Queen Street, P.O. Box 37, Station A, Fredericton, NB E3B 4Y2
Phone: (506) 459-7228 Fax: (506) 459-7228
E-mail: aa821@fan.nb.ca
Deadline: February 14

Cash prizes (first $200, second $100, third $30) are awarded annually in the following categories: poetry, fiction, non-fiction, and children's literature (poetry and prose). Manuscripts can be on any subject and should not exceed 15 pages (4,000 words) for prose, 100 lines or 5 poems; minimum submission of 10 poems in children's category. All awards open to New Brunswick residents only.

The Alfred G. Bailey Prize

An annual cash prize of $400 is awarded for an outstanding unpublished poetry manuscript of at least 48 pages. Some individual poems may have been previously published or accepted for publication.

The Sheree Fitch Prize

A first prize of $200, second of $100, and third of $50 are offered to young writers, aged 14 to 18 as of January 1 in the year of the contest, which alternates yearly between poetry and prose – 1998 is for prose entries, 1999 for poetry. Maximum for poetry is 5 poems or 100 lines; for prose, up to 15 pages or 4,000 words. Work must be original and unpublished.

The Richards Prize

An annual award of $400 goes to the author of a collection of short stories, a short novel, or a substantial portion (up to 30,000 words) of a longer novel. Work must be unpublished although some individual stories may have been.

Writers' Federation of Nova Scotia Awards

Jane Buss, 1809 Barrington Street, Suite 901, Halifax, NS B3J 3K8
Phone: (902) 423-8116 Fax: (416) 422-0881

Atlantic Writing Competition
Deadline: August 7

Six categories for unpublished manuscripts – novel, non-fiction book, short story, poetry, writing for children, and one to be announced – receive small cash prizes of between $50 and $200 for first, second, and third placegetters. All entries receive a brief evaluation. Atlantic residents only. Annual.

Thomas Raddall Atlantic Fiction Award
Deadline: January 16

A $4,000 prize is awarded each year for an outstanding novel or collection of short stories, in English or French, by a native or resident of Atlantic Canada. Co-sponsored by the Writers' Development Trust.

Evelyn Richardson Memorial Literary Trust Award
Deadline: January 16

A $1,000 prize is awarded annually for an outstanding work of non-fiction by a native or resident of Nova Scotia.

Writers Guild of Alberta Annual Awards
c/o Writers Guild of Alberta, 11759 Groat Road, 3rd Floor,
    Edmonton, AB T5M 3K6
Phone: (403) 422-8174 Fax: (403) 422-2663
Deadline: December 31

A $500 prize is awarded annually for excellent achievement by an Alberta writer in each of the following categories: children's literature, drama, non-fiction, novel, poetry, short fiction, and best first book.

The Writers' Union of Canada Short Prose Competition for Developing Writers
The Writers' Union of Canada, 24 Ryerson Avenue, Toronto,
    ON M5T 2P3
Deadline: November 3

An annual award to discover developing writers of fiction and non-fiction. A $2,500 first prize and $1,000 second prize are awarded for the best pieces of unpublished prose up to 2,500 words by a

Canadian citizen or landed immigrant who has not previously been published in book format and does not have a contract with a publisher. The first-placed author agrees to permit publication of the winning entry in *Books in Canada*. Entry fee $25. Apply for full entry conditions.

8

PROVINCIAL & FEDERAL
WRITER SUPPORT PROGRAMS

Outlined below are the main sources of provincial and federal funding for individual Canadian writers. Arts council and other government grants are designed to buy the writer time to devote to his or her work for a specified period in order to support a work-in-progress or the completion of a specific creative project through meeting a varying combination of living, research, travel, or professional-development costs. Such financial support is most often targeted toward the successful published author, but gifted new writers are sometimes also eligible. Several provincial initiatives are open to new as well as established writers.

The single most important source of assistance to writers across the country is the federal Canada Council for the Arts. Since the previous edition of *The Canadian Writer's Market*, the Canada Council's artist-support programs have undergone a major restructuring. Many writers will be relieved to discover that the previous levels of support have been largely retained in the revamped programs. One serious cause for regret is the demise of the Explorations Program, which was one of the few sources of support available to emerging writers. On the other hand, the First Peoples Words scheme is a welcome new addition.

All these programs require applicants to develop detailed project proposals and budgets and to provide writing samples and other support materials.

Alberta Foundation for the Arts

Vern Thiessen, Alberta Foundation for the Arts, 901 – Standard
  Life Centre, 10405 Jasper Avenue, Edmonton, AB T5J 4R7
Phone: (403) 427-6315 Fax: (403) 422-9132

Four categories of writing grants are available to the professional, published writer: The Senior Writer Grant, to a maximum of $25,000, is available to veterans with at least four published books (or equivalent) behind them. The Intermediate Writer Grant, worth a maximum of $11,000, is designed for the professional who has published at least one book (or equivalent). The Junior Writer Grant, of up to $4,000, is open to unpublished writers. In addition, the Special Project Grant of up to $5,000 may be applied for. Competition deadlines are April 1 for the senior category, April 1 and October 1 for the others.

British Columbia Arts Council

Box 9819 Stn. Prov. Gov., Victoria, BC V8W 9W3
Phone: (250) 356-1728 Fax: (250) 387-4099
E-mail: Walter_Quan@tbccc01.tbc.gov.bc.ca
Web site: www.tbc.gov.bc.ca/culture/csb/welcome.htm
Contact: Walter K. Quan, Co-ordinator, Arts Awards Programs

Assistance to a maximum of $5,000 for specific creative projects is available for professional writers of B.C. with at least two published books behind them. Eligible categories are fiction (adult and juvenile), non-fiction, drama, and poetry. One juried competition is held annually. Application deadline September 15.

The Canada Council for the Arts

350 Albert Street, P.O. Box 1047, Ottawa, ON K1P 5V8
Phone: 1-800-263-5588 or (613) 566-4414, ext. 5534 locally or a.h.
  Fax: (613) 566-4410
E-mail: silvie.bernier@canadacouncil.ca
Web site: www.canadacouncil.ca

The Canada Council offers Canadian writers substantial financial support through a variety of programs, most notably Grants for Professional Writers – Creative Writing, Travel and Author Residencies. It should be noted, however, that these grants are not available to new writers. Applicants must have had at least one book published by a professional house or two major texts (short stories, articles, etc.) published on two separate occasions in recognized literary periodicals or anthologies.

Creative Writing Grants help authors working on new projects in fiction, poetry, children's literature, comic art/narrative books, or literary non-fiction. (Literary projects that are innovative or founded on technology may also be eligible.) Grants range from $5,000 to $20,000.

Travel Grants help writers with career-related travel expenses (e.g., speaking at a national or international conference or attending a book launch). Grants are $500 and $1,000.

Author Residencies provide financial assistance to organizations, such as universities, libraries, and writers' associations, to retain the services of a writer-in-residence, thus encouraging exchanges between the author and the community as well as enabling the author to work on a writing project. (Contact Silvie Bernier by e-mail or at ext. 5537.)

The First Peoples Words – Printed and Spoken program offers grants to First Peoples writers and storytellers as well as Aboriginal-controlled publishers, periodicals, and collectives. (Contact Miles Morrisseau, ext. 5482.)

Literary Readings by Canadian Writers in Canada provides opportunities for writers to read from their works and discuss them with the public. (Contact Louise Castonguay, ext. 4573.)

Please note that these programs are subject to change. Write for eligibility conditions and guidelines.

Conseil des arts et des lettres du Québec

79, boulevard René-Lévesque est, 3e étage, Québec, PQ GIR 5N5
Phone: 1-800-897-1707 or (418) 643-1707 Fax: (418) 643-4558
500, Place d'Armes, 15e étage, Montréal, PQ H2Y 2W2
Phone: 1-800-608-3350 or (514) 864-3350 Fax: (514) 864-4160

Created in 1993 as a corporation under the jurisdiction of the Minister of Culture and Communications. The Grant Program for Professional Artists offers several types of grants to creative writers who have published at least one book with a professional publisher or four texts in cultural periodicals, or have broadcast radio scripts. Applicants must be Canadian citizens or landed immigrants, and have lived in Quebec for at least 12 months. The program is open to French and English writers.

Manitoba Arts Council

525 – 93 Lombard Avenue, Winnipeg, MB R3B 3B1
Phone: (204) 945-0422 Fax: (204) 945-5925
Contact: Pat Sanders, Writing and Publishing Officer

Several potential sources of funding for writers: The Writers A Grant, worth up to $10,000, is designed to support concentrated work on a major writing project by professional Manitoba writers who have published two books and who show a high standard of work and exceptional promise. The Writers B Grant, for Manitoba writers with one published book, is worth up to $5,000. The Writers C Grant, worth up to $2,000, for emerging writers with a modest publication background, is available to support a variety of developmental writing projects.

The Major Arts Grant supports personal creative projects of 6 to 10 months' duration by writers of exceptional accomplishment. Covering living and travel expenses, and project costs, this grant is worth up to $25,000. Finally, published Manitoba writers can apply for a Short-Term Project Grant, to a maximum of $1,000, to support significant career opportunities. Write for guidelines, eligibility criteria, and application procedures. Please note that these programs are open to Manitoba residents only.

New Brunswick Department of Municipalities, Culture & Housing

Arts Branch, P.O. Box 6000, Fredericton, NB E3B 5H1
Phone: (506) 453-2555 Fax: (506) 453-2416

Several potential sources of funding support exist for the professional writer in New Brunswick. Funds up to a maximum $6,000 in any two-year period may be applied for in the form of a Creation Grant to support the research, development, and execution of an approved original project. The Arts Awards Program offers study grants worth $1,000 to $2,500 to student and professional writers.

Newfoundland & Labrador Arts Council

P.O. Box 98, Station C, St. John's, NF A1C 5H5
Phone: (709) 726-2212 Fax: (709) 726-0619
E-mail: nlacmail@newcomm.net
Web site: www.nlac.nf.ca

Newfoundland writers can apply to the NLAC for funding support under the Project Grant Program. Project grants are intended to help individuals carry out work in their field and may be used for living expenses and materials, study, and travel costs. Grants generally range from $500 to $2,000 or slightly higher. The amount of grant money available is based on the number of applications.

Northwest Territories Arts Council

Department of Education, Culture and Employment,
    Government of the N.W.T., P.O. Box 1320, Yellowknife,
    NT XIA 2L9
Phone: (867) 920-3103   Fax: (867) 873-0205
Contact: Evelyn Dhont, Arts and Culture Officer
    The mandate of the N.W.T. Arts Council is to promote the visual, literary, and performing arts in the territories. Contributions of up to $19,300 (10 per cent of the total funding budget) may be applied for. Deadlines are January 31. For applications and guidelines, call or write to the Arts and Culture Officer.

Nova Scotia Arts Council

1660 Hollis Street, Suite 302, P.O. Box 1559, Halifax Central P.O.,
    Halifax, NS B3J 1V7
Phone: (902) 422-1123   Fax: (902) 422-1445
E-mail: nsartscouncil@ns.sympatico.ca
Contact: Peter Kirby, Program Officer, Grants to Individuals
    The Arts Council's Grants to Individuals Program is directed to support the creation of new work by professional artists (both established and emerging) in all disciplines, including literary arts; media arts (experimental film, video, and electronic art); performing arts (music, theatre, and dance); visual art and craft; and multidisciplinary work. Applicants must be Canadian citizens or landed immigrants who have lived in Nova Scotia for at least 12 months prior to application deadline.
    Professional Development Grants offer assistance up to $3,000 for formal study programs, mentoring, apprenticeships, and conferences, etc. Deadlines: May 15 and November 15.
    Research Grants offer assistance up to $4,000 to help with research leading to the creation of specific works or research that will benefit the artist's career. Deadlines: May 15 and November 15.

Travel Grants offer assistance up to $3,000 to take part in events and activities that are demonstrably important to the artist's career. Deadlines: May 15 and November 15.

Presentation Grants offer assistance up to $5,000 to help cover direct costs of public presentation of the artist's work. Deadlines: June 15 and January 15.

Creation Grants offer assistance ranging in steps from $2,000 to $12,000 to help with the creation of new work by contributing to the artist's project and living costs. Deadlines: June 15 and January 15.

Ontario Arts Council

Literature Programs – OAC, 151 Bloor Street W., Toronto,
ON M5S 1T6
Phone: (416) 969-7450   Fax: (416) 961-7796

The Ontario Arts Council offers two grant programs for Ontario-based writers. The Writers' Reserve program assists talented new, emerging, and established writers in the creation of new work in fiction, poetry, writing for children, literary criticism, arts commentary, history, biography, or politics/social issues. Writers' Reserve grants are awarded through designated book and periodical publishers, who recommend authors for funding support up to a maximum of $5,000.

The Works-in-Progress program offers support (up to a maximum of $12,000) in the completion of major book-length works of literary merit in poetry or prose by published writers.

Write to the Ontario Arts Council for detailed guidelines and application forms for these programs.

Prince Edward Island Council of the Arts

P.O. Box 2234, Charlottetown, PE C1A 8B9
Phone: (902) 368-4410   Fax: (902) 368-4417

Arts assistance grants to the value of $3,000 are available to support Island writers. Also travel and study grants up to $1,000. Application deadlines: April and October.

Saskatchewan Arts Board

3475 Albert Street, T.C. Douglas Building, 3rd Floor, Regina,
SK S4S 6X6

Phone: (306) 787-4056 or 1-800-667-7526 (SK)
   Fax: (306) 787-4199
   Under the Individual Assistance Program: A Grants, for professional, provincially or nationally recognized artists/writers, offer
up to $20,000 for creative work, up to $10,000 for professional
development, or $5,000 for research. B Grants, for professionals
who have completed basic training or education in their discipline,
offer up to $12,000 for creative work, $7,500 for professional development, or $3,500 for research. C Grants, for emerging profes-
sionals, offer up to $4,000 for creative work, $4,000 for professional
development, or $1,500 for research. Deadlines: March 1 and
October 1 each year.
   Travel grants of up to $1,000 cover travel and related expenses
incurred by artists/writers who wish to enhance their career by par-
ticipating in significant artistic events.
   The Literary Arts Program supports writers as well as book and
periodical publishers and literary organizations. Literary Arts
Project Grants aim to meet the needs of professional or emerging
Saskatchewan writers. The Literary Playscript Commissioning
Program supports the creation, performance, and appreciation of
new literary works by Saskatchewan playwrights. The Literary
Script Reading Program provides, at a subsidized rate, professional
evaluation of manuscripts by other Saskatchewan writers, who
receive a fee for their services.

Yukon Department of Tourism
Arts Branch, P.O. Box 2703, Whitehorse, YT Y1A 2C6
Phone: (867) 667-8592 Fax: (867) 393-6456
   Yukon writers may be eligible for an Advanced Artist Award of
up to $5,000 for a specific project. Funding for the program is
obtained from lotteries revenues and administered by the Arts
Branch.

9

PROFESSIONAL
DEVELOPMENT

Writers at every level of experience can extend their skills and find fresh ideas through all manner of writing courses and workshops. Some believe creative writing is best fostered in the university or college environment, by working with a good teacher who understands literary devices and structures and the power of language. Many skills peculiar to non-fiction writing, generally considered more a craft than an art, can be learned through courses or workshops led by experienced writers who have discovered not only how to refine ideas, but how to research them, transform them into workable structures, and, finally, market them. Some creative writers swear by the hothouse atmosphere, creative exchange of ideas, and collective reinforcement to be found in workshops led by expert facilitators.

Local branches of the Canadian Authors Association, libraries, and adult education classes offered by boards of education are some sources of writing courses and workshops. Regional writers' associations sometimes organize them, too, and are always a good source of information about what's currently available in your area.

This chapter is divided into two parts: first, a review of some of the country's most interesting writing schools, workshops, and retreats; second, a sample of the kind of opportunities for the development of writing skills currently offered by Canadian colleges and universities.

This larger section surveys only some of the more significant writing and journalism programs – in the mainstream and in extension departments – as well as a number of university-based workshops. The list is far from exhaustive. Many universities, colleges of applied arts, and community colleges offer writing courses at some level, depending on staff availability and student demand. Not all courses are taught every year, and programs can change at short notice. Continuing education courses are open to all, but entry to credit courses is generally limited to those with specific academic prerequisites – though experienced writers can sometimes win special permission from the course convenor. Find out where you stand before developing your plans.

The summer courses, generally about a week long and built around daily small-group workshop sessions, offer participants the chance to increase their technical skills, to submit their work to group scrutiny and critical feedback, and to enjoy, and learn from, the company of fellow writers as well as editors, agents, and other publishing people. Courses are sometimes streamed in order to cater to different levels of experience. Workshop facilitators are often nationally or internationally acclaimed authors, and some course participants enrol simply for the chance to work with them, but the best facilitators aren't necessarily the top literary names.

The workshop experience can be intense and demanding, and the rewards elusive. To get most from them, bring at least one well-developed piece of writing with you, be prepared to work hard during and outside the main sessions, but also use the opportunity to rub shoulders with other seekers, to network, and to bask in that all-too-rare sense of being part of a community of writers.

Finally, for those writers harried by family and job obligations, frustrated by the distractions of city living, and with a manuscript they simply must finish, writers' retreats and colonies offer peaceful seclusion, a beautiful rural setting, and a "room of one's own" in which to work without interruption, with meals and accommodation taken care of. Note that these are not teaching situations.

The writer's opportunities for professional development are extraordinarily diverse in Canada. Before you commit yourself, define your needs and carefully evaluate each program to see how it might meet them.

Creative Writing Schools, Workshops, & Retreats

The Banff Centre for the Arts Writing Programs

P.O. Box 1020, Station 28, 107 Tunnel Mountain Drive, Banff,
AB T0L 0C0
Phone: (403) 762-6180 Fax: (403) 762-6345
Office of the Registrar: 1-800-565-9989
E-mail: arts_info@banffcentre.ab.ca
Web site: www.banffcentre.ab.ca/CFAindex.html

All the following programs provide opportunities for professional writers, who must choose the program that best serves their needs and objectives. Banff staff are happy to discuss this individually with applicants. Also contact the Centre to discuss fee schedules and possible funding options.

Aboriginal Arts Program

Program Director: Marie Mumford
Phone: (403) 762-7537 Fax: (403) 762-6238

Aboriginal writers can contact this program directly for information on opportunities specially designed by and for Aboriginal artists.

The Banff playRites Colony

Presented through the alliance of Alberta Theatre Projects and
the Banff Centre for the Arts
August to September
Application deadline: February

An artist-centred program designed to meet the specific needs of each participant. Eligible submissions include works from new or established playwrights, works proposed by theatres and/or script development companies, and works from Canadian translators of Canadian or non-Canadian plays.

Creative Non-Fiction and Cultural Journalism Program

Maclean Hunter Chair: Michael Ignatieff
July
Application deadline: February

Offers eight established non-fiction writers an opportunity to develop a major essay, memoir, or feature piece in the domain of arts and culture. Writers work with experienced and exacting faculty editors, and interact with one another, with guest speakers, and with artists from other fields. Participants bring original projects to Banff in draft form (recommended length 5,000 words). The program requires completion of the projects by the end of the residency since the Centre for the Arts buys and exercises second rights to the material. Each participant receives a $3,000 fee for the completed essay or article.

The Leighton Studios for Independent Residencies
Web site: www.banffcentre.ab.ca/Leighton_Studios/

This year-round program offers three-month working residencies for independent professional artists engaged in the creation of new work and provides opportunities for concentrated focus in a retreat environment. Writers, playwrights, visual artists, composers, songwriters, and performance artists are eligible. The eight fully equipped studios are situated in a beautiful, quiet wooded area. Artists can apply for discounts on the studio fee according to need.

Media and Visual Arts Division
Offers opportunities for theoretical, curatorial, and project writing residencies in media and visual arts-related fields.

Writing for Style
April

A five-day workshop for writers at all levels is led by Program Director Rachel Wyatt. Resource faculty change from year to year. The program provides writers with an opportunity to work on an autobiography, a family history, a journal, unpublished stories, poetry, or non-fiction.

Writing Studio
October
Application deadline: April

Offers a unique, supportive context in which writers who are already producing work of literary merit are encouraged to pursue their own visions and voices. Applicants will normally have produced a body of work (book[s], or stories/poems in magazines or anthologies), and will be working on a book-length manuscript or manuscript-in-progress. Writers spend four or five weeks at the Banff Centre working on their manuscript in individual consultation with senior writers/editors. Enrolment is limited to 20 writers.

The Humber School for Writers

Humber College, Room D149, 205 Humber College Boulevard,
   Toronto, ON M9W 5L7
Phone: (416) 675-6622, ext. 4436 Fax: (416) 675-1249
E-mail: kertes@admin.humberc.on.ca
Contact: Joe Kertes, Director

One of Canada's best schools for writers offers a week-long, immersion summer writing workshop in fiction and poetry in August. A residency option is offered. Workshop fee about $775, plus $230 for full board.

Each year the school also offers a unique 30-week certificate program in creative writing, beginning in January. This extraordinary program offers promising writers the opportunity to send their work-in-progress (novel, short stories, or poetry) directly to their instructor, who provides editorial feedback by mail on a continuing basis throughout the academic year. Current instructors include the distinguished writers Bonnie Burnard, Peter Carey, Timothy Findley, Elisabeth Harvor, Isabel Huggan, Paul Quarrington, Richard Scrimger, Antanas Sileika, D.M. Thomas, and Eric Wright. The Doubleday–Humber Discovery Program ensures that the authors' pick for the best fiction manuscripts to emerge from the workshop are submitted to the editor-in-chief of Doubleday for serious consideration.

Admission is decided on the basis of a 15-page writing sample along with a detailed proposal of the work to be completed during the course. (Each year some students are also admitted without a work-in-progress.) Enrolment, which must be completed by mid-November, is limited. At the time of writing, the fee for Canadians and permanent residents is $989.

Through the Writers' Development Trust, full scholarships are available to cover admission to the program by those who demonstrate writing promise and financial need.

Humber has also established its own literary agency to represent the interests of its best students.

Kootenay School of Writing

112 West Hastings Street, Suite 401, Vancouver, BC V6B 1G8
Phone: (604) 688-6001

Developed on the model of the artist-run centre, this is the only writer-run centre in Canada. Organizes writing workshops, run by practising writers, in poetry, fiction, and theoretical concerns, as well as readings, panels, writer-in-residence programs, seminars, reading groups, book launches, and other events, all of which are open to the public, most for a small charge. The school maintains an archive of readings, colloquia, etc., and also publishes the literary journal *Raddle Moon* (see page 151).

Maritime Writers' Workshop

Department of Extension and Summer Session, University of
  New Brunswick, P.O. Box 4400, Fredericton, NB E3B 5A3
Phone: (506) 454-9153
Contact: Glenda Turner, Co-ordinator

An annual, week-long, limited-enrolment summer program designed to help writers at all levels of experience. Offers instruction in fiction, non-fiction, poetry, and writing for children. As well as workshops and individual tuition, the program includes lecture/discussions, public readings by instructors (all successful published writers), and other special events. All participants are required to submit manuscript samples of their work. Tuition fees are $325 (room and meal charges extra). Scholarships up to the full cost of tuition and board are awarded on the basis of need and talent.

Metchosin International Summer School of the Arts

Pearson College, 650 Pearson College Drive, Victoria, BC V9C 4H7
Phone: (250) 391-2420 Fax: (250) 391-2412
E-mail: missa@pearson-college.uwc.ca
Contact: Meira Mathison, Administrator

Located on the campus of Lester B. Pearson College, this summer school boasts a setting of extraordinary natural beauty, on a wooded hillside of Peddler Bay Inlet. Two workshops are offered in summer 1998: Poetry, a week-long workshop with one of Canada's most highly esteemed poets, Patrick Lane, July 4–10 ($400, including lunches); and Writing, with well-known short story writer Bonnie Burnard, July 6–10 ($300, including lunches). Participants cover a range of aptitude and experience. Accommodation is available. Annual.

Sage Hill Writing Experience
P.O. Box 1731, Saskatoon, SK S7K 3S1
Phone: (306) 652-7395

Sage Hill's 10-day summer writing workshops are held every August at the Sage Hill Conference Centre in rural Saskatchewan, 75 kilometres northeast of Saskatoon, or at St. Michael's Retreat Centre in Lumsden, in the beautiful Qu'Appelle Valley, north of Regina. Both centres have private rooms with writing areas, meeting rooms, recreational facilities, and home-style cooking.

The program offers workshops at introductory, intermediate, and advanced levels in fiction, poetry, and playwriting (though not all these courses are available each year). The low writer-to-instructor ratio (usually 6 to 1) and high-quality faculty (all established writers) help make these workshops among the most highly valued in Canada. Substantial individual tuition time is also considered important.

Fees per course of $495 include accommodation and meals. Scholarships are available. Enrolment is limited. Applicants should send for guidelines. Registration deadline is May 1.

Two annual Youth Writing Camps, for Saskatchewan writers aged 13 to 18, are held in August. For these free, five-day creative writing day camps, held in Saskatoon and Regina, out-of-towners need to arrange their own accommodation and travel. Application deadline is June 1.

A Fall Poetry Colloquium, held in October at St. Peter's College, Muenster, an intensive, three-week workshop/retreat, is also open to writers from outside Saskatchewan. The fee of $775 includes tuition, accommodation, and meals. Application deadline August 9.

Saskatchewan Writers/Artists Colonies & Retreats
c/o P.O. Box 3986, Regina, SK S4P 3R9
Phone: (306) 757-6310 Fax: (306) 565-8554

The Colonies and Retreats were established in 1979 to provide an environment where writers and artists (especially but not exclusively from Saskatchewan) can work free from distractions in serene and beautiful locations. They are not teaching situations but retreats, offering uninterrupted work time and opportunities for a stimulating exchange of ideas with fellow writers and artists after hours. Costs are subsidized by the Saskatchewan Lotteries Trust and the Saskatchewan Arts Board. St. Peter's Abbey is a Benedictine abbey near the town of Humboldt. Emma Lake is in the forest country north of Prince Albert.

A six-week summer colony (July–August) and a two-week winter colony (February) are held at St. Peter's Abbey. Applicants may request as much time as they need, to a maximum of four weeks, but accommodation, in private rooms, is limited to eight people per week. Emma Lake hosts a two-week summer colony in August. Participants are housed in cabins or single rooms. Individual retreats of up to four weeks are offered year round at St. Peter's, with no more than three individuals being accommodated at a time.

Fees, including meals, are $125 per week for Saskatchewan Writers Guild members, and $175 per week for non-members. Applicants are required to submit a 10-page writing sample/slides of recent work, a résumé, description of work to be done at the colony, and two references.

Deadlines: May 1 and January 1 for colonies; two to three months ahead for retreats.

Sechelt Writer-in-Residence Programs

Festival of the Written Arts, P.O. Box 2299, Sechelt, BC VON 3AO
Phone: (604) 885-9631 or 1-800-565-9631 Fax: (604) 885-3967
E-mail: written_arts@sunshine.net

As with so many other enterprises discussed in this book, the Sechelt Programs have faced severe funding shortfalls in recent years. As a result, the five-day writer-in-residence workshops held three times a year had to be suspended – until April 1998, with the first of a new series of three-day workshops. It is hoped that support will be found to continue and expand the school in the future. Past workshops, all led by celebrated established writers, have focused on the writing of fiction in many genres, and of poetry, history, travel, cookbooks, as well as scriptwriting and writing for magazines.

Participants range from beginners to published authors. Classes are limited to 10 to 12 students to allow adequate time for individual tuition. Fees are unconfirmed at this time. Write or phone for further information.

Toronto Writing Workshop
P.O. Box 508, 264 Queen's Quay West, Toronto, ON M5J 1B5
Phone: (416) 260-6621
Contact: Libby Scheier, Director

This independent workshop runs four sessions a year (fall, winter, spring, summer), offering a variety of courses in creative writing. Instructors are experienced professional writers, editors, and/or publishers. In each of the following eight-week workshops, elements of technique are reviewed in the course of discussing participants' work, and a written critique is provided by the instructor. Practical matters, such as publishing and grants, are also addressed. Workshop size is limited to 15. The fee for each course is $235 but can be reduced by early registration.

Introduction to Creative Writing: Addresses fiction, poetry, and creative non-fiction. Open admission.

Intermediate/Advanced Women Writers: For women with some experience of writing fiction, creative non-fiction, or poetry. Admission by phone conversation with instructor.

Intermediate/Advanced Fiction: For writers with some experience. Admission by 5-page writing sample.

Intermediate/Advanced Poetry: For poets with some experience. Admission by 5-page writing sample.

Writing for the Theatre: Reviews basic elements and different styles of theatrical writing. Open admission.

Writing for Children: Covers children's fiction, from picture books to novels for all ages. Open admission.

The following three 1-day workshops are open admission:

Writing the Black Experience: For people of African descent. Discusses fiction, poetry, memoir, family history, historical reconstruction, personal essay, and oral tradition. Work samples of 2 to 5 pages may be brought in for workshopping. The fee for each workshop is $75 but can be reduced by early admission.

Writers' Guide to Publishing: Everything writers need to know about publishing. Bring your questions.

Creative Non-fiction: Literary technique and publishing opportunities in memoir, family history, personal essay, travel and literary journalism, etc. Work samples of 2 to 3 pages may be brought in for workshopping.

University of Toronto Creative Writing Program

Creative Writing Program, School of Continuing Studies,
University of Toronto, 158 St. George Street, Toronto,
ON M5S 2V8
Phone: (416) 978-0765 Fax: (416) 978-6666
E-mail: bruce.meyer@utoronto.ca
Contact: Bruce Meyer, Director

This newly developed program is shaping up to be one of the largest of its kind in Canada. All courses are open admission, non-prerequisite, non-credit, and have an enrolment cap of 18 students. Among the wide range of courses are Introduction to Creative Writing, Short Fiction, Writing the Novel, Writing for Stage, Creativity Theory, and General and Multi-Genre Workshops. Instructors and author participants include Anne Montagnes, Janis Rapoport, Richard Sanger, Cary Fagan, Kim Echlin, Douglas Fetherling, Paul Kropp, James Deahl, Robert Sawyer, Anne Michaels, and Michael Helm. Also features individualized distance learning workshops in multiple genres and personal editorial feedback courses in which students can work toward polishing a completed book-length manuscript.

Regular, open-admission Saturday afternoon seminars with authors and others involved in writing matters are designed to explore areas not covered by core curriculum courses. The 1997/98 Seminars series includes Children's Writing, Horror Writing, Science Fiction, Getting Started as a Writer, Fantasy Writing, Literary Interviewing, and Sports Writing.

The 1998 annual University of Toronto International Summer Writers' Workshop will be held at Hart House, July 14 to July 18. Authors likely to participate include Barry Callaghan, Dionne Brand, Austin Clarke, Cecil Foster, and Olive Senior. Contact the Director for details and cost.

All core curriculum courses are priced according to the following scale: 10 meetings, 20 hours – $275; 20 meetings, 40 hours – $475. Distance and Individual Learning courses, 3 months – $475.

Students who take a second course with the same instructor receive a $75 discount on the second course. Seminars, 3 hours – $40. Students can register by phone by calling (416) 978-2400. To order a Creative Writing Program brochure, call (416) 978-0765 or e-mail the Director.

Victoria School of Writing

P.O. Box 8152, Victoria, BC v8w 3R8
Phone: (250) 598-5300 Fax: (250) 598-0066
E-mail: writeawy@islandnet.com
Web site: www.islandnet.com/vicwrite

This summer school offers four days of intensive workshops in poetry, fiction, playwriting, writing for children, and editing work-in-progress, all focusing on participants' own work. The sessions are led by experienced, established writers from across Canada. Current writers-in-residence include Susan Musgrave, Marilyn Bowering, Patrick Friesen, Rona Murray, Stephen Reid, and Ellen Godfrey. Public readings by author-instructors, optional seminars on matters of interest to writers, and one-on-one consultations are available. The school is held in mid-July at St. Margaret's School in Victoria, set on 22 acres of treed countryside. Registration is $395 ($350 if sent before May 1), and special accommodation deals are offered. Tuition, accommodation, and meals are available in an early-bird package for under $600.

The Writing School

38 McArthur Avenue, Suite 2951, Ottawa, ON K1L 6R2
Phone: 1-800-267-1829 Fax: (613) 749-9551
E-mail: writers@qualityofcourse.com
Web site: www.qualityofcourse.com
Contact: Alex Myers

For the last 14 years, The Writing School has offered creative writing courses by correspondence. These diploma courses are designed to help the student to publish. They give starting writers a thorough and practical understanding of the needs of the market-place, and build creative and technical skills.

The student works with his or her tutor on a variety of assignments, each structured to improve specific skills. All tutors at the School are themselves working writers. Assignments are tailored to reflect the individual interests and abilities of each student. Course fees are $699, which covers all costs, including books, lessons, tapes, and tutorial.

The School offers prospective students a free evaluation of their work. Call the toll-free number for a free brochure detailing course contents and methodology, and for more about the evaluation service.

Creative Writing & Journalism at Colleges & Universities

University of Alberta
Edmonton, AB T6G 2E5
Phone: (403) 492-2181 Fax: (403) 492-8142
Contact: Professor Douglas Barbour, Chair, Creative Writing
   Committee
The Department of English offers courses in writing fiction, poetry, and non-fiction. To make it easier for students to identify these courses and plan their programs, they now have a separate designation – WRITE – and a Combined Honours in Creative Writing has been approved. WRITE courses are open to students from all faculties who fulfil the prerequisites. The department brings a range of new and established writers to read from their work, and sponsors a writer-in-residence program. Opportunities exist for graduate work in creative writing.

There are always one or two creative writing courses offered through extension.

Publishes *The Gateway*.

University of British Columbia
Buchanan Building, Room E462, 1866 Main Mall, Vancouver,
   BC V6T IZI
Phone: (604) 822-0699 Fax: (604) 822-3616
Contact: Creative Writing Program
The Creative Writing Program offers courses of study leading to BFA and MFA degrees. A wide range of creative writing courses are available, including writing for screen and television, the novel and novella, short fiction, stage plays, radio plays and features,

non-fiction, applied creative non-fiction, writing for children, translation, and poetry. A joint MFA with the theatre or film department is also possible. Students may choose to take a double major in creative writing and another subject. A diploma in applied creative non-fiction is open to graduates and those with professional experience.

The literary journal *PRISM international* (see page 149) is edited by program graduate students.

Cambrian College of Applied Arts & Technology

1400 Barrydowne Road, Sudbury, ON P3A 3V8

Phone: (705) 566-8101 or 1-800-461-7145 Fax: (705) 524-7334

Contact: Office of the Registrar

Offers diploma courses leading to a journalism major.

Continuing Education holds evening creative writing classes.

Publishes *The Shield*, a biweekly journalism lab paper.

Camosun College

3100 Foul Bay Road, Victoria, BC V8P 5J2

Phone: (250) 592-1556 Fax: (250) 370-3551

Contact: Cathy Carson, Articulation/Education Liaison Officer

The English Department offers credit courses in prose fiction and poetry as well as in introductory and advanced composition.

A variety of Continuing Education courses in creative writing, including poetry, novel writing, and writing for children, are available.

Credit courses in writing for the print and electronic media are offered as components of the two-year, full-time Applied Communications program. Students write and produce *Camas*, a college news magazine, and some radio and cable television programs.

Continuing Education offers various journalism courses, including Writing for Magazines and other courses to help students in getting their work published.

Students are encouraged to submit material to *The Bound With Glue Review* and the student newspaper *Nexus*.

Canadore College of Applied Arts & Technology

P.O. Box 5001, 100 College Drive, North Bay, ON P1B 8K9

Phone: (705) 474-7600, ext. 5123 Fax: (705) 474-2384

Contact: Mark Sherry, Director of Admissions & Liaison

The two-year print journalism diploma program includes courses in research and interviewing, newswriting, feature writing, keyboard skills, photojournalism, communications, and Canadian politics and economics. Journalism students produce a weekly newspaper, *The Quest*.

Continuing Education offers a course in creative writing and courses in business writing. Canadore's Summer School of the Arts holds week-long creative writing workshops.

Carleton University

Student Liaison and Publication Services, 315 Administration
    Building, 1125 Colonel By Drive, Ottawa, ON K1S 5B6
Phone: (613) 520-3663 or 1-800-267-7366 (ON and PQ)
    Fax: (613) 788-3517
Contact: Jean Mullan, Assistant Director of Admissions (Liaison)

The School of Journalism offers a four-year program leading to an honours Bachelor of Journalism. A one-year master's degree program is available for students with a BJ and journalists with substantial working experience. Students may be eligible for the two-year master's program. Some creative writing courses are also given through the Department of English Language and Literature, including restricted-entry seminars in poetry and fiction.

The Carleton Professional Development Centre offers an introductory course in creative writing and several courses in technical and business writing.

Publishes the student newspaper *The Charlatan*.

Centennial College of Applied Arts & Technology

P.O. Box 631, Station A, Scarborough, ON M1K 5E9
Phone: (416) 289-5000 Fax: (416) 462-8801
Web site: www.cencol.on.ca
Contact: Gary Schlee, Department Co-ordinator

The Communication Arts Department offers a three-year (or a two-year "fast track") diploma program in print journalism, broadcasting, and creative advertising. Also a two-year diploma program in corporate communication. Programs include courses in reporting, editing, scriptwriting, broadcast journalism, production for radio and television, documentary film writing, cinematography, magazine writing, public relations, newspaper feature writing, computer graphics, and more. All programs emphasize practical skills.

Various courses are also offered in the extension program. All courses are held on the East York campus at the small, high-tech Bell Centre for Creative Communications.

Concordia University
1455 de Maisonneuve Boulevard W., Montreal, PQ H3G 1M8
Phone: (514) 848-2656
Contact: Lynne Prendergast, Registrar

The English Department's Creative Writing program offers workshops in playwriting, poetry, and fiction, and gives courses in advanced composition and non-fiction, leading to bachelor's and master's degrees. The Department of Fine Arts offers courses in playwriting through its theatre program.

The Journalism Department has degree programs offering courses in writing and reporting, feature and magazine writing, editing, and writing for radio and television news and public affairs. Undergraduate and graduate programs have quotas, so students are screened for admission.

Conestoga College of Applied Arts & Technology
299 Doon Valley Drive, Kitchener, ON N2G 4M4
Phone: (519) 748-5220 Fax: (519) 895-1085
Contact: F.J. Harris, Registrar

An 80-week journalism diploma program prepares graduates to work as reporters or photographers for newspapers or magazines. Skills can also be used in radio and television, or in advertising and public relations. Graduates are equipped with editing skills such as headline writing and a grounding in design and layout, interviewing, and desk-top publishing. Students with a university degree or those admitted to the Journalism Option at the University of Waterloo are admitted to the 56-week "fast-track" stream. In the UW option the student graduates with both a diploma in journalism and a university degree.

Courses available through the Centre for Continuing Education include Creative Writing and Business Communications I and II.

Douglas College
P.O. Box 2503, New Westminster, BC V3L 5B2
Phone: (604) 527-5400 Fax: (604) 527-5095

Contact: Mary Burns

College credit and university transfer courses in creative writing and communication are available. Courses include Introductory Fiction, Drama, Poetry; second-year courses in short fiction and poetry; screen writing; and personal narrative.

The Print Futures professional writing program is a two-year diploma program preparing students for a professional writing career. Includes courses in writing, research, editorial, and design skills, public relations writing, and writing for magazines and trade publications. For more information, contact the English and Communications Department (ph. [604] 527-5465).

Publishes the literary journal *Event* (see page 141).

Durham College of Applied Arts & Technology
2000 Simcoe Street N., P.O. Box 385, Oshawa, ON L1H 7L7
Phone: (905) 721-2000 Fax: (905) 721-3195
Contact: Director of Arts and Administration Division for CA
    program; Ann-Marie Bambino, Program Officer, Continuous
    Learning Division

Offers a Communication Arts program leading to a two-year diploma in journalism or advertising, or a three-year public relations diploma. Graduates of other colleges and universities may qualify for direct entry into a special one-year program concentrating on practical subjects.

Continuous Learning offers non-credit courses Creative Writing and Getting Published.

Publishes *The Chronicle*, a college newspaper that provides students with experience in writing, editing, design, layout, art, photography, and production.

George Brown College
200 King Street E., Toronto, ON M5A 3W8
Phone: (416) 415-2092 Fax: (416) 415-2699
Contact: Peggy Needham, Co-ordinator

The Communications Department offers the credit courses Poetry, Creating Short Stories, Expressive Writing, Writing for Children, Mystery Writing, Writing for the Theatre, Screenwriting, and Women Writers' Workshop. Creating Short Stories I is offered via the Internet. The Department also offers the journalism credit courses Journalism: Springboard to a Career, Writing for Magazines, and The Complete Travel Writer. The Extension program offers certificates in Technical Communications, Editing, and Creative Writing. A section of Technical Writing I is offered via the Internet. All are evening or weekend courses.

George Brown's biennial Storymakers writing conference (next in 1999), held over a weekend in August, offers a choice of workshops, guest speakers, and readings.

Georgian College of Applied Arts & Technology
1 Georgian Drive, Barrie, ON L4M 3X9
Phone: (705) 728-1951 Fax: (705) 722-5123
Contact: School of Continuing Education

The School of Continuing Education offers a broad range of useful part-time courses on demand, including Writing the Novel, Scriptwriting, Write Better, Creative Writing, Getting Your Writing Published, Writing for Business, Short Story Writing, Fiction Writing, Planning Your Novel, and Writing for Children.

Holland College
140 Weymouth Street, Charlottetown, PE CIA 4ZI
Phone: (902) 566-9591 Fax: (902) 566-9563
Contact: Martin Dorrell, Journalism Instructor

The Media and Communications Department offers a two-year diploma program in journalism.

Publishes *The Surveyor* 11 times in the school year.

Humber College
205 Humber College Boulevard, Etobicoke, ON M9W 5L7
Phone: (416) 675-6622 Fax: (416) 675-1483
Contact: Nancy Burt, Head of Department, Journalism

Offers a three-year diploma course in print and broadcast journalism. Also courses in creative writing and publication editing.

See page 335 for the Humber School for Writers.

University of King's College, School of Journalism
6350 Coburg Road, Halifax, NS B3H 2AI
Phone: (902) 422-1271 Fax: (902) 425-8183
Contact: Office of the Registrar

Two journalism programs are offered: the first, a four-year program, leads to an honours BJ degree, for students entering directly from high school; the second, an intensive one-year program, leads to a BJ, for students who already have a bachelor's degree. Students in the four-year honours program take courses in arts or science at Dalhousie University. All students take courses in broadcast and print journalism, research techniques, interviewing, history of journalism, media law, and journalism ethics, and select from a wide variety of optional courses. Both programs teach journalism from a practical point of view.

Langara College

100 West 49th Avenue, Vancouver, BC V5Y 2Z6
Phone: (604) 323-5511 Fax: (604) 323-5555
Contact: Roger Semmens, English Department Chair

The following creative writing courses receive transfer credit as either Creative Writing or unassigned arts at the second-year level: Short Fiction, Stage Drama, Screenwriting, and Poetry.

The Publishing: Techniques and Technologies Program offers a range of courses relating to different aspects of desk-top publishing. Continuing Education presents courses in QuarkXpress, Adobe PhotoShop, and Adobe Illustrator from time to time.

The Journalism Department offers the following credit courses: Fundamentals of Reporting, Editing and Design, Photojournalism, Broadcasting, Advanced Reporting, Specialty Writing, Deadline Writing, Magazine Writing, Electronic Publishing, Media Law, Media and Society.

The Continuing Education program periodically includes Fundamentals of Reporting, Editing and Publication Design, Broadcasting, and Electronic Publishing.

Lethbridge Community College

3000 College Drive S., Lethbridge, AB T1K 1L6
Phone: (403) 320-3335 Fax: (403) 380-3450
Contact: Jean Phelps, Program Administrator

Continuing Studies offers two useful practical writing courses: Becoming a Writer I aims to encourage creativity by discovering the "writer's voice" in each student through the exploration of various styles of writing, including short stories, novels, and poetry. Becoming a Writer II continues the first course while focusing on fiction, and is ideal for writers working on longer projects or seeking to polish skills acquired in Writer I.

Loyalist College

P.O. Box 4200, Belleville, ON K8N 5B9
Phone: (613) 969-1913 (Post Secondary Admissions Office)
 Fax: (613) 962-0937
Contact: Rob Washburn

The School of Media Studies offers a two-year full-time diploma in print journalism, which includes courses in newspaper production, reporting and newswriting, database research, community reporting, writing for magazines, analytical writing, feature writing, and freelancing for profit. In this hands-on program students are considered to be apprenticing journalists, and work as reporters and editors on the college's award-winning community newspaper *The Pioneer*. At the end, students serve a four-week internship on daily or community newspapers or magazines.

The College also sponsors a six-day creative writing workshop in late July at the Bridgewater Retreat, near Tweed. The cost is $448, with discounts for seniors. Contact Candis Graham at (613) 722-9611 or e-mail bn095@freenet.carleton.ca.

Malaspina University-College

900 5th Street, Nanaimo, BC V9R 5S5
Phone: (604) 753-3245
E-mail: guppy@mala.bc.ca
Contact: Steve Guppy, Chair, Department of Creative Writing

Offers a comprehensive four-year program leading to a BA with a minor in creative writing. Includes introductory courses in journalism, poetry, fiction, and dramatic writing; second-year courses in feature writing and newswriting, poetry, fiction, dramatic writing, and book publishing; and senior level courses in creative non-fiction, feature writing, poetry, short fiction, novel and novella, experimental and speculative fiction, documentary and historical fiction, book publishing, writing for the stage, screenwriting, writing for radio and television, multimedia publishing, and writing for multimedia. These courses are offered on a rotational basis; interested students should consult the Department of Creative Writing to determine which courses will be offered in a given semester.

Publishes a student-edited journal, *Portal*.

Mohawk College

P.O. Box 2034, Hamilton, ON L8N 3T2
Phone: (905) 575-1212   Fax: (905) 575-2378
Contact: Terry Mote, Assistant Registrar

Creative Writing, Writing for Radio, Script Writing, Grammar and Composition for Media are courses within the Media Studies program. Continuing Education offers Creative Writing as a 13-week credit course.

The three-year full-time Broadcast Journalism and Communications Media diploma program includes a range of broadcasting and media courses. Continuing Education has two 13-week credit courses: Report Writing – Business; and Report Writing – Technical.

Publishes the college newspaper *The Satellite*.

Mount Royal College

4825 Richard Road S.W., Calgary, AB T3E 6K6
Phone: (403) 240-0148
Contact: Admissions Advising Centre

The Faculty of Arts and Communications offers an applied degree in Applied Communications with specializations in journalism, technical writing, and public relations, a Professional Writing Certificate program, and a variety of non-credit creative writing courses.

The two-year Journalism Diploma focuses on newswriting, editing, photojournalism, and related subjects taught in a classroom/newsroom setting. Students produce a regular newspaper, and a one-month practicum with an off-campus newspaper is included in the fourth semester. (Contact Communications Department at [403] 240-6909.)

The two-semester, one-year Professional Writing certificate begins every fall and is designed to develop skills in creative, non-fiction, and technical/business writing. (Contact English Department at [403] 240-6451.)

The Creative Writing program offered through the college's

extension faculty offers a wide variety of courses for fiction and non-fiction writers, including Writing for Film and Television, Writing Historical Fiction, and Journal Writing for Men and Women. (Contact the Faculty of Continuing Education and Extension at [403] 240-6012.)

University of New Brunswick

Department of English, Carleton Hall 247, P.O. Box 4400,
   Fredericton, NB E3B 5A3
Phone: (506) 453-4676 Fax: (506) 453-5069
Contact: Ross Leckie, Director of Creative Writing

The English Department offers four credit courses in creative writing, two in poetry and two in fiction.

Continuing Education provides a non-credit fundamentals of writing course.

The university has a writer-in-residence and sponsors the Maritime Writers' Workshop. Also publishes three creative writing journals: *The Fiddlehead* (see page 141), *Qwerty*, and *Journal of Student Writing*.

University of Ottawa

550 Cumberland, P.O. Box 450, Station A, Ottawa, ON KIN 6N5
Phone: (613) 562-5800, ext. 1599 Fax: (613) 562-5104
Contact: Henri Wong, Registrar

The Department of English offers both introductory and advanced workshops in fiction and poetry writing. The department periodically sponsors a prominent Canadian writer as writer-in-residence, and draws in many other distinguished writers to meet formally and informally with students and staff.

Journalism, technical, and business writing courses are available through the Service for Continuing Education and the Department of English.

Continuing Education offers creative writing courses, such as Poetry Workshop, Creative Writing (beginners), Popular Fiction Writing, Advanced Fiction Workshop, and Writing for Results, depending on staff availability and demand.

The Department of English sponsors the monthly journals *Bywords*, *Graffito*, and *Host Box*; the Canadian Short Story Series; and *Reappraisals of Canadian Literature*. It also publishes a series of critical volumes including *The Friday Circle Broadside* and the Chap Book Series. Other campus publications include *Fulcrum*, the student newspaper, and *Alumni News*, a quarterly journal. All accept freelance contributions.

Red River Community College

2055 Notre Dame Avenue, Winnipeg, MB R3H 0J9
Phone: (204) 632-2455 Fax: (204) 632-8352
Contact: Larry Partap, Co-ordinator

The Creative Communications Department offers creative writing courses in fiction; poetry and drama; and magazine and screenwriting. The Department also presents a range of journalism courses: Introduction, Style and Practice, Media and the Law, and Journalism Practicum I, II, and III.

Various courses are also available through the extension program.

University of Regina

Regina, SK S4S 0A2
Phone: (306) 585-4420 Fax: (306) 585-4867
Contact: Wendy Tebb, Secretary to the Director

A four-year Bachelor of Arts in Journalism and Communication (BAJC) is offered, as well as a two-year Bachelor of Journalism. Admission to these programs is limited. Many creative writing courses are available, and although a student cannot major in creative writing, three or four courses may be applied to an English major.

Continuing Education offers journalism and creative writing courses and sponsors writers' conferences (phone [306] 779-4806).

The English Department usually offers credit courses in creative writing, and produces the biannual literary journal *The Wascana Review*.

Ryerson Polytechnic University

350 Victoria Street, Toronto, ON M5B 2K3
Phone: (416) 979-5000
Contact: Faculty of Applied Arts ([416] 979-5319); Continuing
  Education ([416] 979-5180)

One of Canada's most respected schools of journalism. The Faculty of Applied Arts offers a four-year degree program, which also includes courses in English literature and the humanities. Students may choose to specialize in newspaper, magazine, or broadcast streams after second year. Also a two-year program for postgraduate students. Students produce *The Ryersonian*, a weekly newspaper, and the biannual *Ryerson Review of Journalism*, as well as news and public affairs programs for radio and television.

Continuing Education offers a wide range of creative writing courses and workshops, including courses on short story and novel writing, poetry writing, writing for the children's market, science fiction, crime, and romance writing, and family history. Also courses in screenwriting, media writing, and business and technical writing. Instructors in 1997 included Ann Ireland, Christopher Dewdney, Barbara Gowdy, Sarah Sheard, Rhea Tregebov, Peter Robinson, Robert Sawyer, and Barbara Greenwood. (Contact Bonnie Laing, Co-ordinator – Writing Programs, phone [416] 979-5359.)

Continuing Education also offers part-time certificate programs in magazine journalism and publishing. Courses include Feature Writing for the Freelance Market, Freelancing: The Future, and Writing for Print Media.

Seneca College of Applied Arts & Technology

1750 Finch Avenue E., North York, ON M2J 2X5
Phone: (416) 491-5050 Fax: (416) 491-9187
Contact: Office of the Registrar

Options in television and radio scripting, playwriting, and journalism are available to day students in the Broadcasting/Radio & Television program at the School of Communication Arts. A one-year post-diploma program in Corporate Communications offers day students the opportunity to engage in an intensive learning experience designed to graduate mature, flexible communicators with good writing, technical, managerial, and human skills who can quickly become productive in a corporate communications position.

Continuing Education offers courses in various creative writing subjects. These change each semester according to demand and the availability of suitable instructors.

Université de Sherbrooke

Sherbrooke, PQ J1K 2R1
Phone: (819) 821-7681 Fax: (819) 821-7966

Contact: Office of the Registrar

Offers a BA co-operative program in Professional Writing in English. Includes courses in journalism, translation, technical writing, and writing for advertising and public relations. Designed for anglophones, students must also have a working knowledge of French. Co-op students experience paid work terms and gain a full year's professional experience by the time they graduate.

Sheridan College

1430 Trafalgar Road, Oakville, ON L6H 2L1
Phone: (905) 845-9430, ext. 2349 Fax: (905) 815-4051
Contact: Joyce Wayne, Co-ordinator

The Journalism Department offers a two-year diploma in print journalism; also a one-year postgraduate program, Journalism for New Media, which includes training in digital media for broadcast and on-line journalism. These programs are now part of the new Sheridan Centre for Animation and Emerging Technologies. Students produce a weekly newspaper, *The Sheridan Sun* (5,000 copies, 28 times a year), and four issues of *Light Waves*, now an Oakville lifestyle magazine. Courses include digital videography, newswriting for broadcast, magazine writing, coaching/editing, desktop publishing, page design, electronic imaging, Internet, Pagemaker, QuarkXpress, website management, satellite transmissions, and corporate communications.

From May 25 to 29, 1998, Sheridan offers its first annual writers' workshop, an intensive course geared to working writers and journalists who want to upgrade their skills in the new media. Check dates and details with Co-ordinator.

Continuing Education also offers various writing courses.

Simon Fraser University at Harbour Centre

515 West Hastings Street, Vancouver, BC V6B 5K3
Phone: (604) 291-5077 Fax: (604) 291-5098
Contact: Janice Bearg, Co-ordinator

The renowned Writing and Publishing program of the School of Continuing Studies offers 20 to 25 non-credit creative writing courses each fall and winter/spring semester, encompassing a very broad range of professional development courses for writers, editors, and others working in publishing. Includes non-credit certificates in business and technical writing, publishing, and editing, along with courses in newswriting, magazine writing, travel writing, writing for magazines, screenwriting, documentary drama, writing novels, short story writing, and many more.

University of Toronto

Toronto, ON M5S IAI
Phone: (416) 978-4578
Contact: Lynn Snowden, Assistant Vice-Provost,
   Arts and Sciences

Each year the English Department offers credit courses in creative writing. At Erindale campus, a professional writing minor program offers a wide range of courses covering expressive writing, writing for business, scientific and technical writing, and other genres.

The School of Continuing Studies offers non-credit courses in business and creative writing on campus and via distance education. A writer-in-residence gives a non-credit course in creative writing through the English Department.

The University of Toronto Press publishes *U of T Quarterly* and many academic journals. There are two campus newspapers, *The Varsity* and *the newspaper*; individual colleges also publish their own student newspapers. Student literary magazines include *Acta Victoriana* (Victoria College), *Salterra* (Trinity College), and *The Gargoyle* (University College). Hart House publishes a literary annual.

University of Victoria

P.O. Box 1700, Victoria, BC V8W 2Y2
Phone: (250) 721-7306 Fax: (250) 721-6602
Contact: Jennifer Phillips, Secretary, Department of Writing

Through the Department of Writing, students can major in creative writing, choosing courses (lectures and workshops) in fiction, non-fiction, poetry, drama, aspects of journalism, publishing, and multimedia. The Writing Co-operative Education program is open to students working toward a career in writing, publishing, or communications; work terms are designed to combine practical work experience with course study. The department also offers a new one-year post-program diploma in writing and editing.

Publishes *The Malahat Review* and *Inner Harbour Review*.

University of Waterloo
200 University Avenue W., Waterloo, ON N2L 3G1
Phone: (519) 888-4567 Fax: (519) 746-2882
Web site: www/adm.uwaterloo.ca/infoded/cont_ed.html
Contact: Barb Trotter, Publications Co-ordinator

The English Department offers creative writing courses for credit.

The Print Journalism Interdisciplinary Program leads to a concurrent Bachelor's degree from the University of Waterloo and a Diploma of Journalism from Conestoga College, where all the journalism courses are taught.

The Continuing Education Department offers numerous non-credit courses each term, including Creative Writing Workshop for Teens, Writing Picture Books for Children, Getting Started in Writing Fiction, Writing for Publication: Getting Your Non-Fiction into Print, and Technical Writing. Also two credit courses: Technical Writing (on-line) and Introduction to Essay Writing. Current details can be obtained on the Department's web site. Publishes *The New Quarterly* (see page 145).

University of Western Ontario
Graduate Program in Journalism, Faculty of Communications and
    Open Learning, London, ON N6A 5B7
Phone: (519) 661-3383 Fax: (519) 661-3506
Contact: Michael Nolan, Admissions Chair

One of the oldest and most prestigious journalism programs in Canada, and one of only two (Carleton being the other) that bestow a master's degree in journalism.

Under the umbrella of the new Faculty of Communications and Open Learning, undergraduate journalism courses are also offered as part of the new Media, Information and Technoculture undergraduate program.

University of Windsor
Windsor, ON N9B 3P4
Phone: (519) 253-4232/2289 Fax: (519) 973-7050
Contact: Dr. W.H. Herendeen, Chair, Department of English

Writing courses are available at both the general and honours level. Students may take a BA honours or an MA degree in creative writing. The BA requires completion of eight creative writing courses. There is also a BA, general and honours, degree and an MA in communication studies, with courses available in newswriting, scriptwriting, broadcasting, and press studies. An honours co-op MA in English is also offered.

Publishes *The University of Windsor Review*, *University of Windsor Magazine*, and *The Lance*.

York University
4700 Keele Street, North York, ON M3J 1P3
Phone: (416) 736-5910 Fax: (416) 736-5460
Contact: Professor R. Teleky, Co-ordinator, or Sue Parsram, Administrative Secretary

Offers students the chance to major in creative writing, with workshop courses in poetry, prose, fiction, screenwriting, playwriting, and other related subjects.

10

WRITERS' ORGANIZATIONS & SUPPORT AGENCIES

Alberta Department of Community Development
Communications, 7th Floor, Standard Life Building, Edmonton,
   AB T5J 4R7
Phone: (403) 427-6530 Fax: (403) 427-1496

Alberta Foundation for the Arts
9th Floor, Standard Life Centre, 10405 Jasper Avenue, Edmonton,
   AB T5J 4R7
Phone: (403) 427-6315 Fax: (403) 422-9132

Alberta Playwrights' Network
2nd Floor, 1134 – 8th Avenue S.W., Calgary, AB T2P 1J5
Phone: (403) 269-8564 or 1-800-268-8564 within AB
   Fax: (403) 269-8564
E-mail: apn@nucleus.com
Web site: www.nucleus.com/~apn

Alberta Romance Writers Association
223 – 112th Avenue S.W., Calgary, AB T2R 0G9
Phone: (403) 282-6676

Association of Canadian Publishers
2 Gloucester Street, Suite 301, Toronto, ON M4Y IL5
Phone: (416) 413-4929 Fax: (416) 413-4920
Web site: www.can.net/marketplace/pub/acp/acp.htm

Association of Canadian University Presses
35 Spadina Road, Toronto, ON M5R 2S9
Phone: (416) 975-9366 Fax: (416) 975-1839

Book & Periodical Council
35 Spadina Road, Toronto, ON M5R 2S9
Phone: (416) 975-9366 Fax: (416) 975-1839

British Columbia Ministry of Small Business, Tourism & Culture
Cultural Services Branch, 800 Johnson Street, 5th Floor, Victoria,
BC v8v 1X4
Phone: (604) 356-1718 Fax: (604) 387-4099
E-mail: csbinfo@tbc.gov.bc.ca

Burnaby Writers' Society
6584 Deer Lake Avenue, Burnaby, BC v5G 3T7
Phone: (604) 435-6500

Calgary Writers Association
P.O. Box 68083, 7750 Ranchview Drive N.W., Calgary, AB T3G 3N8
Phone: (403) 242-3130

The Canada Council for the Arts
Writing and Publishing Section, 350 Albert Street, P.O. Box 1047,
Ottawa, ON KIP 5V8
Phone: 1-800-263-5588 or (613) 566-4414 local or a.h.
Fax: (613) 566-4410
E-mail: silvie.bernier@canada-council.ca

Canadian Association of Journalists
Carleton University, St. Patrick's Building, Ottawa, ON KIS 5B6
Phone: (613) 788-7424

Canadian Authors Association (National Office)
P.O. Box 419, Campbellford, ON KOL ILO
Phone: (705) 653-0323 Fax: (705) 653-0593
E-mail: canauth@redden.on.ca
Web site: www.CanAuthors.org/national.html

Canadian Children's Book Centre
35 Spadina Road, Toronto, ON M5R 2S9
Phone: (416) 975-0010 Fax: (416) 975-1839
E-mail: ccbc@lglobal.com
Web site: www.lglobal.com/~ccbc

Canadian Copyright Licensing Agency (CANCOPY)
6 Adelaide Street E., Suite 900, Toronto, ON M5C 1H6
Phone: (416) 868-1620 Fax: (416) 868-1621

Canadian Ethnic Journalists' and Writers' Club
24 Tarlton Road, Toronto, ON M5P 2M4
Phone: (416) 488-0048

Canadian Library Association
200 Elgin Street, Suite 602, Ottawa, ON K2P 1L5
Phone: (613) 232-9625 Fax: (613) 563-9895
Web site: www.cla.amlibs.ca

Canadian Magazine Publishers Association
130 Spadina Avenue, Suite 202, Toronto, ON M5V 2L4
Phone: (416) 504-0274 Fax: (416) 504-0437
Web site: www.cmpa.ca

Canadian Poetry Association
P.O. Box 22571, St. George Post Office, Toronto, ON M5S 1V0
Phone: (416) 944-3985

Canadian Science Writers' Association
P.O. Box 75, Station A, Toronto, ON M5W 1A2
Phone: (416) 928-9624 Fax: (416) 924-6715
E-mail: cswa@interlog.com
Web site: www.interlog.com/~cswa

Canadian Screenwriters Alliance
24 Watts Avenue, West Royalty Industrial Park, Charlottetown,
PE CIE IBO
Phone: (902) 628-3880 Fax: (902) 368-1813
E-mail: evie@isn.net

Canadian Society of Children's Authors, Illustrators & Performers (CANSCAIP)
35 Spadina Road, Toronto, ON M5R 2S9
Phone: (416) 515-1559 Fax: (416) 515-7022
E-mail: canscaip@internet.com
Web site: www.interlog.com/~canscaip

CAN:BAIA (Black Artists in Action)
54 Wolseley Street, 2nd Floor, Toronto, ON M5T IA5
Phone: (416) 703-9040

Children's Writers & Illustrators of B.C.
3888 West 15th Avenue, Vancouver, BC V6R 2Z9
Phone: (604) 224-3260 Fax: (604) 224-3261

Conseil des arts et des lettres du Québec
79, boulevard René-Lévesque est, 3e étage, Québec,
PQ GIR 5N5
Phone: (418) 643-1707 or 1-800-897-1707 Fax: (418) 643-4558
500, Place d'Armes, 15e étage, Montréal, PQ H2Y 2W2
Phone: (514) 864-3350 or 1-800-608-3350 Fax: (514) 864-4160

Crime Writers of Canada
P.O. Box 113, 3007 Kingston Road, Scarborough, ON MIM IPI
Phone: (416) 782-3116 Fax: (416) 789-4682
E-mail: ap113@torfree.net
Web site: www.swifty.com/cwc/cwchome.htm

Editors' Association of Canada (EAC)
35 Spadina Road, Toronto, ON M5R 2S9
Phone: (416) 975-1379 Fax: (416) 975-1839
E-mail: editors@web.net
Web site: www.web.net/eac-acr

Federation of British Columbia Writers
890 West Pender Street, Suite 600, Vancouver, BC V6C 1J9
Phone: (604) 683-2057 Fax: (604) 683-8269
E-mail: fedbcwrt@pinc.com
Web site: www.swifty.com/bcwa

Federation of English-Language Writers of Quebec
1200 Atwater Avenue, Suite 3, Montreal, PQ H3Z 1X4
Phone: (514) 934-2485

Island Writers Association (P.E.I.)
P.O. Box 1204, Charlottetown, PE C1A 7M8
Phone: (902) 566-9748 Fax: (902) 566-9748
E-mail: creative@peinet.pe.ca

League of Canadian Poets
54 Wolseley Street, Suite 204, Toronto, ON M5T 1A5
Phone: (416) 504-1657 Fax: (416) 703-0059
E-mail: league@ican.net
Web site: www.swifty.com/lc

Literary Press Group of Canada
2 Gloucester Street, Suite 301, Toronto, ON M4Y 1L5
Phone: (416) 413-4929 Fax: (416) 966-6943
E-mail: claudrum@lpg.ca
Web site: www.lpg.ca

Literary Translators' Association of Canada
3492 Laval Avenue, Montreal, PQ H2X 3C8
Phone: (514) 849-8540 Fax: (514) 538-3651

Manitoba Arts Council
525 – 93 Lombard Avenue, Winnipeg, MB R3B 3B1
Phone: (204) 945-2237 Fax: (204) 945-5925
E-mail: manarti@mts.net
Web site: www.net-mark.mb.ca/netmark/mac

Manitoba Writers' Guild
100 Arthur Street, Suite 206, Winnipeg, MB R3B 1H3
Phone: (204) 942-6134 Fax: (204) 942-5754
E-mail: mbwriter@escape.ca
Web site: www.mbwriter.mb.ca

New Brunswick Department of Municipalities, Culture & Housing
Arts Branch, P.O. Box 6000, Fredericton, NB E3B 5HI
Phone: (506) 453-2555 Fax: (506) 453-2416

Newfoundland & Labrador Arts Council
P.O. Box 98, Station C, St. John's, NF AIC 5H5
Phone: (709) 726-2212 Fax: (709) 726-0619
E-mail: nlacmail@newcomm.net
Web site: www.nlac.nf.ca

Newfoundland & Labrador Department of Tourism, Culture & Recreation
Cultural Affairs Division, P.O. Box 8700, St. John's, NF AIB 4J6
Phone: (709) 729-3609 Fax: (709) 729-0870

Northwest Territories Arts Council
Department of Education, Culture and Employment, Government of the N.W.T., P.O. Box 1320, Yellowknife, NT XIA 2L9
Phone: (403) 873-7551 Fax: (403) 873-0205

Nova Scotia Department of Education & Culture
Cultural Affairs Division, P.O. Box 578, Halifax, NS B3J 2S9
Phone: (902) 424-6389 Fax: (902) 424-0710
E-mail: hflxtrad.educ.waltpa@gov.ns.ca

Ontario Arts Council
Literature Programs, OAC, 151 Bloor Street, Suite 500, Toronto, ON M5S IT6
Phone: (416) 969-7450 Fax: (416) 961-7796
E-mail: info@arts.on.ca

Ontario Ministry of Citizenship, Culture & Recreation
Cultural Programs Branch, 77 Bloor Street W., 2nd Floor,
  Toronto, ON M7A 2R9
Phone: (416) 314-7747 Fax: (416) 314-7460

Ottawa Independent Writers
265 Elderberry Terrace, Orleans, ON K1E 1Z2
Phone: (613) 841-0572 Fax: (613) 841-0775
E-mail: ac615@freenet.carleton.ca

Outdoor Writers of Canada
P.O. Box 1839, Peterborough, ON K9J 7X6
Phone: (705) 743-7052 Fax: (705) 743-7052

P.E.I. Writers' Guild
P.O. Box 2234, Charlottetown, PE C1A 8B9
Phone: (902) 894-9933 Fax: (902) 961-2797

PEN Canada
Canadian Centre for International PEN, 24 Ryerson Avenue,
  Suite 309, Toronto, ON M5T 2P3
Phone: (416) 703-8448 Fax: (416) 703-3870
E-mail: pencan@web.net
Web site: www.pencanada.ca

Periodical Writers Association of Canada
54 Wolseley Street, Suite 203, Toronto, ON M5T 1A5
Phone: (416) 504-1645 Fax: (416) 703-0059
E-mail: pwac@cycor.ca

Playwrights Union of Canada
54 Wolseley Street, 2nd Floor, Toronto, ON M5T 1A5
Phone: (416) 703-0201 Fax: (416) 703-0059
E-mail: cdplays@interlog.com
Web site: www.puc.ca

Prince Edward Island Council of the Arts
115 Richmond Street, Charlottetown, PE C1A 1H7
Phone: (902) 368-4410 Fax: (902) 368-4418

QSPELL (Quebec Society for the Promotion of English Language Literature)

1200 Atwater Avenue, Montreal, PQ H3Z 1X4
Phone: (514) 933-0878 Fax: (514) 933-0878
E-mail: qspell@total.net

Saskatchewan Arts Board

3475 Albert Street, T.C. Douglas Building, 3rd Floor, Regina, SK S4S 6X6
Phone: (306) 787-4056 or 1-800-667-7526 (within SK)
Fax: (306) 787-4199

Saskatchewan Writers Guild

P.O. Box 3986, Regina, SK S4P 3R9
Phone: (306) 757-6310 Fax: (306) 565-8554
E-mail: swg@sympatico.ca
Web site: www.sasknet.com/~skwriter

Victoria Writers Society

P.O. Box 6447, Depot 1, Victoria, BC V8P 5M3
Phone: (604) 920-7154

West Coast Book Prize Society

1033 Davie Street, Suite 700, Vancouver, BC V6E 1M7
Phone: (604) 687-2405 Fax: (604) 687-2405

Writers' Alliance of Newfoundland & Labrador

P.O. Box 2681, St. John's, NF A1C 5M5
Phone: (709) 739-5215 Fax: (709) 739-5215
E-mail: wanl@public.nfld.com
Web site: www.infonet.st-johns.nf.ca/providers/
writers/writers.html

The Writers' Development Trust

24 Ryerson Avenue, Suite 201, Toronto, ON M5T 2P3
Phone: (416) 504-8222 Fax: (416) 504-9090
E-mail: writers.trust@sympatico.ca

Writers' Federation of New Brunswick
404 Queen Street, P.O. Box 37, Station A, Fredericton, NB E3B 4Y2
Phone: (506) 459-7228 Fax: (506) 459-7228
E-mail: aa821@fan.nb.ca
Web site: www.sjfn.nb.ca/community_hall/W/
    Writers_Federation_NB/index.htm

Writers' Federation of Nova Scotia
1809 Barrington Street, Suite 901, Halifax, NS B3J 3K8
Phone: (902) 423-8116 Fax: (902) 422-0881
E-mail: writers1@fox.nstn.ca
Web site: www.chebucto.ns.ca/Culture/WFNS

Writers Guild of Alberta (Edmonton)
11759 Groat Road, 3rd Floor, Edmonton, AB T5M 3K6
Phone: (403) 422-8174 Fax: (403) 422-2663
E-mail: writers@compusmart.ab.ca

Writers Guild of Canada
123 Edward Street, Suite 1225, Toronto, ON M5G 1E2
Phone: (416) 979-7907

Writers in Electronic Residence
24 Ryerson Avenue, Suite 201, Toronto, ON M5T 2P3
Phone: (416) 504-4490

The Writers' Union of Canada
24 Ryerson Avenue, Toronto, ON M5T 2P3
Phone: (416) 703-8982 Fax: (416) 703-0826
E-mail: twuc@the-wire.com
Web site: www.swifty.com/twuc

Writers' Union of Canada (Pacific Regional Office)
3102 Main Street, 3rd Floor, Vancouver, BC V4A 3C7
Phone: (604) 874-1611 Fax: (604) 874-1611

Yukon Department of Tourism
Arts Branch, P.O. Box 2703, Whitehorse, YT Y1A 2C6
Phone: (867) 667-8592 Fax: (867) 393-6456

11

BOOK RESOURCES

For those seeking practical advice and inspiration from books about their craft, there is a cornucopia of writer's resource books on the market: style guides and practical handbooks, personal meditations, teach-yourself marketing primers, as well as more advanced "work-shops" on the narrative and descriptive arts. With more published every year, only a short selection is offered here. As you'll see, the following listing includes books from the United States and Britain as well as from Canada. Most are available in good bookstores here; a few are out of print but may still be held in libraries.

Stylebooks, Handbooks, & Guides

The Canadian Style: A Guide to Writing and Editing, Oxford, Toronto, 1997.
The Canadian Writer's Guide: Official Handbook of the Canadian Authors' Association (12th ed.), Fitzhenry & Whiteside, Toronto, 1997.
The Chicago Manual of Style (14th ed. rev.), University of Chicago Press, Chicago, 1993.
Editing Canadian English, Freelance Editors' Association of Canada, Douglas & McIntyre, Vancouver, 1988.
The Globe and Mail Style Book 1996, Penguin, Toronto, 1996.
Words into Type (3rd ed. rev.), Prentice-Hall, Englewood Cliffs, NJ, 1974.

Appelbaum, Judith. *How to Get Happily Published*, HarperPerennial, New York, 1992.

Ballon, Rachel Friedman. *Blueprint for Writing: A Writer's Guide to Creativity, Craft and Career*, Lowell House, Los Angeles, 1995.

Barker-Sandbrook, Judith. *Thinking Through Your Writing Process*, McGraw-Hill Ryerson, Toronto, 1989.

Begley, Adam, *Literary Agents: A Writer's Guide*, Penguin, Harmondsworth, 1993.

Bernstein, Theodore M. *Watch Your Language*, Atheneum, New York, 1976.

——. *Miss Thistlebottom's Hobgoblins: The Careful Writer's Guide to the Taboos, Bugbears and Outmoded Rules of English Usage*, Simon & Schuster, New York, 1971.

Billot, Diane (ed.). *Money for Writers*, Henry Holt, New York, 1996.

Birkett, Julian. *Word Power: A Guide to Creative Writing*, A. & C. Black, London, 1993.

Blackburn, Bob. *Words Fail Us: Good English and Other Lost Causes*, McClelland & Stewart, Toronto, 1993.

Block, Lawrence. *Telling Lies for Fun and Profit: A Manual for Fiction Writers*, William Morrow, New York, 1994.

——. *Writing the Novel: From Plot to Print*, Writer's Digest Books, Cincinnati, 1979.

Blundell, William E. *The Art and Craft of Feature Writing*, Plume, New York, 1988.

Bly, Robert W. *Secrets of a Freelance Writer* (2nd rev. ed.), Owl, New York, 1997.

Braine, John. *Writing a Novel*, Methuen, London, 1974.

Burgett, Gordon. *The Travel Writer's Guide* (2nd ed.), Prima, Rocklin, CA, 1992.

——. *How to Sell More Than 75% of Your Freelance Writing*, Prima, Rocklin, CA,, 1995.

Buss, Helen M. *Mapping Our Selves: Canadian Women's Autobiography*, McGill-Queen's UP, Montreal, 1993.

Cheney, Theodore A. Rees. *Getting the Words Right: How to Rewrite, Edit & Revise*, Writer's Digest Books, Cincinnati, 1983.

Clayton, Joan. *Journalism for Beginners: How to Get into Print and Get Paid for It*, Piatkus, London, 1992.

Condon, William, and Wayne Butler. *Writing the Information Superhighway*, Allyn and Bacon, Needham Heights, MA, 1997.

Cropp, Richard, Barbara Braidwood, and Susan M. Boyce. *Writing Travel Books and Articles*, Self-Counsel Press, Vancouver, 1997.

Cumming, Carman, and Catherine McKercher. *The Canadian Reporter: News Writing and Reporting*, Harcourt Brace Canada, Toronto, 1994.

Deahl, James (ed.). *Poetry Markets for Canadians* (6th ed.), League of Canadian Poets and Mercury Press, Toronto, 1996.

Derricourt, Robin. *An Author's Guide to Scholarly Publishing*, Princeton UP, Princeton, NJ, 1996.

Dick, Jill. *Writing for Magazines* (2nd ed.), A. and C. Black, London, 1996.

Frank, Thaisa, and Dorothy Wall. *Finding Your Writer's Voice: A Guide to Creative Fiction*, St. Martin's Press, New York, 1994.

Gage, Diane, and Marcia Coppess. *Get Published: Editors from the Nation's Top Magazines Tell You What They Want*, Henry Holt, New York, 1994.

Gardner, John. *The Art of Fiction: Notes on Craft for Young Writers*, Vintage, New York, 1983.

———. *On Writers and Writing*, Addison-Wesley, New York, 1994.

Gerard, Philip. *Creative Nonfiction*, Story Press, Cincinnati, OH, 1996.

Gibaldi, Joseph, and Walter S. Achtert. *The MLA Handbook for Writers of Research Papers*, Modern Language Association of America, New York, 1988.

Giltrow, Janet. *Academic Writing* (2nd ed.), Broadview, Peterborough, 1994.

Goldberg, Natalie. *Writing Down the Bones: Freeing the Writer Within*, Shambhala, Boston and London, 1986.

———. *Wild Mind: Living the Writer's Life*, Bantam, New York, 1990.

Grant, Vanessa. *Writing Romance*, Self-Counsel Press, Vancouver, 1997.

Groves, Dawn. *The Writer's Guide to the Internet*, Franklin, Beedle & Associates, Wilsonville, OR, 1997.

Gutkind, Lee. *The Art of Creative Nonfiction*, John Wiley and Sons, New York and Toronto, 1997.

Hemley, Robin. *Turning Life into Fiction*, Story Press, Cincinnati, OH, 1994.

Hodgins, Jack. *A Passion for Narrative: A Guide for Writing Fiction*, McClelland & Stewart, Toronto, 1993.

Kane, Thomas S., and Karen C. Ogden. *The Canadian Oxford Guide to Writing*, Oxford University Press, Toronto, 1993.

Konner, Linda. *How to Be Successfully Published in Magazines*, St. Martin's Press, New York, 1990.

Levin, Michael. *Writer's Internet Sourcebook*, No Starch Press, San Francisco, 1997.

Lunsford, Andrea, Robert Connors, and Judy Z. Segal. *The St. Martin's Handbook for Canadians*, Nelson Canada, Toronto, 1995.

Malone, Eileen. *The Complete Guide to Writers' Groups, Conferences, and Workshops*, John Wiley and Sons, New York, 1996.

Mandell, Judy. *Book Editors Talk to Writers*, John Wiley and Sons, New York, 1995.

McKeown, Thomas W., and Carol M. Cram. *Better Business Writing*, Clear Communications Press, Vancouver, 1990.

Mencher, Melvin. *News Reporting and Writing* (3rd ed.), W.C. Brown, Dubuque, Iowa, 1984.

Messenger, William E., and Jan de Bruyn. *The Canadian Writer's Handbook* (2nd ed.), Prentice-Hall Canada, Toronto, 1986.

Metter, Eileen. *The Writer's Ultimate Research Guide*, Writer's Digest, Cincinnati, OH, 1995.

Miller, Casey, and Kate Swift. *The Handbook of Nonsexist Writing* (2nd ed.), Harper & Row, New York, 1988.

Novakovich, Josip. *Fiction Writer's Workshop*, Story Press, Cincinnati, 1995.

Peterson, Franklynn, and Judi Kesselman-Turkel. *The Magazine Writer's Handbook*, Prentice-Hall, Englewood Cliffs, NJ, 1982.

Pfeiffer, William S., and Jan Boogerd. *Technical Writing: A Practical Approach*, Prentice-Hall Canada, Toronto, 1997.

Rivers, Dyanne. *The Business of Writing (The Canadian Guide for Writers and Editors)*, McGraw-Hill Ryerson, Toronto, 1994.

Rubens, Philip, ed. *Science and Technical Writing: A Manual of Style*, Henry Holt, New York, 1992.

Smith, Nancy. *The Fiction Writers' Handbook*, Piatkus, London, 1991.

Strunk, William, Jr., and E.B. White. *The Elements of Style* (3rd ed.), Macmillan, New York, 1979.

Taylor, Bob (ed.). *The Canadian Press Stylebook* (rev.), The Canadian Press, Toronto, 1989.

Waller, Adrian. *Writing! An Informal, Anecdotal Guide to the Secrets of Crafting and Selling Non-Fiction*, McClelland & Stewart, Toronto, 1987.

Williams, Joseph M. Style: *Toward Clarity and Grace*, University of Chicago, Chicago, 1990.

Wilson, John M. *The Complete Guide to Magazine Article Writing*, Writer's Digest Books, Cincinnati, 1993.

Zinsser, William. *On Writing Well: An Informal Guide to Writing Nonfiction* (4th ed.), HarperCollins, New York, 1991.

Dictionaries & Thesauruses

The Collins Dictionary & Thesaurus, HarperCollins, London, 1995.

The Concise Oxford Dictionary (9th ed.), Clarendon Press, Oxford, 1995.

Fowler's Modern English Usage (2nd ed.), rev. Sir Ernest Gowers, Oxford University Press, Oxford, 1965.

Funk & Wagnalls Modern Guide to Synonyms, ed. S.I. Hayakawa, Funk & Wagnalls, New York, 1986.

Gage Canadian Dictionary (5th ed.), Gage Educational Publishing Co., Toronto, 1997.

Gage Canadian Intermediate Dictionary, Gage Educational Publishing Co., Toronto, 1998.

ITP Nelson Canadian Dictionary of the English Language, ITP Nelson, Toronto, 1997.

Merriam-Webster's Collegiate Dictionary (10th ed.), Thomas Allen, Toronto, 1993.

The New Fowler's Modern English Usage, ed. Robert Birchfield. Oxford UP, Oxford and New York, 1996.

New Webster's Dictionary & Thesaurus of the English Language, Lexicon, New York, 1991.

The Oxford Desk Thesaurus, Clarendon Press, Oxford, 1995.

The Oxford Writers' Dictionary, R.E. Allen, Oxford University Press, Oxford, 1990.

The Penguin Canadian Dictionary, Penguin Canada/Copp Clark Pitman, Toronto, 1990.

The Penguin Dictionary of Writers & Editors, Bill Bryson, Penguin, London, 1991.

Roget's A to Z, ed. Robert L. Chapman, HarperCollins, New York, 1994.

Webster's New World Dictionary and Thesaurus, Macmillan, New York, 1996.

Yearbooks, Almanacs, & Other Regularly Published Reference Sources

The Book Trade in Canada, Quill & Quire, Toronto. (annual)

The Canadian Global Almanac, John Robert Colombo, gen. ed., Macmillan Canada, Toronto, 1996.

CARD (Canadian Advertising Rates & Data), Maclean-Hunter, Toronto. (monthly)

Canadian Publishers Directory, published biannually as a supplement to *Quill & Quire* magazine.

Literary Agents of North America, Arthur Ormont and Léonie Rosenstiel, eds., Author Aid/Research Associates International, New York. (annual)

Literary Market Place: The Directory of American Publishing, R.R. Bowker, New York. (annual)

Matthews Media Directory, published 3 times a year by Canadian Corporate News.

Novel & Short Story Writer's Market, Robin Gee, ed., Writer's Digest Books, Cincinnati, OH. (annual)

Publication Profiles, published annually as a supplement to *CARD* (see above).

Sources: The Directory of Contacts for Editors, Reporters & Researchers, published biannually as a supplement to *Content* magazine.

Writers' & Artists' Yearbook, A. & C. Black, London. (annual)

Writer's Market, Mark Kissling, ed., Writer's Digest Books, Cincinnati, OH. (annual)

Some Major Canadian Magazine Publishers

Bowes Publishers Ltd., P.O. Box 7400, Station E, London,
ON N5Y 4X3. Phone: (519) 473-0010. Fax: (519) 473-2256.
(farm)

Camar Publications Ltd., 130 Spy Court, Markham, ON L3R 5H6.
Phone: (905) 475-8440. Fax: (905) 475-9246. (consumer)

Canada Wide Magazines Ltd., 4180 Lougheed Highway, Suite
401, Burnaby, BC V5C 6A7. Phone: (604) 299-7311. Fax: (604)
299-9188. (consumer and business)

Family Communications Inc., 37 Hanna Avenue, Unit 1, Toronto,
ON M6K 1X1. Phone: (416) 537-2604. (consumer)

Kerrwil Publications Ltd., 395 Matheson Boulevard E.,
Mississauga, ON L4Z 2H2. Phone: (905) 890-1846. Fax: (905)
890-5769. (business and consumer)

Key Publishers Ltd., 59 Front Street E., 3rd Floor, Toronto,
ON M5B 1B3. Phone: (416) 364-3333. (consumer and business)

Maclean Hunter Ltd., 777 Bay Street, Toronto, ON M5W 1A7.
Phone: (416) 596-5000. (consumer and business)
1001 de Maisonneuve ouest, Suite 1000, Montreal, PQ H3A 3E1.
Phone: (514) 845-5141. (consumer and business)

Naylor Communications Ltd., 100 Sutherland Avenue, Winnipeg,
MB R2W 3C7. Phone: (204) 947-0222. (business)
920 Yonge Street, 6th Floor, Toronto, ON M4W 3C7. Phone:
(416) 961-1028. Fax: (416) 924-4408. (business)

Southam Inc., 1450 Don Mills Road, Don Mills, ON M3B 2X7.
Phone: (416) 445-6641. (business)
3300 Côte Vertu, St.-Laurent, PQ H4R 2B7. Phone: (514) 339-
1399. Fax: (514) 339-1396. (business)

Telemedia Publishing, 25 Sheppard Avenue W., Suite 100, North
York, ON M2N 6S7. Phone: (416) 733-7600. Fax: (416) 733-
8272. (consumer)
2001 University Street, Suite 900, Montreal, PQ H3A 2A6.
Phone: (514) 499-0561. (consumer)

INDEX FOR CONSUMER, LITERARY, & SCHOLARLY MAGAZINES

HOW TO BUY A COMPUTER
MYLES WHITE

"White covers all the bases, and then some…. All his explanations are wonderfully clear, simple, and well-researched." – QUILL & QUIRE

For a writer, the computer has become as indispensable as the pencil and eraser. But buying a computer can be a daunting experience. Myles White, one of Canada's leading writers on the new technology, provides the information the average consumer needs to understand computer terms and the pros and cons of various options. He gives sound advice on how to avoid retailers' tricks and traps, and about what new developments to look for and what to avoid. This book provides all the information you need to buy intelligently and get the best system to suit your needs.

$19.99 • trade paperback • 252 pages

HOW TO AVOID BUYING A NEW COMPUTER
MYLES WHITE

"White's no-nonsense approach to his subject matter makes it a refreshing read…. This book is hard to beat." – THE COMPUTER PAPER

Tempted to mortgage the house to buy a new computer system with all the bells and whistles? Well, think again. Your solution may not be an expensive new computer but a simple upgrade of the one you already own.

Myles White takes you under the hood of your computer and shows – with clear, step-by-step instructions – how easy it is to choose the component you need and install it. Within minutes you can add: circuit boards for sound, video, or Internet access; more memory, both RAM and cache; a CD-ROM drive, another hard drive or floppy drive, a tape backup drive, and more; a more powerful CPU; and even a new motherboard.

Make your system run as fast as it can and be capable of whatever you want it to do – for a fraction of the cost of a new computer.

$19.99 • trade paperback • 308 pages

THE 1998 CANADIAN AND WORLD ENCYCLOPEDIA

"Far more material than … Encarta." – VANCOUVER SUN

"A must-have for all Canadians." – TORONTO STAR

This 2 CD-ROM set includes: The Canadian Encyclopedia; The Columbia Encyclopedia; The Gage Canadian Dictionary; Roget's Electronic Thesaurus; French-English, English-French Dictionary; *Maclean's* Year in Review.

The Number 1 best-selling Canadian multimedia reference
More than 100,000 copies sold • NEW! *Lives and Times of the Prime Ministers*
Now more than 51,000 articles • More multimedia
More than $1^1/_2$ hours of video, $4^1/_2$ hours of audio • Internet updates and links

$79.77 • 2 CD-ROM set • www.tceplus.com